Denis Murphy

Cromwell in Ireland

A history of Cromwell's Irish campaign

Denis Murphy

Cromwell in Ireland
A history of Cromwell's Irish campaign

ISBN/EAN: 9783337125035

Printed in Europe, USA, Canada, Australia, Japan

Cover: Foto ©ninafisch / pixelio.de

More available books at **www.hansebooks.com**

CROMWELL IN IRELAND:

A HISTORY OF

CROMWELL'S IRISH CAMPAIGN.

BY THE

REV. DENIS MURPHY, S. J.

"'Twas not lack of men, nor food, nor raiment,
Nor th' enemy's strength wrenched from them Eire,
But, to one another, not being faithful."
The Dirge of Irelana.

BOSTON:
THE PILOT PUBLISHING CO.
1893.

Electrotyped and Printed by
CASHMAN, KEATING & Co.,
611 Washington St., Boston.

To the Memory

OF THE

Most Rev. John Mac Hale,

ARCHBISHOP OF TUAM,

I DEDICATE

THIS HISTORY OF ONE YEAR'S SUFFERINGS

OF THE IRISH PEOPLE

FOR THEIR FAITH AND COUNTRY.

Preface.

THE object of this work is to give an account in full detail, as far as is possible, of Cromwell's Irish campaign, which began in August, 1649, and ended in May, 1650. It is a portion of history but little known. It lies for the most part in a few books, some of them difficult of access by reason of their scarcity, others written in a lnaguage not intelligible to the greater number of readers. Traditions, indeed, there are still surviving of the doings of Cromwell and his followers, many of them having, no doubt, a foundation of truth ; but many, too, exaggerations at best, and not a few wholly unfounded and false. In truth, there is hardly a ruined church throughout the length and breadth of the land, the destruction of which is not attributed to Cromwell, or a crumbling castle of which it is not said that

" Oliver Cromwell
He did it pommel,
And made a breach
In its battlement."

Evil deeds are attributed to him as done where he never set foot, and names are given to places that would seem at first sight to record his presence there, but in reality have had their origin in the wish of his followers to perpetuate their leader's fame, or in the hatred of those among whom they dwelt, who would hand down the record of his cruelties by an appellation which in their minds summed up all manner of evil.

Many years ago Sir William Wilde expressed a wish that some one would write the history of "Cromwell's Irish campaign, one of the most defective portions of modern Irish history." He adds that Mr. Hardiman, whose services in the field of Irish research have been such as to make us regret that his works are so few, had made a collec tion of all the documents relating to Cromwell in Ireland. I have made inquiry for these wherever I head any part of his manuscripts were — at the British Museum, Markree Castle, the Royal Irish Academy, and the monastery of Errew — but in none of these places were there any tidings to be had of them.

So little has been done hitherto in monographs of even the most important facts of Irish history, and that little under such difficulties, that it is no wonder Cromwell's doings have not been written of. Mr. Prendergast's invaluable work, *The Cromwellian Settlement of Ireland*, has begun a new era of Irish history. It shows that materials are at hand in abundance, if only an enlightened industry will search for them and put them in order. State papers, hitherto accessible only to a few, are now within the reach of all. Collections of rare books, both public and private, are thrown open to the student more freely than formerly. A work on the history of Ireland, if it has merit, need not rely for its success on the comparatively few readers within the narrow limits of this country; it will readily reach to another Ireland beyond the sea, where the story of the old land is read, its traditions and legends repeated, the recollection of its sufferings and its wrongs treasured up with tender care : —

> " Deep in Canadian woods we've met,
> From one bright island flown ;
> Great is the land we tread, but yet
> Our hearts are with our own."

The plan pursued in this work is to follow Cromwell step by step in his progress through Ireland. Other matters treated of in the first chapters needed to be touched on, in order to show what the state of the great political parties both in England and Ireland was at the time. Cromwell's letters are so numerous and so full of details, that there is no difficulty in tracing out his line of march, hour by hour, from the first moment he landed in Dublin up to his setting sail from Youghal. The newspapers of the time, too, give day by day an account of the successes of the Parliamentary army. There are naratives of some of the more remarkable events, written by eye-witnesses, actors or sufferers in the scenes which they describe, some of these being Irish ecclesiastics who had escaped from the carnage or had been banished, and " from the place of their refuge," set down for perpetual remembrance, the record of what they and their countrymen endured. I have allowed each of the chief actors to tell the part which he took, and in his own words, too, when it was possible to do so. The extracts from contemporary writers have been set down just as they are given in the originals. Their very quaintness will often help to bring the scenes which they describe more vividly before the reader's eyes than a more elaborate, but perhaps less faithful, description. Each statement has its reference, not merely to enable the reader to test its truth, but still more to point out to him the works in which he will find further details, which, though not admissible within the limits of a small work, may interest those who wish to study the subject more fully. I have confined myself to a simple narrative of the facts ; for to use the words of Montaigne, which one of the most learned of Irish historians has taken for his motto : "J'aime les historiens ou fort simples ou excellents ; les simples, qui n'ont poin de quoy mesler quelque chose du leur, et qui n'y apportent que le soing et la diligence de ramasser tout ce qui vient à leur notice et d'enregistrer à la bonne foy toutes choses, sans chois et sans triage, nous laissent le jugement entier pour la connaissance de la verité."

This is not the place to enter on any inquiry into the character, either military or political, of Cromwell. That he was a brave man, that he was far-seeing, that he knew how to choose his instruments and to use them, that he did his work in Ireland —from his stand-point — well, thoroughly, no one will deny. But that he was "a heaven-sent messenger," that his conduct, even as a public man, was not contrary to the first principles of morality, that another Cromwel' would be the best panacea for Irish discontent, no one ever so little acquainted with the history of his doings will assert, unless his mind is wholly warped by prejudice of race or religious rancour. Whoever examines, even his brief career in Ireland, with impartiality, must admit the truth of Clarendon's saying, that he was a great, bad man.

I cannot conclude without acknowledging my obligations to Mr. Prendergast, for the great help which I have derived from his *Cromwellian Settlement of Ireland.* From Mr. Gilbert's edition of the *Aphorismal Discovery*, and from the valuable notes which he has appended to it, I have borrowed largely. The high character which both these writers bear for research and accuracy, is the best warrant for the truth of the many statements which I have made on their authority.

The dates throughout are given according to the New Style, which makes the year begin with January 1st, not March 25th, as was the custom formerly.

LIMERICK, Feast of St. Patrick, 1883.

Contents.

CROMWELL IN IRELAND.

CHAPTER I.

THE PEACE OF 'FORTY-EIGHT.

Terms of the Peace — Execution of Charles I.— Ormonde's Authority— The Commissioners of Trust — Overtures to Jones and Coote — The Fleet under Prince Rupert — Owen Roe O'Neill — Treaty with Monk — Defeat of Ferrall — Seige of Derry raised — Monk and Coote censured by the Parliament.

On the 17th of January, 1649, a peace was concluded between the Marquis of Ormonde, acting on behalf of King Charles I. and the General Assembly of the Confederate Catholics. Substantially its terms were the same as those of the treaty which the Catholic party had refused the year before. But the position of the Confederates was much changed within the twelvemonth. The country, impoverished by the long continuence of the war, was no longer able to support a standing army. There was no further hope of aid from abroad. The ambassadors, sent by the Assembly to Rome, were told that the Papal exchequer was almost exhausted, and that the resources of the government were hardly sufficient to meet the dangers that threatened southern Italy. Most opportunely for the royal interests, the Remonstrance of the Puritan army in England was published while the negotiations for the treaty were on foot, "demanding that the parliament should proceed against the King in the way of justice, as the capital and grand author of all the troubles and woes which the kingdom hath endured, and that he should be brought to justice for the treason, blood and mischief he hath been therein guilty of."[1] No ground was left any longer for doubting about the intentions of the party. All who had any regard for the royal authority forgot for a time prejudice and resentment, to secure the King's safety. The Protestants became more tolerant; many Catholics, who had held aloof from Ormonde hitherto, were gained over by the concessions now made on behalf of their religion. The Assembly conceded some points still in dispute, and "in consideration of his Majesty's present condition and of their own hearty desires of spending their lives and fortunes in maintaining his rights and interests, they resolved unanimously to accept the Marquis of Ormonde's answer to their propositions for religion."[2]

[1] Lingard's *History of England*, vol. viii. p. 106; London, 1855. See "The Chief Heads of the Army's Remonstrance," presented to the House of Commons November 20th, 1648, in the Appendix to Clarendon's *History of the Rebellion*, p. 89; London, 1717.

[2] Carte's *History of James Duke of Ormonde*, vol. ii. p. 49; London, 1736. "That desperately wicked remonstrance, whatever mischief it may do, hath yet done this good, that it put us quite from all disputes upon the necessity of conditions, and was no small cause of the speedy, and, I hope, happy conclusion of the peace." — Letter of Ormonde to Lord Jermyn, Jan. 24th, 1649; *ibid.*, vol. iii p. 602.

By the terms of the treaty it was agreed that the Irish people should be free to practice their religion, without prejudice to their persons or estates; that they should no longer be obliged to take the oath of supremacy — for this a new form of oath was substituted, professing allegiance to his Majesty — and that all acts and ordinances of parliament in dishonor of the Catholic faith, passed since August 7th, 1641, should be vacated. They were assured, moreover, that they should not be molested in the possession of the churches and church livings which they then held, or in the exercise of their jurisdiction, until such time as his Majesty, in a free parliament to be held in Ireland, should declare his further pleasure.[1] The peace was confirmed later by Charles II., who professed himself satisfied in every respect with its terms. Yet just eighteen months after he declared it null and void, adding, "that he was convinced in his conscience of the sinfulness and unlawfulness of it and of allowing the liberty of the Popish religion."[2] Ormond was no better than his master. The "Declaration" of Jamestown shows how shamelessly he violated it in its most important points.[3] After the Restoration he was accused of having been on too friendly terms, during the insurrection, with some of the Irish ecclesiastics; he exculpated himself by saying that his aim was to work disunion among the Romish clergy.

A few days after the signing of the treaty the news of the King's execution reached Ireland. By all parties it was received with horror and indignation.[4] Profiting by the feeling of sympathy shown everywhere for the royal family, Ormonde, who was then at Youghal, had the Prince of Wales proclaimed King, under the title of Charles II., with all solemnity, in every town in Ireland that owned subjection to his authority. His own position remained unchanged by the King's death. A fresh commission was issued to him by the new King, on the 17th of February, renewing his powers as Lord Lieutenant and

---

[1] This was called "The Peace of Forty-eight," old style. The Articles, thirty-five in number, are given in Cox's *Hibernia Anglicana*, Appendix xliii.; London, 1690. Milton wrote, in opposition to it, *Observations on the Articles of the Peace.*

[2] Carte's *Collection of Original Papers*, vol. i. p. 400; Dublin, 1759. It is strange how long the Irish continued to show their affection to the Stuart dynasty, not one of whom displayed the least gratitude for the many sacrifices made on their behalf. "The ancient Irish," says M'Geoghegan, "revered the Milesian blood which ran in the veins of James I., and looked on him as a prince descended from themselves. They knew that Edward Bruce, brother of Robert Bruce, from whom James was descended, had been chosen by their ancestors to be their sovereign. It was well-known too, that Edward had been actually crowned King of Ireland."— *History of Ireland*, translated by O'Kelly, p. 552; Dublin, 1844. Roderick O'Flaherty, in the *Epistola Dedicatoria* prefixed to his *Ogygia*, addressing the Duke of York, calls Ireland "Antiquissima majorum tuorum incunabula.' The *Ogygia* was published in 1685. The demands of the Irish gentlemen, who had suffered for the royal cause, afforded to Charles II. and his profligate courtiers, after his Restoration, constant food for their indecent and heartless mirth.

[3] "See the Declaration of the Archbishops, Bishops, and other Dignitaries of the secular and regular clergy against the continuance of his Majesty's authority in the person of the Marquis of Ormonde," dated at Jamestown, August 12th, 1650 in Cox's *Hib. Angl.*, Appendix xlviii.

[4] "How gladly would I draw a curtain over that dismal and unhappy 30th of January, wherein the royal father of our country suffered martyrdom! Oh! that I could say, 'They were Irishmen that did that abominable fact,' or that I could justly lay it at the door of the Papists."— *Hib Angl.*, vol. ii. p. 206. "Resentment and spleen had a good share in forming that work (Cox's); for it carries too much the air and complexion of satire."— Introduction to *Clanricarde's Memoirs*, Dublin, 1744.

confirming all he had done, in virtue either of the commission of the late King or of his own confirmation of the powers or rights thereof.

Almost the whole of Ireland had now declared for Charles. Nearly all the leading men of the Catholic party were united with Ormonde, and threw themselves heart and soul into the defence of the royal cause. Preston, Taaffe, Clanricarde, Muskerry, and Castlehaven forgot their mutual jealousies for a while and thought only of the common interests. Once more Inchiquin changed sides,[1] now for the last time. He had not found among his Puritan friends the gratitude which he expected in return for his treachery and cruelty. Henceforth no one was more zealous than he in supporting the King and Ormonde.

The King had full confidence in the Lord Lieutenant, but even the moderate Catholics made no secret of their distrust in his promises. That this distrust was well founded is clear, from a letter of his to Prince Charles, in which he owns that "for want of force to keep any dependent on the King's authority only, and for obtaining such a peace as might reduce the army and the Confederates under the King's obedience, he had been constrained to subject his Majesty's power to compliances agreeable with neither." One of the charges brought against him in the "Declaration" of Jamestown was, "that his Excellency, when prospering, put no trust of places taken, into the hands of Catholics: by this his diffidence in Catholics, and by other his actions and expressions, the Catholic army had not heart to fight or be under his command; and feared greatly, if he mastered the enemy, and with them the Commissioners of Trust, or the greater part of them, and many thousands of the kingdom also feared he would have brought the Catholic subjects and their religion to their old slavery." According to the terms of the Peace, his powers as Lord Lieutenant should still continue, but he should be assisted in the government by a council of twelve members chosen from the Assembly of the Confederates, whose chief duty it was to look to the due performance of the Articles, "until they should be ratified in a full and peaceful convention of the parliament." These, styled "Commissioners of Trust," and sometimes "Interval Commissioners," were Lord Dillon of Costello, Lord Muskerry, Lord Athenry, Alexander M'Donnell, Sir Lucas Dillon, Sir Nicholas Plunkett, Sir Richard Barnwall, Geoffrey Browne, Donogh O'Callaghan, Turlogh O'Neill, Miles O'Reilly, and Gerald Fennell. They were, jointly with Ormonde, vested with power to levy soldiers, raise money, erect garrisons, and appoint governors; he could do nothing of importance without the consent of a majority of them. It was not without a struggle that he accepted such restraint and limitation to his power; but he felt that in the face of the present dangers union should be purchased at almost any price. Besides, most of the Commissioners were partisans of his own, and "their affections and abilities were so well known and approved by

---

[1] This poor wavering panther, Inchiquin, with so many jumps and leapings from King to Parliament, from Parliament to King, and now the fourth or fifth of his inconstant whirlings to Ormond."—*Aphorismal Discovery of Treasonable Faction*, vol. i. p. 182; edited by J. T. Gilbert; Dublin, 1879. See Appendix ii. : "Morrough O'Brien, Lord Inchiquin."

him that, having most of them inclined to the same good end with him, he presumed he should, with the less difficulty, be able to persuade them which were the nearest and most natural ways that conduced thereunto."

Soon after the conclusion of the Peace, in order to gain over the Parliamentarians in Ireland, who still retained some respect for the oath of allegiance which they had taken to serve the Sovereign and the Parliament, Ormonde published a declaration, in which he reminded them of the regard he had at all times shown for the interests of the Protestant religion, in proof whereof he appealed to the Articles of the Peace, "the sum of which," he declared, "was the indulging of some moderate concessions to the Catholics, made until such time as the Act of Oblivion should be passed in Parliament; that he had specially excepted from the advantage of the Peace those who had any part in the crimes committed in the beginning or the course of the rebellion. The Articles were not agreed to until all hope of a treaty between the King and the Parliament was at an end, and the army had proclaimed their purpose to commit a horrid and execrable paracide in the sacred person of his Majesty. The blame thereof, if any, might be laid on those who made such a treaty necessary." He wrote conciliatory letters to Michael Jones,[1] governor of Dublin, and to Sir Charles Coote,[2] who was in command of the fortress of Derry, inviting them and the forces under their command to return to their allegiance and submit to the King's authority. Jones rejected his overtures, pretending that "he felt himself bound in honor to obey those who had entrusted him with the important office which he held." Coote had frequently professed "that if at any time he should discover the least purpose in the Parliament of England to change the government, or to wrong the King either in his person or posterity, he would sooner beg his bread than be a minister to their proceedings." In reply to Ormonde's letter, he renewed his profession of fidelity, and protested that "as soon as the King or his fleet, or any person lawfully authorized by him, should lay the command on him, and showed

---

[1] He was one of the four sons of Dr. Lewis Jones, a Welshman, Protestant bishop of Killaloe from 1633 to 1646. Another of his sons, Henry, was bishop of Clogher and scoutmaster general to Cromwell, "a post," says Ware, "not so decent for one of his function." *Works of Sir James Ware*, edited by Harris, vol. i. p. 160; Dublin, 1764. "In May, 1652, Dr. Henry Jones, then bishop of Clogher and scoutmaster general, appeared at the council of general and field officers of Ludlow's army, held at Kilkenny and made the officers protest, through a dread of the Lord they trusted, against their General's too great aptness to mercy, so they termed it, and sparing those whom the Lord was pursuing with his great severity."— Letter of the General and Field officers, &c., to the Speaker of the House of Commons, in *The Kilkenny Archæological Journal* for 1867, p. 62. Theophilus was a colonel in the Parliamentary army and governor of Leighlin in 1651.

[2] This was Sir Charles Coote the younger. The elder was killed at the siege of Trim in 1642, having been shot through the body by one of his own troopers, whether by design or accident was never known. "His body was brought to Dublin and there interred with great solemnity, floods of English tears accompanying him to the grave."—Borlase's *Rebellion*, p. 79. He was interred with the ensuing epitaph:

> "England's honor, Scotland's wonder,
> Ireland's terror, here lies under."

Aphor. Disc., vol. i. p. 32.

The same author says the miraculous statue of Our Lady of Trim was burned by his son, Richard Coote.— *Ibid.* The cruelties of both father and sons are still household words throughout Ireland.

a probable appearance of power and success to make him hope for security, nobody should more freely and fully evidence the sincerity of his affection to the King's service than himself."[1] But these protestations were only meant to gain time until succors were sent him from England. Two months later, a mutiny broke out among some of the regiments under his command, in consequence of the imprisonment of their officers, who were found to be in correspondence with Ormonde. The men ran to arms, rescued the prisoners, and took possession of the town and fortress of Enniskillen. Encouraged by the success of their comrades, several officers of the old Scotch regiments in the north, sent to assure the Lord Lieutenant of their readiness to serve the King with the forces under their command. They had opposed the royal authority, not with a view of extinguishing the monarchy, but for the purpose of restraining the prerogative within due limits. Now they loudly professed their abhorrence of those who had compassed the King's death. But unhappily their abhorrence of the Irish was equally violent; they would take no part with the Confederates. They asked that commissioners should be appointed to arrange the terms on which their services would be accepted, and that 1,000 horse should go to their aid. Ormonde sent the Commissioners, and promised that Inchiquin, with 4,000 foot, should be despatched immediately to Athlone, in order to support them. They, too, rose in arms and blocked up their commander, Sir Charles Coote, in Derry.

Towards the end of January the royal fleet, numbering sixteen frigates,[2] under the command of Prince Rupert,[3] arrived off the coast of Munster. A few days later it arrived in Kinsale Harbor. Owing partly to the Prince's jealousy of Ormond, partly to the intrigues of those about him, he remained almost wholly inactive. At rare intervals some of his ships put to sea, and cruising off the southern coasts, seized on English merchantmen. At first the prizes were abundant, but soon the traders learned to avoid the danger by choosing another route or by remaining safe within the English ports. Ormonde besought him " to remember that the ships could not be employed more

---

[1] Cox, in the preface of his *Hibernia Anglicana*, speaking of the different parties then in Ireland, says : " That these distinctions may appear to be neither trivial nor merely notional, it will be necessary to give instances of these several factions in the late Irish wars. First, there was an army of all mere Irish, not an English Papist among them, commanded by the Bishop of Clogher; and another of mere English,.all Papists, under General Preston; and secondly, there was an army of old English and Irish under the Lords Mountgarrett, Taaffe, &c.; and an army of new English, commanded by the Earls of Ormonde, Inchiquin, &c.; and thirdly, there was an army of Papists under the Nuncio; and an army of Protestants. commanded by the Marquis of Ormonde." See also *Account of the Carte MSS.*, by Rev. C. W. Russell and J. P. Prendergast, p. 114; London, 1871.

[2] " In May 1648, the fleet, then stationed in the Downs, declared for the King, and without any leader above the degree of boatswain, sailed for Holland, where the Duke of York, and later the Prince of Wales, took command of them." Guizot's *History of the English Revolution*, p 380; London, 1846.

[3] Rupert was the son of the Elector Palatine Frederick V. and Elizabeth, daughter of James I., King of England. At the beginning of the Civil War he got from his uncle, Charles I., the command of a regiment of horse. His dashing bravery, become a proverb ever since, was often marred by his rashness. In 1648 he was appointed to the command of the royal fleet. After the Restoration he devoted his time to physical and chemical researches. The glass toy, known as Prince Rupert's drop, has its name from him.

usefully than in helping to reduce Derry and the fort near it; the officers would thus become absolute masters of that side of the north, and be able to lend considerable assistance towards the reduction of any other part of the kingdom. He added that he was well assured all the shipping belonging to the rebels on the coast of England towards Ireland was no more than three frigates, which were appointed to convoy over some forces, designed and lying ready at the waterside, for the relief of Dublin ; and of those three, there was only one of any considerable strength, and she carried but thirty guns. The interruption which might be given to that access of strength to Jones would, in all probability, render the work against him easy ; whereas, on the contrary, if he was supplied, it would be almost a desperate undertaking, and himself should be forced to a defensive war. This being the state of affairs about Dublin and Derry, he humbly left it to his Highness to consider how these supplies, so much to be feared, might be easily prevented, the good success of the King's service in that kingdom chiefly depending thereon." But Rupert continued inactive at Kinsale, nor would he furnish Ormonde with the prize-money which the King had ordered him to pay over for the public service. Soon after he was blocked up in that port by the Parliamentary fleet under Blake and Deane, and prevented from rendering any assistance whatever to the land forces, during the whole summer.

Owen Roe O'Neill was almost the only person of importance among the Catholics who held aloof. He was essentially a representative man, the leader of the old Irish, and accepted by them as such. The prestige of that party and of their leader had been lessened by the departure of the legate Rinuccini, who, consistent to the last in upholding the rights, civil and religious, of the Irish people, had quitted Ireland only when he despaired of the successful issue of such a line of policy.[1] O'Neill was still supported by the townsmen of Limerick, Waterford and Galway. On his side, too, were his sturdy clansmen of the North. But a few years before, six of the northern counties had been seized on by the English government and planted with English and Scotch undertakers. The natives were driven from their homes ; from the rich valleys and plains, and forced to seek shelter and support on the barren mountains and in the wild woods.[2] Many of the generation that had then been mercilessly plundered had passed away; they had perished of hunger and disease, or they had fallen in the unequal fight, while attempting to recover the homes which they had lost ; but they left to their children the legacy of revenge. However much they loved their native land, they loved

---

[1] Rinuccini set sail from Galway February 23d, 1649. He had passed nearly three years and a half in Ireland, having landed at Kenmare October 22d, 1645. His letters from Ireland were published in Florence in 1844, under the title : *Nunziatura in Irlanda di Monsignor G. B. Rinuccini, negli anni 1645 a 1649.* A translation by Miss Hutton was issued in Dublin in 1873.

[2] The author of the *Aphorismal Discovery* describes them as "being hunted out by General Leslie like deer or savage beasts, and bleeding under the force of two warlike nations, the English and the Scotch."— *Aphor Disc.*, vol. i. p. 42. In the "Remonstrance of the Ulster Irish," presented to Charles I. in 1641, they say: "We may boldly affirm that we are the most miserable and most unhappy nation of the Christian world."—*Ibid.*, p. 455, Appendix Ii.

their faith still more. By them no settlement was reckoned satisfactory unless it secured absolute freedom for the exercise of the Catholic faith and the complete restoration of all its ancient rights and privileges. Hence, the war in which they were engaged was to them a holy war; a war waged in defence of religion against heresy and unbelief. O'Neill had at this time under his command an army more numerous and better disciplined than that of the Confederates. His forces amounted to 5,000 foot and 300 horse. At the head of such an army he hoped to be able to maintain his ground until a favorable opportunity offered of insisting on his own rights and those of his clansmen.

Ormonde strove to gain him over to his side; for he knew that if O'Neill stood out, the quarrel would be still kept up between the Nuncio's and the King's parties, the forces of the kingdom would be divided, and many of the cities would refuse to pay the taxes imposed on them. Two of the Commissioners of Trust were appointed to treat with him. His first demand was that the six counties of Ulster, lately confiscated, should be restored to the native Irish. But these and the other terms which he proposed were not found acceptable, and the conference came to nothing. Indeed the envoys made no secret of their enmity to him and their unwillingness to accept from him any terms short of an absolute and unconditional surrender. "Their aversion and malice to me and my party," he wrote to Ormonde, "are such as that they will study and devise all the ways they can invent to hinder any settlement or union between your Excellency and us."

O'Neill had been proclaimed "a traitor and rebel against the King and the fundamental laws of the land; a common disturber of the peace, tranquility and quiet of the kingdom, and a manifest opposer of the government of the Confederates, contrary to his oath." [1] Stung with honest indignation, he turned to the Parliamentary party and sought to make terms with them In truth there was little room for choice left him. From his camp, at Cavan, he wrote to Rinuccini on the 18th of May: "We are almost reduced to despair. On the one hand, Ormonde entreats us to join him; on the other, the Parliamentary party seeks our friendship. God knows we hate and detest both alike." And writing about the same time to Massari, Dean of Fermo, who had followed the Nuncio to Ireland, he says: "Either course is worse to me than death. . . . Yet so pressing are our wants, that we must unite with one or the other, unless we get help very soon."

While the preparations for the Irish campaign were making in England, it was found necessary to have recourse to various expedients for the preservation of the places which were still in the hands of the Parliament. One of these was to gain over to the cause of the party the Catholics of the two kingdoms. Conferences were held through the Spanish Ambassador with some Irish ecclesiastics, and with Sir Kenelm Digby and Sir John Winter, on behalf of the Eng-

---

[1] See the proclamation against Owen O'Neill by the General Assembly of the Confederate Catholics in *Aphor. Disc.*, vol. i. p. 747; it was issued September 30th, 1648. Ormonde had landed the day before from France.

lish Catholics. It was proposed that toleration should be granted for
the exercise of the Catholic religion, and that Catholics should in turn
disclaim the temporal pretensions of the Pope, and maintain 10,000
men for the service of the Commonwealth. An order had been lately
made by Parliament, admitting Catholics to compound for their estates
on easy terms, and allowing them to take a form of oath confined
solely to temporal matters. O'Neill did not trust this sudden show
of friendship; at the head of his army he preferred to bide his time.
One thing he needed very urgently — ammunition.[1] In the beginning
of May he summoned a meeting of his followers at Belturbet. There
it was agreed to accept Sir Charles Coote's proposal, made some time
before, that commissioners should be appointed by both parties to
confer together on the terms of a treaty. They met at Newtown,
near Dromahaire, in the county of Leitrim. O'Neill demanded liberty
of conscience for himself and all his followers; an act of oblivion for
all done since 1641; restoration of all the confiscated lands in Ulster
to their original owners, and the possession of a seaport in that
province; for himself a competent command, and provision for his
army as the rest of the forces. These terms were agreed upon.
To meet O'Neill's present wants, it was further agreed that he
should receive thirty barrels of powder, with ball and match in proportion, and 300 beeves or £400, on condition that he should march
to the relief of Derry, then blockaded by the Scots, under Lord
Montgomery of Ardes.[2] But Sir Charles Coote refused to abide by
the articles agreed to by his Commissioners. O'Neill next addressed himself to Colonel Monk, and offered him the same terms.
These Monk gladly accepted, and on the 8th of May he agreed to a
cessation of hostilities for three months.[3] He was then at Dundalk;
and hearing of Inchiquin's approach, after the taking of Drogheda,
and of Lord Montgomery's advance from the north to join Ormonde,
then investing Dublin, he sent word to O'Neill, in pursuance of the
Articles made between them, to draw his forces together, and be in
readiness for his relief, as soon as the enemy drew near. O'Neill
replied that he was in want of ammunition; to obtain this he marched
to Glasdroman, within seven miles of Dundalk. From that place he
sent 1,200 of his best foot and 200 horse,[4] under the command of his
Lieutenant General Ferrall.[5] They received from Monk thirty bar-

---

[1] "There was a mighty scarcity of powder and shot, and he was destitute of all human
way to come by it." *Aphor. Disc.*, vol. ii. p. 41.

[2] Hugh, Viscount Montgomery of Ardes, had been appointed by the Parliament commander of the horse in Ulster. He was taken prisoner at Benburb, but released soon after,
in exchange for the Earl of Westmeath. In the Carte MSS. there is a letter of Owen Roe
to Charles I., declining to obey the order of his Majesty "for the enlargement of so notorious
a rebel." See Rev. C. P. Meehan's *Flight of the Earls*, p. 499; Dublin, 1870.

[3] *The Perfect Diurnal* of August 15th, 1649 gives " The reasons reducing Colonel Monk
to make a cessation with Owen Roe O'Neill, and the Articles agreed on between them."

[4] Cox says 500 foot and 300 horse; *Hib. Angl.*, Reign of Charles II., p. 4.

[5] Ferrall had come from Flanders in 1643; he and Henry O'Neill, Owen Roe's son,
landed at Wexford with a few officers and arms for one troop of horse. He was the trusted
friend of Owen Roe. See O'Connor's *History of the Irish Brigades*, p. 44; Dublin, 1855.
The author of the *Aphor. Disc.* always speaks in the highest terms of O'Farrell's bravery and
skill.

re's of powder, with match and bullets in proportion. Inchiquin had intelligence of the movements of the convoy, and sent six troops of horse, under Colonel Trevor, to intercept it. They met on an open road. The escort was totally routed. Farrall, with about thirty horse, escaped by flight; the infantry were nearly all cut to pieces, not above forty of them escaping. From some of the prisoners Inchiquin learned the weak condition of Dundalk. Two days later he invested the town. The garrison forced Monk to surrender. The greater number of them joined Inchiquin; "the soldiers ran over the trenches to him, swearing deep oaths that they would not engage with Monk, who had entered into a confederacy with Owen Roe, the head of the native Irish." A few days after Trim surrendered, owing to the treachery of Captain Martain; the garrison here too joined Inchiquin.

O'Neill marched to Clones. There an express reached him from Sir Charles Coote, informing him that Derry was still closely besieged by the Scots, under Lord Montgomery, and the garrison reduced almost to extremities, and accepting his former proposals, on condition that he would raise the seige. O'Neill set off at the head of his army and came to Ballykelly. The Scots, hearing of his approach, retired from before the town, and posted away at full speed, by day and night, till they crossed the Bann and reached their own country. He encamped before the town, on the Tyrone side of the river. Coote came to return him thanks, and invited him and his chief officers into the town, and entertained them sumptuously.

Though the treaty saved Derry, it did not prevent a spirit of distrust from spreading throughout the Parliamentary army. By many it was pronounced an apostasy from the principles for which they had fought. The horrors of the massacre of 1641 were once more recalled to mind, and the resolution taken to avenge the blood shed by the Irish. To appease the growing discontent, the Parliament at first deferred the ratifying of the treaty; but the clamor growing louder, it feigned great indignation. O'Neill, finding the cessation would not be renewed, sent an agent to London, proposing to submit with his army to the Commonwealth, if they obtained indemnity for the past, and an assurance of their religion and estates for the future. His agent was asked by the "grandees" "why he applied to them and refused to treat with Ormonde." He replied, "because the late King had always made them fair promises; but when they had done him service, and he could make better terms with their enemies, he had always been ready to sacrifice them." "Why, then, did he not apply to the Parliament sooner?" "Because the men in power then had sworn to extirpate them; but those in power now professed toleration and liberty of conscience." His conditions were refused. Monk was recalled from Ireland, displaced, and for some time imprisoned. "He was brought before the House and asked several questions, which he answered at the bar of the House, touching that business; and though he gave good reasons for what he had done, and pointed out the advantages which the Parliament had gained thereby, yet he was told that if he escaped punishment, it was owing to his

good intentions.   On the 10th of August, the House declared that it
did disapprove of what Colonel Monk had done, in concluding a treaty
with the grand and bloody Irish rebel, Owen Roe O'Neill, and did
abhor the having anything to do with him therein.   Three days later
the House passed the following resolution : —

Resolved, &c. — That this House doth utterly disapprove of the
proceedings of Colonel Monk, in the treaty and cessation made between him and Owen Roe O'Neill ; and that the innocent blood which
had been shed in Ireland is so fresh in the memory of this House,
that this House doth detest and abhor the thoughts of closing with
any party of Popish rebels there who have had their hands in the
shedding that blood.   Nevertheless, the House being satisfied that
what the said Colonel Monk did therein was, in his apprehension,
necessary for the preservation of the Parliament of England's interest, the House is content that the further consideration thereof, as to
him, be laid aside, and shall not at any time hereafter be called in
question.

The Parliament also disapproved of Coote's treaty with O'Neill,
though well satisfied of his diligence and integrity in preserving the
garrison of Londonderry.   He strove to soften their anger " by re-
minding them that it was no new thing with the most wise God to
make use of wicked instruments to bring about a good 'design for the
advancement of his glory.   Yet, many were of opinion that all that
was done both by Sir Charles Coote and by Monk, was transacted by
the privity, if not consent, of the grandees in England ; but the
grounds to fasten this upon them could never be found, though the
business was narrowly searched into."   The Council of State declared Sir Kenelm Digby " a dangerous person ; " he was ordered to
depart the Commonwealth within twenty days, and not to return into
any of the dominions of England without leave of the House, under
pain of death and confiscation of estate.   Three days later it declared
that all persons who had served the Parliament of England in Ireland
and had betrayed their trust, and had adhered, or should adhere to,
or aid, or assist Charles Stuart, eldest son of the late King, were
traitors and rebels, and ordered that their lands should be confiscated
and their persons proceeded against by martial law.

CHAPTER II.

THE BATTLE OF BAGGOTRATH.

Ormonde's army—Charles II. urged to come to Ireland—Muster of the Army—March through Carlow and Kildare—Encampment before Dublin—Inchiquin takes Drogheda and Trim—Dublin invested—Arrival of Reinforcements—Battle of Baggotrath—Cause of the Defeat—Ormonde's Movements—Jones' letter—Orders of the Council of State.

ORMONDE next set about putting an army on foot. It was no easy task to bring together men differing in nationality and religion; to unite those who for eight years had waged a bitter war against each other. The Commissioners of Trust were bound by the terms of the treaty to supply him with 15,000 foot and 2,500 horse. But the provinces, wasted by a long-continued war, plundered by friend and by foe alike, could not maintain such a number. A tax of £60,000 had been assessed on the kingdom; when the money was called for, it was found that none of it had been collected. Ormonde applied to several of the cities and towns for aid. These declined to obey any orders of the General Assembly, and granted or denied supplies as it suited them. At Waterford he raised £7,000 by mortgaging the King's rents and customs; £5,000 was promised by Limerick and Galway on the same terms. The securities were reluctantly accepted, and the money slowly paid in.

In his distress he turned to the King for help. He earnestly besought Charles to come to Ireland, assuring him that his presence there would unite the contending parties and bring the whole nation under his allegiance; it would encourage those who were loyal; it would draw to his standard most of the Parliamentary forces; Jones' men were deserting every day in considerable numbers; perhaps Jones himself would come over; even O'Neill would be reconciled, since he had already, by a private messenger, given the King the strongest assurances of his fidelity, and of his readiness to submit immediately on his arrival. But he suppressed very carefully the main reason why he wished the King to come. The chief power, civil and military, was in the hands of the Commissioners of Trust; they carried on the government of the country. The King's presence would, of course, cause all this power to be transferred to himself, or rather, seeing the yielding nature of Charles' character, to the hands of Ormonde—a consummation he anxiously wished for and strove to bring about by every means in his power. Charles seemed convinced that it was his duty to come and take up the defence of his own cause. When the Scotch commissioners attended him at the Hague, he deferred giving them an answer until his arrival in Ireland. His heavy baggage and his inferior servants were actually landed. But three months were wasted in the vain hope of getting assistance from the States General of the United Provinces. When he reached Jersey, on his way to Ireland, the opportunity was lost, the time for action had gone by.

Ormonde, anxious to take the field early in spring, appointed the 4th of March for the muster of the forces in the county of Tipperary. By the beginning of May he had got together about 2,000 foot and 300 horse at Cashel. At their head he put Lord Castlehaven,[1] and bade him attempt the strong places still held by O'Neill in Leinster, which it would be dangerous to leave behind in the hands of the enemy when the army advanced on Dublin. He captured in quick succession the castles of Maryborough, Athy, and Rheban.[2] Inchiquin was appointed lieutenant-general of the army, and Lord Taaffe master of the ordnance. Meantime news reached him that the Laggan forces in the north had risen in mutiny and besieged Sir Charles Coote in Derry, and that Sir George Munroe, who was at the head of the Royalist army in Ulster, having by the aid of the Marquis of Clanricarde reduced the Parliamentary garrisons, was on his way to join them; that Lord Montgomery and the Earl of Clanbrasil, with the officers and gentlemen of Down and Antrim, had taken up arms against Monk, and made themselves masters of Coleraine and all the fortresses in those counties, except Lisburn, which could not hold out much longer, since it was not provided with supplies for a seige.

The grand aim of Ormonde was to get hold of Dublin. The possession of the capital, he supposed, would not only secure the King's interest in Ireland, but also cause an extensive rising in his favor throughout England. He appointed a general rendezvous for the whole army at Clogrennan.[3] At the end of May he had under his command 14,500 foot and 3,700 horse; he had but four pieces of artillery. In the beginning of June he put himself at the head of this army and set out for Dublin. On the evening of the first day he appeared before

---

[1] James Touchet, Earl of Castlehaven and Baron of Orier, in Ireland, Baron Audley of Hilleigh, in England. His grandfather had received extensive grants of forfeited lands, chiefly church property, from James I. in Wexford, Kildare, Tipperary, Carlow, and Cork; he took his title from a small village near Castletownsend, in the county of Cork. Soon after the surrender of Galway in April, 1652, he entered the service of the great Condé. He died at his sister's house at Kilcash, near Clonmel, in 1684. In 1680 he published his *Memoirs of the Engagement and Carriage of the Civil War of Ireland from 1642 to 1651*. He prepared a second edition of the work, with a dedication to James II., in which he says: "I lay these Memoirs at your Majesty's feet, and pass them on my word not to contain a lie or mistake to my knowledge." This was published in 1685. See Hill's *Plantation of Ulster*, pp. 135 and 335; Belfast, 1877; and Carte's *Life of Ormonde*, vol. i. p 298.

[2] Rheban Castle, two miles north of Athy, was erected by Richard de St. Michel, who got a grant of lands here from William Marshal, Earl of Pembroke, in the reign of King John. This castle and Dunamaise were seized in 1325 by Lysagh O'More, and held by him and his descendants long after. In 1424 it passed to Thomas Fitzgerald, later 7th earl of Kildare, by his marriage with Dorothea, daughter of Anthony O'More. As it commanded a pass over the Barrow, it was reckoned of great importance in time of war. *Anthologia Hibernica*, vol. ii. p. 162; Dublin, 1793.

[3] On the western bank of the Barrow, two miles below Carlow. The fine old castle is still standing. It belonged to a junior branch of the Ormonde family. When the second duke was attainted, it passed into the hands of the Rochforts, in whose possession it is now.

Talbotstown,[1] which, together with Castletalbot,[2] was within three days surrendered to him. At Kildare he was forced to halt for three days for want of provisions. He hoped to meet Inchiquin there, who, with 2,000 Munster men, was marching to join him. He purposed falling on Jones, who was then with a foraging party at Johnstown. He crossed the Liffey and encamped at Naas ; here he was joined by Inchiquin and his party. A council of war was held, at which it was debated whether he should first take Drogheda, Trim, and the other garrisons still in the hands of the Parliament, or march directly on Dublin and lay seige to it. The general officers were of opinion that Dublin should be attempted immediately. They had secret information that the city was at that moment in a very distressed state, that the stock of provisions would not last ten days, that a considerable part of the garrison was disaffected, and that whole companies with their officers impatiently awaited his approach to desert. If Dublin was taken, the other strong places would surrender immediately. If time was wasted in other lesser enterprises, supplies might meanwhile arrive from England, and the capture of Dublin would no longer be possible. Still a want of supplies hindered his advance. Most opportunely, however, Lord Taaffe arrived with a sum of £2,000, contributed by the province of Connaught towards the support of the army.

Crossing the Liffey at Lucan on the morning of June 19th, the army advanced to Castleknock. Jones, the governor of Dublin, had drawn his horse outside the walls. Some slight skirmishes took place between these and Ormonde's outposts. On the evening of the same day Ormonde drew off and encamped at Finglas, three miles to the north of the city. The next day he sent a detachment to show itself before the walls, in the hope that its presence might raise a tumult among those within who were not well affected towards the Parliament. Some of the garrison deserted to him. Having learned that Jones, distressed for want of forage for his horses, had detached a part of his cavalry to Drogheda, he sent Inchiquin in pursuit with a large body of horse ; he surprised a whole troop, and defeated Colonel Coote at the head of three hundred of their number ; the rest fled in great disorder to Drogheda. He sent news of his success to Ormonde, and expressed a hope that he might be allowed to follow up his advantage. A council of war was held. It was agreed that Dublin was so well fortified that an attempt to take it by assault would be hopeless, that the army under Ormonde's command was not sufficiently numerous to invest it wholly, especially as O'Neill and Monk, with the garrisons of Drogheda and Trim, threatened to fall on the lines of the besiegers ; that Ormonde should continue encamped before Dublin with 5,000 foot and 1,500 horse, to prevent supplies from entering and to support any revolt within the city ; that Inchiquin, with the same number of

[1] Talbotstown, two miles south of Baltinglass. There is no trace of the castle, but the site is still pointed out.

[2] Castletalbot, two miles from Talbotstown ; so says Clarendon, *Hist. View*, p. 79. The site is not known. Robert Talbot of Castletalbot was one of the Commons' Representatives in the General Assembly of the Confederate Catholics which met at Kilkenny January 10th, 1647. Ledwich's *History of Irishtown and Kilkenny*, p. 471 ; Dublin, 1804.

horse and 2,000 foot, aided by Colonel Mark Trevor, who had lately declared for the King, should block up Drogheda. An attempt was made to surprise the latter town. Two of the gates were fired : about two hundred of the assailants succeeded in effecting an entrance ; but they were soon repulsed with considerable loss. Two pieces of cannon were sent from Dublin ; when these were planted in position, the town surrendered, the garrison being allowed to march out to Dublin. The greater number took service under Inchiquin. We have already spoken of his success in preventing the supplies sent by Monk from reaching O'Neill and of the capture of Dundalk. He then set out for Dublin and joined Ormonde while he lay at Finglas.

Ormonde now prepared to invest Dublin on all sides, though his army, consisting of 7,000 foot and 1,700 horse, was hardly sufficient to carry on the seige of so extensive a city with effect.[1] He left Lord Dillon[2] with 2,500 men to press the seige on the north side ; with the remainder he crossed the Liffey and encamped at Rathmines, intending to extend his works to the east, so as to command the entrance to the river and prevent any supplies coming in by that way. His confidence in the loyalty of his men was unbounded. "That which only threatens any rule to our success," he wrote, "is our wants, which have been and are such that soldiers have actually starved by their arms, and many of less constancy have gone home ; many of the foot are weak ; yet I despair not to be able to keep them together, and to reduce Dublin if good supplies of all sorts come not speedily to relieve it. I am confident I can persuade one half of our army to starve outright, and I shall venture upon it rather than give up a game so fair on our side and so hard to be recovered if given over."

Before he could carry out his plans, the garrison was strengthened by the arrival of Colonel Venables from England, on the 22d of July, with a strong body of foot ; three days later, Colonel Reynolds[3] came with a regiment of horse ; the next day, Colonel Huncks,[4] with a still larger body of horse and foot ; these reinforcements amounted to 1,600 foot and 600 horse. They brought word that the Parliament, considering the capital sufficiently protected and aware of the disaffection of the southern towns, had sent orders to Cromwell to proceed with his

[1] "This was," Ormonde says, "the largest list given by the officers. Of these I am sure there were 2,000 sick and over-reckoned by the officers for gain and fear of reforming. Besides the two regiments sent to Drogheda and Trim, the army was not I am sure 8,000 effective men." Carte's *Collection*, &c., vol. ii. p. 396.

[2] Lord Dillon, a favorite of Ormonde's was made commander of the Leinster horse in 1647, though he had never seen a sword drawn in a field before, and though Colonel Pierce Fitzgerald MacThomas had been appointed to that post by the Assembly. *Aphor. Disc.* vol. i. p. 155. In the *Nunziatura*, p. 176, an account is given of his conversion and reception into the church by Rinuccini in 1646.

[3] Reynolds was brother-in-law of Lord Henry Cromwell. After the Irish campaign, he had the command of the forces sent to Dunkirk to aid Turenne and the French to take Mardyke from the Spaniards. On his return, in December, 1657, he was lost on the Goodwin Sands.

[4] The King's death-warrant was addressed to Colonels Hacker, Huncks, and Phayre, "willing and requiring them to see the sentence of death executed on him the following day." It was dated Jan. 29th, 1649 ; D'Aubigné's *The Protector*, p. 49 ; Edinburgh, 1849.

army to Munster,[1] and that he waited only for a favorable wind to set sail. The following detailed account of the events that followed was sent by Ormonde to the King.

"Some two or three days before the defeat at Rathmines, we had it from many good hands out of England and from Dublin that Cromwell was at the sea-side, ready to embark for this kingdom with a great army, and that his design was for Munster, where we were sure he had intelligence, and which, if lost, not only the best ports of the kingdom would fall into his hands, but his Majesty's fleet riding in them, blocked up with a mastering number of the rebels' ships, would doubtless be lost. So that if we had taken Dublin, which was very doubtful, and lost those parts, which it was very evident we should if he landed there, as they were then guarded, it was but an ill exchange; but if these places were lost and Dublin not gained, our army must inevitably have come to nothing, and the kingdom fallen to the rebels without resistence. These considerations at a council of war produced these results: first, that the Lord Inchiquin, with two regiments of horse,[2] should then immediately march to secure the province of Munster; that the army should lie still where it was till Rathfarnham[3] should be taken in; and that done, we should remove to a securer quarter at a place called Drimnagh,[4] not far from Rathfarnham, if after the taking of Rathfarnham we found not cause to change that part of our determination. The next day, or the next day but one, Rathfarnham was taken by storm; all that were there were made prisoners; and though five hundred soldiers had entered the castle before any officers of note, yet not one creature was killed, which I tell you by the way, to observe the difference between our and the rebels making use of a victory."

Inchiquin's departure at such a critical moment was a severe loss. Ormonde now gave up all hope of carrying on the siege. He summoned a council of war, at which he proposed to raise the siege and retire to Drogheda, Trim, and the other garrisons still in the possession of the Royalists, and from thence endeavor to distress Dublin, and make an offensive or defensive war, as occasion should offer. His army was not numerous enough, and his present position was too open to an attack. The Irish officers were wholly opposed to such a movement; they contended that it would be little better than a disgraceful retreat; that the reduction of the city was not a difficult task; they need but possess themselves of the old castle of Baggotrath;[5] this they could fortify sufficiently in a few hours, so as to resist any attack from the city; and from it they might advance their works eastwards towards the River Liffey, without hindrance, and seize on the meadows near it, which was the sole pasturage left for the horses of the garrison.

---

[1] One of Ormonde's spies wrote to him: "I find Cromwell hath some friends in Munster, and more he hopes to make with his money. which may work much, when it is known he has it, among needy men." *Aphor. Disc.*, vol. ii. p. 223, appendix xvi.

[2] In all about 1,100 horse, according to Castlehaven, *Memoirs*, p. 114.

[3] Rathfarnham Castle was built by Adam Loftus, one of the favorites of Queen Elizabeth, who came to Ireland in 1559. He became successively archbishop of Armagh, archbishop o Dublin, and lord chancellor. He died in 1605. See *Lives of the Lord Chancellors of Ireland*, by J. R. O'Flanagan, vol. i. p. 263; London, 1870; and *The Lord Chancellors of Ireland*, by O. J. Burke, B. L., p. 65; Dublin, 1879.

[4] This castle, still standing, is between Crumlin and Clondalkin, about three miles from Dublin, close to the Grand Canal. Probably it was built by Hugh de Bernivale, who got a grant of the lands of Drimnagh and Terenure from King John. In the reign of James I., the property passed, after much litigation, into the hands of Sir Adam Loftus. *Irish Penny Journal*, No. 43; Dublin, 1841.

[5] Baggotrath castle stood close to the place now occupied by Begger's-Bush barracks. In 1280 Robert Bagot obtained a grant of the manor of Rath, near Dublin; a castle was soon after erected there, which was called Baggotrath. Dalton's *King James' Army List*, vol. ii. p. 570; Dublin, n. d.

" It was then taken into consideration," continues Ormonde, " what was to be done, and it was held necessary that we should possess a place called Baggotrath and fortify it ; which, if effected, must necessarily have starved all their horses within, which, by access of new forces whilst we lay at Finglass, were 1,200 ; and besides, that place being well fortified, it was easy then to have approached to the river side, that a work being cast up there, it would be impossible for any further succour of men to have got into them. I should have told you that we had a strong party of horse and foot left on the other side of the river, which hindered their grazing that way, and hay they had none in the town. Thereupon it was ordered that my Lord of Castlehaven, General Preston, and Major-General Purcell,[1] should view the place ; and if they found it capable of strengthening in one night's work, then to cause men with materials to be sent as soon as it was dark. Accordingly, the Major-General conducted thither 1,500 foot ; but he met with so ill guides that, though it was within half a mile of our leaguer, he got not thither till a full hour before day.[2] I sat up myself all that night, as well to be ready to answer any falling out of the enemy as to finish my despatches then ready for France. But as soon as day broke, I rode down to Baggotrath, where I found the place itself not so strong as I expected, nor the work at all advanced, and strong parties of the enemy drawn out under their works ; yet they hid themselves the best they could behind some houses at Lowsy Hill, and in a hollow betwixt us and the strand. Hereupon I considered whether I had best go on with the work or draw off my men ; draw them off I could not without great danger, but by drawing near them the whole army, and doing that, their work might be as well countenanced as their retreat. Then I called to me the Major-Generals of the horse and foot, Purcell and Sir W. Vaughan,[3] and showed them where I would have the horse and foot drawn, desiring them accordingly to see it done, telling them and all the officers there that I was confident Jones would hazard all to interrupt our work, which effected would so much annoy him. With these orders I left them, determining to refresh myself with a little sleep for the action I expected, and in my way to my tent I caused all the regiments to stand to their arms.

" It was by this time about nine of the clock, and I had not slept above an hour, when I was awakened by volleys of shot, which I took to be much nearer me than Baggotrath. However, before I got an hundred yards from my tent, all those I left working were beaten out, and the enemy had routed and killed Sir W. Vaughan, and after him divers parties of horse drawn up in closes, into which the enemy could not come to them but through gaps and in files. This was the right wing of our army ; and it was not long before I saw it wholly defeated, and many of them running away towards the hills of Wicklow, where some of them were bred and whither they knew the way but too well. Hereupon I went to the battalia,[4] consisting of my Lord Inchiquin's foot, commanded by Colonel Giffard, with whose

---

[1] " The illustrious Sir Patrick Purcell, Vice-General of all Munster, noble-hearted, and a most accomplished warrior, renowned for his services in Germany against Sweden and France under Ferdinand III. of august memory, after the capture of Limerick, was hanged, his head cut off and fixed on a stake over the southern or St. John's gate of the city." Morison, *Threnodia Hiberno-Catholica*, p. 68 ; Innsbruck, 1659. " It has pleased God to deliver into our hands two persons of principal activity and influence in the late obstinate holding out, the Bishop of Emly and General Purcell, whom we presently hanged, and have set up their heads on the gates." Letter of Ireton to Lenthall, in Rev. C. P. Meehan's *Rise and Fall of the Franciscan Monasteries*, p. 362 ; Dublin, 1877.

[2] It was said that this mishap was owing to the treachery of the guides. According to Taylor, *History of the Civil Wars of Ireland*, vol. ii. p. 11 ; Edinburgh, 1831 ; and Borlase, *Rebellion*, p. 315, when Dr. Edmond O'Reilly, the primate, was tried some years after for burning the castle of Wicklow and murdering the garrison during a cessation of arms, he pleaded in his defence that the guide had led the detachment astray by his directions, and his life was spared in consequence. See also Warner's *History of the Rebellion*, &c., p. 467. But this statement is refuted by the Most Rev. Dr. M'Carthy in his *Collections of Irish Church History*, vol. i. p. 51 ; Dublin, 1861. It was one of the many calumnies published by Fr. P. Walsh against those who opposed him. See his *History of the Remonstrance*, pp. 583 and 689.

[3] Ormonde had given him the command that same morning in his displeasure against Purcell. One of the charges brought against Ormonde in the " Declaration" of Jamestown, August 12th, 1650, was " that Catholic commanders, instanced by the Commissioners of Trust, and therefore by his Excellency's commission receiving their command in their army, as Colonel Patrick Purcell of Major-General in the army, and Colonel Pierce Fitzgerald alias MacThomas, Commissary of the Horse, were removed without the consent of the said Commissioners and by no demerit of the gentlemen, and the said places given to Daniel O'Neill, Esq., Protestant, and to Sir William Vaughan, knight, and, after his death, to Sir Thomas Armstrong, both Protestants." *Aphor. Disc.*, vol. ii. p. 101.

[4] Battalia, i.e. the main body of an army in array.

assistance I put them into the best position I could; and desired my brother[1] and Colonel Reilly to stand in a field next these foot, where I left them till I should either come or send them orders. How they were forced thence, or upon what occasion they charged, I know not; but I soon after perceived the enemy's horse had gotten round and was going through a lane, close by Giffard's foot, where I stood, to meet a party of foot of their own that were coming up in front of us. Giffard's foot gave good fire at them and so disordered them, that had not the two regiments, which for that purpose I left there, been forced, or by some appearing advantage drawn off, but had charged those disordered horse in the rear, it is probable they had been driven over their foot; to which when they had come, they rallied by them, and with them advanced against us, who by this time were environed; another party of theirs of horse and foot being then coming behind us into the field we stood in, and giving fire both ways at us. At this and at the running away of Reilly's regiment, our foot were so discouraged that they fought no more. On the contrary, I heard the enemy offer them quarter and observed them inclined to hearken to it. Then, leaping over a ditch, I endeavored to get to our left wing, hoping to find it form; but they had no sooner apprehended and too well seen how the world went with the right wing and battalia, and had most of them, horse and foot, provided for themselves. It is true that a great reserve of the enemy stood all this while facing them; which was the reason why I drew not to the assistance of the rest of the army, and that made them think themselves desperate. Yet some of them I rallied; but as I advanced a step towards the enemy, they broke away behind me, even upon the sight of their own men running away, taking them for the enemy."[2]

The victors were prevented from pursuing the fugitives by the sudden appearance of Sir Thomas Armstrong, at the head of 1,000 fresh horse, who had just come to Ormonde's aid. The battle lasted but two hours; yet 600 of Ormonde's men were slain.[3] Most of them were butchered after they had laid down their arms on promise of quarter, and been for nearly an hour prisoners. Some Walloons, who were taken for Irishmen, were also put to the sword. Many, too, were murdered after they had been brought within the walls of the city. Among those who were taken prisoners were Ormonde's brother, Colonel Richard Butler, his half-brother, George Mathew, and Christopher, second earl of Fingal; the last died a fortnight after in the castle of Dublin, where he was confined.[4]

Lord Taaffe escaped across the river, and besought Lord Dillon to attempt the recovery of the field with the 2,500 men under his command; but "so great was their consternation, that they could not be prevailed upon to try their fortune, or hardly to provide for their own safety without confusion; though at length they did observe the Lord Lieutenant's orders, of going half to Drogheda and half to Trim, to secure these garrisons."

Ormonde lost his baggage, arms, ammunition, and money-chest containing £4,000. He narrowly escaped being taken prisoner. Colonel Reynolds, who had taken the Marquis' brother, threatened

[1] Richard Butler, of Kilcash, made governor of the county of Waterford by the Confederates. In the army he held the rank of lieutenant-general.

[2] The spot where this battle was fought is said to be the same where some three hundred of the citizens of Dublin, besides women and children, were slaughtered by the "mountaineers," the O'Tooles and O'Byrnes, on Easter Monday, in the year 1209, since called for that reason Black Monday. For an account of this massacre see Hanmer's *Chronicle of Ireland*, p. 370; Dublin, 1809.

[3] Ormonde admitted this number to have been slain on his side. See his letter to the King in Carte's *Collection*, &c., vol. ii. p. 396. According to Bate, 3,000 were slain, and 2,100 common soldiers and 150 officers taken prisoners; 8,000 stand of arms, with the tents, provisions, guns, and baggage, fell into the hands of the enemy. See *Elenchus Motuum Nuperorum in Anglia*, vol. ii. p. 22; London, 1663.

[4] The *Aphor. Disc.* says he died of mere melancholy and grief that he was ever of Ormonde's party; vol. ii. p. 46.

to pistol him if he did not point out to him the Marquis ; he was then quite near, with only a few horse. Reynolds and Captain Otway charged them ; but Ormonde set spurs to his horse and escaped.

Jones' utmost design was to make a sortie, to beat up the enemy's quarters, and to drive them from Baggotrath. But he was led on by his success step by step ; and what he intended to be merely a sortie resulted in the total rout and destruction of the Royalist army.[1] The capital was relieved from further apprehension. By some the defeat was attributed to Ormonde's incapacity, by others to his neglect. In the " Declaration " of the Prelates at Jamestown, a year later, it was said that "the conduct of the army was improvident and unfortunate ; that nothing happened in Christianity more shameful than the disaster at Rathmines, where his Excellency, as it seemed to ancient travellers and men of experience who viewed all, kept rather a mart of wares, a tribunal of pleadings, or a great inn of play, drinking and pleasure, than a well-ordered camp of soldiers. Some even ventured to hint that treason was at work. To silence these murmurs, the King sent him the garter.[2] In truth the defeat did not prove that the troops were deficient in courage or the commander in ability : it only showed how little reliance can be placed upon a mob, no matter how eager to fight, when opposed to a well-disciplined army.[3] It was the close of Ormonde's military career ; for his power was so broken that he never after ventured to meet the Parliamentary army in the field.

Immediately after the battle he set off for Kilkenny. The next day he came with a few horse to Ballysonan,[4] a strong castle in the county of Kildare, and summoned it to surrender. The governor, thinking that Dublin was in the hands of the Royalists, and that their army was approaching, gave up that important place without hesitation. As soon as he reached Kilkenny, he strove to bring together the shattered remnant of his army. A week after, he went to Trim at the head of 300 men, all that he could rally. He summoned troops from every quarter, thinking to make another attempt at the capital. Few responded to his call. Hearing that Jones was besieging Drogheda, he set off to relieve it. Lord Moore had defended it ably ; the besiegers, hearing of Ormonde's approach, raised the siege and returned to Dublin.

Soon after Ormonde wrote to Jones, asking for a list of his pris-

---

[1] Colonel Jones hath found out a fine way of gaining intelligence by sending cunning beggars into Ormonde's camp, who bring him notice of what he can observe there also. Some soldiers that seem to run thither, are of purpose employed to gain intelligence. *Cromwell's Embarcation* in *Aphor. Disc.*, p. 224, appendix xvi.; from the Carte MSS., vol. xxv. p. 25

[2] " We, weighing the eminence of your brother and family, and, above all, the great and extraordinary services done by you for many years past and still continued in the condition of Lord Lieutenant in that our kingdom, together with your singular courage and fidelity, &c." King's warrant to make Ormonde a Knight of the Garter, in Carte's *Collection*, &c., vol. ii p. 394

[3] According to Clarendon, Jones' army consisted of 6,000 foot and 1,900 horse, a greater force than Ormonde had under his command. *Hist. View*, &c., p. 91.

[4] Five miles south-west of Kilcullen Bridge.

oners. Jones replied : "Since I routed your army, I cannot have the happiness to know where you are, that I may wait on you."

On receipt of the news the Council of State ordered, "That Colonel Jones' letter relating to the victory of August 6th, of the forces of the city of Dublin against Ormonde's army, with the list of prisoners and ammunition taken, and Captain Otway's narrative be printed and published; and that it be sent to the Lord Mayor of London, and to all the ministers within his jurisdiction, who are to publish the same to-morrow in their congregations ; so that there may be an acknowledgement of God's goodness to the Commonwealth in so seasonable a victory." For never was a day in Ireland like this, to the confusion of the Irish and raising up of the spirits of the English and restoring their interest, which, from their first footing in Ireland, was never in so low a condition as at that time, there not being one considerable landing-place left for them but Dublin only, and that almost lost. The Parliament, for their high and extraordinary sense of so signal and seasonable a mercy, thought it fit and their duty to set apart a time for public and solemn thanksgiving, to be rendered to the Lord, the author of that mercy. And they did therefore enact and ordain that Wednesday, the 29th of August, be observed and kept as a day of public and holy rejoicing and thankfulness to the Lord in all churches and chapels within the Commonwealth.

Jones received the thanks of Parliament. A former vote, settling on him lands to the value of £500 for his success at Dungan's Hill,[1] two years before, was revived. Another vote, granting him and his heirs for ever lands to the value of £1,000 for his service, was now passed. Six of the best horses in Tilbury Race were ordered to be chosen by the trustees for the sale of the late King's goods for General Jones, as a gratuity from the House. It was ordered that £200 be given to Captain Otway who brought the news.

Yet in spite of Jones' success at Rathmines, he was still in great straits. His funds were quite exhausted ; to pay his men he was forced to levy a weekly tax off the city of Dublin. The harbor had only two frigates left to protect it. Throughout the rest of Ireland there were only two fortresses, Derry and Culmore, in the hands of the Parliament.

---

[1] Near Summerhill, in the county of Meath, where he defeated the Confederate army under the command of Preston. 3,000 foot, being deserted by their own cavalry, retreated to a bog, and threw down their arms. They were surrounded and cruelly put to death to a man. See *The Exact Relation of the great victory obtained against the rebels at Dungan's Hill*, by H. M.'s forces under the command of Colonel Michael Jones, August 8th, 1647, in Rev. C. P. Meehan's *Confederation of Kilkenny*, appendix, p. 308; Dublin, 1882.

CHAPTER III

Rebellion of 1641—The King and the Parliament—Character of the Rebellion—The Act of Subscription—An Irish war popular — Lord Wharton Commander-in-Chief—Lord Forbes' Expedition—The Parliament and the Army—Lord Lisle Lord Lieutenant—Inchiquin changes sides—Reinforcements for Dublin—The Cobbler of Aggavam.

On the 23d of October, 1641, the Irish of Ulster rose in rebellion,[1] and seized on many of the strong places in the North.[2] The flame spread rapidly. Two months after, all the walled towns and fortresses were in the hands of the insurgents, except Derry in the north; Cork, Youghal, Kinsale and Bandon, in the south; Dublin, Drogheda, Dundalk, and the castle of Carrickfergus, in the east.[3] The King, who was then absent in Scotland, wrote to the parliament that to it he committed the care of Ireland, and ordered provision to be made for the suppression of the rebellion. By this course he hoped to free himself from the suspicion of being too faint a prosecutor of an enemy whose insurrections it was said he had himself fomented. The popular party in the parliament pretended to understand this passage as giving them the control of the war to the exclusion of the King, and interpreted it in the most unlimited sense. Six months later, April 8th, 1642, he sent another message to the parliament, that he intended to put himself at the head of an army and go into Ireland to chastise those wicked and detestable rebels, odious to God and all good men. But the leaders of the popular party

[1] " We imagine we are in no rebellion ourselves, but do really fight for our Prince in defense of his royal crown and prerogative, wherein we shall continue and die to the last man." Letter of Owen Roe O'Neill to Sir Robert Stewart, June 18th, 1643, in the *Carte MSS.*, vol. v. p. 272.

[2] See in *Desid. Curios. Hiber.*, vol. ii. p. 78; *The Heads of the Causes that moved the Northern Irish and the Catholics of Ireland to take arms;* it is reprinted in Curry's *Civil Wars of Ireland*, vol. ii. p. 371, and in *Aphor. Disc.*, vol. i. p. 450, appendix li. The native Irish being well informed, as they thought, that they must either turn Protestants, or depart the kingdom, or be hanged at their own doors, took up arms in their own defence, especially in Ulster, where the six counties had been forfeited. Anderson's *Royal Genealogies*, in Curry, vol. i. p. 190. It was blazed abroad by the best note of Protestants that all Ireland, by that time twelvemonth must either go to church, be executed, or endure banishment or exile. *Aphor. Disc.*, vol. i. p. 12. The Catholics were urged to rebellion; and the Lords justices were often heard to say, that the more there were in rebellion the more lands would be forfeited. Castlehaven's *Review of the Civil Wars of Ireland*, p. 28. The oath of association of the Catholic Confederation is given in Borlase's *Rebellion*, p. 95. The motto on their seal was: PRO DEO REGE ET PATRIA HIBERNI VNANIMES. Curry's *Civil Wars*, vol. i. p. 271.

[3] Though the Irish were at first a popular rout of unarmed clowns, the English durst scarce peep out of the gates of their great garrisons of Dublin and Drogheda. *Queries, &c.*; London, 1644, quoted in Prendergast's *Cromwellian Settlement of Ireland*, p. 56; Dublin, 1870.

had already laid their plans to take the management of the war out of
his hands; they feared the attempt made by Strafford, some years
before, to raise an Irish army which should be not only wholly independent of the parliament but entirely under the control of the King,
might be again renewed and their liberties endangered. They declared
they would consider his departure from England equivalent to a formal abdication of the throne.[1] Day by day the rebellion grew in
strength; its character soon became changed. It was no longer a
sudden outburst of wrath; it was a war directed by leaders skilled in
warfare and supported by a nation eager to avenge centuries of wrong.
The King's exchequer was empty, drained by James I. to satisfy the
hungry cravings of his Scotch favorites. The parliament forced the
King to assent to a scheme, which was afterwards embodied in an
Act,[2] for the advancing of money towards the raising and paying a
private army for subduing the Irish rebels, and offering as security
2,500,000 acres of forfeited Irish lands. The money should be paid
to a committee composed half of members of the House of Commons,
half of subscribers to the fund. The subscribers, or Adventurers,[3] as
they were more commonly called, on payment of ready money, would
have estates allotted to them on the following terms: £600 for 1,000
acres in Leinster; £450, £300, and £200 for the same quantity respectively in Munster, Connaught and Ulster. The allotment was
to take place as soon as the Lords and Commons in parliament assembled should declare the rebels subdued and the war appeased and
ended. The King suggested that such a wholesale confiscation would
make the Irish desperate. This was just what the parliament wanted.
The army would be kept employed far away, where it could not be
used by the King in support of his rights. Besides, the appointment
both of the commander and the officers should be entirely in the
hands of the Adventurers; the King had merely the signing of their
commissions.

An Irish war was at all times popular in England. Sir John
Bulstrode Whitelocke[4] declared that if these measures were carried
out, they would put an end to the long and bloody conflict foretold

---

[1] On the 8th of April, 1642, the Parliament declared that the King's going to Ireland
would be against the law, and that whosoever should assist him on his journey to Ireland
should be an enemy to the Commonwealth. Borlase's *Rebellion*, p. 70.

[2] It went by the name of the Adventurer's Act, or the Act of Subscription. February
26th, 1642, "The House of Commons passed the Bill for the Adventures for Ireland:
That every one that would bring in and adventure money for the reducing of Ireland
should have so many acres of the Irish Rebels' lands, proportionable to the money which
they brought in, and very good bargains; whereupon very great sums of money were
brought in for that service." Whitelocke, p. 54. See *A Declaration of both Houses of
Parliament concerning the Affairs of Ireland;* whereunto are added twelve arguments to
promote the work of subscription; London, 1641, reprinted by P. Traynor; Dublin, 1879;
and *Account of the Carte MSS.*, p. 160. It received the Royal assent March 19th, 1642.

[3] See the "List of the names and subscriptions of the Adventurers for lands in Ireland"
in the '*Cromwellian Settlement*, p. 403. The number of the original Adventurers was 1,360;
the sum total subscribed by them was £43,406 5s. od. *Ibid*, p. 448.

[4] Bulstrode Whitelocke, Esq., a member of the House, is given in the "List of Adven-
turers for land in Ireland." *Crom. Sett.* p. 405. The sum which he ventured was £400.
A namesake of his, probably a descendant, holds lands now near Corofin, in the county of
Clare.

with so much truth by Giraldus Cambrensis ;[1] another asserted that
it would bring in such sums as would soon bring the war to an end ;
that the work of Elizabeth and James I. would now be perfected ; that
the Irish would be rooted out by a new and overwhelming plantation
of English, and another England would speedily be founded in Ireland.
In this way a private army of 5,000 foot and 400 horse was
raised.[2] Lord Wharton was appointed commander-in-chief and lord-
general for Ireland.[3] This force assembled at Bristol in August,
1642, ready to embark for Munster ; they only waited for the signing of
the officers' commissions by the King, according to his promise. But
the Civil War having burst out when the royal standard was displayed
at Nottingham, the King refused to sign the commissions, fearing
that these forces might be employed against himself, as in fact happened. For being directed by the parliament to march against the
Royalist army, they took part in the battle of Edgehill, on the 23d of
October. The Adventurers finding that the funds that they had
raised to conquer lands in Ireland were misused by the parliament,
would not risk any further subscriptions, though the measure of land
was enlarged to the Irish standard,[4] and afterwards doubled for any
one who would pay in a sum equal to a fourth of his original subscription. The military part of the scheme failed. But the plan of pledg-
ing the land in Ireland for moneys to be advanced by parliament,
sometimes to relieve the gasping condition of the Protestants there,
but oftener to carry on the war against the King in England, was
continually extended. The sums brought in did not answer the purpose. In order to induce merchants and traders, foreign Protestants
as well as English, to embark in this speculation, the parliament
offered the principal sea-ports in Ireland for sale ; Limerick, with
12,000 acres contiguous, for £30,000 and a rent of £625, payable to
the state ; Waterford, with 15,000, at the same rate ; Galway, with
10,000, for £7,500 and a rent of £520. But the offer, however
tempting, found no bidders.

For the next few years the Parliamentary army was kept busily
employed at home. All the energy its leaders could display, all the

---

[1] Speech at a conference between the Lords and Commons, February 13th, 1642. "The
Irish have four national prophets who, speaking of the conquest of Ireland, all agree that
it will be stained by frequent battles, by numerous murders, and a contest continued to late
ages ; but in the end, a little only before the Day of Judgment, they promised complete conquest of the island to the people of England, and to have it garrisoned from sea to sea."
Giraldus Cambrensis, *Expugnatio Hibernica*, B. II. c. 34, edited by Dymock, vol. v. p. 385 ;
London, 1867.

[2] See *The List of Field Officers* chosen and appointed for the Irish expedition by the
Council, Guildhall, London, for the regiments of 5,000 foot and 500 horse, under the command of Philip, Lord Wharton, Baron of Scarborough, Lord-General of Ireland, first published in 1642, and reprinted by Hotten ; London, 1863. Among the names on the roll of
the officers is that of ensign Oliver Cromwell.

[3] Wharton, though a firm adherent of the Parliament during the Civil War and a personal friend of Cromwell, was not one of the Adventurers ; but Dame Philadelphia, his
mother, appears in the list as a subscriber of £200. Besides, by right of his wife, he was
entitled to the joint adventure of John and Robert Goodwin, members of the Long Parliament, for £600, as she was their heiress. See "The Case of Lord Wharton," in *Account of
the Carte MSS.*, p. 160.

[4] 100 acres Irish measure are very nearly equivalent to 162 English.

resources they could command, were needed to make front against the bravery of the Cavaliers. "Their votes," says Hume, "breathed nothing but death and destruction to the Irish rebels ; but no forces were sent, and little money was remitted." A few buccaneering expeditions from time to time visited the coast of Munster, like that which was headed by Lord Forbes in 1642. He set sail with six ships and 1,200 men. These, too, had been raised under an ordinance of the House of Commons, which accepted the proposal of certain adventurers to equip a force at their own expense ; the outlay to be repaid by the confiscated lands of the Irish. He landed at Kinsale and laid waste the surrounding country. The people took up arms and obliged him to raise anchor. He next landed at Galway, got possession of the abbey, dug up the graves, and burnt the coffins and bones of the dead, and required the citizens to sign "a submission, expressing their belief that there was no other means of saving them from extirpation and banishment." He next sailed up the Shannon, and spoiled the mansions on the riverside. He seized on Bunratty, a castle belonging to the Earl of Thomond, and left in it a garrison to hold it for the Parliament.[1]

In the beginning of 1647, the Presbyterian leaders were anxious to get rid of the army. The support of an army of between 20,000 and 30,000 men was a heavy burden. They strove to disguise their real motives under the pretense of the national advantage, "for it was observed by some that a victorious army out of employment is very inclinable to assume power over their principals ; and this occasioned the parliament's greater care for their employment in Ireland." Besides, such a large force had ceased to be any longer necessary, now that royalty was subdued. It was agreed that 12,000 men should be employed in Ireland ; those only should be sent who volunteered for that service : the remainder should be disbanded. The proposal to go encounter the Irish rebels was not very acceptable to them. They demanded their arrears of pay, and forty weeks' pay for the horse and eighteen for the foot ; indemnity for acts done in war, and a clear discharge according to contract, no service in Ireland except under known commanders. A letter was presented to the House on behalf of eight regiments of the army of horse, wherein they expressed "some reasons why they could not engage in the service of Ireland under the present conduct, till they were satisfied in their expectations and their first desires granted." Extra pay was offered to them. About two hundred of Sir Thomas Fairfax's officers met the Commissioners from the Derby House Committee.[2] The encouraging votes of the House were communicated to them, as two months' pay at present and a month's on shipboard, and other particulars. The

---

[1] *Life of Ormonde*, vol. i. p. 346 ; Hardiman's *History of Galway*, p. 117 ; Dublin, 1820 ; Hugh Peters was Lord Forbes' chaplain during his expedition, and his lordship was much guided by his advice. *Life of Ormonde*, vol. i. p. 347. No mention is made of this expedition in Admiral Forbes' *Earls of Granard* ; London, 1868.

[2] So called from the place where it first met. It was superseded by the Council of State, consisting of 38 members, which was appointed February 14th, 1649. This too held its meetings for a time at Derby House ; but towards the end of May it removed to Whitehall. *Domestic State Papers* (1649-50), preface xv.

officers desired to know what answer was given to their former desires of a general. It was answered that Major-General Skippen was voted general.[1] They replied that he had written to the House desiring to be excused. The officers with much civility, yet much affection, cried : "A Fairfax or a Cromwell." These they had experience of, and their conduct had been so blessed of heaven, that they should be encouraged much for Ireland, if that were declared. It was answered that they came to speak and to treat with those who would go under whomsoever the parliament should appoint ; others were at liberty to stay at home. About 12,000 enrolled themselves on this condition, but parliament refused its consent.

In the spring of this year Colonel Castle's regiment was sent to the aid of Ormonde. He was followed by Colonel Hungerford's regiment and Colonel Long's. The Commissioners, who arrived in June, to take possession of Dublin and the other fortresses betrayed to them by Ormonde,[2] brought with them 1,400 foot and 600 horse. By the end of that year both King and Parliament were subdued. Cromwell's first step was to make the army completely his own. The following written perhaps at his suggestion, will show what his plans were :

> It is a great pity the militia of this country should be disbanded. We hear of some overtures made by the army for engaging them and all the supernumeraries of the kingdom. The service will be gallant, and the design superlative ; and if old Noll, or any man of gallantry and fidelity do accept of that brigade, he cannot want men or money.

When the hopes of the Royalists were extinguished by the death of the King and the banishment of the Stuart dynasty, the leaders of the Parliamentary party could turn their whole attention to the affairs of Ireland, and proceed vigorously against those whom they styled the Irish rebels. When it was known that Charles II. had been proclaimed King in Ireland, and that the whole population had rallied in support of the royal cause under Ormonde's standard, it was resolved that he should be attacked in his last stronghold. Religious hatred was employed to stir up those who were callous to other motives. The following extract from a political pamphlet of the time will show the sentiments of the Puritans towards the Irish Catholics :

> A word of Ireland : not of the nation universally, nor of any man in it that hath so much as one hair of Christianity or humanity growing on his head or beard, but only of the truculent cut-throats, and such as shall take up arms in their defence.
>
> These Irish, anciently called Anthropophagi (man-eaters), have a tradition among them, that when the devil showed our Saviour all the kingdoms of the earth and their glory he would not show him Ireland, but reserved it for himself. It is most probably true, for he hath kept it ever since for his own peculiar aim ; the old

---

[1] April 2d, 1647, the House voted that the Commander in-Chief of the Forces in Ireland should be styled Field-Marshal and allowed £6 per diem, and appointed Major-General Skippen to be Field-Marshal, and Colonel Massey Lieutenant-General of the Horse under him. Whitelocke, p. 246.

[2] He handed over to the Parliament Dublin, Drogheda, Trim, Naas, and the other garrisons then held by him in Ireland, June 7th ; on the 25th of July he delivered up the regalia. Cox's *Hib. Angl.*, vol. i. p. 93. Jones took possession of the castle of Dublin for the Parliament. Curry, vol. i. p. 385. See Appendix i.

fox foresaw that it would eclipse the glory of the rest ; he thought it wisdom to keep it for a hoggards for himself and all his unclean spirits employed in this hemisphere, and the people to do his son and heir — I mean the Pope — that service for what Louis XI. kept his barber Oliver, which makes them to be so blood-thirsty. They are the very offal of men, dregs of mankind, reproach of Christendom, the bots that crawl on the beast's tail. I wonder Rome itself is not ashamed of them.

I beg upon my hands and knees that the expedition against them may be undertaken whilst the hearts and hands of our soldiery are hot. To whom I will be bold to say briefly: Happy is he who shall reward them as they have served us : and cursed is he that shall do the work of the Lord negligently. Cursed be he that holdeth back his sword from blood ; yea, cursed be he that maketh not his sword stark drunk with Irish blood, that maketh them not heaps on heaps, and their country a dwelling place for dragons, an astonishment to nations. Let not that eye look for pity, nor that hand be spared that pities or spares them. And let him be accursed that curseth them not bitterly.

The general insurrection that took place the following year, the revolt of the navy, and the rising of the Scots so obstructed the counsels of the Parliament that little was done towards the relief of Ireland. The sending over of Lord Lisle as Lord Lieutenant helped to alienate Inchiquin, one of the most active and unscrupulous partisans of the Parliament. In a fit of jealous disappointment he made overtures to the Royalist party, and brought over to them all the Munster garrisons.

CHAPTER IV.

CROMWELL GENERAL.

The Army for Ireland — The Lord Lieutenant — Waller and Lambert — Cromwell appointed — Officers' Petition — 12,000 men to be sent to Ireland — Committee to provide Ships — Cromwell Commander-in-Chief. His Humility — Committee for the Affairs of Ireland — Provision for the forces — Conference with the Common Council of London — £120,000 advanced for the Service of Ireland — Casting of Lots — The Regiments for Ireland — The General's Order.

EARLY in 1649 news reached Ireland, that "great preparations were making in England forthwith to send a great fleet and army for Ireland, which, it was said, should be commanded by Cromwell." There were many who ambitioned the post of Lord Lieutenant.[1] Waller[2] and Lambert[3] were the chief candidates for public favor. It was a question whether the Presbyterians or the Independents should have the upperhand. The former supported the claims of Waller; the latter, headed by Cromwell, insisted that the chief command should be given to Lambert, who already held the second place in the army. He was known to be as much opposed to Presbyterianism as to royalty. But Cromwell was jealous of Lambert; he thought the government of Ireland and the command of such an army as would be needed there, too great a trust for him. Therefore some of Cromwell's friends, who were always ready at hand in such emergencies, on a sudden proposed that Cromwell should command the expedition. Cromwell was absent when the proposal was made. The Presbyterian party thought it was only a trick to defer the service, and that he had no intention of going to Ireland, or if he did go, his absence from England would give them all they wished for; they

---

[1] "The government of Ireland is administered sometimes by a single person in the nature of a viceroy; sometimes by two or three persons called Lord Justices, who derive their authority by commission, sometimes from the Viceroy, sometimes from the Crown. The chief governors in the early ages have been called by divers names, as Custos, Judiciary, Lord Lieutenant, and Lord Deputy." Ware's *Antiquities of Ireland*, vol. ii. p. 89. From the close of the twelfth century the governor of the Anglo-Norman colony in Ireland was called Chief Justiciary, a title applied in England to the chief officer of the King's court. The title of Lord-Lieutenant seems to have been reserved for court favorites or persons of acknowledged eminence. Cromwell's predecessors in that dignity were the Earls of Leicester and Strafford, Lord Mountjoy, and the Earl of Essex. Ware gives the titles borne by each of the chief governors. *Ibid.*

[2] He was one of the leaders of the Presbyterian party in the House of Commons, and had distinguished himself in the early part of the Civil War. He retired from the House in June, 1647, when the eleven members were impeached by the army.

[3] Lambert had distinguished himself by his bravery, especially at Naseby and Fife. He was, of all the officers in the army, second to Cromwell in courage, prudence and capacity. Cromwell regarded him with a jealous eye; and upon his refusal to take the oath to be faithful to the Government, deprived him of his commission, but granted him a pension of £2,000, more through prudence than generosity; for he knew that such a man as Lambert, rendered desperate by poverty, would be capable of anything. Grainger's *Biographical History*, vol. iii. p. 18; London, 1769.

OLIVER CROMWELL.

should be able to regain to their party Fairfax, who had already begun
to show a dislike to his new friends. And so both parties agreed, and
Cromwell was declared Lord Lieutenant, with as ample and independent a commission as could be prepared.

Feb. 19th. — At a Council of the army holden at Whitehall, there were voted
10,000 men to go over into Ireland, amongst which the Lieutenant-General Cromwell's own regiment is one; by which it is probable he may command in chief.
Some regiments are already drawing northward.[1]

March 2d. — The House being informed that there were several officers of
the army at the door, they were called in, and Colonel Whaley told Mr. Speaker
that the General Council of the officers of the army had sent these gentlemen to
present the House with this petition. . . . That it is their desire that the House
would take it into their serious, effectual, and speedy consideration. . . . That the
sad and distressed condition of Ireland may be immediately considered; and, ere
it is too late, such seasonable supplies sent thither as may require the English power
and interest; for which work we humbly offer and earnestly desire that such forces
as are already raised and can be spared, which we conceive will be, with some little
addition, a considerable strength, may be forthwith appointed for that service, with
some equal provision for maintenance as the forces here shall have provided, and
under such conduct and conditions as may encourage faithful men for that employment; by which means you will probably in a great measure secure this nation, in
fact ease the people of their pressure, and, by the blessing of God, recover that
kingdom out of the hands of the rebels. Upon the reading of the petition, the
Commons voted, That the matters contained in the said Petition . . . be taken
into immediate consideration; that Mr. Speaker do return thanks to the Petitioners.
. . . The House ordered that it should be referred to a Council of State to consider
of that business concerning Ireland.[2]

March 3d. — Lieutenant-General Cromwell, Sir Henry Mildmay, Sir Henry
Vane, Sir Arthur Hesilrigge, Colonel Jones, Colonel Martin, Colonel Walton, Mr.
Scott, and Mr. Robinson to be a committee to consider the order of March 2d,
concerning the forces in England and Wales, and which are fit for service in
Ireland.

March 5th. — That 12,000 horse and foot must be sent to Ireland . . . to
suggest to the House that the £20,000 a month tax be continued for the Irish army.

March 9th. — Order in parliament, referring it to the Council of State to confer with the Army Committee how the forces that are to go to Ireland may be
modelled for the best advantage.

March 9th. — The Council of State to the Lord-General: Parliament has
this day ordered 12,000 men to be sent to Ireland; equal provision to be made for
them as for these here; and have referred the care of this business to us. We
desire you to call together your Council of War, and to consider what regiments
shall go thither of horse, foot, and dragoons,[3] and under what commander.

March 12th. — Lieutenant-General Cromwell, Sir Henry Mildmay, Mr. Holland, Colonel Walton, to be a committee to consult the Navy Commissioners, as to
which ships out of the eight ordered may be soonest made ready; how sufficient
shipping may be sent to Chester and Liverpool. They are to certify how many ships,
and of what burden will suffice, and at what rates, and how they may be had.

March 13th. — A committee of the Council was appointed to report to the
House that the Lord-General and his Council of War have been consulted with
about the modelling of the forces for Ireland, in pursuance of the order of the 9th

---

[1] *The Kingdom's Faithful and Impartial Scout,* Feb. 16th to 23d; in *Cromwelliana,* p.52.

[2] *Perfect Diurnal,* Feb. 27th to March 3d. The duties of the Council of State were:
1st, to command and settle the Militia of England and Ireland; 2d, to set forth such a
Navy as they should think fit; 3d, to appoint magazines and stores and to dispose of them;
4th, to sit and execute the powers given them for a year. Whitelocke, p. 376.

[3] "Dragoon, a kind of soldier that serves indifferently either on foot or on horseback."
Johnson. According to Merrick, they were so called not after the draconarii of the Romans,
but because they carried a short blunderbuss having a dragon's head at its muzzle. *Inquiry
into Ancient Armour;* in glossary ad verb.; London, 1842.

of March; and that he thinks nothing can be done until the Commander-in-chief is nominated[1]. The Council wishes to know the pleasure of the House concerning his nomination, which being determined, the rest will proceed with more expedition.

March 14th. — Report was made to the House from the Council of State as to the proceedings in order to the sending of forces for Ireland. And upon debate, the House referred it to the Council of State to nominate a General and other chief officers for Ireland, and to report with speed to the House, that the work may be hastened, of which there is great need.

March 15th. — The Council of State upon the business of Ireland: Lieutenant-General Cromwell is by them in nomination to be General for Ireland; and in order to this also, at a General Council of the Army at Whitehall it was resolved upon, that the business of Ireland cannot be well taken into consideration before the Commander-in-chief be nominated and other arrangements propounded, which are under debate by the Council of State to be reported to the House.

March 23d. — This day the committee of officers appointed by the General Council of the Army sat at Whitehall. They named some officers to propose some particulars for the encouragement of those who shall engage for Ireland by present pay, provisions, stating of accounts, &c., and resolved, That so many regiments as shall be designed of the army for that service shall be drawn by lot.

The Council of the Army met again, and named two officers of every regiment of horse and foot of the army and divers garrisons of the kingdom, to meet the next morning to seek God, to gather what advice to offer to the General concerning the expedition for Ireland, and to make a report to the Council on Monday next by three of the clock in the afternoon. The Lieutenant-General Cromwell is to give in his answer to the Council of State on Tuesday next (March 27th) whether he will go for Ireland or not.

On Easterday (March 25th), the army had a day of humiliation and fast for their future undertakings, especially concerning Ireland. Peters[1] performed his old office of blowing the trumpet, and told them that he hoped none of them would refuse to go into Ireland. Yet they could not but go with more cheerfulness when they knew that they had a particular call from God, which he promised them within three days.

March 26th. — The General Council of the Army sat at Whitehall, and had before them the debate of several particulars for the better encouragement of those as shall engage for the service of Ireland; the particulars agreed on are many, and which are to be rendered to the parliament for confirmation.

The following test to be taken by Colonel Tuthill and all the officers going to Ireland: "To be faithful to the Commonwealth, without King or House of Peers, to obey the orders of parliament, or his superiors appointed thereby, to do nothing to prejudice the Commonwealth, and to discover any conspiracies against it." A week later, an order was issued to Colonels Tuthill and Reynolds to offer this test to every private soldier of their respective regiments, those not taking the test to be discharged.

March 27th. — Lieutenant-General Cromwell having intimated his willingness to serve the parliament in the war of Ireland, care being had for necessaries for the army, as money, &c.; they considered of that peculiar war in several things, and did vote, among other things, some money for the faithful and valiant Governor of Dublin.

March 28. — Lieutenant-General Cromwell this day was, by the House of Commons, voted General for Ireland, and declared to the House his acceptance to go for that service; and for the better supply of that service, several things were debated to this purpose: — 1°. That Lieutenant-General Cromwell shall go Commander-in-chief of the forces for Ireland. 2°. That such regiments as shall be

---

[1] Peters in early life was expelled from Cambridge for irregular behavior. He afterwards took to the stage, and there acquired the habit of buffoonery which he practiced later in the pulpit. Being obliged to fly from England, he went to Rotterdam, and became pastor of the English church there. He was one of the first to justify rebellion. The Sunday after the trial of Charles I. began, he preached at Whitehall and "spake old Simeon's words, that he had seen his salvation, that is, Kings in fetters and Princes in chains." Carte's *Collection*, &c., vol. i. p. 212. He was executed in 1660 with other regicides. See *The Trial of the Regicides*, p. 149: London, 1724; Ludlow's *Memoirs*, pp. 308 and 367.

allotted for the Irish service may have all their arrears audited, stated, and debentures given for their respective services. 3°. Visible security to be given, so that any friend or other, being entrusted with a debenture, may receive it at a time prescribed by the parliament. 4°. Those that go for Ireland to be first satisfied for their arrears since 1645. 5°. That out of the £120,000 per mensem for England and Ireland, three months' pay shall be given for those that go. 6°. The private soldiers and non-commissioned officers to receive two months' pay of arrears, and commissioned officers under captains one month's pay. 7°. That magazines for provisions be settled at Bristol, Chester, Liverpool, Beaumaris, and Milford. And that in order to the latter and for the better victualling of the ships, as occasion requires, that the chief officers of the respective towns and garrisons of Bristol, Chester, Liverpool, Beaumaris, the Isle of Anglesea, and Milford in South Wales, shall observe such orders and commands as they shall receive from the sai l chief commander. 8°. A sufficient squadron of ships to be on the Irish coasts, to be at the command of the Commander-in-chief of the land forces in Ireland. 9°. The ships to be victualled at Dublin, Liverpool, and Beaumaris; and a Court of Admiralty to be erected at Dublin, to prevent their coming into England to dispose of prizes and so neglect the service. 10°. The pay of the officers and soldiers to be according to the Irish establishment, only the officers to receive for the present the same pay as here. 11°. An hospital for sick and maimed soldiers to be erected at Dublin. 12°. The parliament's forces already in Ireland, and those now to go over, to be one army and one establishment. 13°. 5,000 quarters of bread-corn, 200 tons of salt, and 200 tons of cheese, to be transported with those who now go over. 14°. A competent train of artillery, with arms for both horse and foot, ammunition and other things necessary, to be provided for that service. 15°. That effectual care be taken to send over recruits of men and horse, with furniture complete, as occasion requires. 16°. That there be recruits of horse, foot, arms, saddles, &c., ready to supply the service of Ireland, to be sent over as need shall require. The whole was referred to the Council of State for some small amendments. The House ordered money to be advanced to Colonel Jones, Governor of Dublin.

The next day Cromwell appeared in the House full of confusion and irresolution. After much hesitation and many expressions of his own unworthiness and disability to support so great a charge, and of the entire resignation of himself to their commands, and absolute dependence upon God's providence and blessing, from which he had received many instances of His favor, he submitted to their good will and pleasure, and desired them that no more time might be lost in the preparations which were to be made for so great a work. "For he did confess that kingdom to be reduced to so great straits that he was willing to engage his own person in the expedition, purely for the difficulties which appeared in it, and more out of hope, with the hazard of his life, to give some obstruction to the success which the rebels were at present exalted with, and so preserve to the Commonwealth some footing in that kingdom till they might be able to send fresh supplies, than out of any expectation that with his strength he should be able in any signal degree, to prevail over them.[1]

[1] Clarendon's *History of the Rebellion*, vol. iii. p. 322; Echard's *History of England* vol. ii. p. 672; London, 1718. Cromwell was unwilling to accept the office, as it lessened the authority of his General. He acquaints him with it and assures him that he will never accept of it, though threatened with the greatest punishment if he do not comply, or tendered the highest reward if he do. By this little instance Fairfax perceived how much more deserving Cromwell was than himself, whom he before knew to be no way his inferior; and at the same time he vied in kindness, and showed that he deserved well of his country by refusing the charge, and assigned it wholly to Cromwell. Peck's *Memoirs of O. Cromwell*, p. 44; London, 1740. Cromwell was made General-in-chief of all the forces June 26th, 1650, Fairfax having resigned, being unwilling to march with the army into Scotland. Ludlow's *Memoirs*, p. 122. His friend Godwin used to say that it was one of the peculiarities

March 30th. — Upon report from the Council of State, that Lieutenant-General Cromwell accepted of the service of Ireland, and would endeavor to the utmost of his power, with God's assistance, to carry on that work against the rebels and all that adhere to them, the House did approve of Lieutenant-General Cromwell to be Commander-in-chief of all the forces sent to Ireland · and to take off any reflection on the General (Fairfax), or dislike to him, it was also voted, That the Lord Fairfax be general of all the forces of the parliament both in England and Ireland."

March 31st. — By order of the Council of State, Sir William Armayne, Sir Henry Vane, Lieutenant-General Cromwell, Sir John Danvers, Mr. Scott, and Colonel Jones to be a committee for the civil and military affairs of Ireland, with power to advise with Sir Robert King, Colonel Hill, Sir Hardress Waller, and others.

April 11th. — This day the Council of State made report to the House of their proceedings, and further propositions agreed on as to the forces that shall go to Ireland.

Resolved by the Commons assembled in parliament : 1°. That effectual provision be made for maimed soldiers during their lives, and for the widows and orphans of such as shall be slain in the service; and that for the present one or more hospitals be appointed and prepared at Dublin, or elsewhere, for the recovery of sick and lame soldiers. 2°. That such backs, breasts, and pots [1] as shall be wanting, shall be provided for every trooper who shall be employed in the service, and these to be transported to such places as the Commander-in-chief shall direct. 3°. That it be referred to the Council of State to treat with the officers of the forces that are to go into Ireland, upon what terms the arms, horse, and furniture to be provided may be continued and maintained. 4°. That it be referred to the Council of State to confer with the said officers of the said army touching the sending over recruits of horse and men, &c., for the forces on the service of Ireland as occasion may require.

It was also informed that the army are upon so good a way of forwardness for the advance of the service of Ireland, as that this day the officers of the army were appointed to meet about the casting of lots which regiments shall engage in that service.

April 12th. — A report was this day made from the Council of State of the necessity to advance a speedy and considerable sum for the service of Ireland. The House upon debate voted, That the sum of £120,000 should be borrowed of the City of London for the service ; and for the speedy affecting thereof, they elected a committee, consisting of Sir Henry Vane, Lieutenant-General Cromwell, &c., to go to the Common Council of the City, to treat with them for borrowing the sum of £120,000 upon security of the two last months' assessments of the £9,000 per mensum, and meet with the said Common Council this afternoon ; and that ten members more should be added to the said Committee.

Those who were appointed to go to the Common Council about the furnishing £120,000 came to Guildhall. The first that spoke was Mr. Lisle ; after him Mr. Whitelocke, who very notably urged the accommodating the parliament with the sum appointed for the service of Ireland. After whom the Lord Chief Baron Wilde did press the same with many arguments ; and, among others, he rightly distinguished the state of the war in that kingdom, as being not between Protestant and Protestant, or Independent and Presbyterian, but Papist and Protestant, and that was the interest there : Papacy or Popery being not to be endured in that kingdom, which notably agreed with the maxim of King James, when first King of the three Kingdoms : " Plant Ireland with Puritans, and root out Papists, and then secure it." The last that spake was the Lieutenant-General, who first excused himself as designed for that service, and so might be thought to seek himself ; after he cleared up divers things by way of satisfaction, and particularly these : 1°. Whereas it was reported money would be endeavored, and then nothing done for Ireland. 2°. That it was said the army would not go. Both which he asserted were false, and that the

---

of Cromwell's frame, whether the causes were bodily or mental, that he always had tears at command. *History of the Commonwealth*, vol. ii. p. 360 ; London, 1824.

[1] The cuirass, originally of leather ; as the name imports, but later of iron, covered the body both before and behind ; it consisted of two parts, a breast and a back-piece of iron, fastened together by means of straps ; the pot was an iron hat with a broad brim. Grose's *Military Antiquities*, vol. ii. p. 244 and 249 ; London, 1801.

expedition would be for Ireland, and that the officers were unanimous for the service, and, he doubted not, the soldiers; only it was necessary they be accommodated. As for any divisions or distractions in the army, there was none, though it had been attempted. For the service he professed a readiness to do it to his utmost. The Common Council considered of the security, viz., the two last months' assessment and fee-farm rent, but looked not upon it as sufficient, and therefore ordered a committee of six aldermen and six commoners, to consider how security might be satisfactory, which is like to involve the Dean and Chapters' lands. It is thought this will be the security accepted of, if it can be procured. The Common Council did, by their recorder, Mr. Glyn, return thanks to the Lord-General for his great service done for the kingdom, and particularly for London; they thanked the parliament for him, and for making him Generalissimo of England and Ireland, also for the good choice they had made of appointing the Lieutenant-General chief for reducing Ireland.

April 13th. — The Committee appointed yesterday to go into the city and treat with the Common Council concerning the advance of £120,000 for the service of Ireland made report this day: That the Common Council declared that it would be ready and willing to contribute their utmost endeavors for the advance of this sum for the relief of that distressed nation of Ireland. The thanks of the House were given them for their willingness to promote the business. And for the better carrying out of the business of Ireland by the advance of this £120,000 of the city, the House ordered that there should be addition made to the Committee for sale of fee-farm rents, and the Committee was ordered to make a speedy report of the business.

April 20th. — This day, according to appointment, the General Council of the Army met at Whitehall, about casting of lots what regiments should go for the service of Ireland; where, after a solemn seeking of God by prayer, they cast lots what regiments of the old army should be designed for that service: 14 regiments of horse and 14 of foot of the established forces came to the lot; and it being resolved that four regiments of horse and four of foot should go upon that service, ten blanks and four papers with *Ireland* written upon them were put in a hat, and being shuffled together, were drawn out by a child; who gave to an officer of each regiment in the lot the lot of that regiment; so that it was done in so impartial and inoffensive a way, as no regiment can take any just exception. The regiments to whose lot it fell to go were, of horse, Commissary-General Ireton's, Colonel Scroop's, Colonel Horton's, and Major-General Lambert's; of foot, Colonel Ewer's, Colonel Cook's, Colonel Hewson's, and Colonel Dean's; of dragoons, Major Abbott's, Captain Mercer's, Captain Fulcher's, Captain Garland's, and Captain Bolton's troops. The officers of each regiment which were allotted expressed much cheerfulness at the decision. There are three more regiments already in forming, besides those of the army, viz., a regiment of foot of Lieutenant-General Cromwell, Colonel Venables' regiment, and the Kentish regiment under Colonel Phayre.

April 23d. — The parliament enacted that Thursday, the third of May, be set apart and appointed for a public and solemn day of fasting and humiliation, earnestly to seek unto Almighty God that He will be graciously pleased to give a blessing to the forces of the parliament now in Ireland and such as are to be shortly sent thither and at last to establish his pure worship in this nation.

April 24th. — Colonel Tuthill's regiment is shipped, in all 1127, besides a company that is coming up of 100 men. Two days later, letters from Chester informed the House, that the vessels on which this regiment had embarked were driven by a strong north-west wind upon the coast of Wales, near Beaumaris; where, if they have not a supply of victuals, they will come to land; the consequences whereof will be the spoil of 1,250 good soldiers, the ruin of the country, and the non-relieving of Ireland, and particularly of Dublin, which place is, we fear, begirt by Ormonde.

April 30. — This day Colonel Hewson's regiment marched to Rumford, in order to the advance for Ireland.

An order was issued by the Lord-General to the officers of every regiment of the army, that none entertain any of the forces designed for Ireland: Whereas divers officers of regiments designed for Ireland go off from the same, with an expectation to be entertained in other regiments that stay in this nation; these are therefore required upon sight hereof to forbear to list or entertain any soldiers whatsoever, either horse or foot, in their regiments for the space of six months from the date hereof, without special order from himself.

CHAPTER V.

THE LEVELLERS.

Mutiny among the Troops — Cromwell's Ambition — "The Hunting of the Foxes" — His Nepotism — Spread of the Sedition — Defeat of the Insurgents — Thanks given to the Generals — Readiness of the Army to go for Ireland — Transports — The General Officers — Cromwell's Delay — His Commission, Life-guard and Allowance.

THE expedition was delayed for a time by a mutinous spirit, which showed itself in several of the regiments destined for service in Ireland. Many of the common soldiers had become infected with the doctrines of the Levellers, a sect which was intent on establishing a theocracy, which they called "The Dominion of God and his Saints." They first appeared near Cobham, in Surrey, busy in digging the ground and sowing it with roots and beans. One Everard, once of the army, who termed himself a prophet, was their chief. They were thirty men, and said they should shortly be four thousand. They invited all to come and help them, and promised them meat, drink, and clothes. Everard and Winstanley, the chief of those that had assembled at St. George's Hill in Surrey, came to the General and made a declaration to justify their proceedings. Everard said, " He was of the race of the Jews; all the liberties of the people were lost by the coming in of William the Conqueror; and ever since, the people of God had lived under tyranny and oppression worse than that of our forefathers under the Egyptians. There lately had appeared to him a vision, which bade him 'Arise, and dig and plough the earth, and receive the fruits thereof;' their intent was to restore the creation to its former condition, to restore the ancient community of enjoying the fruits of the earth." While they were before the General they stood with their hats on; and being demanded the reason thereof, they said, "Because he was their fellow creature." Being asked the meaning of the phrase: "Give honor to whom honor is due," they said, "Your mouths shall be stopped that ask such questions."

The mutiny first broke out on the night of April 26th, among a troop of Colonel Whaley's regiment, at the Bull in Bishopsgate. This regiment was not allotted for Ireland; but the men refused to quit London, as they were ordered. Fairfax and Cromwell hastened to the place and forced them to march. Fifteen were seized and tried by court-martial. Five of this number were condemned to be shot; four of these were pardoned by the General. The next day the fifth was shot in St. Paul's Churchyard. His name was Lockyer, one who had for seven years served in the army with equal courage and constancy to any trooper, being at his death about twenty-three years of age; he was, it is said, a pious man, and of excellent parts and much beloved. His death, far from quelling the sedition, seemed rather to spread it ; among all classes it produced a profound impression of grief and anger. At the funeral, two days after, "about one hundred persons went before the corpse, five or six in a file ; the corpse was bosught, with six trumpets sounding a soldier's knell ; then the trooper's horse came, clothed all over in mourning, and led by a foot-man. The corpse was adorned with bundles of rosemary, one half-stained in blood. Some thousands followed in rank and file, with black and green ribbons on their heads and breasts. At the new churchyard in Westminster, some thousands more of the better sort met them, who thought not fit to march through the city.

Cromwell's ambitious purposes would seem to have been suspected by many for a long time. The French Ambassador wrote from London to Cardinal Mazarin, in June, 1649 : "Cromwell, according to the belief of many, carries his ideas beyond even the suggestions of the most undisciplined ambition." In a pamphlet entitled, "The Hunting of the Foxes ; or, The Grandee Deceivers Unmasked," the authors, "five private soldiers," after censuring the Council of State as "adorning itself with all the regal magnificence and majesty of courtly attendance," proceed in the following strain :

"Was there ever a generation of men so apostate, so false, and so perjured as these ? Did ever men pretend a higher degree of holiness, religion, and zeal to God and their country than these ? They preach, they fast, they pray, they have nothing more frequent than the sentences of Sacred Scripture, the name of God and of Christ in their mouths ; you shall scarce speak to Cromwell about anything but he will lay his hand on his breast, elevate his eyes, and call God to record ; he will weep, howl, and repent, even while he doth smite you under the first rib. O Cromwell ! whither art thou aspiring ? He that runs may read and foresee the intent, a new regality." See 128th page.

The pamphlet was declared by the House to contain much false, scandalous and reproachful matter, highly seditious, and destructive to the present government, its authors and distributors guilty of high treason, to be proceeded against as traitors ; and the Council of State was enjoined to carry these resolutions into effect. At a council of officers, held at Whitehall at the end of February, it was resolved to take severe measures against all intrigues. Fairfax issued a general order to the army, forbidding all meetings and deliberations as contrary to discipline ; but admitting the right of the soldiers to petition, provided they first informed their officers of their intention to do so. Five soldiers who presented a petition to complain of the obstacles thrown in their way, were severely punished. Colonel Lilburne petitioned against the Council of State and the High Court of Justice. Obtaining no redress, he printed the petition, with the title, "England's new chains discovered." He was committed to the Tower, on suspicion of high treason, for being the author, contriver, framer, or publisher of a seditious book.

Cromwell was openly charged with nepotism too.

Truly, if you knew what a large family the Lieutenant-General hath in the army, you could not much blame him for being so craving daily for money, whereof honest John Lilburne hath given a perfect muster — 1°. Himself, Lieutenant-Gen eral and Colonel of horse. 2°. One of his sons, Captain of the General's Life-guard. 3°. His other son, Captain of a troop in Colonel Harrison's regiment. 4°. His brother-in-law, Desborough, Colonel of the General's regiment of horse. 5°. His son-in-law, Ireton, Commissary-General of the horse and Colonel of horse. 6°. His brother, Ireton, Quartermaster-General of the horse and Captain of horse. 7°. His cousin, Whaley, Colonel of horse. 8°. And his brother, Whaley, lately made Judge Advocate. And all these are the Lieutenant-General's creatures at command.

The flame of sedition spread rapidly through the ranks of the army. A week later, news reached London that insurrections had broken out in Oxfordshire and Gloucestershire; that several troops of Scroop's, Reynolds', and Ireton's regiments had revolted from command and driven away their officers, and the most of the men of Harrison's, Ingoldsby's, and Horton's regiments were already in correspondence with the mutineers and disposed to join them. A party of two hundred men, under the command of one Captain Thompson, left their quarters at Banbury; they demanded justice on the murderers of Lockyear, and threatened that if a hair of Lilburne's were hurt they would avenge it seventy-and-seven fold upon the tyrants! Reynolds was sent in pursuit of them. Some returned to the ranks, others were taken prisoners. Thompson escaped with a few of his companions. Meantime, at Salisbury, where the headquarters were, a body of about a thousand strong, headed by Cornet Thompson, rose in mutiny. The parliament left the generals to act as they thought best. Fairfax and Cromwell reviewed the two regiments which they commanded in person. Both professed the utmost zeal in the cause of the parliament. Colonel Whaley and his officers issued a " Declaration," that divers had wickedly gone about to divide the army, to persuade those soldiers to whose lot it was fallen to go for Ireland to refuse that service. They disclaimed those traitorous plots and actions, and utterly abhorred them, and resolved to continue their due allegiance to the parliament, the general, the lieutenant-general, and others in authority, and engaged to stand or fall with them.

A few days after, the generals, Fairfax and Cromwell, came up with the insurgents at Burford, in Oxfordshire. Cromwell entered the place suddenly, in the night, with 2,000 men. Reynolds posted himself with a strong party outside the town. The mutineers defended themselves for a short time; but soon losing all hope, about four hundred of them surrendered; the rest succeeded in making their escape. Fairfax summoned a court-martial, which decided that they should be decimated. Three were shot, the others were pardoned, after having been reproached for having so wickedly imperilled the cause of God and of their country. "They wept, they retired to Devizes for a time, were then restored to their regiments, and marched cheerfully for Ireland."

A new sedition broke out at Oxford in Colonel Ingoldsby's regiment. The soldiers seized their officers and cast them into prison. The Colonel himself, who had been sent down to repress the mutiny, was not spared. They fortified themselves in the buildings of New College, and from that stronghold renewed the demands of the Levellers. The revolt died away of itself ten days after it broke out.

May 26th. — Lieutenant-General Cromwell being come post to town last night, made a narrative this day to the House of the army's proceedings against these termed Levellers, and how they are suppressed, the discontents in the Isle of Wight, Portsmouth, and other castles thereabout allayed, and all in quiet. The House hereupon ordered that the thanks of the House should be given to Lieutenant-General Cromwell for his great care and courage in this business against the Levellers. Mr. Speaker, according to the said resolution, stood up and gave the hearty thanks of the House accordingly.

And that so great a deliverance may not easily be forgotten, the House ordered that there should be a day of thanksgiving set apart for this great mercy, not only for the city and suburbs, but likewise for the whole Commonwealth; and therefore ordered that Thursday come fortnight should be set apart for this duty in the city and suburbs, and late lines of communication; and Thursday come three weeks for all the nation. Mr. Thomas Goodwin and others were appointed to preach that day before the parliament.

Lieutenant-General Cromwell has caused his tent to be put up, and it is agoing; and he and his officers and forces are preparing for a sudden advance for Ireland, they being much satisfied in the Act passed for their accounts. Colonel Stubberds has mustered his regiment of foot designed for Ireland, on Hounslow Heath, and read the Act for Accounts at the head of them; they were full and all unanimous. Colonel Phayre's regiment, Colonel Venables', and Colonel Huncks' regiment of foot also are ready to march. Colonel Reynolds hath almost completed his regiment of horse, and Major Shelburne's regiment is nigh ready. Those regiments taken out of the standing army, will be new moulded before they be sent, but all will be ready for march about three weeks hence, for Ireland.

May 29th. — Report was made to the House by Lieutenant-General Cromwell, of the readiness of the forces to go for Ireland, and, if money were in readiness, to be shipped away presently; some already are far on their march. The House hereupon made some further progress for the encouragement of such as shall advance money upon Dean and Chapters' lands; and also passed further orders for the advance of money and provisions for the service of Ireland.

May 31st. — The humble representation and resolutions of the officers and soldiers in Lieutenant-General Cromwell's regiment : —

" The manifold experiences we have of your Excellency's happy conduct ever since the goodness of God has sent you over to us, and the many signal victories He hath been pleased to make you instrument in, to the twice total subduing of a powerful enemy, together with our sensibleness of God's love to this present parliament in carrying them through so great and glorious undertakings for the good of the commonwealth, the benefit of which we hope all honest men will be sensible of. In consideration of these things, we are at a loss within ourselves that any generation of men amongst us (especially of such large professions), who have tasted of the same mercy we have done, should now, through the pride and ambition of their hearts, so manifestly disown God, by such an unchristian and unheard of rejection through pride and ambition, in casting off the authority of this present parliament and your Excellency, as divers of late have endeavored. Therefore we, the officers and soldiers of Lieutenant-General Cromwell's regiment, do in all humility represent to your Excellency that we have been and are sadly afflicted in our spirits with the thoughts of that horrid and unnatural defection so lately made from the parliament's and your Excellency's authority; and each of us in particular profess that we do from our hearts disavow the having any hand directly or indirectly in advising or countenancing the revolt or capitulation of any of the twelve troops of your army, or any others lately or now opposing the parliament's or your Excellency's authority. And that we neither did nor do own or countenance any of those late papers which have scandalized the parliament, Council of State, or your Excellency's authority derived from them. And we desire to bless God, who hath enabled your Excellency so seasonably to reduce those who otherwise, by their destructive principles, might have brought great confusion upon the nation. And for the manifestation of our faithfulness and obedience we further profess that we shall, by the grace of God, hazard our lives and all that is dear unto us for the preservation of this parliament, the supreme authority of the nation, the just authority of the people, according to their late acts and declarations; and while we are soldiers, we shall cheerfully submit unto your Excellency's authority over us, under them, and to the discipline of the army now practised amongst us, against any person or persons, that, under any notion or pretence whatsoever, shall go about, to be obedient to your Excellency in putting into execution your commands, according to the power and authority given you by parliament; withal resolving to use our utmost endeavors to discover all such persons as shall, by way of agitators or otherwise, endeavor disturbance amongst us, to break the present government and peace of the army. And because it hath been rumored that this regiment had an intention to have seized upon the person of the Lieutenant-General, in order to the carrying on that rebellious design, we profess for our parts we never had the least knowledge of any such thing; and if any person or persons lately amongst us, at any meetings in London or elsewhere, have promised or engaged in the name of the regiment anything tending thereunto, it hath proceeded from the treachery of their own hearts, with whom we leave it; no doubt but God will, in due time, find out such deeds of darkness; and as we hope our desire of avoidance of such from amongst us, whose principles might lead them to such an action, will in some measure vindicate us, so we further add that it could not but have been a detestable crime for any part of the army to have attempted (much more to have done) such an act, so in us, by how much the nearer we stand related to him as being our Colonel, and of whose fidelity we have had such ample testimony, it would have been most wicked and abominable.

Lieutenant-General Cromwell is to have a regiment of horse for Ireland, consisting of fourteen troops, and a lieutenant-colonel and two majors to be designed for the regiment.[1]

June 5th.— The Council of State gave orders for Flemish ships to transport the horse into Ireland, and for the regiments to march to Chester and the other ports, and not to stay above one night in a place. Letters from Sir George Ascough, that he had furnished Dublin with provisions, and sent others to Sir Charles Coote, and had blocked up Prince Rupert's ships at Kinsale.

June 7th.— The general officers for Ireland, besides Lieutenant-General Cromwell, are said to be Major-General Lambert, Major-General of the whole; Colonel Jones, Lieutenant-General of the horse; Colonel Horton, Commissary-General of the horse; and Colonel Monk, Major-General of the foot.

June 13th.— Mr. Whalley, agent at Chester, was ordered by the Council of State to make stay of all ships that are now or shall come into a port of Cheshire, Lancashire, or Wales, capable of transporting horse, that they may be ready and no time lost.

June 15.— Upon a report from the Council of State, the House approved of Commissionary-General Ireton to go into Ireland next Commander-in-Chief unto Lieutenant-General Cromwell.

Cromwell still delayed his departure under various pretexts. The parliament began to feel anxious, for it was chiefly to get rid. of Cromwell and to find employment for the army that the war had been undertaken with such vigor and at so much cost. The French Ambassador in London wrote to Mazarin : "They still say that Cromwell will start at the end of this month, at the latest. The opinion which I have to the contrary is so conformable to that of many intelligent persons, that I cannot retract it ; and until I am convinced by the news of his journey into that country, I shall persevere in the opinion. It can hardly be possible that Cromwell, who, according to the belief of many, carries his ideas even beyond the suggestion of the most undisciplined ambition, can resolve to abandon this king-

---

[1] Whitelocke. p. 391. This was the day on which Cromwell's army was supposed to have begun its march from London for the reduction of Ireland. and from it the soldiers' service was afterward reckoned in the distribution of the forfeited lands of the Irish. They were the first that were paid. *Cromwellian Settlement*, p. 187. The troops that had served against the Irish before Cromwell came over were called the old Protestants. See *Life of Ormonde*, vol. ii. p. 134.

dom to the mercy of the plots which may be formed in his absence, and which his presence can prevent from being so much as undertaken." [1]

June 19th.—An order from the Lord General to Lieutenant-General Cromwell and the other officers designed for Ireland was issued, bidding all to take care that from henceforth they entertain none who had left other regiments designed for the service of Ireland, without taking a particular account of them, what troops they came from, and what they received upon their discharge as arrears; and upon mustering of any such, to set their names distinct in the muster rolls, with such particular account as aforesaid concerning each man.

June 20th. — Ordered that the Commission should be brought into the House for Lieutenant-General Cromwell to go commander over the forces for Ireland on the morrow.

June 22d.— A report this day made to the House from the Council of State, that, according to the order of the House, they had prepared and drawn up the Commission to be given to Lieutenant-General Cromwell as to his service of Ireland. The Commission was read in Latin and after in English; the House, approving thereof, ordered that the Lord Commissioners of the Great Seal of England should be required and authorized to pass the said Commission under the Great Seal unto the said Lieutenant-General Cromwell. The House spent some time in debate how long this Commission should continue, and at last resolved it should be in full force for three years. They then considered of settling the civil power of the nation of Ireland, whether by commissions or otherwise. The House, after a short debate, voted that Lieutenant-General Cromwell be Chief Governor of Ireland, and likewise that the civil and military power of that nation be settled in him during the time of his Commission. Instructions were ordered to be prepared for the Commander-in-Chief by the Council of State, and reported to the House with all speed.

June 25th.— The extraordinary charges of Lieutenant-General Cromwell as Chief Governor and Commander-in-Chief of Ireland as to this preparatory expedition into that nation, referred to the consideration of a committee to consider thereof and report.

July 2d.— The Commons ordered the Lord-Lieutenant's life-guard of 50 to be made up to 70, and they paid according to the former establishment by the Committee of the Army, and Mr. Owen to go his chaplain, and £100 per annum to be allowed to his wife and children in his absence, to be paid quarterly, until the House shall take further order; which was referred to a committee to consider how it may be settled. The House then seriously debated concerning the speedy conduct of the army for Ireland, under the command of the Lord Lieutenant of Ireland, for relief of our friends there in necessity; and hereupon ordered Wednesday next, July 10th, should be set apart for solemn fasting and humiliation for the city and suburbs, and all parts within the late lines of communication, to wait upon God for his blessing and good success upon the said army against the Irish rebels; the same to be observed and kept in all churches and chapels on a more distant day throughout all England.

Letters that Colonel Jones put all the Roman Catholics out of Dublin; that Sir George Ascough secured the harbor for the army to land from England.

July 5th. — The Lord Lieutenant, taking his leave this day, feasted many chief friends, and intends to set out from London by Monday or Tuesday next. The train of artillery was shipped for Ireland.

July 6th. — The House ordered that Wednesday next should be set apart for a day of humiliation for the city and suburbs, and all parts within the late lines of communication, to wait upon God for his blessing and good success of the army against the Irish rebels. The House then considered what ministers should be appointed to preach on next Wednesday.

July 7th — The Lord Lieutenant of Ireland, intending to advance on Tuesday morning next from London towards the relief of our distressed brethren of Ireland,

---

[1] The rebels seem to prepare to send forces into Ireland, and Cromwell gives forth he will go with them, which few believe. Letter of Sir E. Nicholas to Ormonde, June 9th, 1649; in Carte's *Collection*, &c., vol. i. p. 294.

desired the House to give him leave to offer some petitions to their consideration, on behalf of several of their friends, to whom he engaged himself to use his utmost endeavors to promote their requests to the House before his departure. The House gave him favor herein accordingly, and his Lordship presented several petitions, which were read and debated.

July 12th. — In pursuance of an order of the House, the Lord Lieutenant of Ireland is to be allowed from the date of his patent £10 a day, as General of the forces in Ireland, during his continuation in England ; from the time of his arrival in Ireland, he is to receive, as General of the forces thereof, £2,000 per quarter, which is not to be understood as any of the salary which by his patent he is entitled to receive as Lord Lieutenant ; £3,000 to be immediately advanced to him for his transportation and furnishing himself with provision.[1]

On the day of his departure his friends assembled at Whitehall. Three ministers invoked the blessing of God on the cause of the saints ; and two officers, Goff and Harrison, and the Lord Lieutenant himself, expounded the Scriptures excellently well and pertinent to the purpose.[2]

---

[1] In March, 1648, a sum of £1,680 a year was settled on Cromwell, and £5,000 on Fairfax, out of the Marquis of Worcester's estate. . Of this sum Cromwell forgave the State £1,000 per annum for six years towards the expenses of the war in Ireland, if it should continue so long, to be employed as the parliament should be pleased to appoint. The House accepted the free offer of Lieutenant-General Cromwell, testifying his zeal and good affection. *Mod. Intell.*, March 23d, 1648 ; in *Cromwelliana*, p. 38.

[2] Heath, in his *Flagellum*, says Ireton was absolutely the best prayermaker and preacher in the army, though Oliver came little behind him.

CHAPTER VI.

CROMWELL SETS OUT FOR IRELAND.

Departure from London — Journey to Bristol — The Rendezvous — Mutiny — Idolaters to
be extirpated — News of Jones' Victory — The Fleet sets sail — The Regiments and
their Commanders — Reception in Dublin — Proclamations — The . Buff Coat in the
Dublin pulpits.

CROMWELL's departure was thus announced in *The Moderate In-
telligencer* of July 10th : This evening, about five of the clock, the
Lord Lieutenant of Ireland began his journey by way of Windsor
and so to Bristol. He went forth in that state and equipage as the
like hath hardly been seen ; himself in a coach with six gallant Flanders mares, whitish grey ; divers coaches accompanying him, and very
many great officers of the army ; his life-guard consisting of eighty
gallant men, the meanest whereof was a Commander or Esquire, in
stately habit, with trumpets sounding almost to the shaking of Char-
ing Cross, had it been now standing. Of his life-guard many are
colonels ; and, believe me, it's such a guard as is hardly to be paralleled
in the world. And now have at you, my Lord of Ormonde ! You
will have men of gallantry to encounter, whom to overcome will be
honor sufficient ; and to be beaten by them will be no great blemish
to your reputation. If you say, " Cæsar or nothing," they say, " A
Republic or nothing." The Lord Lieutenant's colors are white. Thus
he was conducted to Brentford, where the gentlemen who accompanied him took their leave, wishing him a prosperous issue to his undertaking, whom he answered again with great civility and respect.
From thence he posted directly for Bristol, by Windsor, Reading,
Newbury, Marlborough, and Bath.

On Saturday evening, July 14th, he entered Bristol, where he
was royally entertained by the soldiers and officers in arms and others
who held offices by order of Parliament. The citizens likewise expressed much joy at his coming, and entertained him with great
respect. The people thronged from the surrounding country to see
him. His wife and several other members of his family came to
pass some days with him. There, for reasons which it is not possible
to ascertain, he remained for a whole month, coming and going between the different places along the coast, and receiving numerous
visitors. He seemed still to hesitate, and to quit the soil of England
with great doubtfulness and effort. Thence, by way of Tenby, which
he reached on the 2nd of August, and Pembroke, he went to Milford Haven. He had already issued orders for the troops to ren-

dezvous there.[1] The parliament ordered transports to put into that port, to be ready for the conveyance of the troops. Twenty ships were sent round the coast with a convoy. The Council of State issued orders to James Powell, Bristol, to stay all ships in the ports of Bristol, Minehead, Barnstaple and Appledare, fit for transporting horse and foot to Dublin, and to send them to Milford Haven. He had sent a dispatch to Chester, directing Colonels Venables, Huncks and Reynolds to embark. Their regiments, consisting of 1500 foot and 600 horse, well supplied with clothing and all other necessaries, set sail without delay, and being favored with a prosperous wind, reached Dublin on the 25th of July, the day before Ormonde sat about investing the city.[2] Some of the troops were disheartened at the news of Ormonde's approach to Dublin at the head of an army of 30,000 men, and made no secret of their unwillingness to engage in so hazardous an enterprise as the landing in Ireland under such disadvantages. Colonel Horton's regiment refused to embark, and disbanded themselves. Colonel Cook's regiment rose in mutiny at Minehead; many of the men deserted. With difficulty the officers appeased those who remained and got them on board. At Bristol a whole battalion refused to embark.[3] Cromwell suddenly appeared among them, and their complaints were hushed; at the same time preachers labored strenuously to work on their prejudices. They were compared to the Israelites proceeding to extirpate the idolatrous inhabitants of Canaan, and described as the chosen instruments by which heaven was to overthrow the empire of Babylon and establish in its stead the New Jerusalem. Wednesday, August 1st, was kept by Act of Parliament a public fast throughout England and Wales, to call upon God for a blessing upon the Lord Lieutenant Cromwell's forces against the enemies of the parliament in England and in Ireland.

But the welcome tidings of Jones' success gave them courage; they loudly expressed their desire to proceed to Ireland. Cromwell embarked the day after the good news reached him. From on board the ship John, at Milford, he wrote to his "loving brother," Richard Mayor, whose daughter had just been married to his eldest son, Richard Cromwell, expressing to him his joy at Jones' victory. "This is an astonishing mercy," he wrote, "so great and seasonable, that indeed we are like them that dreamed. What can we say? The Lord fill our souls with thankfulness, that our mouths may be full of his praise, and our lives too; and grant we may never forget his goodness to us. These things seem to strengthen our faith and love against

---

[1] July 21st. The Lord Lieutenant appointed Milford Haven the general rendezvous of all the forces for Ireland. Whitelocke, p. 399.

[2] Reynolds and his party were detained by contrary winds for some time. This delay caused a report to go abroad that it was intended to make a descent on Munster, which unhappily divided Inchiquin and a good body of men from Ormonde, as he marched towards Dublin. Clarendon's *Hist. of the Rebellion*, vol. iii. p. 322.

[3] Many of Colonel Tuthill's soldiers have manifested great disaffection, and threatened to run to the enemy, when transported . . . . Colonel Levesy's regiment, designed for Ireland, a great burden. by their disorderly carriage, expressing great disaffection to the Commonwealth . . . . Some of Colonel Reynold's troopers disorderly, swearing they will not go to Ireland. Colonel Horton's regiment refused to go to Ireland and disbanded themselves. . . . . Major Bethel and other officers refused to go.

more difficult times. Sir, pray for me, that I may walk worthy of the Lord in all that he hath called me to."

On Monday, August 13th, he sat sail with the van of his army in thirty-two ships. Commissary-General Ireton,[1] his son-in-law, followed two days after, with the main body of the army in forty-two vessels. His chaplain, Hugh Peters,[2] with twenty sail brought up the rear. Three regiments were left behind for want of shipping. "There was much seeking of God by prayer for a blessing upon them, and the country people prayed heartily for a fair wind for them. The wind proved favorable ; the second day following they landed at Kingsend, near Dublin, Sir George Ascough[3] having secured the harbor for them with his ships. Cromwell's original design was, that a part of the army, under Ireton, should effect a landing somewhere in Munster, "for the Irish did account that province to be the key of the kingdom, both by reason of the cities and walled towns (which are more than all the little island besides), the fruitfulness of the country, being reputed the garden of Ireland, and the commodious harbors lying open both to France and Spain." Besides, he had secret assurances from the friends of the parliament in the southern towns, that his forces would be received there with favor.[4] But Jones' success and the necessity of recovering some garrisons near Dublin, for want of which the forces within the city would soon be reduced to great extremity, made him alter his plan, and order that all should land at Dublin. Inchiquin, too, was master of a great part of the south, and for the moment he was on the King's side.

The invading army was made up of Ireton's, Scroop's, Horton's, Lambert's, and Cromwell's own regiments of horse ; of Abbott's, Mercer's, Fletcher's, Garland's, and Bolton's troops of dragoons ; and

---

[1] Ireton, two years before, had married Bridget, Cromwell's eldest daughter. This connection and his own merits, for he had distinguished himself at Naseby, soon obtained for him speedy promotion in the army. He was the chief cause of the King's death, having intercepted a letter in which Charles declared his intention of putting Cromwell to death. He was made president of Munster in 1650, and later Lord Deputy. He died in the zenit of his successes at Limerick, Nov. 15th, 1651. His body was taken to England and buried with the English sovereigns in the chapel of Henry VII. at Westminster Abbey. After the Restoration it was exhumed and burned at Tyburn. Lingard's *Hist of England*, vol. ix. p. 8. His widow married Fleetwood, who succeeded him as Lord Deputy.

[2] Peters, at the beginning of the troubles in Ireland, had a brigade against the rebels, and came off with honor and victory, and the like was now expected of him. Whitelocke, p. 410. He fell sick, and returned to Wales immediately after the capture of Wexford, and there seems to have been employed looking to the shipping of recruits, supplies, &c., while Cromwell was in Ireland.

[3] Ascough had fought against Van Tromp and De Ruyter. When the fleet revolted o the Prince of Wales, he declared for the parliament, and brought the Lion man-of-war, which he commanded, into the Thames. The following year the parliament appointed him Vice-Admiral, and ordered that he should have the command of the Irish seas, giving him "a ship proportionable to that great honor, and at present greatest service." *Perfect Diurnal*, March 2nd, 1649. He did much towards reducing the whole island to the obedience of the republic. Granger's *Biog. Hist. of England*, vol. v. p. 158 ; London, 1824.

[4] Ireton seems to have sailed for Munster, and to have been forced by stress of weather to land at Dublin. "Major-General Ireton designed for Munster, hovering at Cabell Island, near Youghal, some days, did not see ground to put in there ; the 10th day from his putting out from Milford, he landed at Dublin with seventy sail ; after him the third squadron, commanded by Colonel Horton, consisting of 18 sail ; in all 113."

of Ewer's, Cooke's, Hewson's,[1] Deane's, and Cromwell's regiments of foot, and Colonel Phayre's Kentish regiment. The divisions of Jones and Monk, already in Ireland for some time, were also under his command. The whole force at his disposal must have been over 17,000 men, most of them well trained to war, and in good heart on account of their past successes. He had, besides, several pieces of artillery, an abundant supply of military stores, and £200,000 in money.[2] Among the officers were many whose names are familiar to the readers of Irish history, Henry Cromwell, the Protector's second son, and later Lord Deputy; Jones, Blake, Sankey, Ingoldsby,[3] and others equally prominent in bringing about the King's death and raising up the Commonwealth.

On his arrival in Dublin, "he was most heroically entertained with the resounding echo of the great guns round about the city, and a great concourse of people to see him." When nearly in the heart of the city, where the concourse was greatest, he halted, and rising in his carriage, with his hat in his hand, he made a very grateful speech to the people. "He did not doubt," he said, "that as God had brought him thither in safety, so he would be able, by divine Providence to restore them all to their just liberties and properties. All those persons whose hearts' affections were real for the carrying of the great work against the barbarous and bloodthirsty Irish and all their adherents and confederates, for the propagating of the Gospel of Christ, the establishing of truth and peace, and restoring of this bleeding nation of Ireland to its former happiness and tranquility, should find favor and protection from the parliament of England and from himself, and withal receive such rewards and gratuities as should be answerable to their merits." This speech was received with great applause by the people, who all cried out, "We will live with you and die with you."

It must be borne in mind that two years before this time, soon after Dublin was surrendered by Ormonde to the parliament, the new governor, Colonel Michael Jones, ordered all the "Papists" to quit; they were forbidden to return under severe penalties; under pain of death no one should pass the night within the city walls. This order was renewed by the parliament, with the additional clause, that anyone giving shelter to a priest or Jesuit, even for a single hour, should

---

[1] Hewson, the one-eyed cobbler, who from a mender of old shoes became a reformer of government and religion. His bravery in the field soon raised him to the rank of colonel. Cromwell had such a high opinion of him that he made him governor of Dublin. Later he became a member of the Barebones Parliament, a Lord of the Upper House, and a member of the Council of Safety. After the Restoration he fled to Amsterdam, where he died in obscurity.

[2] Hill says he brought with him also an immense supply of Bibles and a vast store of scythes. *McDonnells of Antrim*, p. 275; Belfast, 1873. "Last Monday, Colonel Hewson, with a considerable body of horse, marched into Wicklow. He doth now intend to make use of the scythes and sickles that were sent over in 1649, with which they intended to cut down the growing corn in those parts, which the enemy is to live upon in winter time, and thereby, for want of bread and cattle, the tories may be left destitute of provisions, and so forced to submit and quit these places." Letter of the Commissioners for Ireland to the parliament, Dublin, July 1st, 1650; in *The Cromwellian Settlement*, p. 78.

[3] "Dick Ingoldsby, who can neither pray nor preach; I'll entrust him before ye all."

lose his life and forfeit his property. At Ormonde's approach to the city Jones again "put out all the men, Roman Catholics, out of Dublin ;[1] but their wives and children were allowed to stay."

On the 23d of August he published the following proclamation ; it was dated from Dublin Castle :

"Whereas God Almighty, in the abundance of his mercy and goodness, hath been pleased from time to time to vouchsafe preservation and deliverance unto this city from the rage and cruelty of a bloody enemy, and in a special manner to manifest his . . . *numerous army of rebels encamped about this city; which continual mercies do justly call for a thankful acknowledgement of his gracious goodness, by a sincere and earnest endeavor as well as to maintain the honor of his most holy name as to oppose and take away such offences, being contrary and displeasing to his divine will. And yet notwithstanding, by the frequent practice of profane swearing, cursing, and drunkenness, his holy name is daily dishonored and blasphemed to the scandal and grief of all good men, although the said offences are prohibited by the law of God, the known laws of the land, and the known articles of war ; whereby we have just cause to fear that, without a thorough reformation of such sins, he may deservedly break off the continuance of his wonted kindness towards this place and give us over to destruction. And forasmuch as it is a duty required at the hand of the magistrate, who ought not to bear the sword in vain, but to improve the power committed into his hand for the punishment and prevention of offences, we therefore sadly taking the premises into consideration, and resolving that the said offences be strictly proceeded against and punished according to the utmost severity and rigor of the law, do, by this our proclamation, strictly charge and command that as well the mayor of this city and other officers and ministers of justice in the same city whom the same shall concern, as also that all officers of the army, do respectively cause the said laws and articles to be put in execution against all such persons as shall offend against the same. And we do further charge and command all officers of the army to be aiding and assisting to the said mayor of this city and other the said officers and ministers of justice therein, for the apprehending of all and every the said offenders which shall be members of the army, and for the bringing of them before their proper officers, whereby they may be severely punished according to the said articles of war. And we do hereby declare our full resolution to punish the neglect and contempt of this our proclamation with the severest punishment which by law may be inflicted upon the contemners thereof."

The following day he issued another proclamation. The army was deeply imbued with a horror and detestation of the Irish rebels, the result of the continual reports of the atrocities alleged to have been perpetrated on their Protestant brethren. Hence they were ready to interpret most liberally the orders given them to treat the Irish people as the Israelites in Joshua's time were bidden to treat the Canaanites, to utterly destroy them, to show them no mercy.[3]

"Whereas I am informed that, upon the marching out of the armies heretofore and of parties from garrisons, a liberty hath been taken by the soldiers to abuse, rob, and pillage, and too often to exercise cruelties upon the country people ; being resolved, by the grace of God, diligently and strictly to restrain such wickedness

---

[1] An exception seems to have been made in favor of Father Nicholas Netterville, S. J., who was on terms of great intimacy with Cromwell, often dining at his table and playing chess with him. Captain Foulkes having accused him of saying Mass, he replied : " I am a priest, and the Lord General knows it. And tell all the town of it, and that I will say Mass here every day." Gilbert's *History of the City of Dublin*, vol i. p. 56; Dublin, 1861.

[2] Some words are wanting in the original here.

[3] Deuter. vii. 2. On Cromwell's arrival in Dublin he addressed his soldiers, and declared no mercy should be shown to the Irish, and that they should be dealt with as the Canaanites in Joshua's time.

for the future, I do hereby warn and require all officers, soldiers, and others under my command, henceforth to forbear all such evil practices as aforesaid, and not to do any wrong or violence towards country people or persons whatsoever, unless they be actually in arms or office with the enemy, and not to meddle with the goods of such without special order. And I further declare that it shall be free and lawful to and for all manner of persons dwelling in the country, as well gentlemen and soldiers as farmers and other people, such as are in arms or office with or for the enemy only excepted, to make their repair and bring any provisions unto the army, while in march or camp, or unto any garrison under my command; hereby assuring all such that they shall not be troubled or molested in their persons or goods, but shall have the benefit of a free market, and receive ready money for the goods and commodities they shall so bring and sell. And that they, behaving themselves peaceably and quietly, and paying such contributions proportionably with their neighbors as have been, or shall be duly and orderly imposed upon them for maintenance of the parliament's forces and other public uses, shall have free leave and liberty to live at home with their families and goods, and shall be protected in their persons and estates, by virtue hereof, until the 1st day of January next, by or before which time all such of them as are minded to reside and plough and sow in the quarters, are to make their addresses for new and further protection to the attorney-general, residing at Dublin, and to such other persons as shall be authorized for that purpose. And hereof I require all soldiers and others under my command, diligently to take notice and observe the same, as they shall answer to the contrary at their utmost perils; strictly charging and commanding all officers and others in their several places carefully to see to it, that no wrong or violence be done to any such person as aforesaid, contrary to the effect of the premises. Being resolved, through the grace of God, to punish all that shall offend contrary thereunto, very severely, according to law or articles of war; to displace and otherwise punish all such officers as shall be found negligent in their places, and not see the due observance hereof, and not to punish the offenders, under their respective commanders. Given at Dublin, the 24th of August, 1649."

This last proclamation was a shrewd piece of policy. No previous invader had thought of conciliating the peasantry by promises of justices and protection. The Royalist army, especially that portion of it that was commanded by Inchiquin, had plundered friend and foe alike without mercy; even the Confederates had shown little scruple in their dealings with the tillers of the soil. The opinion spread rapidly abroad, that Cromwell was more favorably disposed to the native Irish than the Royalists under Inchiquin or the descendants of the original invaders who sat in the Council of Kilkenny. Nor were his threats of punishment idle words. On his way to Drogheda he ordered two of his private soldiers to be put to death in the face of the whole army for stealing two hens from a poor Irishwoman. On the strict observance of this proclamation, and on the positive assurance given by his officers that they were for the liberties of the Commons: that every one should enjoy the freedom of his religion, and that those who served the market at the camp should pay no contribution, the country people flocked in with all kinds of provisions; and due payment being made for the same, his army was much better supplied than even that of the Irish had ever been.[1]

According to tradition, he occupied during his stay in Dublin,

[1] When Cromwell possessed himself of Ireland, several merchants in Dublin and other towns, to supply a scarcity of small change, coined pence and halfpence of copper and brass, with their name and place of abode on them, which they were obliged to make good afterwards.

the old house which stood at the corner of Castle Street and Werburgh Street.[2]

"The buff coat, instead of the black gown, appeared in Dublin pulpits, that being a furtherer of preferment if valor accompanied it; to use two swords well is meritorious. Not a word of St. Austin or Thomas Aquinas, nor any such hard words; only downright honesty was now given forth." In spite of this display of religion, the troopers' horses were stabled in St. Patrick's cathedral.

---

[2] This house was demolished in 1812 by order of the Commissioners of Wide Streets, and the materials sold for £40.

CHAPTER VII.

THE SEIGE AND CAPTURE OF DROGHEDA. ¡

Muster of the Army — The March — Finglas Cross — Defences of Drogheda — The Garrison — Sir Arthur Aston — The Fortifications — Cromwell's Account of the Siege — The Assault — No Quarter — Death of Ashton — Official List of the Slain — The Bloody Street — The Survivors.

AFTER a few days' rest — for the men and horses had been so so sick at sea that they could not march any sooner,[1] — and a public thanksgiving for their safe arrival, Cromwell determined to take the field. His present plan of action was wholly different from that which he professed to have in view while the expedition was in preparation. He felt that the fiercest passions of the Protestants and Republicans were roused against the Catholics and the Royalists, and could be readily made to serve his purposes. The instructions which he now received from the parliament were inspired by the news of Jones' victory. The scheme to gain O'Neill over was at an end ; the negotiations with the Catholics were broken off wholly.

Friday, August 31st, was appointed for a general muster of the forces under his command. They assembled to the number of 15,000 men. From these he chose twelve regiments, in all about 10,000 "stout, resolute men for the present service " ; at their head he crossed the Liffey, and encamped about three miles to the north of Dublin "in the field of Lord Barnwell." [2] The next day he began the march to Drogheda, probably by the high road passing through Swords and Balbriggan ; in the evening he pitched his camp "at Ballygarth, close to the Nannywater," twenty miles from Dublin. There is still standing in the churchyard of Finglass an ancient cross ; it was held in such veneration that two baronies of the county of Dublin, Upper and Nether Cross, have had their names from it. The emblem of our salvation was to the Puritans "the mark of the Beast," and they directed against it their pious rage. It is said that a detachment of the soldiers pulled it down, intending to break it in pieces. Fortunately they did not carry out their purpose wholly. The inhabitants buried it, in order to save it from further desecration. On the return of the army, a fortnight later, it could not be found.[3] Baldungan

---

[1] *Perfect Diurnal*, Aug. 22d. "The Lord Lieutenant was as sick at sea as any man I ever saw in my life." Letter of Peters from Milford, Aug. 16th.

[2] Letter from Ireland in *Cromwelliana*, p. 64 ; probably at Turvey; the castle, formerly the residence of the Barnwells, is still standing. The proprietor then was Nicholas Barnwell, created Viscount Barnwell of Turvey in 1645.

[3] Taylor's *Civil Wars*, vol. ii. p. 15. It was discovered by the Rev. Dr. Walsh, author of the *History of Dublin*, in 1816. It is of granite, and stands on a pedestal about eight feet high.

castle was battered by the ships.[1] Coming to Gormanstown, Cromwell attempted to get possession of the heir, then a child in arms.
The boy was saved by the exertions of the parish priest, who fled with
him to France, and later had him brought up in the Catholic religion.[2]
As the enemy advanced, the Irish forces along the coast and in the
adjoining parts of Meath hastened to obstruct his passage. But owing
to the promptness of his movements, they could do no more than
make sudden onsets and retreat before him.

Drogheda[3] is a seaport town, on the east coast, about twenty-three
miles due north of Dublin. Cromwell felt that the possession of this
place would be of the utmost importance to him. Being the passport
to the Northern parts of Ireland, it was essential to the security of
the metropolis and the keeping up of communication with those parts ;
as a seaport situated opposite the English coast, it afforded the most
direct means of intercourse with England. Hence, it was resolved
by the confederates in a council of war, consisting of fifteen members,
held August 23d, that "Drogheda was to be maintained." The governor of the town gave orders to destroy the castles of Belgard,
Athcairne, Dardistown, and Bellewstown, and sent out a party for that
purpose. But the enemy had anticipated him, and coming up, got
possession of some and secured, by advancing with a great body of
horse, the rest of them. Ormonde, judging it would be the first place
attacked, applied his utmost industry to supply it with all things
that it needed. He ordered the fortifications to be repaired, and provisions and ammunition to be thrown into it, as well as the shortness
of the time would allow. All suspected persons were forced to quit.
He hoped to put it in such a state of defence that it would occupy
the besiegers a considerable time and cause them some loss; meantime he would employ himself in recruiting his shattered forces and
in preparing further means of resistance. He then withdrew to Trim
with his horse and a small body of foot, whence he sent orders to
Lord Inchiquin to bring up whatever forces he could muster, all fears
of Cromwell's landing in Munster being now at an end. He remained
in the town till the last moment, making arrangements for its defence.

---

[1] Baldungan castle, fourteen miles north of Dublin, formerly belonged to the Knights
Templars. After their suppression it passed into the hands of the Barnwells, and through
them by the female line to the Berminghams and St. Laurences. In the war of 1651 it was
held by Thomas Fitzwilliam for the Confederates. D'Alton's *History of Drogheda*, vol. i. p.
113 : Dublin, 1844.

[2] This must have been Jenico, 7th viscount Gormanstown. His father, Nicholas, the
6th viscount, took a leading part among the gentlemen of the Pale in the war of 1641 ; for
which he was outlawed and excepted from pardon for life or estate. In 1688, the 7th viscount
took the side of James II., and was in consequence outlawed. The outlawry was reversed
and the estates recovered, after a tedious suit by his nephew.

[3] Droched Atha, i., e. the Bridge of the Ford : it is Latinized Urbs Pontana and Vadi-
pontum ; by the English it was called Treoid and Tredagh. In 1228, Henry III. granted to
the good men of Drogheda tolls for one year for the building of their bridge. In 1234, a
murage charter was granted to the town at both sides of the river. The part to the north
of the Boyne is called in ancient documents Drogheda towards Uriel, the southern part
Drogheda towards Meath. Great dissentions subsisted between the two parts, which were
often attended with bloodshed. By the exertions of F. Philip Bennett, O. P., a reconciliation took place in 1412 ; the result was a petition to Henry VI. to unite the town under one
mayor and form it into one special county. A burlesque used to take place yearly, on
Shrove Tuesday, in memory of this ancient feud.

Though anxious to share the dangers with the garrison, he could not allow himself to be shut up there and thus prevented from issuing orders to the rest of the forces. Some days later he went to Tecroghan[1] and thence to Portlester,[2] and awaited there Inchiquin's coming up before making any attack on the enemy.

Yet, in spite of the efforts, the town was but indifferently supplied. Only a week before Cromwell appeared, the governor wrote to Ormonde : " Yesternight there came from Dundalk .ten barrels of powder, but very little match ; and that is a thing most wanting here ; and for round shot not any at all. I beseech your Excellency to be pleased to give speedy orders for same, as also for the sudden coming of men and moneys. Bellyfood, I perceive, will prove scarce amongst us, but my endeavors shall never be sparing to approve myself." He was much embarrassed, too, by the movements of Lady Wilmot and other ladies, his near relatives, then in Drogheda, whom he discovered to be in communication with Colonel Jones and other officers of the Parliamentary army in Dublin.

The town was garrisoned by 2,221 foot and 320 horse, nearly all of whom were Irish, viz.,[3] Ormonde's regiment of 400 men, under the command of Sir Edward Verney ; Colonel Byrne's Colonel Wall's, and Colonel Warren's regiments, amounting to about 2,000 men ; Lord Westmeath's, 200 ; Sir James Dillon's, 200 foot and 200 horse ; besides 500 foot sent in under Lieutenant-Colonel Griffin Cavenagh while Cromwell lay before the town. The horse were divided into five troops, commanded respectively by Major Butler, Captain Harpole, Sir John Dungan, Sir James Preston, Lieutenant-Colonel Dungan, Captains Plunket, Fleming, and Finglas. The entire force of artillery in the town consisted of one master-gunner, two gunners, and three gunner's mates. The commander to whom this important place was confided by Ormonde, with the full consent of the Commissioners of Trust, was Sir Arthur Aston, a Catholic,[4] of an ancient

---

[1] Tecroghan, five miles north of Trim, belonged to Sir Luke Fitzgerald. As it guarded the passage by the head waters of the Boyne, it was called " one of the pillars of Ireland." See the " Declaration " of Jamestown.

[2] Portlester, a great secure fastness, five miles west of Trim. It was one of the strongholds of Silken Thomas, in 1556. The lordship of Portlester, which extended to Bellewstown, near Bective, passed to the earls of Kildare, by the marriage of Gerald, 8th earl, with Alison, daughter and heiress of Sir Rowland FitzEustace, who died in 1495. See Dean Butler's *Trim and its Antiquities*, p. 134 ; Dublin, 1861. The castle has been demolished.

[3] Ludlow, *Memoirs*, p. 116, Bate, *Elenchus*, &c., vol. ii. p. 24, and others say the garrison was composed almost wholly of English. Mr. Froude repeats this statement, perhaps to extenuate Cromwell's cruelties to the Irish. *The English in Ireland*, vol. i. p. 123 ; London, 1872. But Ormonde expressly says the contrary in his answer to the 13th Article of the Jamestown " Declaration " ; " Drogheda was put into the hands of Sir Arthur Aston, a Catholic ; and of the soldiers and officers of the garrison, the greater part were of that religion." See the Appendix to *The History of the Remonstrance*, p. 117. In the Essex MSS. at Stowe, too, it is stated that the majority of the officers and soldiers were Catholics. D'Alton's *Hist. of Drogheda*, vol. ii. p. 162 ; from which we may fairly conclude they were Irish. If the garrison consisted mainly of English, how could Cromwell say that " their death was a righteous punishment for having imbrued their hands in innocent blood ? "

[4] " Whom the Papists, notwithstanding, would not acknowledge for a Papist." Clarendon's *Rebellion*, vol. ii. p. 153. " He had the misfortune to be much esteemed where he was not known, and very much detested where he was." *Ibid.*, p. 527.

Cheshire family, allied to Viscount Moore, who had distinguishe[d] himself both at home and abroad. He had served in the army of Sigismund, King of Poland, against the Turks.[1] When the civil war broke out he returned to England and was appointed colonel-general of dragoons; with them he did good service at Edgehill. Later he was made governor of Reading and Oxford. Clarendon says there was not in the King's army a man of greater reputation, or one of whom the enemy had greater dread. So confident was he of the strength of his position and of the courage of the garrison, that he wrote to Ormonde, "he would find the enemy play, and that the garrison, being select men, was so strong that the town could not be taken by assault; that they were unanimous in their resolution to perish rather than deliver up the place." Hence he advised to hazard nothing by hastening to his relief. Ormonde, therefore, might fairly reckon on a lengthened resistance; and he well knew that a tedious siege would be disastrous to the assailants, no matter how well disciplined and cared for, as it would of necessity expose them to all the hardships of a winter campaign in a hostile country.

The fortifications of the town consisted of a wall more than a mile and a half in length, enclosing an area of about sixty-four acres Irish measure. Its height was about twenty feet, its thickness from four to six, diminishing towards the summit so as to allow a space of about two feet behind the embrasures for the soldiers to stand on. In later times this space was widened by the addition of three or four feet supported by columns and arches of stone, on which there was a passage leading round the town, with doorways through the gates, castles, and turrets. This wall exists still on the Louth side, running from the west gate to the river, from St. Laurence's gate to the quay, bounding Dominic Lane on the west side, and Scarlet Street and Patrick Street to the south. On the Meath side the line can be traced from the Butter Tower to the foot of the Millmount, and from Blackbut Lane to Priest's Lane; it encloses the burial-ground of St. Mary's parish to the south and east. There is a fragment also between St. James Street and the Boyne.

The gates guarding the northern part of the town were, taken in regular order, the West gate, near the end of West Street, composed of two towers and a portcullis between; Fair gate, adjoining the place where fairs were held, no longer identified; Sunday's gate, so called from the Dominican or St. Sunday's friary near it;[2] this was also

[1] In the Harleian MSS. 2149, there are various testimonies of foreign princes lauding his conduct in the wars; one is a record of a yearly pension of 700 florins by Sigismund. D'Alton's *Hist. of Drogheda*, vol. i. p. 268. During the siege he resided in the old house at the corner of Patrick's Well Lane, formerly belonging to the Elcock family, as may be seen by the arms and inscription on the slab let into the gable. James II. is said to have slept in this house the night before he went to the camp at Donore. See Wild's *Boyne and Blackwater*, p. 308; Dublin, 1850.

[2] Sunday, i. e., *dies dominica*. The Dominican priory, founded in 1224 by Luke Netterville, Archbishop of Armagh from 1217 to 1227, was under the invocation of St. Mary Magdalen. Here on March 16th, 1395, four of the Irish kings, O'Neill, O'Donnell, O'Hanlon, and M'Mahon, made their solemn submission to Richard II. See Ware's *Works*, vol. ii. p. 186. Thomas, 8th earl of Desmond, beheaded by the Lord Deputy Tiptoff, February 15th, 1467, was buried in this church. The stately monument erected over his grave was

called the Cow gate ; the only fragment of it now existing is the gable of a forge ; it was a square castle, having near it two towers, the Tooting and Boulter's ; St. Laurence's, still standing ;[1] St. Catherine's, somewhere at the edge of the river ; its site is not known. On the Meath side were St. James' or the Dublin gate, at the end of St. James' Street, where the stream that flows through the Dale falls into the Boyne ; the Blind gate ; Duleck gate, on the Duleck road ; St. John's gate, the entrance to the old priory of St. John of Jerusalem,[2] which stood on the grounds of Ball's Grove ; and lastly, the Butter gate, an octagon perforated with an arched passage.[3]

But Cromwell's activity and boldness soon frustrated Ormonde's plans and put an end to his hopes. He was too well aware of the evils that would result from a long delay before the town, and determined to spend no time in the common forms of approaches and turnings. Sir George Ascough's ships, which had attended his army on the march from Dublin, blocked up the entrance to the harbor, and prevented any aid from coming in by sea. Ormonde's hope of succor from Inchiquin was vain ; for many of his horse were English and did not care to fight against their countrymen ; whole squadrons deserted.

We shall let the Lieutenant-General tell the history of his successes, as he related them to the parliament, supplementing his narrative from other sources : —

" For the Right Honorable William Lenthal,[4] Esquire, Speaker of the Parliament of England. These :

Dublin, 17th of Sept., 1649.

" SIR, —

" Your army being safely arrived at Dublin, and the enemy endeavoring to draw all his forces about Trim and Tecrogan, as my intelligence gave me, from whence endeavors were made by the Marquis of Ormonde to draw Owen Roe O'Neill with his forces to his assistance, but with what success I cannot yet learn ; I resolved, after some refreshment taken for our weather-beaten men and horses, and accommodations for a march, to take the field. And accordingly upon Friday, the 30th of August last,[5] I rendezvoused with eight regiments of foot and six of

---

removed to Christ Church, Dublin, by order of Sir Henry Sidney, and placed in the room of Earl Strongbow's, which had been wholly demolished by the fall of that part of the church. Archdall's *Monasticon*, p. 457 ; Dublin, 1786.

[1] The priory of St. Laurence stood near the gate of the same name ; to it belonged the burial-ground called the Cord.

[2] This was made subject to the prior of St. Keenan's, Duleck, by Walter de Lacy ; a portion of the funds for its support came from tolls on butter taken at the Butter gate. All these gates existed up to 90 years ago. There were, besides, two castles on the Meath side, built soon after the invasion ; the one called the Castle of Drogheda, the other Blackagh. D'Alton's *Hist. of Drogheda*, vol. i. pp. 42 and 91.

[3] Drogheda was besieged by the Irish under Sir Phelim O'Neill in 1642. Sir Henry Tichborne was then governor, and Lord Moore was in command of the cavalry. An interesting account of this siege is given in *The Whole Proceedings of the Seige of Drogheda*, by Nicholas Bernard, Dean of Ardagh. Dublin, 1736.

[4] On the 5th of November, 1640, the Commons chose him to be their Speaker, and two days after presented him to the King with the usual ceremonies. Clarendon's *Rebellion*, vol. i. p. 171.

[5] Should be 31st ; this error about the day of the month runs through the whole of this letter.

horse, and some troops of dragoons, three miles on the north side of Dublin. The design was to endeavor the regaining of Drogheda, or tempting the enemy upon hazard of the losing of that place to fight."

On the night of September 2d, a body of horse encamped about two miles from the town. Early the following morning Aston was abroad with his horse ; but finding the enemy too strong to deal with, he returned and left Captain Finglas on the field, with orders not to engage but upon advantage, and only with small parties, to discover their motions. In the afternoon news was brought him that about 500 of the enemy's horse were drawing towards the fort at Oldbridge. In a letter written about two in the afternoon of the same day, he apprised Ormonde that the enemy's army, or the greater part of it, had appeared. "Their foot," he wrote, "being convoyed over by an overawing power of horse, hath taken all the advantageous places without the walls, insomuch that I am very confident this night they will make their batteries, the which (all places being so serviceable to them) we can hardly prevent. . . . I have lost one captain of Colonel Warren's regiment, who was slain by a musket shot. Major Butler hath lost two horses, the one of them shot under himself, the other a trooper's, a soldier or two wounded ; and this is all hitherto."

"Your army came before the town upon Monday following,[1] where having pitched, a speedy course was taken as could be to fix our batteries, which took up the more time because divers of the battering guns were on shipboard."

Tradition says the site of one battery was about 400 yards to the east of St. Mary's church-yard, at a spot called Bevrack Mount, which has been recently levelled. The place now goes by the name of Cromwell's Mount. The position of the battery to the south cannot be traced. Some interruption was caused from time to time by sallies of the garrison, in which a few men were slain on both sides. Sir Thomas Armstrong, at the head of 200 men, made a sortie ; "but they were so well entertained, that every one of them was taken prisoner, except Sir Thomas, who escaped by the goodness of his horse." On the 8th of September Aston reported he had made another strong sally with both horse and foot on the enemy's camp. The position of the town was ill suited to sallies. Besides his ammunition was failing, as he had to spend four barrels every day. Provisions, too, were growing short. He asked Ormonde "to attempt an assault on the greater camp speedily, and he will, if he have notice, beat up those upon St. John's Hill."

"Upon Monday, the 9th of this instant, the batteries began to play ; whereupon I sent Sir Arthur Aston, the then governor, a summons to deliver the town to the use of the parliament of England : —

---

[1] Cromwell always looked on the 3d of September as his fortunate day. On two successive anniversaries of that day he gained the victories of Dunbar and Worcester ; on that day, too, he died, as Waller says in his *Panegyric to the Lord Protector :* —
         "In storms as loud as his immortal fame,"
which Godolphin parodied thus : —
         "In storms as loud as was his crying sin."
See Timbs' *Curiosities of History,* p. 139; London, 1862.

"*September* 10*th*, 1649.

SIR,

Having brought the army belonging to the parliament of England before this place, to reduce it to obedience, to the end effusion of blood may be prevented, I thought fit to summon you to deliver the same into my hands to their use. If this be refused, you will have no cause to blame me. I expect your answer and rest,

Your servant,

O. CROMWELL."

" To which receiving no satisfactory answer, I proceeded that day to beat down the steeple of the church [1] on the south side of the town, and to beat down the tower [2] not far from the same place, which you will discern by the chart enclosed."

As this summons was disregarded, he immediately took down the white flag which hung over his quarters, and put out a red ensign instead.

"Our guns [3] not been able to do much that day, it was resolved to endeavor to do our utmost the next day to make the breaches assaultable, and, by the help of God, to storm them. The place pitched upon was that part of the town-wall near a church called St. Mary's; [4] which was the rather chosen, because we did hope, if we did enter and possess that church, we should be better able to keep it against their horse and foot, until we could make way for the entrance of our horse; and we did not conceive that any part of the town would afford the like advantage for that purpose with this."

The wall bounded a part of the church-yard of St. Mary's. It was twenty feet high, and strengthened with towers, and pierced with portholes. It seems strange that this spot, which was most difficult of access and very strongly fortified, should have been the first chosen for attack. Towards the east it runs along the brink of a deep, precipitous valley, called the Dale, through which a stream flows. On the south the approach was not so difficult, but the wall was as high, protected by towers at intervals, and strengthened by buttresses on the inside. In the church-yard there are still the remains of a regular bastion and platform for cannon, the only vestiges of modern fortifications in the entire circuit of the town-wall. Perhaps he

[1] This must have been St. Mary's, as it was the only church on that side of the river that had a steeple.

[2] This tower stood at the south-eastern angle of the wall, and was then a modern work compared with the rest of the defences. The ruins of it show that the ancient wall was demolished, and this tower and a bastion erected in its place. It was built on an arch, and resembled the Magdalen tower in shape. In 1750 it was 50 feet high.

[3] Said by Aston to be " eight pieces of battery, the least whereof shot twelve pounds, and one of them a thirty-pounds' bullet." Letter to Ormonde in *Aphor. Disc.*, vol. ii. p. 259, appendix lxi.

[4] This church, originally founded by the citizens of Drogheda for the Carmelite Order, was called St. Mary's of Mount Carmel. It stood on the most elevated part of the southern division of Drogheda, and filled the southeastern angle of the town-wall; its defences were formed by nature and are exceedingly strong. D'Alton's *Hist. of Drogheda*, vol. i. p. 41. The extent of the friary may be judged from the broken walls at the east end of the present building. The church of St. Mary, now standing, is the second erected on the spot since Cromwell demolished the original one; the only remains of which are the walls of a small vestry, near the east end of the present building, and the foundations of an old tower about 150 feet distant. See Wild's *Boyne and Blackwater*, p. 308; and *The Dublin Penny Journal*, vol. i. p. 284. This convent should not be confounded with St. Mary's de Urso, belonging to the Crouched Friars of St. Austin, on the Louth side of the river, between West Street and the Boyne, the tower and church walls of which are still standing.

chose it because, if once taken, it afforded a more secure lodgment for the first assailants than any other point within the fortifications.[1] The besieged had planted guns on the summit of the church-spire; these and some long fowling-pieces gave great annoyance to the assailants.

"The batteries planted were two; one was for that part of the wall against the west end of the said church, the other against the wall on the south side. Being somewhat long in battering, the enemy made six retrenchments, three of them from the said church to Duleek gate; and three of them from the east end of the church to the town-wall, and so backward. The guns, after some two or three hundred shot, beat down the corner tower, and opened two reasonable good breaches in the east and south wall.

"Upon Tuesday, the 10th of this instant, about five o'clock in the evening, we began the storm;[2] and after some hot dispute we entered, about seven or eight hundred men, the enemy disputing it very stiffly with us. And indeed, through the advantages of the place and the courage God was pleased to give the defenders, our men were forced to retreat, quite out of breath, not without some considerable loss; Colonel Castle,[3] whose regiment was one of those that stormed, being there shot in the head, whereof he presently died: and divers officers and soldiers doing their duty killed and wounded. There was a tenalia[4] to flanker the south wall of the town between Duleek gate and the corner tower before mentioned, which our men entered, wherein they found some forty or fifty of the enemy, which they put to the sword; and this tenalia they held; but it being without the wall, and the sally-port through the wall into that tenalia being choked up with some of the enemy who were killed in it, proved of no use for an entrance into the town that way. Captain Brandly did with forty or fifty of his men very valiantly storm it, for which he deserves the thanks of the State.

"Although our men that stormed the breaches were forced to recoil, as is before expressed, yet, being encouraged to recover their loss, they made a second attempt, wherein God was pleased so to animate them, that they got ground of the enemy, and, by the goodness of God, forced him to quit his entrenchments.[5] And,

---

[1] The town-wall at this point is still in the ruinous condition to which Cromwell reduced it, except that the breach on the eastern side has been partially filled up. The parapet on that side is completely demolished. The breach on the south side has been greatly enlarged; but the part of the wall still standing is about 20 feet high and 6 feet thick. The range of buttresses, connected by circular arches on the inner side, is still standing.

[2] Our word was, "For Him that we shall find with us in Ireland, as well as we did in England, our Lord God." The enemy's word was "Ormonde." Letter from Dublin, in *Cromwelliana*, p. 64.

[3] He is called by Wright and others Cossell. *Hist. of Ireland*, vol. ii. p. 77. He was sent by the parliament with his regiment in the beginning of 1647, to take possession of the garrisons surrendered by Ormonde. On the 8th of April, 1652, it was resolved by parliament, That it be referred to the Commissioners of parliament now in Ireland, to take present care for the good education and maintenance of the two children of Colonel Castle deceased, and to allow for that purpose, out of the revenue of Ireland, such sum as they shall think fit, not exceeding the sum of four score pounds a year, and to settle lands of inheritance of the value of one hundred pounds a year of the lands forfeited to the Commonwealth, at the common value the same lands were in the year 1640, upon the said children and their heirs. — Henry Scobell, clerk of the parliament. MSS. in the Library of the Royal Irish Academy.

[4] Tenalia, now called tenaille, by engineers, a kind of advanced defensive work, which takes its name from its resemblance to the lips of a pair of pincers. It stood in the orchard which now occupies the ground from the south-east angle of the wall to Duleek Street; there was a small, arched doorway in the wall, now filled up, which perhaps was the sally-port mentioned here. These tenalia were small towers, originally placed at regular distances round the town-wall. Only one now remains, at the rear of the Millmount. *Dublin Penny Journal*, vol. i. p. 286.

[5] "The besiegers loaded some of their guns with bullets of a half a pound, and fired on the enemy's horse, drawn up somewhat in view; this forced them to retire. The foot,

after a very hot dispute, the enemy having lost both horse and foot, and we only foot, within the wall, they gave ground, and our men became masters both of their retrenchments and of the church; which, indeed, although they made our entrance more difficult, yet they proved of excellent use to us; so that the enemy could not now annoy us with their horse; but thereby we had advantage to make good the ground, so that we might let in our own horse, which accordingly was done, though with much difficulty."

Some further details are given by Whitelocke under the date October 1st, taken from " more letters of the particulars of the taking of Drogheda." "That the breaches not being made low enough, the horse could not go in with the foot, but the foot alone stormed and entered the town ; but by reason of the numerousness and stoutness of the enemy, who maintained the breach as gallantly as ever men did, and by the death of Colonel Castle, whose regiment was one of those that stormed (and he was slain at the storm), our men were dis-heartened and retreated, which my Lord Lieutenant seeing, went himself to the breach,[1] and after a little time a fresh reserve of Colonel Ewer's men fell on with the rest very courageously, and God abated the courage of the enemy ; they fled before us till we gained the town, and they all agreed in the not giving of quarter." " The garrison," says Froude, "fought with extreme courage; twice, after forcing their way into the town, the storming parties were beaten back through the breach. The third time, as the light was waning, Cromwell led them in person, forced Aston back upon his inner lines, stormed these lines in turn, and before night was master of the town." Colonel Wall who commanded the regiment stationed nearest to the trenches, was killed by a shot in the breast ; his men became confused and dispirited by the loss of their leader.

Then it was, probably, that quarter was offered and accepted. " All the officers and soldiers," says Ormonde, "promised quarter to such as would lay down their arms, and performed it as long as any place held out ; which encouraged others to yield. But when they had once all in their power and feared no hurt that could be done them, then the word 'no quarter' went round, and the soldiers were forced, many of them against their wills, to kill the prisoners." A contemporary author says Cromwell could not take the town until its defenders had received the promise of their lives from some persons of high rank in his army.[2] As soon as the town was in the assailant's power, Jones, the governor of Dublin, who was second in command, told Cromwell that now he had the flower of the Irish army in his hands, and could deal with them as he pleased. He then issued an order that the life of neither man, woman, nor child should be spared ;

---

deprived of their support, began to break and shift for themselves, when charged a second time." Ludlow's *Memoirs*, p. 116.

[1] The sword worn by Cromwell at Drogheda is preserved in the United Service Museum, London. Marmion's *Maritime Ports of Ireland*, p. 256 ; London, 1858.

[2] *Cambrensis Eversus*, vol. iii. p. 187 ; Dublin, 1851. Ludlow says, positive orders had been given by Cromwell to give no quarter to any soldier. *Memoirs*, p. 117. " All conclude that no man had quarter with Cromwell's leave." Letter of Inchiquin to Ormonde, Sept. 15th, 1649 ; in *Aphor. Disc.*, vol. ii. preface xxviii. In November, 1649, the Irish, under Inchiquin, laid siege to Carric-on-Suir, then held by Col. Reynolds, and used to cry at the walls, that they would soon give them " Tredagh quarter." *Crom. Sett.*, p. 189.

and when one of his officers pleaded for mercy for the unresisting victims, "he would sacrifice their souls," he said, "to the ghosts of the English whom they had massacred."

And thus a body of 3,000 men was totally destroyed and massacred,[1] with which, in respect of experience and courage, the Marquis would have been glad to have found himself engaged in the field with an enemy though upon some disadvantage.

> "Divers of the enemy," continues Cromwell, "retreated to the Millmount,[2] a place very strong and of difficult access, being exceeding high, having a good graft, and strongly palisadoed. The Governor, Sir Arthur Aston, and divers considerable officers being there, our men getting up to them, were ordered by me to put them all to the sword. And, indeed, being in the heat of action, I forbade them to spare any that were in arms in the town; and I think that night they put to the sword about 2,000 men."

It was manned with 250 of the best men; when they saw their companions retreat, they were so disheartened that they thought it useless to make further resistance. "Lieutenant-Colonel Axtell of Colonel Hewson's regiment, with some twelve of his men, went to the top of the Mount and demanded of the Governor the surrender of it, who was very stubborn, speaking high words; but at length was persuaded to go into the windmill at the top of the Mount, and many of the chiefest as it could contain, where they were disarmed and afterwards slain."

Sir Arthur Aston was among the first who fell; he was killed "after quarter given by the officer who first came there." "A great dispute there was," says Ludlow in his *Memoirs*,[3] "among the soldiers for his artificial leg, which was reputed to be of gold; but it proved to be but of wood, his girdle being found to be better booty, wherein 200 pieces of gold were found quilted." A. Wood says he was believed to have hid away his gold for security in his wooden leg. This they seized upon as a prize when he fell; but finding nothing in it, they knocked out his brains with it and hacked his body to pieces. Sir Edward Verney, Colonels Warren, Fleming, Boyle, and Byrne, were slain in cold blood.[4]

---

[1] Dr. Fleming, archbishop of Dublin, in a letter to the Propaganda, dated June 6th, 1650, sets down the number of the slain at 4,000. See *Spicil. Ossor.*, vol. i. p. 340. Belling says that number of Catholic soldiers and citizens was killed. *Vindiciæ, &c.*, p. 210. Bate gives the same number. *Aphor.· Disc.*, vol. ii. p. 275, appendix lxxiv. See also Castlehaven's *Memoirs*, p. 114. The official list brings the numbers of officers and soldiers killed up to nearly 3,000.

[2] The Millmount is close to the S. W. angle of the town-wall. It is an artificial mound, said to have been erected over the grave of the Tuatha de Danaan chief Colpa, who was drowned at the mouth of the Boyne, or over the wife of Goban the smith. See Wilde's *Boyne and Blackwater*, pp. 180 and 202. It has its present name from a windmill which was on its summit. It formerly belonged to a family named Delahoyde; they were said to have received a grant of it from Cromwell in return for having supplied him with corn during the seige. D'Alton's *Hist. of Drogheda*, vol. ii. p. 280. The hill is now occupied by a martello tower; it is connected by a causeway with a high bank rising abruptly from the Boyne, on which barracks for infantry and a hospital have been erected.

[3] p. 117, Clarendon says he was given to such an immoderate love of money, that he cared not by what unrighteous ways he exacted it. *Hist. of the Rebellion*, vol. ii. p. 527.

[4] "Verney, Finglas, Warren, and some other officers were alive in the hands of Cromwell's officers twenty-four hours after the business was done." Inchiquin to Ormonde, *ut supra*.

As every part of the town was commanded from the Millmount, further resistance was hopeless. The assailants in full force passed through the two breaches, crossed the bridge, and were soon in possession of the whole of the north side. There the work of slaughter was continued.

"Then our horse and foot followed them so fast over the bridge, which goes over a broad river; and being very long, and houses on both sides, yet they had not time to pull up their drawbridge, and our men fell violently upon them, and I believe there was 2,000 of them put to the sword."

The following is the official list of the principal officers slain at Drogheda:

Sir Arthur Aston, governor; Sir Edmund Verney,[1] lieutenant-colonel to the Lord of Ormonde.

Of the horse commanded by Major Butler: Lieutenant-Colonel Finglas, Captain Plunket, the Lord of Desme's (Dempsey's) son, and Colonel Fleming slain.[2]

Of Foot: Colonel Warren, Colonel Wall, Captain Butler, Major Tempest, Major Fitzgerald, Major Wilkins, Lieutenant-Colonel Gray, — Stevens, Captain-Lieutenant Street, Captains Cooley and Bagnall; Colonel Byrne, Lieutenant-Colonel Boyle,[3] Major Doudle, Captains Croker, Beuss, Fisher, Geffess, Birns. In all, 44 captains, all their lieutenants and ensigns, 220 reformadoes[4] and troopers, and 2,500 foot soldiers.[5]

Such was the fate of those who had surrendered because quarter had been promised them. There were others who put no faith in these promises, and, knowing the certain death that awaited them, resolved to sell their lives as dearly as possible.

"Divers of the officers and soldiers being fled over the bridge into the other part of the town, where about a hundred of them possessed St. Peter's church-steeple,[6] some of the West gate, others a strong round tower[7] next the gate called St. Sunday's. These being summoned to yield to mercy, refused, whereupon I ordered the steeple of the St. Peter's church to be fired, when one of them was heard to say in the midst of the flames, 'God damn me, God confound me, I burn, I burn.'"

---

[1] The son of the King's standard bearer who fell at Edgehill.

[2] Colonel Fleming was the nephew of Dr. Fleming, Archbishop of Dublin.

[3] Lieutenant-Colonel Richard Boyle was son of Richard Boyle, Protestant Archbishop of Tuam, a relative of the Earl of Cork; his brother Michael, who was later Archbishop of Armagh, was chaplain-general to the King's army in Munster, during the rebellion. See *Records of Cork, Cloyne, and Ross*, by the Rev. Maziere Brady, vol. iii. p. 91; Dublin, 1864.

[4] Reformado, according to Webster, an obsolete word, was an officer, who for some disgrace was deprived of his command, but retained his rank, and perhaps his pay.

[5] The above list of officers who were slain, is taken from the *Perfect Diurnal* of October 2d, 1649.

[6] In 1548, the steeple of this church, then said to be one of the highest in the world, was thrown down by a violent tempest. It was replaced by one of wood. *D'Alton's Hist. of Drogheda*, vol. i. p. 19. It had several chapels and oratories, erected by the piety of the inhabitants of the town. In 1740, the old church was removed, and the present one erected on the same site.

[7] This tower stood to the east of the Sunday gate, not on the town wall, but a little detached from it; perhaps it was one of the Irish round towers. *Dublin Penny Journal*, vol. i. p. 286.

His first intention was to blow it up, and for the purpose he had put a quantity of powder in the subterranean passage; but changing his plan, he set fire to the steeple. Those who rushed out to avoid the flames were slaughtered. Only one person escaped; he leaped from the tower, and received no other hurt·than a broken leg. He had quarter given him by the soldiers "for the extraordinariness of the thing." [1]

The street leading to St. Peter's church retained, even within the memory of the present generation the name of "Bloody Street;" it is the tradition of the place that the blood of those slain in the church formed a regular torrent in this street.

"The next day the two other towers [2] were summoned, in one of which was about six or seven score, but they refused to yield themselves, and we knowing that hunger must compel them, set only good guards to secure them from running away until their stomachs were come down. From one of the said towers, notwithstanding their condition, they killed and wounded some of our men. When they submitted, their officers were knocked on the head, and every tenth man of the soldiers killed, and the rest shipped for the Barbadoes. The soldiers in the other tower were all spared (as to their lives only), and shipped likewise for the Barbadoes."

Three or four officers of name and good families, who had found some way, by the humanity of some soldiers of the enemy, to conceal themselves for four or five days, being afterwards discovered, were butchered in cold blood. Captain Teige O'Connor, who was left among the dead, at night returned to his home, and afterwards recovered. Garrett, Dungan, and Lieutenant-Colonel Cavenagh also escaped. Cromwell saved Dr. Bernard, dean of Kilmore and Ussher's chaplain, and afterwards made him his almoner.

Except these and some few others who during the assault escaped at the other side of the town, and others who, mingling with the rebels as their own men, disguised themselves so as not to be discovered, there was not an officer, soldier, or religious person belonging to that garrison left alive, and all this within the space of nine days after the enemy appeared before the walls.

---

[1] Bate's *Elenchus*, &c., vol. ii. p. 25. Bate was Cromwell's physician. He got in with the Royalists at the Restoration, by his friends' report that by a dose given to Oliver he had hastened him to his end. He was made chief physician to Charles II. and a member of the Royal Society. *Athen. Oxon.*, vol. iii. col. 827; London, 1817.

[2] Bolton Tower and West Tower.

CHAPTER VIII.

ONE of the English soldiers who was present at the siege and took part in the assault, was Thomas, eldest brother of Anthony à Wood, the well-known historian of Oxford. He was a Captain in Colonel Ingoldsby's troop. The vivid description given by him of the manner in which the Puritans carried on the war furnishes an excellent commentary on the language of Cromwell. "He returned," says Anthony, "from Ireland to Oxford for a time to take up the arrears of his studentship at Christ Church. It was the winter after the siege. At which time, being often with his mother and brethren, he would tell them of the most terrible assaulting and storming of Drogheda, wherein he himself had been engaged. He told them that three thousand at least, besides some women and children, were, after the assailants had taken part, and afterwards all, the town, put to the sword, on the 11th and 12th of September, 1649. At which time Sir Arthur Aston, the governor, had his brains beat out and his body hacked to pieces. He told them that when the soldiers were to make their way up to the lofts and galleries in the church, and up to the tower where the enemy had fled, each of the assailants would take up a child, and use it as a buckler of defence when they ascended the steps, to keep themselves from being shot or brained. After they had killed all in the church, they went into the vaults underneath, where all the flower and choicest of the women and ladies had hid themselves. One of these, a most handsome virgin, arrayed in costly and gorgeous apparel, kneeled down to Thomas à Wood, with tears and prayers, to save her life ; and being struck with a profound pity, he took her under his arm, and went with her out of the church, intending to put her over the works to shift for herself. But a soldier, perceiving his intentions, ran his sword through her body. Whereupon à Wood, seeing her gasping, took away her money and jewels, and flung her down over the works." Mr. Froude has been unlucky that he did not fall in with this detailed account given by one "who was himself engaged in the storm." It proves his assertion to be wholly false, that there is no evidence from an eye-witness that women and children were killed otherwise than accident-ally.[1]

"It is remarkable," says Cromwell, "that these people, at the first, set up the Mass in some places of the town that had been monasteries, and afterwards grew so insolent, that the last Lord's day before the storm, the Protestants were thrust out of the great church called St. Peter's, and they had public Mass there,[2] and in this very place near 1,000 of them were put to the sword, fleeing thither for safety."

The sight of the ruin which surrounded him does not seem to have wrought any compunction in his soul :

"I am persuaded," he says, "that this is a righteous judgment of God upon these barbarous wretches, who have imbrued their hands in so much innocent blood, and that it will tend to prevent the effusion of blood for the future, which are the satisfactory grounds of such actions, which otherwise cannot but work remorse and regret. The officers and soldiers of this garrison were the flower of their army. And their great expectation was, that our attempting this place would put fair to ruin us, they being confident of the resolution of their men and the advantage of the place ; if we had divided our force into two quarters, to have besieged the north town and the south town, we could not have had such a correspondency between the two parts of our army, but that they might have chosen to have brought their army and have fought with what part they pleased, and at this same time have made a sally with 2,000 men upon us, and have left their walls manned, they having in the town the number hereinafter specified, some say near 4,000.

"And now give me leave to say how it comes to pass that this work was wrought. It was set up in some of our hearts that a great thing should be done, not by power or might, but by the spirit of God. And is it not so, clearly ? That which caused your men to storm so courageously, it was the spirit of God, who gave your men courage and took it away again ; and gave the enemy courage and took it away again ; and gave your men courage again, and therewith this happy success. And therefore it is good that God alone have all the glory !"

And writing to the President of the Council of State, he says :

"This hath been a marvellous great mercy. . . . I wish that all honest hearts may give the glory to God alone, to whom, indeed, the praise of this mercy be-longs."

What the fate of the ecclesiastics was who were found within the walls, it is not hard to conjecture.

"I believe all the friars were knocked on the head promiscuously but two ; the one was Father Peter Taaffe, brother to Lord Taaffe, whom the soldiers took the next day and made an end of.[3] The other was taken in the round tower, under

---

[1] "It is possible that in such a scene women and children may have been accident-ally killed ; but there is no evidence of it from an eye-witness. and only general rumors and reports at second hand." *The English in Ireland*, vol. i. p. 124.

[2] "One thing is very remarkable and ought not to be omitted, and that is, that though there were several Protestants in the town, yet were the Papist soldiers so insolent and so unjust to their Protestant companions, even in the midst of their adversity, that on Sunday, the 8th of September, they thrust the Protestants out of St. Peter's church, and publicly celebrated Mass there, though they had monasteries and other convenient places besides for that purpose." Cox's *Hib. Angl.*, Reign of Charles II., p. 8.

[3] This was Peter, a prior of the Order of St. Austin, sixth son of Sir John Taaffe, who was made Baron of Ballymote and Viscount Taaffe of Corren, by patent bearing date August 1st, 1628, for services rendered to the English against O'Donnell, and brother of Major-General Lucas Taaffe, governor of Ross, of whom more hereafter. Archdall's *Peerage*, vol. iv. p. 293. Bruodin says he was tempted by Cromwell to renounce his faith, but refused. *Prop. Fid. Cath.* p. 719.

the repute of a lieutenant ; and when he understood that the officers in that tower had no quarter, he confessed he was a friar, but that did not save him."

A manuscript history of these events, written at the time by one of the Jesuit Fathers employed on the Irish mission, and preserved in the archives of the Irish College at Rome, gives some further details of the cruelty exercised towards the priests that were seized.

"When the city was captured by the heretics, the blood of the Catholics was mercilessly shed in the streets, in the dwelling-houses, and in the open fields ; to none was mercy shown ; not to the women, nor to the aged, nor to the young. The property of the citizens became the prey of the parliamentary troops. Everything in our residence was plundered : the library, the sacred chalices, of which there were many of great value, as well as all the furniture, sacred and profane, were destroyed. On the following day, when the soldiers were searching through the ruins of the city, they discovered one of our Fathers, named John Bathe,[1] with his brother, a secular priest. Suspecting they were religious, they examined them, and finding that they were priests, and one of them, moreover, a Jesuit, they led them off in triumph, and, accompanied by a tumultuous crowd, conducted them to the market-place, and there, as if they were at length extinguishing the Catholic religion and our Society, they tied them both to stakes fixed in the ground, and pierced their bodies with shots till they expired. Father Robert Netterville,[2] far advanced in years, was confined to bed by his infirmities ; he was dragged thence by the soldiers, and trailed along the ground, being violently knocked against each obstacle that presented itself on the way ; then he was beaten with clubs ; and when many of his bones were broken, he was cast out on the highway. Some good Catholics came during the night, bore him away, and hid him somewhere. Four days after, having fought the good fight, he departed this life, to receive, as we hope, the martyr's crown."[3]

Two Fathers of the Dominican Order, Dominick Dillon, prior of the convent of Urlar, who had been appointed chaplain to the Confederate army by the Nuncio Rinuccini, and Richard Oveton, prior of the convent of Athy, were seized and taken outside the walls of the Puritan camp. There, in the presence of the whole army, they were

---

[1] Father Bathe entered the College of Seville in 1630, and returned to Ireland in 1638, where he was employed in missionary work up to his death. *Ecclesiastical Record*, vol. ix. p. 219; Dublin, 1873. He was probably a native of Drogheda. The family mansion of the Bathes occupied the angle formed by the junction of Laurence Street and Ship Street, the principal front being towards the latter. A print of it is given in the *Dublin Penny Journal*, vol. i. p. 189. It was pulled down in 1824. Athcarne castle also belonged to the family. D'Alton's *Hist. of Drogheda*, vol. i. p. 104.

[2] In Oliver's *Collectanea* S. J., Exeter, 1830, F. Netterville is said to have been put to death June 15th, and F. Bathe August 16th, both when Drogheda was taken by the heretics. The MSS. History of Seville College gives the date of F. Bathe's death as August 16th. *Eccls. Record, ut supra.* This difference of dates, taken with the fact that such cruelties could not well have taken place when the Royalists captured the town in June, goes to show that both were put to death by Cromwell's soldiers.

[3] MSS. in the Arundel Library, Stonyhurst. See, also, F. M. Tanner's *Societas Jesu usque ad sanguinem pro Christo militans;* Prague, 1675, and Broudin's *Propugnaculum,* &c., p. 697.

put to death through hatred of their religious calling and of the Catholic faith.

The massacre continued for five whole days in succession. "During all that time," says Clarendon, "the whole army executed all manner of cruelty, and put every man that belonged to the garrison, and all the citizens who were Irish, man, woman, and child, to the sword." Well might Ormonde say, that on "this occasion Cromwell exceeded himself and anything he had ever heard of in breach of faith and bloody inhumanity ; and that the cruelties exercised there for five days after the town was taken, would make as many several pictures of inhumanity as are to be found in *The Book of Martyrs* or in *The Relation of Amboyna.*"

Ludlow calls it an "extraordinary severity." Of the inhabitants only thirty survived, and these by a dubious mercy were shipped to the West Indies, and sold as slaves to the planters. Richard Talbot, who was later the famous Duke of Tyrconnell, was at Drogheda when the town was taken. The sights he witnessed, though he was but a child at the time, made a lasting impression on his mind, and inspired him with a horror of the Puritans all his life long. According to a tradition still current in Drogheda, the slaughter was stayed by a touching incident which aroused the lingering spark of humanity in Cromwell's breast. Walking through the streets, he noticed, stretched in the pathway, the dead body of a newly-made mother, from whose breast her miserable infant was striving to draw sustenance.

The number of those who fell in the assault was very small, if we believe Cromwell's statement —

"A great deal of the loss in this business fell upon Colonel Hewson's, Colonel Castle's, and Colonel Ewer's regiments ; Colonel Ewer having two field-officers of his regiment shot, Colonel Castle and a captain of his regiment slain ; Colonel Hewson's captain-lieutenant slain. I do not think we lost 100 men upon this place, though many were wounded.[1]

"I humbly pray the parliament may be pleased that the army may be maintained, and that a consideration may be had of them and of the carrying on affairs here, as may give a speedy issue to this work, to which there seems to be a marvellous fair opportunity offered by God. And although it may seem very chargeable to the state of England to maintain so great a force, yet surely to stretch a little for the present in following God's providence, in the hope the charge will not be long, I trust it will not be thought by any unfit for me to move for a constant supply, which, in human probability as to outward things, is most likely to hasten and perfect this work ; and indeed, if God please to finish it here as He hath done in England, the war is likely to pay itself.

"We keep the field much, our tents sheltering us from the wet and cold ; but yet the country sickness[2] overtakes many, and therefore we desire recruits and

[1] In another letter he gives the number killed as 20 or 30 ; of wounded as 40. *Cromwelliana*, p. 64.

[2] The country disease or country sickness, of which Cromwell so often complains, was a kind of dysentery, "reigning in no country so epidemically as in this kingdom, not sparing natives more than strangers." See Dineley's *Tour in Ireland*, in *Kilk. Arch. Journal* for 1856, p. 178. "Against this disease," says Peter Lombard, "they employ a remedy, which is common and easy to be had, as is well known, viz., a certain most excellent liquor, which they call usquebagh, so well mixed that it has the power of drying up, and does not inflame, like that which is made in foreign countries." *De Hibernia Insula Sanctorum*, p. 38 ; Dublin, 1868. "They use, to aid digestion, a certain fiery draught commonly called usquebagh." Stanihurst's *De Rebus Hibernia*, p. 38 ; Antwerp, 1584.

some fresh regiments of foot may be sent us. For it is easily conceived by what the garrisons already drink up, what our field army will come to if God shall give more garrisons into our hands. Craving pardon for this great trouble,

"I rest,

"Your most obedient servant,

"OLIVER CROMWELL."

Peters' letter, written from Dublin on the 15th September, and received by the House on the 26th, was more laconic —

"The truth is, Drogheda is taken, 3,552 of the enemy slain, and 64 of ours; Colonel Castle and Colonel Symonds of note. Aston, the governor, killed — none spared. We have also Trim and Dundalk, and are marching to Kilkenny. I came now from giving thanks in the great church. We have all our army well landed."

On the receipt of these letters, October 2d, the parliament ordered: 1°, that a letter of thanks should be sent to the Lord Lieutenant of Ireland and communicated to the officers there, taking notice that the House doth approve of the execution done at Drogheda, as an act both of justice to them and mercy to others who may be warned by it; and that the Council of State prepare a letter to be signed by the Speaker; 2°, that it having pleased God to bless the endeavors of the forces of the Commonwealth against the Irish rebels and their adherents at Drogheda, which was taken by storm, there being in it a strong garrison of Ormonde's army, and 3,000 of the enemy being slain, and only sixty-four privates and two officers of the English; all ministers in London, and within the lines of communication publish the same to-morrow, Sunday, the 30th instant, and stir up the people to give thanks. This order to be printed and sent to the Lord Mayor, who is to send a copy to all ministers within his jurisdiction. It was further ordered in parliament, October 11th, that 12,000 of the Acts for a day of public thanksgiving be forthwith printed and sent to the sheriffs of the several counties, to be dispersed to all the ministers of the parishes in England and Wales and the town of Berwick; and that the Council of State give order accordingly. In obedience to the order of the Council of State, the ministers of London acquainted the people with the great successes of the Parliamentary forces in Ireland and returned thanks to God for the same.

The first of November was observed as a general day of thanksgiving throughout the whole kingdom, for the foregoing victory at Drogheda, and others since obtained in Ireland. On the same day an order was issued, "that £100 be given to Captain Porter, who brought the news of the great success in Ireland, for his pains and travel therein, the Council of State to see to it."

The *Irish Monthly Mercury* for December, 1649, printed at Cork, thus unfeelingly triumphs over this defeat:

"Not long after the sally at Dublin, which the enemy out of modesty, call the battle of Rathmines, the Lord Lieutenant landed at Dublin, with an army so nourished in victory that they never saw any defeat but those they gave their enemies. The first design we undertook was the gaining of Tredagh, in which Ormonde had placed above 3,000 of his select men, and Sir Arthur Aston for commander, one as unable to stand to it as to run away; and it may be that's the reason he fell in the service; doubtless he was better for a retreat, since every step he would make a halt. In a word, if the rule be true, of judging Hercules by his foot, we may conclude this a wooden governor; yet he had made so good earthen fortifications, that, by trusting to his works, he showed what religion he was of. Their first entrenchment against us was the church, out of which they were soon dislodged; and I dare say it was the first time they ever went from church unwillingly, this being done, too, by some ordinances of Parliament, 'tis not unlikely the grave Presbyterians (if ever the drowsy assembly come into play again) may question their proceeding, and aver we have a mind our enemies should still continue Papists, by so frequently evincing there was no salvation for them in our Church. At length, the breach being found assaultable (more from the rent than the longness of it), our army were so little courtiers as to enter the town without so much as knocking at the gate, where all lost their lives but those that saved them. Of the first qualification there were about 3,000, of the latter 30, be it more or less."

How little such a result was expected by the Royalist party in England, is seen from the closing paragraph of the *Mercurius Pragmaticus* of September 17th, 1649, where having said that "Lord Noll had turned his nose[1] towards Tredagh, thinking to fire the town; but the sea had formerly so cooled it that it looked as if he had wrapped it in an indigo bag, to keep it from firing the gunroom"; the writer concludes:

"More certain news, that Cromwell hath now his ironsides banged to purpose, and is, as one letter speaks, beat back into Dublin with a very great loss, at least 4,000 slain and 600 taken, himself wounded, but not mortal. The Junto (i. e., the parliament) have caused proclamation to be made at all seaports for letters, that this news should not be divulged : but, as secret as they carry it, it is sufficiently known for truth. The King is said to be landed in Ireland, which adds new life and valor in the commanders and common soldiers, that by the next year you will go near to hear of Dublin being besieged, if not stormed, all their forces now drawing that way. There is good store of money in the castle, which will make the soldiers storm lustily."

Ormonde strove to excuse himself for not aiding Drogheda, though at the time he had over 3,000 men under his command. "Many of them had come off from the rebels to us in the time of our better fortune, as the Lord Moore's and Sir Thomas Armstrong's horse, and of these our numbers diminished daily by the revolt of some officers and many private soldiers, the rest showing much dejection of courage, and upon all occasions of want, which are very frequent with us, venting their discontent in such dangerous words, that it was held unsafe to bring them within that distance of the enemy as was necessary to have kept them united, and consequently one side of the town open to receive continual supplies.

Cromwell and his party did not err in their conjecture. The speedy capture of Drogheda and the merciless massacre of its inhabitants had the effect which they desired. It spread abroad the terror of his name; it cut off the best body of the Irish troops, and disheartened the rest to such a degree, that it was a greater loss in itself and more fatal in its consequence than the rout at Rathmines. Ormonde wrote to the King: "It is not to be imagined the terror that

---

[1] Cromwell's ruby nose was productive of much nonsense and buffoonery; "the blazing of his beacon nose," "the glowworm glistening in his beak," "Oliver is a bird of prey, as you may know by his bloody beak." Jesse's *Court of England under the Stuarts,* vol. iii. p. 30; London, 1840.

these successes and the power of the rebels have struck into the people. They are so stupefied, that it is with great difficulty I can persuade them to act anything like men towards their own." When Owen
Roe O'Neill heard the sad news, he swore a great oath, that, as
Cromwell had taken Drogheda by storm, if he should storm hell he
would take it. Immediately after, 180 of Inchiquin's men deserted
and passed over to Cromwell's army.

According to popular tradition, Cromwell held a council of war in
the drawing-room of the large house with an oriel window, formerly
belonging to the Drumgoole family, and now forming part of Kirk's
hotel.

Two days after the fall of Drogheda, Cromwell dispatched Colonel Chidley Coote with two regiments of horse, his own and Jones',
and Colonel Castle's regiment of foot, to take possession of Dundalk.
Ormonde had ordered this place and Trim to be abandoned and burnt
when Drogheda was taken ; but fear so possessed the garrison that
they did not carry out his orders. A messenger was sent forward
with the following summons to the Governor :

"For the Chief Officer commanding in Dundalk; These:

"12th September, 1649.

"Sir,
"I offered mercy to the garrison at Tredagh, in sending the Governor a sum-
mons before I attempted the taking of it, which being refused brought their evil
upon them.
"If you, being warned thereby, shall surrender your garrison to the use of the
Parliament of England, which by this I summon you to do, you may thereby pre-
vent effusion of blood. If, upon refusing this offer, that which you like not befalls
you, you will know whom to blame.
"I rest,
"Your servant,
O. CROMWELL."

The enemy abandoned the place, and possession was taken of it.
There is a tradition that Cromwell came to Dundalk, and received
there a wound which marked his face. He was watering his horse at
the ford where the bridge was built afterwards. Lord Plunkett, ancestor of Lord Louth, one of the Royalist officers, who was in the neighborhood enlisting men for the Confederates, was riding by, and his
horse, wishing to drink, stopped short at the same ford. Seeing the
reflection of Cromwell's star in the water, Plunkett determined if possible, to kill him ; and, not being near enough to reach him with his
sword, he flung the naked blade at Oliver's head and gashed his
prominent nose. A rush was instantly made by Cromwell's attendants, but the Royalist officer escaped by a subterranean vault leading
into Lord Roden's demesne. A large reward was offered for his
apprehension. He was traced by a faithless servant named Taaffe
and betrayed. He was seized and brought captive to Castle Cumberland. Cromwell's wound was undergoing surgical treatment at the
moment. Several of the Parliamentary officers suggested a variety
of cruel deaths, in order that the sufferer might select that which he
deemed most painful to the prisoner. But Cromwell would not adopt

any of their savage plans, and said he preferred to leave the selection to Lord Plunkett himself. When the captive was asked how he wished to die, he replied boldly : "With my good sword in my hand, and any two of your officers before me ready to execute your orders." This reply so gratified the General, that he spared the prisoner's life, on condition that there should always be an Oliver in the family. The name, however seems to have been common among the Plunketts before the event here mentioned took place.

> "A party of horse and dragoons was sent to a house within five miles of Trim, there being then in Trim some Scots companies which the Lord of Ardes [1] brought to assist the Lord of Ormonde. But upon the news of Tredagh, they ran away, leaving their great guns behind them, which we also possessed."

Major Ponsonby was left at Trim with a small garrison ; the rest returned to the army. The "house" was the castle of Trubly ; [2] here Cromwell passed a night. He battered down a part of the Yellow Steeple, and blew up a tower of the castle. Some years ago a number of lead and iron bullets were found in the ruins. Dean Butler doubts whether Cromwell visited Trim ; but there is a tradition that Scurlock of Scurlockstown and his brother of the Rock had a skirmish with him at a place since called Cromwell's Hill, near Grange ; and that Rathmore Castle, then held by the Plunketts, was blown down by balls from guns planted on the Hill of Ward. A stone over the door of Ballinlough castle recorded that the estates were given back to the owner by Cromwell in return for the good entertainment he received there. There is in the keeping of the family an old document which shows he visited the place. He passed a night in the old church of Taghmon, when besieging the castle ; the Nugents, the owners of it, escaped being massacred by flight during the night. [3]

Thus ended the hopes that Ormonde had placed on the long resistance which he supposed would be offered by Drogheda. He left his quarters at Trim and Tecroghan,[4] and at the head of 5,000 men retreated southwards, having given orders to the garrisons which he left behind to set fire to the places committed to their keeping in case the enemy should approach. But fear so possessed them that

---

[1] Hugh Montgomery, second viscount Ardes, was son of the sixth laird of Braidstones, one of the Scotch favorites of James I. His uncle, the first viscount, was dean of Norwich ; but seeing that a good fortune might be made in Ireland, he got himself appointed to the sees of Derry, Clogher, and Raphoe, which three dioceses comprising the chiefest part of Ulster, were now united for one man's benefit. He was one of the Commissioners appointed by the King to seize on the lands of the Irish for the Church and the Crown. If the lands were found to belong to the sept, they were declared forfeited to the Crown, in consequence of O'Neill's rebellion ; if they belonged to the Church, then the Bishop entered on the possession of them. In either case the natives were plundered. See Rev. C. P. Meehan's *Flight of the Earls*, p. 56.

[2] Trubly was the property of the Cusack family from the time of Richard II.

[3] The translator of *Cambrensis Eversus* says the garrison and citizens of Moate surrendered on terms to Cromwell himself. But nothing of the kind is said in the original. The passage clearly refers to the Millmount near Drogheda. See *Camb. Ever.*, vol. iii. p. 187.

[4] Tecroghan was surrendered to Col. Reynolds and Sir Theophilus Jones, June 16th, 1650, by its governor, Sir Robert Talbot. This castle belonged to Sir Luke Fitzgerald ; his wife was called by the soldiers Colonel Mary. She was greatly misled by the confidence she placed in Talbot. *Aph. Disc.* vol. ii p. 91.

they did not execute these orders, nor destroy the fortifications as they were directed; the enemy thought it worth while to take possession of them and garrison them. Cromwell deemed it wisest not to pursue him through a hostile country, the roads of which he was entirely ignorant of. His forces, too, were somewhat weakened by the detachments left in the different strongholds which he had seized, especially at Drogheda, which he took special care to secure against any sudden assault. He returned to Dublin, where, no doubt, he was welcomed with joy.

CHAPTER IX

Venables' Expedition — The Ulster Scots — Surrender of Carlingford and Newry — Defeat of Trevor — Surrender of Belfast and Coleraine — Further Successes — Cromwell's Letter.

THE capture of Dundalk opened up the road to the north and enabled Cromwell to continue his successes in that quarter. When leaving Dublin, he had despatched northwards by sea 1,000 foot, and a plentiful supply of wheat and "other things necessary for their accommodation;" 500 horse were sent by land. Two large battering guns were sent in a man of war; this was to attend upon the party during the expedition. Venables, who was in command, was ordered to effect a junction with Sir Charles Coote, then shut up in Derry. He was told also to sound the Scotch planters and, if possible, to gain them over to the side of the Commonwealth. The Ulster Scots were divided among themselves; some still held out for the King; a considerable number sided with the Parliament. ' These had sent messengers to Cromwell when he lay before Drogheda, asking for aid. Venables was soon in a position "to send information which promised well towards the northern interest." He found these disciples of Knox were but too ready to make common cause with the Puritan party against the Catholic Confederates.

On the 18th of September, the land force came before Carlingford. The same day the ship entered the harbor and passed the fort at its mouth without being harmed in any way, though several shots were fired at her as she sailed past. That night Venables encamped in the open country to the south of the town. The next day preparations were made to land the cannon and erect the battery; but before either was done, the garrison beat a parley and surrendered upon articles. He found in the three castles and in the fort commanding the town forty barrels of powder, seven pieces of cannon, about a thousand muskets, and nearly five hundred pikes.

The following day, with Jones' regiment he marched by the river side under the mountain to Newry,[1] and crossed the river at a ford, a mile below the town; the rest of the party was left with Coote on the other side of the mountain. On Venables' approach, the governor came out to treat with him. He allowed the horse to march through the town, cross the bridge, and take up quarters on the Down side of

---

[1] Newry, anciently called Iubhar cinn Tragha, the yew-tree at the head of the strand, said to have been planted by St. Patrick. See *Annals of the Four Masters*, ad ann. 1162; Dublin, 1856. In after ages the name was shortened to Iubhar, which, by prefixing the Irish article, gave rise to the present form of the name. See Joyce' *Irish Names of Places*, pp. 22 and 52, first series; Dublin, 1869.

the river ; he then surrendered the castle upon articles. Venables with his regiment rested there for three days ; he was then joined by the rest of the troops.

Meantime word was brought him from Lisnagarvay (Lisburn) by some deserters, that the town would surrender if he showed himself before it. Leaving an ensign and some few men in the castle of Newry, he continued his march Northwards, and lay the first night at Dromore. He encamped by the road side in a field to the south-west of the town, well enclosed with hedges. He was not aware that any of the enemy was in the neighborhood ; besides, both officers and men had grown careless, owing to their constant success, and did not think there was any danger to be feared from an enemy whom they despised. About three hours after they had encamped, news was brought from Dundalk that Colonel Mark Trevor, who had been sent by Ormonde to intercept them, was advancing with a considerable party of horse, intending to attack them unawares before morning. Orders were immediately issued for the horse to draw off into the enclosed field where the fort lay. But, owing to the carelessness of the officer who gave the order, or of the messenger who delivered it, little notice was taken of it ; it did not reach half the horse ; the dragoons were totally ignorant of it. The omission was near proving the utter ruin of the entire party. Trevor had followed them all day. His scouts gave him certain intelligence of their movements. When darkness set in, he sent some of his men to reconnoitre the camp and to find out when an attack would be made. Before daybreak he fell on them. The guards were surprised and ran off towards the camp, closely pursued by the assailants. The sudden onset threw the main body into confusion : they, too, fled in dismay. Fortunately for the fugitives, the greater part of the encampment was surrounded by a high hedge, behind which was a bog. Hence they could not readily find a way of escape ; had they dispersed, they would have been knocked on the head by the peasantry or cut to pieces by the enemy. Owing to the darkness of the morning, Trevor was not aware of the advantage he had gained. With 500 horse he took up his position on the neighboring hill. From the small resistance he had heard made, he concluded that the enemy was totally defeated and could not rally ; when daylight appeared, his cavalry would be ready to capture any that survived the attack. As soon as day broke, Venables saw his danger ; about fifty of his horse rallied and drew up on a mound within the field. Those who had concealed themselves in holes and ditches took up their arms again and joined on to the horse ; so that before Trevor's men could see what the enemy was doing, there had got together four or five bodies of horse and a party of 400 foot, all ashamed of the confusion into which they had fallen and eager to redeem their fault by a display of bravery. After a sharp skirmish Trevor was forced to retire towards the Bann ; two officers, who had been taken prisoners, and two standards were retaken. The same day Venables advanced to Lisburn ; there he was joined by Major Bruffe with a troop of the county horse. They marched to Belfast, which surrendered within four days upon articles. Eight hundred

Scots were afterwards turned out of the town, whither they had brought their wives and children to plant themselves. About the same time Colerain surrendered to Sir Charles Coote ; he imitated the example of Cromwell at Drogheda in putting the garrison to the sword. He entered the counties of Down and Antrim, and forced Sir George Munroe to retire. By the end of September, every port and every important place in the North — Carrickfergus alone excepted — was in the hands of the Parliament. There being no longer any occasion for such a large body of horse in those parts, Jones' regiment was sent back to reinforce the army in Dublin. When announcing these successes to the parliament, Cromwell ends his letter thus :

"I have sent these things to be presented to the Council of State for their consideration. I pray God, as these mercies flow in upon you, He will give you a heart to improve them to His glory alone ; because He alone is the Author of them and of all goodness, patience, and long suffering extended towards you.

"P. S. — I desire the supplies moved for may be hastened. I am very persuaded though the burden be great, yet it is for your service. If the garrisons we take swallow up your men, how shall we be able to keep the field ? Who knows but the Lord may pity England's sufferings, and make a short work of this ? It is in His hand to do it, and therein only your servants rejoice. I humbly present the condition of Capt. George Jenkins' widow. He died presently after Tredagh storm. His widow is in great want."

CHAPTER X

THE KING AND ORMONDE.

Ormonde tries to collect Supplies — The King's Journey to Ireland — His Character — Intrigues of the Scotch Envoys — He decides to go to Scotland — Taaffe joins Ormonde — Refusal of the Cities to contribute.

IMMEDIATELY after the capture of Drogeda Ormonde left Portlester with the remnant of his army and marched towards Kilkenny; here he expected to be joined by Inchiquin, who had still a considerable force of horse and foot in Munster, and by Lord Montgomery of Ardes at the head of the Ulster troops. But he had neither money nor provisions to keep an army together even for a single day. The Commissioners of Trust were dispersed; the collectors employed by them were not so diligent as they should have been in getting in either corn or money. Ormonde issued warrants for raising both; this the Commissioners declared a breach of the articles of the treaty; some even spoke of making terms with the enemy.

Once more, in his perplexity, Ormonde turned to the King. About the middle of June Charles had left the Hague and gone to St. Germain's to visit the Queen, his mother, intending after a stay of eight days, to proceed on his journey to Ireland, "as a place where he might conveniently unite the forces and interests of both kingdoms against the common enemy." At this time the royal interest was predominant in Ireland. The fleet under Prince Rupert road triumphant along the coast; the Parliamentary commanders, Jones in Dublin, Monk in Belfast, and Cook in Londonderry, were almost confined within the limits of their garrisons. Inchiquin in Munster, the Scotch regiments in Ulster, the great body of the Catholics throughout the whole country had proclaimed the King, and acknowledged the authority of his lieutenant. Just then Charles was asked by Ormonde to come to Ireland; he consented. But his own pleasures or the intrigues of his counsellors detained him for three whole months at St. Germain's. Meantime news reached him of the defeat at Rathmines. His first impulse on hearing of it was to set out for Ireland and bear a share in the struggle. To those who reminded him of the dangers he would encounter he replied, "Then must I go there to die, for it is disgraceful to live anywhere else." But Charles was even then essentially a man of pleasure; his good purposes through life were writ in water. One of his courtiers described his character to Ormonde: Foreign princes begin to look on him as a person so lazy and careless in his own business that they think it not safe, by contributing anything to his assistance, to irritate so potent enemies as they fear his rebellious subjects are likely to prove. Charles soon felt that his presence was by no means desirable at St. Germain's.

Mazarin gave him plainly to understand that a longer residence there would embarrass the court of France, which had no desire to quarrel with the Commonwealth of England. Queen Henrietta Maria urged him to take the Cardinal's hint. It was remarked that after he had learned that Cromwell had assumed the government of Ireland, he hesitated still more, lest he might meet such a formidable adversary. He sent Colonel Warren and Mr. Henry Seymour, gentlemen of his bedchamber, to obtain from Ormonde a true account of the state of affairs in Ireland and his opinion concerning the expediency of the journey. On the 27th of September Ormonde replied to the King as follows : —

" Your Majesty's commands in your letters and in the message by Colonel Warren, were to give you an account of the present state of affairs here and my opinion touching your Majesty's coming into this kingdom. The first, Sir, is briefly this : The rebels are strong in their numbers, exalted with success, abundantly provided with all necessaries, likely to want for nothing that England can afford them ; and, in the pride of all this, are either marched out or ready to march out, to pursue their victories. On the other side, to withstand them our numbers are inferior, discouraged with misfortunes, hardly and uncertainly provided for, the people weary of their burdens, wavering in their affections, through the advantages taken to pervert them by those disloyally inclined, and our towns defenceless against any considerable attempt. After such a stating of our condition, your Majesty may wonder that I, who, in my opinion concerning the hazarding of your person into this kingdom, was doubtful, or rather plainly against it, only upon fallible resolutions taken of Cromwell's coming over, before the defeat near Dublin, which made easy the better half of his work in this kingdom, and before the loss of Drogheda with above two thousand of our best foot and above two hundred horse, should now change my opinion, and hold it absolutely necessary for your Majesty to appear here in person.
" This seeming preposterous change proceeds not from a less care of your Majesty's safety, but from a greater desire of your glory, consisting in your being restored to your kingdoms by the blessing of God upon your immediate conduct of your affairs and armies ; for which by a special providence they seem to be reserved, and without which it is evident, not only to me, but to all that for faith or judgment I hold capable of such a debate, that this kingdom will very shortly eject all signs of obedience to your Majesty, and revert to the condition it was in when your Majesty commanded me hither, or rather to a much worse. For all such as have contributed towards the restitution of your Majesty's government at the conclusion of the last peace and would persevere to the end in their loyalty, will now infallibly, in the first place, be singled and marked out for destruction. So that if your Majesty conceive the preservation of any footing in this kingdom may be at any time necessary towards the recovery of the other two, it can, reasonably speaking, be no other way hoped for than by your presence ; and by that it may. When there was a possibility of reducing this kingdom without this or any personal hazard to your Majesty, and that by the reduction of it, your Majesty might have no more to do but to command the transportation of an army hence for any design more worthy the venture of your person than this then seemed to be, and that I saw it was needful to put something upon unequal trial rather than abide the threatened invasion, I held it my duty to dissuade your Majesty to come in at the end of our success, when it was to be feared the formidable forces then designed and since come against us would give a check unto it. But now that the rebels are so exalted in their pride, even as high success and the lowest contempt of an enemy can raise them, and that any check given by your Majesty to them will hazard the ruin of their usurpation and the restoring of your Majesty, it will be ruin to them if the progress of their arms be now stopped, and to your Majesty's infinite honor to have attempted it with such disadvantage, whatever the event be. Yet I should not dare to advise the purchase of it at so desperate a rate, nor your coming into this kingdom, if I did not believe your Majesty may have as safe a residence here and retreat hence as I conceive that in or from Jersey to be."

Meantime, about the middle of September, Charles had set out for St. Germain's, by way of Normandy, for the island of Jersey, the only part of his dominions of which he retained possession, in order to be so much nearer to Ireland, in case he should be advised to go there. Prince Rupert was at Kinsale with sixteen frigates of the royal fleet, well equipped and ready to put to sea, awaiting orders to set sail and escort the King to Ireland.

Ormonde's letter reached the King at Jersey. Owing to the intrigues of the Scotch envoys and to the artful insinuations of some of his counsellors, who secretly feared that if he was once at the head of a Catholic army, he would listen to the demands of the Catholic party for the re-establishment of their religion, and to a disinclination on his own part to show himself to the Protestants of England and Scotland surrounded by a Catholic people as his chief supporters, he had already changed his mind and was now determined to go to Scotland. All thoughts of the expedition to Ireland were at an end. Ormonde had nothing left him but to strive to unite for a common effort the various parties that still professed allegiance to the Crown. He went to Graigue, in the county of Kilkenny, and encamped there : here he was joined by Major-General Luke Taaffe, at the head of 1,000 foot and 300 horse, which the Marquis of Clanricarde had sent to his assistance from Connaught. But he was utterly deficient in supplies. The only course open to him was to place these troops in garrisons, where they would be most likely to hinder the advance of the enemy. Even for this the consent and authority of the Commissioners of Trust were needed. Not only did they refuse the necessary permission, but the very cities and towns which were most likely to be attacked were those which were most determined in refusing to admit any of his soldiers. Wexford, Waterford, and Limerick would make no terms with him ; they declared they would not obey his orders further than they thought fit.

CHAPTER XI.

OWEN ROE O'NEILL.

Ormonde's Overtures to O'Neill — Terms of the Treaty — His Illness and Death — His Character — Letter to Ormonde — Early Life of O'Neill — The School of Mars — The Sword of Red Hugh — Benburb — His Forces join Ormonde.

Soon after Ormonde's defeat at Rathmines, he sent Daniel O'Neill to his uncle Owen Roe, to make him offers of friendship and to propose to him the same terms for the union of the parties which he had offered before in vain ; for O'Neill would accept of none but such as the nuncio Rinuccini had approved of. Ormonde was anxious to gain him over to the King's side, for, as Carte, no friend of O'Neill, admits, "the Marquis had a very high and advantageous opinion as well of his honor, constancy, and good sense, as of his military skill, from which he proposes as much advantage to the King's affairs as he did from the force of his troops." The King, too, urged Ormonde, " by all fair invitations to draw General O'Neill and his party to submit to their lawful sovereign." By this time O'Neill had found that little reliance was to be put in the promises of the Puritans. Just before the battle of Rathmines he had signified that he was anxious to renew negotiations. Owing to the exertions of Heber MacMahon, bishop of Clogher, a treaty was brought out between them, and assented to by the officers of the northern army. O'Neill should have the command of 3,000 foot and 800 horse, subject to the orders of the Lord Lieutenant. He and his party should enjoy the benefit of the Articles of the Peace in their demands touching the Plantation in Ulster, and all the other advantages derivable under these Articles ; an act of oblivion was to be passed, to take effect from the 22d of October, 1641. He agreed to join Ormonde at Carrickmacross in the middle of December. So eager was he to show his good will and his entire forgetfulness of past injuries, that, even before the treaty was signed, he sent 3,000 men under Lieutenant-General Ferrall to Ormonde's assistance. He strove to follow, himself, in all haste ; but at this critical moment he was struck down by a fatal illness. None of his biographers have given any detailed account of the symptoms of his disease. According to Carte, "it was a defluxion in the knee, which was so extremely painful, that he could neither ride nor endure to be carried on a litter. By some it was imputed to poison from a pair of russet boots sent him by a gentleman named Plunkett, in the county of Louth, who afterwards boasted he had done the English good service in dispatching O'Neill out of the world." Colonel Henry

Tully O'Neill, too, gives this as the cause of the illness.[1] Others say he was poisoned by Coote, when entertaining him with a great parade of hospitality and extraordinary plenty. Coote is said to have given him at table some subtle poison, which paralyzed his energies so that he could no longer mount his horse; it was of a lingering operation, weakening its victim gradually, giving him little pain, but causing his hair and nails to fall off by degrees. During the first month of his illness, O'Shiel,[2] his physician, was absent; the physician in attendance on him, mistaking his malady, treated him for gout. For some time he battled against the disease, hoping he might so far recover as to be able to place himself at the head of his army, a thing he was infinitely fond of doing. From Derry, where he was first attacked about the middle of August, he advanced slowly and painfully through Tyrone and Monaghan into Cavan. From Ballyhaise he was carried to Cloughouter,[3] the residence of his brother-in-law, Philip Maelmora[4] O'Reilly. The author of the *Aphorismal Discovery*, his secretary, describes his last moments thus: "He died in our Lord, the 6th of November, 1649, a true child of the Catholic religion,[5] in sense and memory; many of both secular and regular clergy assisting him in such a doubtful transit, behaving himself most penitently. Being most devout unto all regular orders in his life, and specially to the

---

[1] *Desid. Cur. Hib.*, vol. ii. p. 520. Rev. C. P. Meehan, in his *Franciscan Monasteries*, p. 346, says, "it is sad such a crime should have been attributed to a Plunkett of Louth, who, we presume was a Catholic." But he seems to forget that the old English of the Pale showed themselves at all times to be the most inveterate enemies of O'Neill and his party. Lord Dunsany, a Plunkett, used to display his loyalty by cruelty to the Irish people. *Crom. Sett.* p. 256. "The Anglo-Irish of four hundred years standing, especially those of the Pale, were extremely averse to the rebellion, and offered their service to the State against the rebels, remembering their own origin and choosing to adhere to the English Government, which they were apprehensive would be thrown off by the natives. They were afraid also of losing a considerable part of their estates, which were Church property, if the old Irish got the power of the nation into their hands." *Nunciatura*, p. 391. The San Pietro, on board of which Rinuccini came to Ireland, was pursued by a renegade called Plunkett and obliged to put into Kenmare bay, though the Legate wished to land at Waterford. *Ibid.*, p. 64. In Lord Dunraven's *Memorials of Adare*, p. 48, Oxford, 1864, there is an account of the murder of F. Cornelius O'Connor and his companion, F. Eugene Daly, Irishmen, of the Order of the Holy Trinity for the Redemption of Captives, who, a short time before, were seized by the heretical pirate John Plunkett, and thrown into the sea.

[2] He had studied in the chief seats of learning abroad, and on account of his skill was styled "the Eagle of Medicine" by his contemporaries. The nobles and gentry of Limerick paid him an annual pension, that they might have his services at call. He accompanied Preston in his campaigns, but afterwards united his fortunes to those of O'Neill. He was slain in the battle in which Henry O'Neill was taken prisoner. See an account of the O'Shiels in Rev. C. P. Meehan's *Franciscan Monasteries*, p. 377; and of Owen O'Shiel in *Aphor. Disc.* vol. ii. p. 89.

[3] Cloghouter, Cloch Iocha Uachtair, the stone fortress of the upper lake; it is built on a rock in the middle of a lake, about six miles to the west of the town of Cavan. The ruins are still in existence, showing that the architectural details closely resemble those of Reginald's Tower in Waterford. See *Annals of the Four Masters*, vol. ii. p. 646; Dublin, 1856. In the island there was an abbey of Premonstratensians dedicated to the Blessed Trinity, from which it has its present name of Trinity Island. See O'Curry's *MSS. Materials of Irish History*, p. 108; Dublin, 1861. It was founded in 1251 by Clarus O'Mulchonry, dean of Elphin.

[4] This is a family name of the O'Reillys. O'Donovan translates it "Illustrious Chief.' *Irish Penny Journal*, p. 415.

[5] "Owen Roe, the most cordial Roman Catholic in the world." *Perfect Diurnal*, Feb. 28th, 1649.

order of St. Dominick, he wore his habit,[1] as a sure buckler against the rigor of future judgment, but was interred in the monastery of St. Francis of Cavan, to oblige both patriarchs."[2]

It may be that O'Neill's death at such a critical moment has been the principal reason for the suspicion of poison ; the coincidence, at least, is strange. This much is certain, that it was the greatest calamity that could then befall the Irish nation. Many of his clansmen did not believe that he could die at a time when he was so much needed, "some deeming that God, in his divine clemency, would not deal so strait with this poor nation as to bereave them of this their only champion ; but rather, the world being unworthy of so good a masterpiece, lulled him to sleep and snatched him away to some secret corner of the world, as another Elias, to keep him there for future better purposes." He had in truth all the qualities that constitute a leader of men : a clear, sound judgment, chivalrous valor, bravery in the field, skill in profiting of every advantage offered by the enemy, caution which left nothing to chance, and earned for him from our historians the title of the Irish Fabius. For seven years he kept together an army, created by his own genius, without a government at his back, without regular supplies ; enforcing discipline and obedience, gaining victories, and maintaining a native power even in the very heart of the kingdom. Always intent on the welfare of his country, he rose high above the petty jealousies and intrigues that surrounded him. In nothing did he show more magnanimity than in the noble self-denial that made him sink his own greatness and follow the leadership of those whom he knew to be his inferiors. Early in 1648 he wrote to Lord Muskerry : "I do protest, swear, and vow before Almighty God, that I never harboured the least thought of ambition in anything yet, but that which I assuredly thought and imagined to redound to the freedom, preservation, and liberty of my King, country, religion, and nation ; and that, during the remainder of my days, no private interest of my own, neither love, hatred, inducement, nor suggestion of any will persuade me to the contrary." When the news of Ormonde's defeat at Rathmines reached him, instead of rejoicing at the downfall of one who had ever been his bitterest foe, he called together his officers and asked them what they thought best to be done as affairs then stood. They all submitted to his better judgment. "Gentlemen," he replied, "to show to the world that I value the service of my King and the welfare of my country, as I always did, I now forget and forgive the Supreme Council and my enemies their ill practices and all the wrongs they did me from time to time ; and I will now embrace that peace which I formerly denied out of good intention."

---

[1] " Whereas in this province (Ireland) the pious practice has grown up, that the faithful of both sexes should wear the religious habit of the different orders, each one according to his devotion, and desire to die wearing it, we grant to all those who shall wear our habit or scapular, that they shall be sharers in all the blessings (beneficia) and in the good works done throughout the whole order." See Acts of the General Chapter of the Dominican Order held in Rome in 1644, in *Hib. Dom.*, p. 116.

[2] *Aphor. Disc.*, vol. ii. p. 62. Colonel H. T. O'Neill says he was buried in the old Francisan monastery of Cavan. *Desid. Cur. Hib.* vol. ii. p. 521. There is a tradition in Cavan that his burial-place was concealed lest it should be violated by the English.

Only a few days before his death he wrote the following touching letter to Ormonde : —

" May it please your Excellency, —

"Being now on my death-bed, without any great hope of my recovery, I call my Saviour to witness that (as I hope for salvation) my resolution, ways, and intentions, from first to last in these unhappy wars, tended to no particular ambition or private interest of mine own (notwithstanding what was or may be thought of to the contrary), but truly and sincerely to the preservation of my religion, the advancement of his Majesty's service, and the just liberties of this nation ; whereof, and of my particular reality and willingness to serve your Excellency above any other in this kingdom, I hope that God will permit me to, give ample and sufficient testimony in the view of the world ere it be long. However, if in the interim God pleaseth to call me away, I do most seriously recommend to your Excellency's care my son and heir, Colonel Henry O'Neill, praying and desiring that your Excellency may be favorably pleased not only to prescribe a present course that he may participate of the late peace, but also of the benefit of such conditions, concessions, and creation as his Majesty intended for me and was assured for me by your Excellency in his Majesty's name, by an instrument bearing date Kilkenny, the 29th of September last. And that, in case of my death, your Excellency will not only assure him thereof under hand and seal, but likewise by aiding and assisting him in the timely procurement thereof. And in so doing your Excellency will highly oblige me, my said son, and the posterity of

" Your Excellency's most humble servant,

OWEN O'NEILL." [1]

Little is known of the earlier part of O'Neill's life. He seems to have left Ireland in his infancy. An entry in the records of the College of Salamanca shows he studied there ; it states also that Eugenius Rufus O'Neill had been appointed to a sergeancy of halberdiers, the foot-guards of the Spanish monarchs. He was transferred to the Netherlands, probably about 1625. In the State Paper Office is a "List of Irishmen abroad," sent in by some one of the numberless spies whom the English kept constantly employed in foreign countries, "that might be dangerous to the peace of Ireland in the event of a war with Spain ; they have been long providing of arms for any attempt against Ireland, and have in readiness five or six thousand arms laid up in Antwerp for that purpose, bought out of the deduction of their monthly pay ; and it is thought they have now doubled that proportion by this means." From internal evidence it is probable that this list was made out about 1640. [2] Among the names we find that of Owen O'Neill, sergeant-major of the Irish regiment. He learned the science of war in "that great school of Mars," the Low Countries, and won the highest distinctions in the Spanish service. [3] He left rank and station abroad at the call of his countrymen,

---

[1] *Carte MSS.*, vol. xxvi. p. 49. The promise alluded to above was that he should have the title of Earl of Tyrone. See *Account of the Carte MSS.*, p. 121.

[2] This very curious document is given in the *Nation* of February 5th, 1859.

[3] An account of his gallant defence of Arras against the French, in 16,0, is given in the appendix to O'Connor's *History of the Irish Brigades*, p. 437. The articles for the surrender of Arras, between the generals of Louis XIII. and Owen O'Neill, commander of the town for King Philip of Spain, are given in *Aphor. Disc.*, vol. i. p. 352, appendix xvii. He landed at Castle Doe, on the coast of Donegal, July 13th, 1642, "having come by sea from Dunkirk and taken on his way two prizes ; he came with many commanders, old beaten soldiers of his own regiment in Flanders ; and for his security during his abode there did man Castle Doe." *Aphor. Disc.* vol. i. p. 43.

to aid them in the struggle for their rights. On his coming to Ireland he was welcomed with joy, and called on by the unanimous voice
of the people to be their leader : —

> Owen Roe — our own O'Neill!
> He treads once more our land ;
> The sword in his hand is Spanish steel,
> But the hand is an Irish hand.

When General Leslie expressed to him regret that a person of
his experience and reputation abroad should come to Ireland to second
so bad a cause, and besought him earnestly to return whence he had
come, he replied with scorn, that he had more reason to come to
relieve the deplorable state of his country than he had to march at
the head of an army to England against his King, to force him to
give unreasonable conditions to himself and his countrymen at a time
when all Scotland was their own. Father Luke Wadding sent to him
from Rome the sword[1] of his ancestor, the great Red Hugh, that
spread terror among the foe at the Yellow Ford, and well and bravely
did he wield it for faith and fatherland. In the forty battles which
he fought against the English, only once did he suffer defeat. No
treachery or inhumanity ever sullied his victories. At the battle of
Benburb, gained with far inferior numbers by his skill and gallantry,
3,000 Scots were left dead on the field, and many more were slain in
the pursuit. "The Lord hath rubbed shame on our faces, till we are
humbled," wrote their general, Monroe. On the side of the Irish
only seventy fell.[2] The colors taken from the enemy, thirty-two in
number, were sent by F. Hartegan, S. J., to Rinuccini, then in Limerick. They were borne in solemn procession to St. Mary's Cathedral,
where a *Te Deum* was sung in the Nuncio's presence in thanksgiving
for the success that the God of Hosts had granted to the Catholic
army. Had the confederate leaders united with him then, and allowed
him to follow up this victory ; or even now, had he been spared to
meet Cromwell under the walls of Drogheda, or to carry out the plan
of defence which he urged Ormonde to adopt, viz., to avoid an open
engagement unless at a great advantage, and to defend the mountain
passes of Wicklow and retard the enemy's advance until the winter
should set in ;[3] like his Roman model,

---

[1] "This heirloom," says Rinuccini, "was accompanied with the papal blessing for
Don Eugenio, and so irritated Preston and his Anglo-Irish adherents, that they gave out
that his Holiness' next gift to Eugenio will be a crown." *Nunziatura*, p. 309. It was brought
over by Massari, dean of Fermo, who came to Ireland in 1647.

[2] June 5th, 1646. See an account of this battle in *Aphor. Disc.* vol. i. p. 113;
Transactions of the Ossory Archæol. Soc., vol. i. p. 307 ; Kilkenny, 1879, and Rinuccini's *Em-
bassy*, p. 173. Even his enemies said he was the best soldier and the wisest man among the
Irish rebels. Clarendon's *Rebellion*, vol. ii. p. 614.

[3] "He would not have Cromwell fought with but upon great advantages, for he believes our men are much out of heart, and that the passes and season must beat Cromwell
more than any forces we can bring against him." Letter of Daniel O'Neill to Inchiquin,
25th Sept., 1649, in *Aphor. Disc.*, vol. iii. p. 277, appendix lxxvi.

> Whose wise delay
> Restored the fortunes of the day,

he might have saved his country.[1] But it was not to be.

> He lived for Erin's weal, but died for Erin's woe.

Finding himself unable to advance, he ordered his favorite officer, Lieutenant-general Ferrall, to take 3,000 of his men and march with all possible haste to the help of Ormonde. The country through which they had to pass was full of marshes and lakes; and supplies were so difficult to be had, that the men were obliged to scatter far and wide. Their advance was, in consequence, so much retarded, that it was only on the 25th of October they reached Kilkenny.[2] Most of those that remained in the north continued to serve under Heber MacMahon and the officers who were in the confidence of their former leader; but many of them dispersed soon after his death, and never after reassembled.[3]

---

[1] All writers, even the sceptical Dr. O'Conor, of Stowe, admit that had Owen Roe lived, he would have saved Ireland. Appendix to Davis' *Poems*, p. 221; Dublin, 1859. Here is a specimen of the way in which history is sometimes written: "Owen Roe O'Neill is the only one of the Irish leaders of parties in Ireland then who, by his successful audacity and his continual defections, has obtained any name in history. Guizot's *Hist. of Oliver Cromwell*, p. 46. Et c'est ainsi qu'on écrit l'histoire!

[2] "A very considerable body of good foot and very cheerful in the service." Ormonde to the King, in *Aphor. Disc.*, vol. ii. p. 446, appendix 42.

[3] Owing to the system of irregular warfare among the Irish and the want of supplies, it was difficult to keep an army together for any time. After the battle of Benburb, Owen Roe's army dispersed over Monaghan, Cavan, Leitrim, and Longford, until the crops should be ripe. Journal of Sir Phelim O'Neill, in Haverty's *Hist. of Ireland*, p. 562.

CHAPTER XII.

THE MARCH TO WEXFORD.

Cromwell's Plan — Capture of Killincarrick — Cromwell's Plot — Capture of Limbrick, Ferns, and Enniscorthy — Wallop — Encampment before Wexford — Spirit of the Citizens — The Garrison Reinforced — The Governor — Summons to Surrender — The Reply — The Batteries Planted — Propositions of the Governor — Cromwell's Answer.

Less than a fortnight after his return from Drogheda Cromwell set out on his expedition to the south. Winter was fast approaching ; no time could be lost if the southern part of the island was to be subdued. Besides, it was of the utmost importance to follow up the blow that had been so successfully struck at Drogheda, and to prevent by a rapid advance the union of the scattered forces of the Irish, which a sense of their common danger and the presence of so fierce an enemy could not fail to bring about, as soon as they had recovered from the panic wrought by the late atrocities.

Before he set out, "he caused many taxes to be taken off that were laid upon the well-affected English Protestants about Dublin ; whereupon he gained exceedingly upon the good affection of the people ; and divers of the gentlemen of Ireland voluntarily tendered their services to him, and at their own charge rode along with his life-guard.[1] Major Byrne reckoned that "he had four great pieces, the one of 66 bullet, the second of 44 bullets, the other of 36 bullets apiece, and two small pieces of 12 bullet apiece ; 4,000 effective foot, whereof some are intended to be left at Wexford ; 1,200 horses and 400 dragoons." He chose Colonel Michael Jones to act as his lieutenant, and left in his place, as governor of Dublin, Colonel Hewson. He took the route along the coast, in order to secure direct communication at all times with England by the capture and garrisoning of the seaports.[2] The fleet attended him and kept within sight of land, to support him and allow him to embark in case he found it expedient to do so. The proclamation he had issued, forbidding the soldiers to take anything from the inhabitants without payment under the pain of death, made the country people bring to his camp an abundant supply of provisions. He took care to have the report spread abroad that he had come to check the arbitrary power of the nobility, and to restore to the people the free exercise of their religion.[3] Ormonde ordered Colonel Hugh

---

[1] *Perf. Occur.*, Oct. 5th to 12th, in *Cromwelliana*, p. 65.

[2] "No hope of our being quiet at sea unless the English army by land deprive the Irish of all their harbors by taking the towns thereupon, as Wexford, Waterford, Kinsale, Cork, Limerick, Galway." Letter from Ireland in *Perf. Diurnal*, April 3d to 9th, 1649.

[3] "Wexford being his next design, he wrote to the inhabitants, and courted them to submit to his authority and to quit the royal interest, and that they should enjoy all their possessions and fortunes, and be as well used as any others under his power." Gale's *History of Corporations in Ireland*, appendix cxxv. ; London, 1834.

Byrne to march with the regiment of foot under his command to Powerscourt, in the county of Wicklow, in order to destroy all the strongholds thereabouts of which the enemy might possess himself; and to distress him by preventing any one bringing supplies, either to the army in the field or to the garrison in Dublin. The following letter gives the details of the march to Wexford :

"For the Honorable William Lenthall, Esquire, Speaker of the Parliament of England ; These :

Wexford, 14th October, 1649.

SIR,

The army marched from Dublin about the 23d of September into the county of Wicklow, where the enemy have a garrison about fourteen miles from Dublin, called Killincarrick,[1] which they quitting, a company of the army was put therein. From thence the army marched through almost a desolate country until it came to a passage of the river Doro,[2] about a mile above the castle of Arklow, which was the first seat and honor of the Marquis of Ormonde's family, which he had strongly fortified : but it was, upon the approach of the army, quitted, wherein he left another company of foot."

Arklow was taken on the 28th of September, the guns having fired at it from the opposite side of the river. In the lower part of the town there is a piece of ground still called Cromwell's Plot. It is said that at this time it was held by a namesake of the Lord Lieutenant. Hearing that one bearing the same name lived in the town, Cromwell had him summoned to his presence, and asked him what service he could do him. The other replied that he wished for nothing more than to be left in the quiet possession of his plot. This Oliver promised him, adding, "a poor man I find you, and a poor man I leave you." Three months later the town was besieged by the O'Tooles and O'Byrnes. Hewson set out from Dublin with 1,000 horse and foot to relieve it ; at his approach the besiegers retired. When he had supplied it plentifully with provisions he returned to Dublin. It was attacked a second time in the following January. The garrison, commanded by Captain Barrington, made a sudden sally, and slew many of the assailants ; the rest fled.

On his march through Wicklow he lost many of his horse in the mountain passes ; they were cut off by Brian MacPhelim O'Byrne's party. Cromwell's own horse and furniture were carried off from the camp by Christopher Tuohill ; his father was sent by Cromwell to offer him a sum of £100 for the horse, "but for gold or silver he would not give him back, but preferred to keep him as a monument."

"From thence the army marched towards Wexford ; wherein on the way was a strong castle called Limbrick,[3] the ancient seat of the Esmondes, where the enemy had a strong garrison, which they burnt and quitted the day before our coming

---

[1] Five miles beyond Bray, on the high road to the town of Wicklow. The castle is now in ruins. In the Usurper's time, Captain Barrington, garrisoned at Arklow, murdered Donogh O'Doy of Killincarrick and above 500 men, protected by himself. Pamphlet published in London in 1662, quoted by O'Connell in his *Memoir of Ireland*, p. 264 ; Dublin, 1843.

[2] The Daragh joins the Avoca river four miles north-west of Arklow.

[3] In 1606 Sir Laurence Esmonde obtained from James I. a peerage and a grant of the manor of Limbrick in return for his services to the Crown in Holland and Ireland. He and

thither. From thence we marched towards Ferns, an episcopal seat, where was a castle,[1] to which I sent Colonel Reynolds with a party to summon it, which accordingly he did, and it was surrendered to him,[2] where we, having put a company, advanced the army to a passage over the river Slaney, which runs down to Wexford ; and that night we marched into the fields of a village called Enniscorthy, belonging to Mr. Robert Wallop, where was a strong castle, very well manned and provided for by the enemy ; and, close under it, a very fair house belonging to the same worthy person, a monastery of Franciscan friars, the considerablest in all Ireland : they ran away the night before we came. We summoned the castle, and they refused to yield at the first ; but upon better consideration they were willing to deliver the place to us, which accordingly they did, leaving their great guns, arms, ammunition and provisions behind them,"

Enniscorthy was part of the territory given by Strongbow to Maurice de Prendergast, one of his companions in arms ; he built the castle. The manor afterwards came into the possession of the Mac-Morroughs, and was given by Donald Cavenagh, surnamed the Brown, head of his sept, to the Franciscan monastery which he founded for Friars Minors of the Strict Observance, in 1460. After the dissolution of the religious houses, it was bestowed by Queen Elizabeth on Sir Henry Wallop, knight, treasurer at war to the Queen in Ireland, for his eminent services to the crown.[3] The "worthy person" who at this time dwelt in the "fair house," was his grandson ; he had been member for Andover, one of the judges presiding at the trial of Charles I., and member of the Council of State. After the Restoration, he was sentenced to be imprisoned for life in the tower of London, where he died in 1667.[4] His great-grandson was created Earl of Portsmouth in 1743.[5]

This castle was retaken soon after by the following stratagem. Some Irish gentlemen feasted the soldiers of the garrison, and sent in women to sell them "strong water," of which they drank too much. The Irish fell on them, took the garrison, and put all the officers and Captain Todd, the governor, his wife, and all his men to the sword, except four, who had betrayed the place for a sum of £7. Colonel Cooke, the governor of Wexford, stormed it, and slew the whole of the Irish garrison soon after. The Lord Lieutenant hearing of the treachery of some of the garrisons, ordered that the Irish should be put out of all those belonging to the Parliament.

Sir William Parsons plundered the O'Byrnes of a great part of their territory, " a case," says Carte, " very extraordinary, containing such a scene of iniquity and cruelty, that, considered in all its circumstances, is scarce to be paralleled in the history of any country." *Life of Ormonde*, vol. i. p. 27. Some part of the castle and bawn-wall are still standing.

[1] One of the finest of Anglo-Norman style now found in Ireland, supposed by O'Donovan to have been built by William FitzAdelm, ancestor of the de Burgos.

[2] " The garrison left their arms, ammunition and provisions behind them." Letter c Cromwell in *Aphor. Disc.*, vol. ii. p. 283, appendix lxxxvii.

[3] He came to Ireland in 1580. Later he was appointed one of the Lords Justices, Commissioner of Forfeited Estates and of the Munster Plantation. He obtained from Si John Perrott "three little abbeys and a friary " in Adare. See *Memorials of Adare*, p. 59.

[4] He was sentenced to be drawn on a sledge under Tyburn gallows with a halter roun; his neck. He owed his life very probably to the fact that he had not signed the warrant fc the King's execution. Hall's *Ireland*, &c., vol. ii. p. 171.

[5] His descendant Isaac Newton Wallop, fifth earl of Portsmouth, is at present owne of ..,198 acres in the county Wexford, the yearly valuation of which is £9,280. See *7*. *Landed Proprietors of Ireland*, by U. H. De Burgh ; Dublin, 1878.

On Saturday, September 29th, the Parliamentary fleet appeared off the harbor of Wexford ; and the second day after, October 1st, Cromwell with his army encamped before the walls. The possession of this town was most important to him. It was through it principally that the Confederates obtained the necessary supplies of arms and ammunition, and communicated with their friends in foreign countries ; for its inhabitants, guided by their faithful bishop, Nicholas French, had never for a moment wavered in devotion to their country and religion. There, too, he would find secure anchorage for his fleet. The "intelligence he had in the town" made him hope that its capture would be an easy task. "Hugh Rochfort," says Carte, "a lawyer, recorder of the town, was now in correspondence with Cromwell, through Mr. Nicholas Loftus, who was at this time a very active instrument in engaging all the inhabitants of the town to be subservient to Cromwell's purposes. Rochfort carried on the same work with still greater artifice, pretending to be zealous for the Irish cause ; and having done all he could to intimidate the townsmen and persuade them to capitulate, he quitted the place upon Cromwell's approach and retired with his goods to the fort of Passage, letting them see by that action his own terror, and inviting them to follow his example." [1]

Ormonde was aware of these intrigues, and had given timely notice to the Commissioners of Trust of the approaching danger. They relied on the mayor and townsmen ; but these had little time to prepare for the defence. He was determined to leave no means untried to save so important a place. His forces had been considerably increased by the arrival of 1,000 foot and 300 horse, which the Marquis of Clanricarde had sent to his assistance, under the command of Major-General Lucas Taaffe. Two regiments of Inchiquin's horse had also joined him ; but these he could put little faith in, as after the capture of Drogheda they took every opportunity of deserting to the enemy. Inchiquin was hindered from coming by a conspiracy of his officers. Besides, the townsmen distrusted Ormonde. They knew that often before he had treated with the enemy ; that he had basely surrendered the capital. Nor was their confidence in him increased when they learned that he had lately made common cause with Inchiquin, who had sacked Cashel and slaughtered some hundreds of his countrymen there. No wonder, then, that he did not wish to admit his troops, and that they preferred to trust to their own arms and to the justice of their cause. It was only when the fleet appeared before the town that they accepted David Sinnott, lieutenant-colonel of Preston's regiment, as governor ; "and if Sir Edmund Butler," says Carte, "had not come himself, they would have opposed Sinnott's entrance with his men, and delivered the town to the enemy at the first summons."

"On Monday, being the 1st of October," continues Cromwell, "we appeared before Wexford, into which the enemy had put a garrison of their army, the town

---

[1] This is Carte's account. *Life of Ormonde,* vol. ii. p. 91. Rochford, like the Marquis of Antrim and many others of the old Irish, was anxious to come to terms with Cromwell, relying more on him than on Ormonde. See Hill's *MacDonnells of Antrim,* p. 277.

until then having been so confident of their own strength that they would not at any time suffer a garrison to be imposed upon them. The commander that brought these forces was David Sinnott, who took upon him the command of the town."

The following letters passed between the commanders :[1]

(1.)   To the Commander-in-Chief of the Town of Wexford.

Before Wexford, 3d October, 1649.

SIR,

Having brought the army belonging to the Parliament of England before this place, to reduce it to its due obedience, to the end effusion of blood may be prevented and the town and country about it preserved from ruin, I thought fit to summon you to deliver the same to me, to the use of the State of England. By this offer I hope it will clearly appear where the guilt will lie, if innocent persons should come to suffer with the nocent. I expect your speedy answer and rest,

Sir, your servant,

O. CROMWELL.

(2.)   For the Lord General Cromwell. These :—

Wexford, 3d October, 1649.

SIR,

I have received your letter of summons for the delivery of this town into your hands. Which standeth not with my honor to do myself ; neither will I take it upon me without the advice of the rest of the officers and Mayor of this corporation, this town being of so great consequence to all Ireland. Whom I will call together and confer with, and return my resolutions unto you to-morrow by twelve of the clock.

In the meantime, if you be so pleased, I am content to forbear all acts of hostility, so you permit no approach to be made. Expecting your answer in that particular, I remain,

My Lord,

Your Lordship's servant,

D. SINNOTT.

The mayor and aldermen were so courteous, that in the interval before they returned their positive answer, they sent Cromwell a present of sack, strong waters, and strong beer. The next day about twelve o'clock, the following answer was sent :—

(3.)   To the Commander-in-Chief of the Town of Wexford.

SIR,

I have received your resolutions to return your answers by twelve of the clock to-morrow morning, which I agree unto ; but for your other part of your letter to forbear all acts of hostility, I consider that your houses are better than our tents, and so shall not consent unto that. I rest,

Sir, your servant,

O. CROMWELL.

(4.)   For the Lord General Cromwell.

Wexford, 4th October, 1649.

SIR,

I have advised with the Mayor and officers, as I promised ; and I am content that four whom I shall employ may have a conference with four of yours, to

---

[1] The letters throughout this work are taken from Cary's *Memorials of the Civil War,* vol. ii. p. 168, &c., who professes to give them exactly as they are found in the Tanner MSS. Commonly they are given as altered by the parliament to adapt them better for public reading. The order is the same as that followed by Carlyle.

see if any agreement may be begot between us. To this purpose I desire you to send mine a safe-conduct, as I do hereby promise to send to yours when you send me their names. And I pray that the meeting may be had to-morrow at eight o'clock in the forenoon, that they may have sufficient time to confer together and determine the matter; and that the meeting and place be agreed upon, and the safe-conduct mutually sent for the said meeting this afternoon. Expecting your answer hereto, I rest, My Lord,

Your servant,

D. SINNOTT.

Send me the names of your agents, their qualities and degrees. Those I fix upon are: Major James Byrne, Major Theobald Dillon, Alderman Nicholas Chevers, Mr. William Stafford.

(5.) To the Commander-in-Chief of the Town of Wexford.

Before Wexford, 4th October, 1649.

SIR,
Having summoned you to deliver the town of Wexford into my hands, I might well expect the delivery thereof, and not a formal treaty; which is seldom granted but where things stand upon a more equal foot.

If, therefore, yourself or the town have any desires to offer, upon which you will surrender the place to me, I shall be able to judge of the reasonableness of them when they are made known to me. To which end, if you shall think fit to send the persons named in your last, intrusted by yourself and the town, by whom I may understand your desires, I shall give you a speedy and fitting answer, and I do hereby engage myself that they shall return in safety to you.

I expect your answer hereunto within an hour; and rest your servant,

O. CROMWELL.

(6.) For the Lord General Cromwell.

Wexford, 4th October, 1649.

SIR,
I have returned you a civil answer to the best of my judgment; and thereby I find you undervalue me and this place so much, that you think to have it surrendered without capitulation or honorable terms, as appears by the hour's limitation in your last.

Sir, had I never a man in this town but the townsmen and the artillery here planted, I should conceive myself in a very befitting condition to make honorable conditions. And having a considerable party with them in the place, I am resolved to die honorably, or make such conditions as may secure my honor and life in the eyes of my own party.

To which reasonable terms if you hearken not, or give me time to send my agents till eight o'clock in the forenoon to-morrow with my propositions, with a further safe-conduct, I leave you to your better judgment and myself to the assistance of the Almighty; and so conclude. Your servant,

D. SINNOTT.

To this letter Cromwell returned no answer. The following day the Governor again made overtures to him.

(7.) For the Lord General Cromwell.

Wexford, 5th October, 1649.

SIR,
My propositions being now prepared, I am ready to send my agents with them to you; and for their safe return, I pray you to send a safe-conduct by the bearer to me, in the hope an honorable agreement may thereupon arise between your Lordship and, my Lord, your Lordship's servant,

D. SINNOTT.

A permit was accordingly given, allowing the agents to come and return in safety.

While these papers were passing between us," continues Cromwell, "I sent the Lieutenant-General with a party of dragoons, horse and foot, to endeavor to reduce their fort which lay at the mouth of their harbor, about ten miles distant from us. To which he sent a troop of dragoons ; but the enemy quitted their fort, leaving behind them about seven great guns, and betook themselves, by help of their boats, to a frigate of 12 guns lying in the harbor within cannon-shot of the fort. The dragoons possessed the fort ; and some seamen belonging to your fleet coming happily in at the same time, they bent their guns at the frigate, and she immediately yielded to mercy, both herself, the soldiers that had been in the fort, and the seamen that manned her. And whilst our men were in her, the town, not knowing what had happened, sent another small vessel to her, which our men also took."

Meanwhile he was investing the town closely on the south and west. Alarmed at such formidable preparations, the townsmen asked Ormonde to give them further reinforcements. The next day he sent to their aid another Ulster regiment, under the command of Lord Iveagh,[1] in all 1,500 men. Lord Castlehaven, who knew the country, escorted them with 200 horse. "Taking a great compass, he came before day to the ferry near Sir Thomas Esmonde's house at Bally-brenan. The foot crossed the arm of the sea in boats and entered the town by the only side still open. Castlehaven returned with the horse to Ormonde. After their arrival, Sinnott sent out the following despatch :

(8.)   For the Lord General Cromwell.

Wexford, 5th October, 1649.

My Lord,

Even as I was ready to send out my agents to you, the Lord General of the horse came hither with relief. Unto whom I communicated the proceedings between your Lordship and me, and delivered to him the propositions I intended to despatch unto your Lordship, who hath desired a small time to consider them and to speed them unto me, which, my Lord, I could not deny, he having a commanding power over me.

Pray, my Lord, believe that I do not do this to trifle out time, but for his present content ; and if I find any long delay in his Lordship's returning them back unto me, I will proceed of myself according to my first intention ; to which I beseech your Lordship give credit, at the request,

My Lord, of your Lordship's ready servant,

D. SINNOTT.

(9.)   To the Commander-in-Chief of the Town of Wexford.

Wexford, 6th October, 1649.

SIR,

You might have spared your trouble in the account you give me of your transaction with the Lord General of your horse, and of your resolutions in case he

---

[1] This was Arthur Viscount Magennis of Iveagh, who was attainted in 1642. In Cromwell's self-denying ordinance he was excepted from pardon for life and estate ; he was afterward restored. The territory of the Magennis tribe included the whole of Down ; it was limited at a later period to Ilyveagh, a territory of Dalriada, in the county of Down, now forming part of the baronies of Upper and Lower Iveagh, with some other parts of the same county including Moy Innis, now the barony of Lecale. M'Geoghegan's *History of Ireland,* pp. 119 and 121 ; O'Callaghan's *History of the Irish Brigades in the Service of France,* p. 330 n. ; Glasgow, 1870. Bryan Viscount Iveagh was a colonel in the Irish army of James II. ; at the end of the war he entered the Austrian service. He died without issue. *Ibid.*

answered not your expectation in point of time. These are your own concernments, and it behooves you to improve them, and the relief you mention to your best advantage.

All that I have to say is, to desire you to take notice, that I do hereby revoke my safe conduct from the persons mentioned therein. When you shall see cause to treat, you may send for another. I rest, Sir,

Your servant,

O. CROMWELL.

The same day Cromwell landed his artillery and stores, and began to erect a battery that would command the ferry and prevent all communication with the town. The position which he chose was the rising ground to the south of the town, now occupied by the residence of Mr. Cormack and still known as Cromwell's Fort. A battery of four guns was erected on the top of the Trespan Rock, close by.[1] The governor was in some apprehension for the safety of the place, chiefly on account of the scarcity of supplies. But if a body of five hundred men, well supplied with provisions, was sent him, he made no question of defending it against the enemy, who began already to suffer for want of forage. Ormonde resolved to attempt the relief of the place in person. Leaving General Taaffe with a Connaught regiment to garrison Ross, he set out with the rest of his army, and crossing the Slaney, came on the evening of October 11th to the ferry on the north side of the town. He sent a message to the mayor, that he had come to give the townsmen any further help they pleased. Some of the aldermen came to express their thanks, and declared they were willing to receive any number of men he might wish to send. Sir Edmund Butler, governor of the county, succeeded in entering the town with 300 foot and 100 horse ; on account of his great experience and well-known bravery he was appointed military governor of the town with the consent of the townsmen.

The batteries were ready for action on the evening of the 10th. At an early hour the following morning they began to play on the castle, which stood outside the walls on the south side of the town. Against this the besiegers directed the whole force of their artillery, seeing that if it was captured, the town would soon follow. By noon the battlements of the castle were beaten down, and three great breeches were made in two of the towers. When about a hundred shots were fired, "the Governor's stomach came down." He demanded a parley, and asked that four persons chosen by him should go out and propose certain terms of surrender.

(10.) For the Lord General Cromwell.

Wexford, 11th October, 1649.

MY LORD, —

In performance of my last, I desire your Lordship to send me a safe conduct for Major Theobald Dillon, Major James Byrne, Alderman Nicholas Chevers, and Captain James Stafford, whom I will send to your Lordship instructed with my desires. And so I rest,

My Lord, your servant,

D. SINNOTT.

---

[1] The breastwork of this battery was standing up to the year 1829. It has been effaced since by the working of the quarry near.

"Which desire I condescending to," says Cromwell in the letter to the Speaker of the parliament, "two field officers with an alderman of the town and the captain of the castle, brought out the following propositions, which for their abominableness, manifesting also the impudence of the men, I thought fit to present to your view, together with my answer :"

"*The propositions of Colonel David Sinnott, Governor of the town and castle of Wexford and on behalf of the officers, soldiers, and inhabitants in the said town and castle, to General Cromwell :* —

"1. That all and every the inhabitants of the said town from time to time, and at all times hereafter, shall have free and uninterrupted liberty publicly to use, exercise, and profess the Roman Catholic religion, without restriction, mulct, or penalty, any law or statue to the contrary notwithstanding.

"2. That the regular and secular Roman Catholic clergy now possessed of the churches, church-livings, monasteries, religious houses, and chapels in the said town and in the suburbs and franchises thereof, and their successors, shall have, hold, and enjoy to them and their successors for ever the said churches, &c., and shall teach and preach in them publicly, without any molestation, any law or statute to the contrary notwithstanding.

"3. That Nicholas, now Lord Bishop of Ferns, and his successors, shall use and exercise such jurisdiction over the Catholics of his diocese as since his consecration hitherto he used.

"4. That all the officers and soldiers of whatever quality and degree soever in the said town and castle, and such of the inhabitants as are so pleased, shall march with flying colors, and be conveyed safe with their lives, artillery, ordnance, ammunition, arms, goods of all sorts, horses, moneys, and whatever else belongs to them, to the town of Ross and there to be left safe with their own party ; allowing each musketeer towards their march a pound of powder, four yards of match, and twelve brace of bullets ; and a strong convoy to be sent with the said soldiers, within twenty-four hours after the yielding up of the said town.

"5. That such of the inhabitants of the said town as will desire to leave the same at any time hereafter, shall have free liberty to carry away out of the said town all their frigates, artillery, arms, powder, corn, malt, and other provisions which they have for their defence and sustenance, and all their goods and chattels, of what quality or condition soever, without any manner of disturbance whatsoever, and have passes and safe-conducts and convoys for their lives and said goods to Ross, or where else they shall think fit.

"6. That the mayor, bailiffs, free burgesses, and commons of the said town may have, hold, and enjoy the said town and suburbs, their commons, their franchises, liberties and immunities, which hitherto they enjoyed ; and that the mayor, bailiffs, and free burgesses may have the government of the said town, as hitherto they enjoyed the same from the realm of England, and that they have no other government, they adhering to the State of England and observing their orders and the orders of their governors in this realm for the time being.

"7. That all the burgesses and inhabitants, either native or strangers, of the said town, who shall continue their abode therein, or come to live there within three months, and their heirs shall have, hold, and enjoy their several castles, houses, lands, tenements, and hereditaments within the land of Ireland, and all their goods and chattels, to them and their heirs to their own several uses for ever without molestation.

"8. That such burgess or burgesses, or other inhabitants of the said towns, as shall at any time hereafter be desirous to leave the said town, shall have free leave to dispose of their real and personal estates respectively to their best advantage ; and further, have full liberty and a safe-conduct respectively to go into England or elsewhere, according to their several pleasures who shall desire to depart the same.

"9. That all and singular the inhabitants of the said town, either native or strangers, from time to time, and at all times hereafter, shall have, reap, and enjoy the full liberty of free-born English subjects, without the least incapacity or restriction therein ; and that all the freemen of the said town shall be as free in all the seaports, cities, and towns in England, as the freemen of all and every the said cities and towns ; and all and every the said freemen of the said cities and towns to be as free in their said town of Wexford as the freemen thereof, for their greater encouragement to trade and commerce together on all hands.

" 10. That no memory remain of any hostility or distance, which was hitherto between the said town and castle on the one part, and the Parliament or State of England on the other part ; but that all acts, transgressions, offences, depredations, and other crimes of what nature and quality soever, be they ever so transcendent, attempted or done, or supposed to be attempted or done, by the inhabitants of the said town or any other, heretofore or at present adhering to the said town, either native or stranger, and every of them, shall pass in oblivion, without chastisement, challenge, recompense, demand, or questioning for them or any of them, now or at any time hereafter."

(11.) For the Commander-in-Chief in the town of Wexford.

Before Wexford, 11th October, 1649.

" Sir,

" I have had the patience to peruse your propositions ; to which I might have returned an answer with some disdain. But, to be short, I shall give the soldiers and non-commissioned officers quarter for life, and leave to go to their several habitations, with their wearing clothes : they engaging themselves to take up arms no more against the Parliament of England ; and the commissioned officers for their lives, but to render themselves prisoners. And as for the inhabitants, I shall engage myself that no violence shall be offered to their goods, and that I shall protect their town from plunder.

" I expect your positive answer instantly ; and if you will upon these terms surrender and quit, and in one hour send to me four officers of the quality of field-officers and two aldermen, for the performance thereof, I shall thereupon forbear all acts of hostility.

" Your servant,

" OLIVER CROMWELL."

CHAPTER XIII.

THE CAPTURE OF WEXFORD.

Courage of the Townsmen — Discord — Treachery of Stafford — Surrender of the Castle — Entrance of the Besiegers — Massacre of the Inhabitants — Contemporary Writers — Letter of Dr. French — His Apologia — Massacre of the Franciscans — "They knelt around the cross divine " — Terror of the Commissioners of Trust — Ormonde's Plans.

As soon as the inhabitants of Wexford learned the answer to the terms of surrender proposed by the Governor, they prepared themselves for a stern resistance. To the soldiers, quarter and liberty; to the officers, quarter, but not liberty; and to the inhabitants freedom from pillage: these were the conditions on which the town should be surrendered within an hour. Yet matters were not so desperate within the walls that such terms need be accepted. The town was, according to Cromwell's description, "pleasantly seated and strong," having a rampart of earth fifteen feet thick within the walls.[1] It was garrisoned by over 2,000 men, commanded by an officer who had given many proofs of his bravery and fidelity. In the fort and elsewhere in and about the town there were near a hundred cannon; in the harbor, three vessels, one of them of thirty-four guns, another of about twenty guns; and a frigate of twenty guns on the stocks, built up to the uppermost deck. Winter was setting in — it was the middle of October — and the "country sickness" would soon begin to tell on troops encamped under the open sky. Ormonde's army was at Ross, only twenty miles off, watching, no doubt, for a favorable moment to fall on the rear of the besieging lines, whose numbers were too few to keep up a complete investment and, at the same time, to repel a sudden attack that might be made on any point either from within or without.

Unhappily within the town there was that which marred many of these advantages — discord, a want of mutual confidence between Ormonde and the inhabitants — and so far did it go, that the townsmen seem to have thought there was little room left them for choice between those who called themselves their friends and those whom they well knew to be their enemies. The day before Cromwell encamped before the town, Sinnott, the governor, wrote to Ormonde:

"I find no resolution in the townsmen to defend the town; but to speak the truth nakedly, I find and perceive them rather inclined to capitulate and take con-

---

[1] Some portions of the town-wall with five of the towers, three square and two round, are still in a sufficient state of preservation to show that the walls were 22 feet high, and were supported on the inside by a rampart of earth 21 feet thick.

ditions of the enemy. In so much as I cannot as yet find admittance for those few assigned hither for the defence of the place, nor a muster of the townsmen to know what strength they have for the defence thereof. In which respect seeing I am not able to do his Majesty any service, I am resolved to leave the town without I find out their undelayed conformity."

With difficulty he induced them to admit the reinforcements from the Royalist army within the walls; it was only at his urgent request that they consented to receive a second body of troops, though these were much needed for the defence of the town. Some went so far as to propose that Cromwell should be treated with, in the hope that a peaceful surrender might secure to them not only life and liberty, but a part of their goods, and perhaps their homes. But worse than this — they had in their midst a traitor. Such was the confidence of the Council of the Confederate Catholics in Captain James Stafford,[1] that the government of the county of Kilkenny had been entrusted to him jointly with Sir Thomas Esmonde,[2] and when it was known that Cromwell was marching on Wexford, he was sent to act as governor of the castle there,[3] a most important post, since the possession of it insured the safety of the town. Sir Edward Butler had good reason to suspect his fidelity, but he dared not displace him, as he was himself too much under the control of the Commissioners of Trust.

On the 11th of October, about noon, some breaches having been made in the walls of the castle, the Governor of the town asked for a safe conduct for four persons to treat of surrender on honorable terms. What these terms were we have already seen. One of the four persons chosen on behalf of the townsmen was Stafford.

"While I was preparing the answer to the propositions," says Cromwell, "studying to preserve the town from plunder, that it might be of more use to you and your army, the captain, who was one of the Commissioners, being fairly treated, yielded up the castle to us."

It is obvious that the advantage taken by Cromwell of "treating" Stafford and entering the town while the terms of surrender were under discussion, was fraudulent and treacherous. The local tradi-

[1] In the Jamestown "Declaration" the loss of Wexford is attributed to the "unskilfulness of the governor, a young man, vain and unadvised." Cox's *Hib. Anglic.*, appendix xlviii. The author of the *Aphor. Disc.* calls Stafford "a vain, idle, young man, nothing practiced in the art military." Vol. ii. p. 54.

[2] He was the son of Sir Laurence Esmonde. In the Civil War of 1641 he deserted the King and held Duncannon for the parliament. The fort was taken by Preston after a siege of two months. Esmonde died of grief soon after. His first wife was sister of O'Flaherty, chief of Iar Connaught. She fled with her son Thomas, in order to bring him up a Catholic. Esmonde, in his anger, affected to consider the marriage invalid, on the ground that his wife was "of the Irishry." Thomas was brought up by his mother's relatives, and through their influence obtained the rank of baronet. During the usurpation of Cromwell his extensive estates were granted to Colonel Monk. He died while engaged in a lawsuit for their recovery, leaving a son, Sir Laurence, then a minor. The Duke of Buckingham, as his next friend, succeeded in recovering a considerable part of them; these are now in the possession of Sir Thomas II. Esmonde. The recognition of the peerage did not follow that of the title to the property, for Sir Thomas though declared "an innocent papist," yet, as such, labored at that time under peculiar disadvantages. See *Annals of the Four Masters*, ad. ann. 1597, note and appendix, and *The Kilkenny Arch. Journal* for 1856, 1862, and 1870.

[3] A portion of the outer wall of the castle is still standing.

tion says that Cromwell and Stafford had a meeting at midnight by the riverside. Carte's words leave no room for doubting of the Governor's guilt: "The enemy entered the gates by the treachery of Captain Stafford." And again: "Stafford having privately received Cromwell's forces into the castle, which commanded the part of the town which lay next it, they issued suddenly from thence, attacked the wall and gate adjoining, and soon became masters of the place." Clarendon is still more explicit: "Stafford gave up the place to Cromwell, and took conditions under him, and thereby gave entrance to him into the town."

The castle[1] was about three hundred paces outside the wall, so close that the communication could not be cut off between them. The gates were immediately thrown open to admit those who were outside, and the whole army poured in. They entered so suddenly, that the townsmen were first made aware of Stafford's treachery by seeing the enemy's colors floating from the summit of the castle and the guns turned against the walls. In great consternation they abandoned that portion of the works, and retreated into the town. The assailants seeing the walls without defenders, rushed forward with their scaling-ladders, and crossed over without hindrance. An attempt was made to prevent the advance of the cavalry by placing ropes and chains across the street. Meantime the garrison were retreating to the market-place; there the townspeople had already gathered together.

Then the scenes that took place at Drogheda were renewed at Wexford.[2] We have Cromwell's own account of these atrocities, in his letter to the speaker of the parliament, from before Wexford, 11th October.

"When they (the townsmen and the garrison) were come into the market-place, making a stiff resistance, our forces broke them; and then put all to the sword that came in their way. Two boatfuls of the enemy, attempting to escape, being overprest with numbers, sank, whereby were drowned near three hundred of them. I believe, in all, not less than two thousand; and I believe not twenty of yours from first to last of the siege. And indeed, it hath, not without cause, been deeply set upon our hearts that we intending better to this place than so great a ruin, hoping the town might be of more use to you and your army, yet God would not have it so; but by an unexpected providence, in his righteous justice, brought a just judgment upon them, causing them to become a prey to the soldier, who in their piracies had made preys of so many families, and made with their bloods to answer the cruelties which they had exercised upon the lives of divers poor Protestants! Two (instances) of which I have been lately acquainted with. About seven or eight score poor Protestants were by them put into an old vessel, which being, as some say, bulged by them, the vessel sank, and they were all presently drowned in

[1] Cox says the castle was surrendered within two hours after Sir Edward Butler and the force sent with him had entered the town.

[2] "Cromwell's forces entered and made almost as great slaughter as at Drogheda." Castlehaven's *Memoirs*, p. 116. See also Warner's *History of the Rebellion*, p. 476. "For an hour the fight continued in the market-place, but on unequal terms, for the sword of Cromwell cut down nearly all the townspeople without regard for condition, age, or sex." Bruodin's *Propug.* p. 680. "The enemy put to the sword all those that were found in arms, with an execution as horribly deliberate as that of Drogheda." Leland vol. iii. p. 353. "Great mortality did accompany that fury of both soldier and native; all sex and age indifferently there perished." *Aphor. Disc.* vol. ii. p. 54. "2,000 were slain of Ormonde's soldiers in the town." *Brief Chron. of the Irish Wars*, p. 5.

the harbor. The other was thus: They put divers poor Protestants into a chapel (which, since they have used for a Mass-house, and in which one or more of their priests were now killed), where they were famished to death.

"The soldiers got a very good booty in this place; and had not they (the townspeople) had opportunity to carry their goods over the river while we besieged it, it would have been much more. I could have wished for their own good and the good of the garrison, they had been more moderate. Some things which were not easily portable, we hope we shall make good use of to your behoof. There are great quantities of iron, hides, tallow, salt, pipe and barrel staves, which are under the Commissioners' hands, to be secured. We believe there are near a hundred cannon in the fort and elsewhere in and about the town. Here is likewise some very good shipping; here are three vessels, one of them of thirty-four guns, which a week's time would fit to sea: there is another of about twenty guns, very near ready likewise, and one other frigate of twenty guns, upon the stocks, made for sailing, which is built up to the uppermost deck; for her handsomeness' sake I have appointed the workmen to finish her, here being materials to do it, if you or the Council of State shall approve thereof. The frigate also, taken beside the fort, is a most excellent vessel for sailing, besides divers other ships and vessels in the harbor.[1]

"This town is now in your power, that of the former inhabitants, I believe, scarce one in twenty can challenge any property in their houses. Most of them are run away, and many of them killed in this service. And it were to be wished that an honest people would come and plant here, where are very good houses and other accommodations fitted to their hands, which may by your favor be made of encouragement to them. As also a seat of good trade, both inward and outward, and of marvellous great advantage in the point of the herring and other fishing. The town is pleasantly seated and strong, having a rampart of earth within the wall near fifteen feet thick."

And he concludes with the following pious utterance:—

"Thus it hath pleased God to give into your hands this other mercy"— Drogheda was the first—"for which, as for all, we pray God may have all the glory. Indeed your instruments are poor and weak, and can do nothing but through believing—and that is the gift of God also.

"I humbly take leave, and rest,
"Your most humble servant,
"OLIVER CROMWELL."

On the receipt of this letter, October 30th, orders were issued by the parliament to the Council of State, to prepare a letter of thanks to the Lord Lieutenant of Ireland and to the officers of the army; and to give one hundred pounds to Captain William Raby for bringing the letters from the Lord Lieutenant.

There is abundant testimony of contemporary writers to prove that the cruelties practiced at Wexford on the clergy and people were as great as those of which Drogheda was the scene a month before. Dr. Fleming, Archbishop of Dublin, writing to the Secretary of the Propaganda at Rome, very soon after, says that many priests, some religious, innumerable citizens, and two thousand soldiers were massacred. Father St. Leger, S. J., in a letter to his superiors in Rome, in 1655, containing an account of the events of the preceding years, states that when Wexford was taken, Cromwell exterminated the citizens by the sword. Colonel Solomon Richards, too, says that the

---

[1] A party of his Excellency's foot, by help of some vessels, took the Earl of Antrim's frigate with 14 guns. His Excellency took Wexford by storm, and in it 51 pieces of ordnance besides those in ships, forty vessels in the harbor, and great store of plunder.

town of Wexford was much depopulated in its taking by Oliver Cromwell. In "The Humble Petition of the Ancient Native Inhabitants
of the Town of Wexford, and of the Heirs, Orphans, and Widows of
such of them as are dead, to his Majesty Charles II., July 4th, 1660,"
it is said of Cromwell : "The said usurper entered the town and put
man, woman, and child, to a very few, to the sword ; where, among
the rest, the Governor lost his life, and others of the soldiers and
inhabitants to the number of 1,500 persons." In the west side a great
slaughter was made. Fortunately we have a detailed account of
these events from one whose testimony is beyond all cavil. Dr.
Nicholas French, the Bishop of Ferns, was then lying ill in a neighboring town. In a letter to the Papal Nuncio, written from Antwerp
in January, 1673, he thus describes what took place : [1]

"On that fatal day, October 11th, 1649, I lost everything I had. Wexford,
my native town, then abounding in merchandise, ships and wealth, was taken at the
sword's point by that plague of England, Cromwell, and sacked by an infuriated
soldiery. Before God's altar fell sacred victims, holy priests of the Lord. Of those
who were seized outside the church, some were scourged, some thrown into chains
and imprisoned, while others were hanged or put to death by cruel tortures. The
blood of the noblest of our citizens was shed so that it inundated the streets. There
was hardly a house that was not defiled with carnage and filled with wailing. In
my own palace, a boy hardly sixteen years of age, an amiable youth, and also my
gardener and sacristan, were barbarously butchered ; and my chaplain, whom I had
left behind me at home, was pierced with six mortal wounds and left weltering in
his blood. And these abominable deeds were done in the open day by wicked
assassins ! Never since that day have I seen my native city, my flock, my native
land, or my kindred : and this it is that makes me the most wretched of men. After
the destruction of the town, I lived for five months in the woods, every moment
sought after that I might be put to death. There my drink was milk and water,
my food a little bread : on one occasion I did not taste food for five whole days. I
slept under the open sky, without any shelter or covering. At length, the wood in
which I lay concealed was surrounded by numerous bodies of the enemy, who came
to seize me and send me in chains to England. But, thanks to my guardian angel,
I escaped their hands, owing to the speed and swiftness of my horse."

There is another letter of Dr. French, still extant in the library
of Trinity College ; it is entitled *Apologia*, and seems to be a defence
of his leaving Ireland and seeking safety in a foreign land : —

"You say nothing about my native city, Wexford, cruelly destroyed by the
sword on the 11th of October, 1649; nothing of my palace that was plundered,[2] and
of my domestics impiously slain ; nothing of my fellow-laborers, precious victims,
immolated by the impious sword of the heretic before the altar of God ; nothing of
the inhabitants weltering in their own blood and gore. The rumor of the direful
massacre reached me whilst I was ill in a neighboring town, suffering from a burn-

---

[1] The original is given in *Spicil. Ossor.*, vol. i. p. 347. Dr. French left Ireland in 1651,
having been sent by the Confederates to ask for aid and protection for the Irish Catholics
from the Duke of Lorraine. The laws made against Jesuits, priests, friars, monks, and
nuns, and rigidly enforced, prevented his return to his native land. After some time he went
to Spain, and there acted as coadjutor to the bishop of St. Iago ; these duties he performed
also at Paris and Ghent. He died in the latter place, August 23d, 1678. He is buried
opposite the high altar in the church of St. Nicholas. Over the spot there is a white marble
monument bearing his arms and the motto : *Virtus in angustiis.* The inscription on it will
be found in the *Bishops of Ferns*, by the Most Rev. Dr. M'Carthy, p. 21 ; Dublin, 1874. His
Settlement and Sale of Ireland and *The Unkinde Deserter* were reprinted by Duffy, Dublin,
in 1856.

[2] The soldiers had the plunder of the town for two hours. *Relation, &c.*

ing fever. I cried and mourned and shed bitter tears and lamented; and turning to heaven with a deep sigh, cried out in the words of the prophet Jeremias, and all who were present shared in my tears. In that excessive bitterness of my soul, a thousand times I wished to be dissolved and to be with Christ, that thus I might not witness the sufferings of my country. From that time I saw neither my city nor my people; but, like an outcast, I sought refuge in the wilderness. I wandered through woods and mountains, generally taking my rest and repose exposed to the hoar frost, sometimes lying hid in the caves and caverns of the earth. In the woods and groves I passed more than five months, that thus I might administer some consolation to the few survivers of my flock who had escaped from the merciless massacre, and dwelt there with the herds of cattle. But neither woods nor caverns could afford me a lasting refuge; for the heretical governor of Wexford, George Cooke, well known for his barbarity, with several troops of cavalry and foot soldiers, searching everywhere, anxious for my death, explored even the highest mountains and most difficult recesses; the huts and habitations adjoining the wood, in which I had sometimes offered the Holy Sacrifice, he destroyed by fire; and my hiding-places, which were formed of branches of trees, were all thrown down. Among those who were subject to much annoyance on my account was a nobleman, in whose house he supposed me to be concealed. He searched the whole house with lighted tapers, accompanied by soldiers holding their naked swords in their hands to slay me the moment I should appear. But in the midst of all these perils God protected me, and mercifully delivered me from the hands of this blood-thirsty man."

The following account of the massacre of some Franciscan Fathers of the convent of Wexford, is taken from *A Brief History of the Irish Province of the Friars Minor of the Regular Observance*, by Father Francis Ward.

On the 11th of October, 1649, the octave of our holy father, St. Francis, seven religious of the Order of St. Francis, all men of great merit and natives of the town, perished by the sword of the heretics in Wexford, viz.: Father Richard Synnott, professor of theology, formerly guardian of the convent; F. John Esmonde, preacher, who had singular power in relieving energumenes; F. Paulinus Synnott, who had suffered much for the faith among the Turks, and had received from Pope Urban VIII. full jurisdiction over all the Catholic captives; F. Raymund Stafford, who had left a considerable inheritance, and despising everything for Christ, had chosen to imitate the poverty of Christ under the standard of St. Francis. Fifteen months before his death he had retired to an island, and led there an austere and mortified life, using only once each day lenten fare. F. Peter Stafford, too, was much devoted to prayer. During the times of persecution, in the absence of the secular clergy, he discharged for fifteen years the duties of parish priest with great credit. Brother Didacus Chevers, over seventy years of age and blind; Brother James Rochford, both men of exemplary lives, and devoted to work. Some of these were slain while kneeling before the altar, others while hearing confessions. F. Raymond Stafford, holding in his hand a crucifix, came out of the church to encourage the citizens, and even preached with great zeal to the enemy, until he was slain by them in the market-place. All these were men of most exemplary life, and as they fell, the Lord deigned to show how precious their death was in his sight.

1. When they were fired at, the balls fell close to some of them without doing them any harm whatever. This I heard from a noble lady, Margaret Keating, to whom the enemy related it in presence of her children and servants.

2. Whilst they were being put to death, it happened that a little of their blood fell on the hand of one of the executioners; this he could not wash off ever after, or remove by any means whatever. I heard this from Mr. John French of Ballolonie, who had himself seen the blood, and learned the circumstances from the mouth of the wicked man after the capture of the city; he spoke of the crime with great sorrow, saying that he bore about on his hand the token that he had slain the religious "whose blood you see," and would carry the mark with him to his grave.

3. Mrs. Margaret Keating, the wife of Captain Doran, and daughter of Mr. William Keating, an alderman of Wexford, told me she heard a soldier of the English army, named Weaver, say, that when the religious were mortally wounded and

lay expiring in the streets, through compassion for them and wishing to put an end to their sufferings, he fired at one of them twice. Though the balls touched his cowl, they did not penetrate it; they fell gently near the cowl as if they had no force. He then shot at his body, but the result was the same. Weaver was asked to fire again; he replied, "I have done so already as well as I could; hitherto I have slain none of the Irish, nor shall I do so in future." He left the army and became a Catholic. I was sought for to reconcile him to the Church, but as I was not found, I did not see him. But to a certainty he was reconciled by the Rev. Patrick Hampton, chancellor of Ferns, of pious memory.

4. Some of the soldiers who put on the habits of the religious, died miserably. Mr. William Hore, of Harperstown, told me that he warned in a friendly manner one of the English soldiers who had the habit on, to lay it aside, as it was not right to mock at St. Francis or the other saints. He replied, "that is all nonsense and superstition." "Tell me, I beg you," said Mr. Hore, "to-morrow morning if you have had any dream." He agreed to do so. After he had gone to rest he was tortured by spectres all the night, thinking mad dogs were dragging him about. He was so terrified at these sights that he took sick and died.

5. Francis Whitty, a man of noble birth, told me that he saw one of the English soldiers who had the habit on, die while uttering blasphemies.

6. It is commonly reported that a soldier fired at the crucifix which F. Raymond held in his hand, and that the ball turned aside and killed the captain of the company. This I heard from Sir Thomas Esmonde and from many others.

7. The Rev. John Turner, the parish priest of Maglass, declared that, on the day when the religious and others were slain at Wexford, he saw a beautiful woman ascending towards the sky. This he saw when he was five miles from Wexford, before he heard anything whatever about its capture.

8. Divers mishaps befel those who were daring enough to dwell in the convent that formerly belonged to the religious. Many of them, soon after they came to the place, died, and were buried in the convent garden. Those who survived were frequently troubled during the night by spectres; they told their neighbors that they thought they had done wrong in killing the religious, and that they would remain no longer in the convent, even though they should find no other place to live in. This I heard from some of their neighbors who knew well of their death and burial, and who had heard from these persons that they were tormented in this way by spectres.

I, the undersigned, declare on the word of a priest, that I heard the above facts related by the aforesaid persons, and have set them down in writing exactly as they were told.

FATHER FRANCIS STAFFORD,

Of the Conception, preacher and confessor, and ex-guardian of the Convent of Wexford.

Any other priests who fell into the hands of the soldiers, no doubt suffered the same fate as the Franciscans.[1] About Eastertide, 1654, four Franciscans were arrested in Wexford by Cromwellian officers, and hanged without formality of trial, in the neighborhood of their former convent.

Sir Edmund Butler was killed by a shot that struck him on the head as he was endeavoring to escape by swimming across the ferry.

A tradition, still current in Wexford, says, that 200 women were

---

[1] In the year 1649, there were in Ireland 23 bishops and 4 archbishops. In the cathedrals there were, as usual, canons and dignitaries; the parishes had pastors, a great number of priests, and numerous convents of regulars. But after Cromwell had attained to supreme power, all were scattered. Over 300 were put to death, 1,000 more driven into exile. Four bishops were slain, the others were obliged to fly to foreign countries, except the Bishop of Kilmore, who was too feeble to be removed. MS. in the Arundel Library, Stonyhurst. In 1641 there were in Ireland 43 houses of the Dominican Order and 600 religious. Ten years after, there was not a single house in their possession, and three-fourths of the religious were dead or in exile. *Hib. Dom.* p. 286.

put to death in the public square. They had flocked round the great cross which stood there, in the hope that Christian soldiers would be so far softened by the sight of that emblem of mercy as to spare the lives of unresisting women. But the victors, enraged at such superstition, and perhaps regarding their presence there as a proof that they were Catholics, and therefore fit objects for their zeal, rushed upon them and put them all to death.

M'Geoghegan, who published his history in 1758, was the first writer who made special mention of this incident of the siege,[1] and from the silence of contemporaries, some of our historians have inferred that the tradition refers only to the general massacre of the inhabitants in the market-place. In reply it may be said, that no one of the contemporary writers, whose works have come down to us, intended to give an exhaustive account of all that took place. Besides, it must be borne in mind that M'Gheoghegan had special opportunities of learning the traditions on such points ; he was chaplain to the Irish Brigade in the service of France, at a time when probably it had in its ranks the children and the grandchildren of those who were eye-witnesses of what he relates. "Some have questioned the accuracy of the statement made by M'Geoghegan and Lingard," writes the Most Rev. Dr. Moran, "as to the massacre of these three hundred females around the cross in Wexford : they say Dr. French and other contemporary writers would not be silent in regard of this particular. But these contemporary writers sufficiently describe the wholesale massacre of the inhabitants, without mercy being shown to either age or sex; and any particulars that are added have a special reference to themselves. The same writers, when describing the destruction of Drogheda, are silent as to the massacre in the crypts of St. Peter's church ; and were it not for the narrative of an officer who was himself engaged in that barbarous work, some critics would probably now be found to reject it as fabulous. The constant tradition not only of Wexford, but of the whole nation, attests the truth of the statement of the above-named historians."

The following poem by Michael J. Barry, on this subject, may be new to some of our readers : —

> They knelt around the cross divine,
>   The matron and the maid ;
> They bowed before redemption's sign,
>   And fervently they prayed —
> Three hundred fair and helpless ones,
>   Whose crime was this alone —
> Their valiant husbands, sires and sons
>   Had battled for their own.
>
> Had battled bravely, but in vain —
>   The Saxon won the fight,
> And Irish corpses strewed the plain
>   Where Valor slept with Right.

---

[1] *History of Ireland*, p. 574. He was born in 1701, and was sent at an early age to France, where he entered the Church. For some time he was chaplain to the Irish Brigade. During the latter part of his life he was attached to the church of St. Méry, in Paris. He died in 1764.

And now that man of demon guilt,
    To fated Wexford flew —
The red blood reeking on his hilt
    Of hearts to Erin true!

He found them there — the young, the old,
    The maiden, and the wife;
Their guardians brave in death were cold,
    Who dared for *them* the strife.
They prayed for mercy — God on high!
    Before *thy* cross they prayed,
And ruthless Cromwell bade them die
    To glut the Saxon blade!

Three hundred fell — the stifled prayer
    Was quenched in women's blood;
Nor youth nor age could move to spare
    From slaughter's crimson flood.
But nations keep a stern account
    Of deeds that tyrants do!
And guiltless blood to Heaven will mount,
    And Heaven avenge it too!

The murder of Irish women was nothing new to the Puritans. After the battle of Naseby one hundred females, some of them of distinguished rank, were put to the sword, under the pretext that they were Irish Catholics. In one day eighty women and children, some infants at the mother's breast, were precipitated over the bridge at Linlithgow ; and if any struggled to the bank of the river, they were knocked on the head or thrust in again by the soldiery. Their crime was being the wives and children of Irish soldiers who had served under Montrose.

It was not the inhabitants of the town alone that were slain. Dr. Lynch states that there was throughout the country an indiscriminate massacre of men, women, and children, by which not less than four thousand persons, young and old, were atrociously butchered by the order of Colonel Cooke, appointed governor of the town by Cromwell.

The churches in Wexford and its neighborhood were profaned, and some in part, some wholly demolished. Selskir,[1] St. Patrick's, St. Mary's, St. Bride's, St. John's, St. Peter's, St. Maud's at Maudlenstown were pulled down. The plate of Selskir was seized, and its bells were taken and shipped to Chester. A few years after, they were removed to the old church near River Street, Liverpool, where they remain to this day. According to tradition, the freedom of the town and exemption from the port duties of Liverpool were granted to the freemen of Wexford in lieu of these bells.

Cromwell's cruelties at Drogheda, repeated at Wexford, spread terror far and wide. Towns and strong places fifty miles off declared for the parliament. Even the Commissioners of Trust were so terri-

---

[1] Selskir was called SS. Peter and Paul's of Selskir, i. e., of the holy sepulchre. It belonged to the Canons regular of St. Austin. The prior had a seat in parliament. Archdall's *Monasticon*, p. 755.

fied, that they were on the point of leaving Kilkenny and transferring their sittings elsewhere. They sent one of their number, Dr. Fennell, to consult Ormonde on the subject. He strove to dissuade them from their purpose by assuring them there was no occasion for such alarm, since Ross was not yet taken; that if the place held out, the loss of the besieging army would be so great, that for one year, at least, Kilkenny would be secure from attack; if it were lost, the time needed to march to Kilkenny would be sufficient for them to secure their departure; that their removal could not but discourage others, and make them think of entering into terms with the enemy. By these arguments they were reassured, and continued their sittings at Kilkenny.

After Ormonde had thrown the second relief into Wexford, he began his march back towards Ross, intending to cross the Slaney near Enniscorthy. But Cromwell, having had intelligence of his movements, sent Jones with a considerable detachment to intercept him. Ormonde saw them drawn up on a hill; though their numbers were inferior to his own, he preferred to avoid an engagement, distrusting many of Inchiquin's men. In the dusk of the evening he set off in another direction, and fetching a compass over the mountains of Wicklow, he arrived, after two days' march, at Leighlinbridge. There Colonel Butler, who had escaped by swimming across the ferry, brought him news of the fall of Wexford.

To Ormonde the fall of Wexford was a severe shock; it was wholly unexpected by him, and disconcerted all his plans, for he calculated that the siege of so strong a place would have delayed Cromwell's advance for several weeks, and that in the meantime he could procure such aid from Ulster and Munster as would make him a match for the Parliamentary army. This was not the only mortification he experienced; he learned almost at the same time of the successes of Coote and Venables in the north, and of attempts at revolt made by the southern garrisons. All his plans were disarranged. In his anger he reproached the Catholics with deserting the cause of the King; "They who stood so rigidly with the King upon religion, and, as they called it, on the splendor of it, now could with difficulty be withheld from sending commissioners to Cromwell to entreat him to make stables and hospitals of their churches."

CHAPTER XIV

THE ATTEMPT ON DUNCANNON.

Ireton sent to attempt Duncannon — Its Importance — Roche the Governor — Wogan appointed in his Place — Plan of Defence — Its Success — Reinforcements from Dublin — Inchiquin tries to intercept them — Fight at Glascarrig.

AFTER the capture of Wexford, Cromwell sent Ireton to lay siege to Duncannon. This fort is situated on a rock projecting from the eastern side of the entrance to Waterford harbor, eleven miles southeast of the city. On the face looking towards the sea it was defended by three batteries; on the land side it was protected by a deep ditch, and behind there was a massive and precipitous rampart hollowed out of the rock; on this two watch towers were built. There were also two sally-ports, and between them a draw-bridge. The whole covered about four acres. It had been specially strengthened when the Spaniards threatened a descent in 1558. The possession of it was of the greatest importance to the Royalists, as it secured to them the only approach by water to Waterford, and made them masters of the surrounding country.[1] During the siege of Wexford Ormonde went to take an exact survey of its condition. He distributed money among the soldiers, and assured them that their welfare would be a constant care to him, and that immediate relief would be sent to them. Indeed, so important did he consider the place that he resolved, in case Lieutenant-General Ferrall arrived before its fall with the forces sent by Owen Roe O'Neill, to venture a battle rather than lose it. He appointed Colonel Edward Wogan[2] governor, in place of Captain Thomas Roach, who candidly declared himself unequal to the duties of such a critical position. The Commissioners who had put him in command there, resented the change as a breach of the Articles of the Peace

---

[1] It was taken, after two months' siege, in March, 1645, owing to the valor and skill of General Thomas Preston, who had learned the art of war in Flanders, "that far-famed academy of Mars." Lord Esmonde held it at that time for the parliament. A detailed account of the siege, taken from the diary of Geoffrey Baron, who was present, is given by his brother, Father Bonaventure Baron, in his *Siege of Duncannon*. See Ware's *Writers of Ireland*, p. 253.

[2] Wogan, when a youth of fifteen, had been, by the corruption of his nearest friends, engaged in the parliament service against the King, and had a command of a troop of horse under Ireton; but he abjured that party upon the execution of Charles I., and was appointed by Ormonde to the command of his own guards. He fought very bravely at the battle of Rathmines. He left Ireland with Ormonde in December, 1650. On hearing that the royal standard was set up in the Highlands of Scotland, he took leave of Charles II., who was then at Paris, passed into England, assembled a body of cavaliers at Barnet near London, and traversed the whole of England by marches conducted with so much skill, dexterity and spirit, that he safely united his handful of horsemen with the Highlanders then in arms. After several months of desultory warfare, in which Wogan's skill and courage gained him the highest reputation, he had the misfortune to be wounded in a dangerous manner, and no surgical aid being at hand, he terminated his short but glorious career. See Scott's *Waverly*, chap 29, and Clarendon's *Hist. of the Rebellion*, vol. iii. p. 507.

and an attempt to shake off their authority. But Ormonde found means to elude their objections, and Wogan was permitted to remain. One hundred and twenty English officers of Ormonde's life-guard, whose fidelity had been well tried by long service on the King's side, were sent to aid in the defence. From the citizens of Waterford he got forty barrels of powder and a sufficient quantity of provisions to enable the besieged to make a lengthened resistance. Lord Castlehaven was sent to consult with the Governor on the plan of defence to be followed ; and seeing the situation of the besieging force, they resolved on making a sally on a party of foot belonging to the enemy that lay encamped in the neighborhood.

Castlehaven gives the following account of this affair in his *Memoirs:*

"The Marquis of Ormonde had returned over the bridge at Ross, and encamped on the Kilkenny side. From thence he sent me to Passage,[1] in the county of Waterford, over against Ballyhask, to look after the relieving of Duncannon, besieged by some of Cromwell's people. I think Ireton commanded. And though there were parliament ships before it, I ventured one morning with a boat, and got into the place to the governor, a brave gentleman, one Colonel Wogan, whom the Lord Lieutenant had sent some time before thither to command : and with him, besides the Irish garrison, about a hundred English officers who had served the King in the wars of England. This gentleman, from the highest part of the rampart, showed me how the enemy lay. After I had well considered all, I offered to send him that night, by sea, eighty horses with saddles and pistols, if he could mount them with so many of his English officers, and before day, with them and some foot, make a sharp sally upon the enemy. He liked the proposal extremely, but doubted much my performance, it being about three miles by sea. I desired him to leave that to me, and assured him he should shortly be satisfied of what I undertook. Having thus concluded, I took my boat, returned, and immediately set myself to my business that I might lose no time, because the tide served at the beginning of the night; and having provided boats, I commanded eighty horse to go to the sea-side. I caused them to be boated out of hand and sent them away. They all came to Duncannon safe and undiscovered: all was executed as designed, great slaughter made and the cannon seized. For the confusion among the enemy was great, by reason that they judged it the falling in of an army from abroad, seeing horses come against them, and knowing of none in the fort. Our people retiring before day, the enemy raised the siege in the morning and marched off."

Cromwell's army was already much weakened by the manning of the garrisons in the towns and forts that had surrendered to his army. The country sickness, the effect of a climate especially injurious in the winter season to strangers, was spreading rapidly through the army. Colonel Horton, "a person of great integrity and courage," who had rendered good service in the course of the previous summer in quelling some of the Welsh mutineers, had fallen a victim to it. It was found necessary to send for a reinforcement from Dublin, where many of the soldiers that had been disabled by sickness and wounds had been left behind. About 800 foot and 350 horse accordingly set out, under the command of Major Nelson. They were supported by two troops of Colonel Michael Jones' regiment, under Major Meredith and Captain Otway. They reached Arklow on the first of November.

---

[1] Passage is on the Waterford side of the river, Ballyhack on the Wexford side, about three miles above Duncannon. Ballyhack castle is still standing ; only a small part of the castle of Passage is remaining ; both are close to the water's edge.

A week before, Ormonde, who was then at Kilkenny, had got information from Sir Luke Fitzgerald, that a party of 1,200 foot and 300
hors: was about to march towards Wexford to Cromwell's aid, and
might easily be captured. A council of war was held. With the consent of the Commissioners of Trust, it was agreed that Inchiquin,
who then lay at Tinnehinch in the county of Carlow, should be
despatched through Scollagh Pass with 1,600 foot and 600 horse to
intercept them. He left Tinnehinch, and advanced southward through
the Pass. Cromwell was informed by his spies of Inchiquin's movements, and sent a messenger to warn his friends of the danger; he
bade them march in close order and make all possible haste to join
him at Wexford.

They rested for two days at Arklow to recruit themselves and
make arrangements to have a strong detachment of horse from the
army sent to meet them at Glascarrig,[1] midway between Arklow and
Wexford, where they intended to take up their quarters for the night.
The plan failed; their friends did not meet them at the appointed
place. Yet knowing that the enemy was not far off, they thought it
better, however weary they were, to march seven miles further towards
Wexford and pass the night there : in this way they hoped to deceive
the enemy, who they were told, was lying somewhere in the neighborhood, intending to fall on their quarters early the next morning.
Inchiquin had information from his scouts of their movements. He
hurried off with all his horse and a few light foot in pursuit; the rest
of the foot were ordered to follow with all possible speed. Within
seven miles of Wexford the alarm of his approach was first given, one
of the enemy's officers, who rode some distance in front of his troop,
having caught sight of the cavalry marching after them. Inchiquin,
seeing he had overtaken them, slackened his pace and put his troops
in line. This gave them ample time to form. They drew up their
horse in six single divisions; 160 musketeers were placed on the flanks
of the forward divisions of the horse, 80 on each flank; the main
body of the foot was placed· in the rear. This order they were able
to keep for some time, as the strand was narrow, having on one side
a steep sand-bank and on the other the sea. Such a position was
advantageous to them, since it prevented Inchiquin's horse from
attacking them in full force. The fight began by a volley from the
musketeers; Meredith's horse charging immediately after. The first
division of Inchiquin's men held their ground for some time, and then
fell back in good order to the right and left. The second division, a·
fresh body of 150 horse next advanced against the enemy. These,
being somewhat thrown into disorder by the former charge, were
driven back; most of them ran off till they came to the main body,
who, letting their own horse pass by, waited steadily until the assailants were within pistol-shot, and opened on them a well-directed fire.
Several of the officers were killed. The rest retired in great confusion. Lieutenant Warren, of Cromwell's regiment, who had been in
the midst of the enemy, coming up, cried out that Inchiquin's troops

---

[1] Here "the force of Galls" landed with Dermot MacMorrough, in 1167.

were in great disorder, and called on his men to charge. The horse again advanced. Inchiquin received the charge, but his lines were soon broken. Two of his standards were taken. The loss on both sides was small ;[1] yet trifling as this success was, it tended to keep up the respect with which Cromwell had hitherto awed his enemies. Inchiquin rejoined his foot, and returned to Ormonde at Thomas-town.

[1] "I do not hear that we have two men killed, and but one mortally wounded, and not five that are taken prisoners." Letter of Cromwell to Lenthal, from Ross, Nov. 14th.

. CHAPTER XV.

THE SIEGE OF ROSS.

Cromwell encamps before Ross — Taaffe Governor — Summons to Surrender — The Three-Bullet Gate — No Toleration — No Quarter for Irishmen — No Mercy for Priests — Surrender of the Town — Terms of Surrender — Cromwell's Lodging at Ross.

CROMWELL's soldiers were already weary of the hardships of the winter's campaign, and frequently showed a disposition to mutiny.[1] He quieted them with the assurance that the expedition to Ross should be the last service demanded of them for the year, and that, after the capture of that town, they should go into winter quarters. On the 15th of October he left Wexford. Ballyhaly castle,[2] the residence of the Cheevers family, was besieged; it was destroyed with the exception of the towers, of which there were formerly four. Detachments were sent to Tintern and Dunbrody, which reduced the garrisons there.[3] Two days later, he encamped before New Ross, a walled town situated on the river Barrow, "a very pleasant and commodious river, bearing vessels of a heavy burden." He had with him but three pieces of cannon. Ormonde sent Sir Lucas Taaffe,[4] whose abilities he overrated, with 1,500 foot to defend the place — there were already 1,000 foot garrisoning the town — and hearing of Cromwell's advance, he marched with his army towards Ross, and encamped on the other side of the river, in view of the English army. The enemy, being separated by the river, could offer no opposition to his

---

[1] " His army decays incredibly and will become very inconsiderable unless it be strongly and timely recruited out of England, and had been already wasted, had not towns been poorly given him, and the winter proved fairer than in man's memory any winter hath been." State of Armies in Ireland, in *Aphor. Disc.*, vol. ii. p. 466.

[2] In the parish of Kilturk and barony of Bargy. It was given to Colonel Bunbury, the Cheevers family being obliged to "transplant" to Killyan, in the county of Galway. The castle and estates were sold by the Bunbury family early in the last century. Only one of the towers remains. See *Kilk. Arch. Journal*, for 1863, p. 319.

[3] *Brief Chronicle*, p. 5. These were both Cistercian abbeys. Tintern was founded by William Marshal, Earl of Pembroke, in 1200, in thanksgiving to the B. V. Mary for having saved him from shipwreck. Hence it was called Sancta Maria de Voto. Dunbrody was founded by Hervey de Monte Marisco in 1182; it was called Sancta Maria de Portu. Archdall's *Monasticon*, pp. 752 and 736.

[4] He was the third son of Lord Taaffe. After Cromwell's reduction of the kingdom, he submitted with his brother Francis, a Colonel of the Confederate army, and the forces under their command, upon articles concluded at Dunmore; yet he was excepted from pardon for life or estate. Being forced to leave Ireland, he served for some time as colonel in Italy and Spain. He died in Ireland and was buried at Ballymote. Archdall's *Peerage*, vol. iv. p. 293. By the author of the *Aphor. Disc.*, he is called "a common, cogging gamester, a routebanke, and temporiser fit for any stamp, a prime member of Ormonde's party and faction." Vol. i. pp. 145 and 173.

coming. Before taking over the command, Taaffe came to the camp'
and asked for an order under the Lord Lieutenant's hand for the de‑
fence of the town as long as it was possible ; and for the surrender
when it should be decided by a council of the chief officers that it
could hold out no longer.

On his arrival before the town, Cromwell sent the following sum‑
mons to the Governor : —

(1.) For the Commander-in-Chief in Ross. These :

Before Ross, 17th October, 1649.

S<small>IR</small>,
    Since my coming into Ireland, I have this witness for myself, that I have
endeavored to avoid effusion of blood ; having been before no place to which such
terms have not been first sent as might have turned to the good and preservation
of those to whom they were offered ; this being my principle, that the people and
places where I come may not suffer, except through their own wilfulness.

    To the end I may observe the like course with this place and the people therein,
I do hereby summon you to deliver the town of Ross into my hands, to the use of
the Parliament of England. Expecting your speedy answer,
                     I rest your servant,
                             O<small>LIVER</small> C<small>ROMWELL</small>.

The trumpeter who carried the summons was not allowed to
enter the town ; his message was received at the gates, and he was
told that an answer would be given in due time. The batteries ot
the besieging army were therefore got ready during the night, and
preparations made for storming the outworks. Early on the morning
of Friday, the 19th, the large guns began to play. Soon after the
Governor sent the following answer to the summons : —

(2.) For General Cromwell, or, in his absence, for the Commander-in-Chief of the
        Army now encamped before Ross.

Ross, 19th October, 1649.

S<small>IR</small>,
    I received a summons from you the first day you appeared before this place,
which should have been answered ere now, had not other occasions interrupted me.
And although I am now in far better condition to defend this place than I was at that
time, yet am I, upon the considerations offered in your summons, content to enter‑
tain a treaty, and to receive from you those conditions that may be safe and honor‑
able for me to accept of. Which, if you listen to, I desire that pledges on both sides
may be sent for performance of such articles as may be agreed upon ; and that all
acts of hostility may cease on both sides, and each party keep within their distance.
To this your immediate resolution is expected by,
                     Sir, your servant,
                             L<small>UCAS</small> T<small>AAFFE</small>.

To which Cromwell immediately replied : —

(3.) For the Governor in Ross. These :

Before Ross, 19th October, 1649.

S<small>IR</small>,
    If you like to march away with those under your command, with their arms,
bag and baggage, and with drums and colors, and shall deliver up the town to me,
I shall give caution to perform these conditions, expecting the like from you. As
to the inhabitants, they shall be permitted to live peaceably, free from the injury and
violence of the soldier.

If you like hereof, you can tell how to let me know your mind, notwithstand-ing my refusal of a cessation. By these you will see the reality of my intentions to save blood, and preserve the place from ruin.

        I rest your servant,

            OLIVER CROMWELL.

The batteries still continued to play, and a breach was soon made in the wall, close by the Three Bullet gate. The men were drawn out in line, ready to advance for the storm, Lieutenant-Colonel Ingolds-by being chosen by lot to lead them. Taaffe, seeing how matters stood sent the following reply : —

    (4.) For General Cromwell. These:

           Ross, 19th October, 1649.

SIR,

   There wants but little of what I would propose: which is, that such towns-men as have a desire to depart may have liberty within a convenient time to carry away themselves and their goods; and liberty of conscience to such as shall stay; and that I may carry away such artillery and ammunition as I have in my command. If you be inclined to this, I will send upon your honor, as a safe conduct, an officer to conclude with you. To which your immediate answer is expected by,

        Sir, your servant,

           LUCAS TAAFFE.[1]

To understand the full meaning of Cromwell's answer to the above letter, we must call to mind the spirit that animated the Puri-tans, and the cruelties which they perpetrated on Catholics. Some time before the rebellion broke out, it was confidently asserted that Sir John Clotworthy, who well knew the designs of the faction that governed the House of Commons in England, had declared in a speech, that the conversion of the Papists was only to be effected by the Bible in one hand and the sword in the other. Sir William Parsons positively asserted that within a twelvemonth no Catholic should be seen in Ireland. On the 8th of December, 1641, both Houses of the English Parliament passed a joint declaration, in answer to the demand of the Irish for the full exercise of their religion, that they would born in Ireland out of all capitulations, agreements, and compositions

---

[1] Bate says his spirit was cowed by the noise of six or seven shots. *Elenchus,* &c. pt. 2, p. 28. The tradition in the town is, that he surrendered after the besiegers had fired only three shots; hence the name given to the gate. It was formerly called the " Ladies' Gate "; by some it is thought to have been the same which was built to commemorate the generous gifts of the ladies of Ross towards the building of the walls :

     " Then they said a gate they'd make,
     Called the Ladies' for their sake."

See Appendix vi. : " The Walling of Ross." This beautiful specimen of Early English architecture was pulled down by the Corporation in 1845. A stone fixed in the wall of a corn-store near the site bears the following inscription, recording the wit as well as the taste of that body : —

      This is the west side of
      Bewly Gate, taken down
      In the year 1845, by consent
      Of the Town Commissioners.

Lord Mountjoy, colonel of the Dublin militia, was killed on the same spot when the town was attacked on the 5th of June, 1798. See *Kilk. Arch. Journal* for 1858, p. 206. The Market gate also was taken down some years ago.

hereafter to be made with the enemy; and upon taking of every such Irishman and Papist born in Ireland, forthwith to put such persons to death. On the 23d December, 1646, the Scotch parliament ordained that the Irish prisoners taken at and after the battle of Philipshaugh in all the prisons of the kingdom, should be executed without any assize or. process, conformably to the treaty between the two king- never give their assent to any toleration of the Papist religion in Ire- land, or in any other part of his Majesty's dominions. On the 24th of October, 1644, the parliament of England made an ordinance against giving of any quarter to any Irishman or to any Papist born in Ireland, taken in hostility against the parliament by sea or land. Strict orders were given to the Lord General, Lord Admiral, and all other officers by sea and land, to except all Irishmen and all Papists doms passed in act. "The Parliamentary party," says Clarendon, "had grounded their own authority and strength upon such found- ations as were inconsistent with any toleration of the Catholic religion, and even with any humanity to the Irish nation, and more especially to those of the old native extraction, the whole race whereof they had upon the matter sworn to an utter exterpation." "The orders of the parliament," says Borlase, " were excellently well executed." A con- temporary writer says, the Irish Puritans rioted in the promiscuous slaughter of women, old men, and children, and the English auxiliaries openly avowed that they would strain every nerve to extirpate with- out mercy the Irish race. Some even talked, like Antiochus concern- ing Jerusalem, of making Ireland the common burying-place of the Irish people. Captain Swanly took a transport bound from Ireland to England with 150 men on board, sent by Ormonde to the King. He selected 70 of his captives and threw them overboard, because they were Irish. In the journals of the House of Commons we find that he was called into the House, and had thanks given him for his good service, and a chain of gold to the value of £200. For priests, above all, there was no mercy. The Lords Justices Borlase and Par- sons, in the beginning of the rebellion, had forbidden any quarters to be given to those Catholics whom they found in arms, and principally all priests, as being known incendiaries of the rebellion and prime actors in exemplary cruelty. When any forces surrendered, they were always excepted; they were thenceforth out of protection, to be treated as enemies that had not surrendered. Pym boasted that not a priest would be left in Ireland. " We have three beasts to destroy, that lay burdens on us," said one of the party; " the first is a wolf, on whom we lay five pounds a head; the second beast is a priest, on whose head we lay ten pounds; if he be eminent, more; the third beast is a Tory." "Cromwell," says Lord Macaulay, " resolved to put an end to that conflict of races and religions which had so long distracted Ireland, by making the English and Protestant population decidedly predominant. For this end he gave the rein to the fierce enthusiasm of his followers, waged war resembling that which Israel waged on the Canaanites, and smote the idolaters with the edge of the sword." " During the ten years of Cromwell's government," says Mr. Froude, " the priests and their works were at an end."

(5.) For the Governor in Ross: These:

Before Ross, 19th October, 1649.

SIR,

To what I formerly offered, I shall make good. As for your carrying away any artillery or ammunition that you brought not in with you, or hath not come to you since you had the command of that place, I must deny you that, expecting you to leave it as you found it.

For that which you mention concerning liberty of conscience, I meddle not with any man's conscience. But if by liberty of conscience you mean a liberty to exercise the Mass, I judge it best to use plain dealing, and to let you know, where the Parliament of England have power, that will not be allowed of. As for such of the townsmen who desire to depart and carry away themselves and goods, as you express, I engage myself, they shall have three months' time so to do; and in the meantime shall be protected from violence in their persons and goods, as others under the obedience of the Parliament.

If you accept of this offer, I engage my honor for a punctual performance hereof. I rest your servant,

OLIVER CROMWELL.

(6.) For General Cromwell.

October 19th, 1649.

SIR,

I am content to yield up this place upon the terms offered in your last and first letters. And if you please to send your safe conduct to such as I shall appoint to perfect these conditions, I shall, on receipt thereof, send them to you. In the interval, to cease all acts of hostility, and that all parties keep their own ground, until matters receive a full end. And so remains,

Sir, your servant,

LUCAS TAAFFE.

(7.) For the Governor of Ross.

October 19th, 1649.

SIR,

You have my hand and honor engaged to perform what I offered in my first and last letters; which I shall inviolably observe. I expect you to send me immediately four persons of such quality as may be hostages for your performance; for whom you have this safe conduct enclosed, into which you may insert their names. Without which I shall not cease acts of hostility. If anything happen by your delay to your prejudice, it will not be my fault. Those you send may see the conditions perfected. Whilst I forbear acts of hostility, I expect you forbear all actings within. I rest,

Your servant,

OLIVER CROMWELL.

"This," says an old London newspaper, "was the last message between them, the Governor sending out his four hostages to compose and perfect the agreement, and hereupon the batteries ceased, and our intentions to storm the town were disappointed. Thus, within the space of three days, we had possession of this place, without the effusion of blood; it being a very considerable place, and very good quarter for the refreshment of our soldiers. The enemy marched over the river to the other side, and did not come out on that side of the town where we had encamped." Some five hundred English soldiers that were in the town, most of them the Munster forces, entered the services of the parliament: the rest, to the number of 1,500, followed Taaffe over the river to Kilkenny.

After garrisoning Ross, Ormonde set off for Kilkenny, to meet a part of Owen Roe's army coming to join him under Hugh O'Neill. On the way the next morning, October 19th, he heard the report of Cromwell's cannon, but he had no notion that the town would surrender so soon.

The following were the terms of surrender : —

Articles concluded and agreed upon by and between the Right Honorable the Lord Lieutenant of Ireland of the one part, and the Governor of Ross of the other part, the 19th October, 1649: —

1. It is concluded and agreed, That the Governor of Ross, with all his command, may march into Kilkenny or Leighlin bridge, with their arms, bag and baggages, drums beating, colors flying, bullet in bouche, bandoliers full of powder, and matches lighted at both ends, provided they march thither in three days, and that no act of hostility be committed during the said time.

2. It is concluded and agreed, That such townsmen as desire to depart and to carry away themselves and their goods, shall have three months' time so to do; and in the mean time shall be preserved from violence in their persons and goods, as others under the obedience of the Parliament of England; and that a convoy may be sent with them to secure them in their journeys.

3. It is concluded and agreed, That the inhabitants shall be permitted to live peacefully, and enjoy their goods and estates free from the injury and violence of the soldiers.

4. In consideration whereof, the Governor of Ross is to surrender into my hands the town of Ross, artillery, arms, ammunition, and other utensils of war that are therein, by three of the clock this present day, except such as were brought in by the said Governor, or such as came in since he had the command thereof; and by two of the clock to permit the Lord Lieutenant to put three hundred men into the block-house, gate-house near the breach, and the white tower near the same.

5. For the performance of the Articles on the said Governor's side, he is to deliver four such hostages as I shall approve of.

JAMES CRARFORD, ⎫ *Commissioners*
MATH. LYNELL,   ⎪   *and*
THOMAS GAYNAN, ⎬ *hostages for*
MATH. DORMER, ⎭ *the Governor.*

I do approve and conform these articles.

LUCAS TAAFFE.

An extension of these articles was afterwards granted : —

I do hereby grant and desire that the promises of protection and all other benefits granted to the inhabitants of the town of Ross in the third article concluded upon the surrender of the said town, shall be extended and continued to the said inhabitants, as well after the three months mentioned in the second of the said articles as during that space, they behaving themselves peaceably and faithfully as becometh persons under protection, submitting to the authority of the Parliament of England.
Given at Ross the thirteenth day of November, 1649.

OLIVER CROMWELL.

While Cromwell did continue in Ross, he lodged in the house of the sovereign, Francis Dormer, where did hang a picture of my Lord of Ormonde. Cromwell gazing on it, asked who it was that it represented? Being told, he said, "The man whom the picture concerned was more like a huntsman than any way a soldier;" which was most true, and the very party so inclined by education and nature. Here, too, the churches were plundered.[1] When leaving, he appointed Colonel Daniel Axtell governor of the town.[2]

During the siege, or soon after, a party was sent to seize Ballycerogue castle, five miles south of Ross, then in the possession of the Sutton family. The inmates refused to surrender, and when an attempt was made to capture it, they offered a successful resistance. The assailants, angered at their repulse, set fire to it; twenty-three of the family were consumed in the flames, only two escaped.[3]

The following is Cromwell's official account to the speaker of the parliament of England, dated Ross, October 25th, 1649:

"Since my last from Wexford we marched to Ross, a walled town situated upon the Barrow, a port-town, up to which a ship of seven or eight hundred tons may come.

"We came before it upon Wednesday, the 17th instant, with three pieces of cannon. That evening I sent a summons; Major-General Taaffe being governor, refused to admit my trumpet within the town; but took the summons in, returning me no answer. I did hear that near 1,000 foot had been put into this place some few days before my coming to it. The next day was spent in making preparations for our battery; and in our view there were boated over from the other side of the river, of English, Scotch, and Irish, 1,500 more: Ormonde, Castlehaven, and the Lord of Ardes being on the other side of the water to cause it to be done.

"That night we planted our battery, which began to play early the next morning. The governor immediately sent forth an answer to my summons; copies of all which I make bold to trouble you with; the rather because you may see how God pulls down proud stomachs. The governor desired commissioners might treat, and that in the meantime there might be a ceasing of acts of hostility on both sides. Which I refused; sending in word, that if he would march away with arms, bag and baggage, and give me hostages for performance, he should. Indeed, he might have done it without my leave, by the advantage of the river. He insisted upon having the cannon with him, which I would not yield unto, but required the leaving the artillery and ammunition; which he was content to do, and marched away, leaving the great artillery and ammunition in the stores to me. When they marched away, at least 500 English, many of them of the Munster forces, came to us.

"Ormonde is at Kilkenny, Inchiquin in Munster, Henry O'Neill, Owen Roe's son, is come up to Kilkenny, with near 2,000 horse and foot, with whom and Ormonde there is now a perfect conjunction. So that now I trust some angry friends will think it high time to take off their jealousy from those to whom they ought to exercise more charity.

"The rendition of this garrison was a seasonable mercy, as giving us an opportunity towards Munster; and is for the present a very good refreshment for our men. We are able to say nothing as to all this, but that the Lord is still pleased to own a company of poor, worthless creatures, for which we desire his name to be

---

[1] The bell in the Town Hall to be given back to Father Anthony Mulloy for the Franciscan Abbey of New Ross, formerly deprived thereof by Oliver Cromwell. *Council Book of New Ross Corporation*, anno 1687.

[2] Lieutenant Colonel Axtell, governor of Ross, hath marched from Ross into the rebels' quarters so far as the county of Kilkenny, and from thence into other parts, where he hath been and done good service, and brought away both prisoners and good booty. *Perfect Diurnal*, Jan. 9th, 1650.

[3] *Annuary of the Kilk. Arch. Soc.* for 1855, p 164. Ballycerogue castle was probably built by Roger de Sutton, who came with Robert Fitzstephen to Ireland, and got a grant of land in the barony of Shelburne. William Sutton of Ballycerogue was one of the Commons' representatatives at the General Assembly of the Confederate Catholics held at Kilkenny in 1647. See Ledwich's *Irishtown, &c.*, p. 471. A considerable portion of the castle is still standing.

magnified, and the hearts of all concerned may be provoked to walk worthy of such continued favors. This is the earnest desire of

"Your most humble servant,

"OLIVER CROMWELL."

On the 30th of October it was ordered by the parliament, "that it be referred to the Lord Mayor of the city of London to take care to disperse the said letters and transactions to all the ministers within London and the Liberties, who are required respectively to read the same in their respective congregations on Thursday next, and to take notice of this great and wonderful mercy in giving in the fort and town of Wexford, together with the haven there and the shipping in it, as in addition to the former mercies, for which that day was set apart, and to return all humble thanks to Almighty God for the same."

CHAPTER XVI.

REVOLT OF THE MUNSTER GARRISONS.

Disaffection of the Southern Towns — The English Plantation — Lord Broghill — Commission from the King — Visit of Cromwell — Terms offered him by the Parliament — Return to Ireland — His Retainers — Townsend — Revolt of the Garrisons of Youghal and Cork — Letter of Colonel Deane — Sir Robert Stirling Governor — Flight of Lady Fanshaw — Relation of Colonel Ryves.

CROMWELL's uninterrupted successes brought about the revolt of many of the English garrisons throughout the country, then under the command of Inchiquin in the King's interest. The Parliament had many adherents in the south, with whom Cromwell was " in intelligence," and on whose support he relied. We have already seen that his original design was to land in Munster. The disaffection of the southern towns was chiefly due to the contrivance of Lord Broghill,[1] afterwards Earl of Orrery, third son of Richard Boyle, first Earl of Cork. He was born at Lismore in 1621 ; there he was brought up by his father in the strictest principles of Puritanism. At the beginning of the rebellion he was placed at the head of the troops which his father had raised among the English planters.[2] In the field he displayed both valor and ability. For some time he acted under the Parliamentary commanders ; but the trial and execution of the King made him abandon his new companions in arms. Besides, he was disgusted at the legal toleration granted at the time to the Catholic religion, which he believed to be both sinful against God and injurious to the state. He left Ireland, and withdrew to Marston Bigod, his seat in Somersetshire. There he lived for some time in retirement. He continued, however, to correspond with Ormonde, whose real sentiments accorded with his own. At length, growing weary of repose, he determined to engage again in public life. Very soon after he received a letter from the exiled King, informing him that he had provided two small ships to accompany him to Ireland ; that he knew what great influence the Boyle family had among the Protestants of the south, and would much desire his company. Broghill was flattered by the confidence shown him, and replied that he would soon pay a visit to his Majesty. Some of his letters were intercepted by the vigilance of Cromwell, and copies of them laid before the Parliament, the originals

---

[1] Tuaithe Brothail, i. e. district of Broghill, the name of a manor and castle a little to the west of Charleville, in the county of Cork, formerly belonging to the Fitzgeralds. See Smith's *History of Cork*, vol. i. p. 305 ; Cork, 1815.

[2] He was made baron of Broghill in his eighth year. He was taken prisoner at the battle of Liscarroll, Sept. 3d, 1642, but afterwards rescued by his party. In the same battle his second brother, Lord Kinalmeaky, was killed. His youngest brother was the philosopher, Robert Boyle. Archdall's *Peerage*, vol. i. p. 163. He died in 1679, and is buried in the tomb of the Boyle family in St. Mary's church, Youghal.

having been forwarded to their addresses. Under pretence of ill health he had obtained through the influence of his friend, the Earl of Warwick, permission to pass beyond the seas, in order to visit the German baths. His real intention was to go to Holland and obtain from the King a commission to levy troops in Ireland, in the hope that by displaying zeal in the royal cause, he might get back some part of his estates which had been forfeited.[1] On his way he passed through London. Cromwell, who was then making preparations for the Irish expedition, heard of his arrival, and being anxious to gain him over to the Parliamentary party, sent an officer with a request to know at what hour it would be convenient for his Lordship to receive a visit from the General, as he wished much to converse with him. As Broghill had no previous acquaintance with Cromwell, he was astonished at receiving such a message, and declared that there must be some mistake ; he told the messenger to present his duty to his master, adding that he would wait on him at whatever hour he might appoint. A few minutes after Cromwell entered the room. He began by expressing a great regard for Broghill, and assured him that the great esteem he had for his Lordship was the sole motive for his coming. His Lordship's designs, he said, were well known to the Council of State, and they were fully aware that, instead of proceeding to Spa for his recovery from the gout, he was on his way to Charles Stuart, to obtain a commission to raise men and excite an insurrection in Ireland. Broghill protested that he was innocent of such a crime and incapable of playing so base a part ; he entreated the General to give no heed to such idle reports. Cromwell, however, insisted that he had ample proof of the truth of all he stated, and produced copies of the letters which had been intercepted ; he added, that the Council of State had actually given orders that he should be arrested on his arrival in London and sent to the Tower ; that he had himself interposed, and with some difficulty obtained permission to confer with his Lordship, with a view of diverting him from his design. Broghill found it impossible to dissemble any longer ; he thanked Cromwell for his kindness, and asked his advice. Cromwell replied, that, though till then unacquainted with him personally, he was no stranger to the high reputation he had earned in the Irish wars ; that, as he was himself now appointed commander in Ireland, he had obtained leave from the Council to offer his Lordship a general officer's command ; no oath or engagement should be pressed on him ; he should only be required to fight against the native Irish. Broghill asked for a short time to deliberate. He was plainly told that he must make up his mind on the spot, for it was the purpose of the Council to imprison him should he hesitate to accept these terms. He closed with the offer, and later became the firm adherent and even a personal friend of the Protector.[1]

[1] "The earl of Cork saith he expects his brother. Lord Broghill, here every day, and that he comes with intention to adhere to the King's friends in Ireland upon some inv'ta 'on from your excellency." Letter of Nicholas to Ormonde, from Caen, April 8th, 1649.

[2] Morrice's *Memoirs*, prefixed to Lord Orrery's *State Letter*, p. 9 ; London, 1742. "This earl," says King James in his *Memoirs*. "was famous for changing parties so often, and for making a speech to Cromwell to take the title of King ; his tongue was well hung.

He was told to hasten to Bristol where men should be sent him, and, in due time, ships would call for his transportation; the main body of the army would follow him without delay. He kept his promise well, for when Broghill's name occurs in Irish history, it seems ever a prelude of woe to the Irish people. On his arrival in Ireland,[1] he raised a well-appointed body of 1,500 foot and a troop of horse, among the retainers of his family, English settlers, chiefly from Gloucester, Somerset and Devon, whom his father had planted on the confiscated lands of Gerald, the great Earl of Desmond, purchased by him from Sir Walter Raleigh and other undertakers in Munster.[2] Of these, many having adopted Puritan principles, had been obliged to fly from their homes in England, on account of the heavy penalties to which all professing such opinions were subjected; during the Civil War they were the most decided enemies of the Stuarts. Through these he soon opened a communication with the officers of the different garrisons in the south, who were ready to embrace the first opportunity that offered of breaking what they termed an unholy alliance with the Confederate Catholics.[3]

Colonel Richard Townsend was the chief agent now employed to corrupt the southern garrisons and to induce them to revolt.[4] A year before, he had been found engaged in intrigues of the same nature, and he was in consequence deprived of the command which he held.[5] When he heard of the expedition that was preparing for Ireland, he professed a great hatred of the republican party; in reality, he was a spy sent over by Cromwell to corrupt the Munster army. In spite of his previous misconduct he was restored to his command by Inchi-

---

he had some good parts, and he was reckoned so cunning a man, that nobody would visit him or believe what he said." Macpherson's *Original Papers*, vol. i. p. 43, quoted in Curry's *Review*, &c., vol. ii. p. 102.

[1] Carte says he landed at Wexford in October, 1649.

[2] See O'Flanagan's *Munster Blackwater*, p. 8; London, 1844. "The county of Cork, by the noble plantations made by the earl of that name, became the best inhabited with English of any county in that kingdom." Cox's *Hib. Angl.*, Reign of Charles I., p. 95.

[3] "Upon this occasion I must needs say that, in the bringing in of divers garrisons, his lordship hath been most eminently serviceable unto you; and I do earnestly and humbly desire he may be taken into consideration, his lordship having shrunk from your interest, though under as great trials and necessities as any man, he having his whole fortune under the power of the enemy, which was in Ireland, and that little in England so engaged that I dare say his wants were scarce to be paralleled; and as yet his estate lies in those countries which are in the enemy's power. Sir, I take no pleasure to mention those things of charge; but where eminent services are done, and those enabling the State to give marks of their favor and good acceptance, I trust it will be accounted no fault in me to represent the merits of men to you." Cromwell to Lenthal, Dec. 19th, 1649, in *Aphor. Disc.*, vol. ii. p. 467, appendix 44.

[4] See in Appendix vii. the depositions of each of the conspirators in reference to the part he took in the revolt and capture of the Munster garrisons.

[5] In November, 1648, Colonel Townsend and Colonel Doyley, in the name of the Munster army, sent propositions to the parliament of England. Colonel Temple arrived in the harbor of Kinsale with two frigates, being sent by the Committee of Derby House to treat with them. Ormonde intended to seize them and deprive them of their command. They did not care to stand a trial before a court martial, so quitted their employments and departed for England. *Life of Ormonde*, vol ii. p. 47. Later he passed patents for large estates in the south west of the county of Cork. He was member for Baltimore in the Irish parliament of 1661, and high sheriff of the county in 1671. He was the ancestor of the Castletownsend family. Burke's *Landed Gentry*, p. 1507; London, 1863.

quin, who, constantly changing sides himself for the most trivial reasons, thought that those under his command should be models of fidelity and honor. About the end of September an attempt was made by him and Colonels Gifford and Warden, to get hold of the town of Youghal and to seize on Inchiquin. Sir Piercy Smith, the governor, was also one of the conspirators. An officer to whom they had made known their plans in the hope of gaining him over, rode off in all haste to Castle Lyons, where Inchiquin then was, and told him of the intended revolt. They were immediately seized and imprisoned. Sir Piercy Smith, who had got timely notice of their capture, seized on Colonel Wogan and some Royalists, who were then in the town, and stood upon the defence. Inchiquin invested the place. Smith, seeing that Cromwell could send him no aid, offered to submit upon a promise of indemnity for himself, of release of the officers, and the removal of the Royalists. Either because he had not the means of reducing the place by force, or because he preferred gaining them over by fair means, Inchiquin agreed to these terms.

On the 16th of October the garrison and citizens of Cork threw off their allegiance to the King. The garrison was composed entirely of English ; Inchiquin having stipulated that he should have entire control over the garrisons, had refused to allow any Irish troops to remain within the walled towns. They could not endure the thought of joining with the Irish against their own countrymen ;[1] they declared that the quarrel was no longer between the King and the parliament, but rather a national one between the English and the Irish, which could be brought to an end no other way than by seizing on the lands and reducing the people to the state of serfs. They thought they had as good reason for surrendering now as they had for surrendering Dublin two years before to the parliament. The following account of the revolt is given in a letter of Colonel Deane to the Speaker of the House of Commons, written from Milford Haven, and dated November the 8th, 1649. The writer says he has had a clear narrative of it by one who was an actor in the whole business : —

"The 16th of October, at night, Colonel Townsend, Colonel Warden, and Colonel Gifford, being there prisoners for the business of Youghal, were ordered to be disposed into three different castles. Next day some of the officers in the town came to these gentlemen that night, and told them they were undone unless they would stand by them, for they would else be slaves to the Irish. Upon which the three colonels replied, that if they would fetch for each of them a sword and pistols, they would live and die with them, which was done ; and the guards perceiving them coming down stairs armed, cried out, "We are for you, too ;" and from thence marched to the main guard, and they immediately declared with them, upon this general consent, crying, "out with all the Irish." In which all the townsmen that were English and the soldiers unanimously agreed, and put it presently into execution. They put out next morning their Major-General Starling, and these few that dissented ; and since that Youghal has done the same. And those of Youghal had sent to Colonel Gifford, the present governor of Cork, to send Colonel Warden, with

_____

[1] "The county of Cork, being inhabited and garrisoned with Englishmen, could not endure the thoughts of joining with the Irish against their countryman. They knew that the Irish aimed at their destruction in the end. They remembered the reasons of surrendering Dublin to the Parliament two years before, and they thought they had the same motive to submit now." Cox's *Hib. Angl.*, Reign of Charles ii , p. 12.

a hundred horse, to their assistance, for they had seized on Sir Piercy Smith, their governor, and Johnson, who had betrayed them formerly, and some others, and had secured the castle."

A Cromwellian of the time describes the occurrence in the following strain of quaint humor and malignant triumph : —

"Sir Robert Starling was governor there, who little dreamed of losing his command, yet found he had lost it when he waked. One may truly say he was taken napping; but I must acknowledge, to extenuate his misfortune, that he was divested of his government in the dark, and consequently could not see to prevent it. Sure this major-general lost his way into that office, and was as much surprised at having got that employment as we were to see him in it. His ignorance was so great it passed for his religion, for never any that saw him draw up the army but concluded he relied on Providence for the victory, he made so little use of the means of obtaining it. He has now done that too which he never did to this regiment, I mean exercised ; and the word of command is, 'as you are,' that is, reduced to his primitive existence, which affords him the stoic's motto, *omnia mea mecum porto.*" This makes me that I believe he will think these last eight years a dream, and that he was never really waked out of it but when these rude fellows at Cork presumed to do it.

Lady Fanshawe, the wife of Sir Richard Fanshawe,[1] gives some further details of what Carlyle calls "the universal hurly-burly" that followed on the revolt : —

"I was lying ill in my bed," she writes in her *Memoirs*, "when Cork revolted. It was in the beginning of November.[2] At midnight I heard the great guns go off, and thereupon I called upon my family to rise, which I did as well as I could in that condition. Hearing lamentable shrieks of men, women and children, I asked at a window the cause. They told me they were all Irish, stripped and wounded, and turned out of the town : and that Colonel Jeffries,[3] and some others had possessed themselves of the town for Cromwell. Immediately I packed up my husband's cabinet — by chance he was gone to Kinsale on business that day — with all his writings, and near £1,000 in gold and silver ; and about three o'clock, by the light of a taper, I treaded my way to the market-place, and sought out and found Colonel Jeffries. I reminded him of the many civilities he had received from my husband. Jeffries gave me a pass for myself, family and goods. With this I returned through thousands of naked swords to the Red Abbey.[4] I there hired a neighbor's cart, and with my servants, my sister, and my little girl Nan, got safe to the garrison of Kinsale."

---

[1] *Memoir of Lady Fanshawe*, p. 77 ; London, 1830. Sir Richard was at this time paymaster to the fleet of Prince Rupert. At the Restoration he was appointed ambassador to the courts of Spain and Portugal.

[2] The revolt took place October 16th, as may be seen by the depositions in Appendix vii.

[3] He had command of "ye Watergate"; it stood at the end of Castle Street, where Daunt's Square now is. See *History of Cork*, a lecture by John G. M'Carthy, Esq., M. P., p 44; Cork, 1869 Colonel Jeffries was ancestor of the Jeffrey family of Blarney, his son, Sir James Jeffrey, having purchased, in 1701, this portion of the forfeited estate of the Earl of Clancarty. Smith's *Hist. of Cork*, vol. i. p. 166.

[4] This was the Augustinian friary, founded by Patrick de Courcy, Baron of Kinsale, in 1420. The tower, 64 feet high, and the walls of the church are still standing. It is in the southern part of the city ; the present Cumberland Street runs over part of the ground. See Windele's *Historical Notices of Cork*, &c., p. 64 ; Cork, 1839 At the suppression of the religious houses this priory, with its appurtenances, was granted to Cormac M'Carthy, son of Teigue Lord Muskery. At this time it was inhabited by Dean Boyle, a relative of the first Lord Cork, who was then chaplain general of the Munster army, and later lord chancellor and archbishop of Armagh. See Ware's *Antiquities*, vol. i. p. 130.

A short time before the Irish inhabitants had lost all they had, having been plundered by Inchiquin's soldiers. But bad as was their condition then, it was far worse now, for during the space of twenty-four hours they did not know one the miseries of the other, by which means the poor inhabitants had a greater sense of the last than of the former plunderers.[1]

The good news was made known to the parliament without delay. The House being informed that Colonel Ryves, who brought the letter, was at the door, he was called in, and being come to the bar, gave the House an account of the wonderful providence of God in bringing in several garrisons in Munster without striking a blow. The relation was to this effect : —

"That the said Colonel Ryves, being in Cork, where there were only 120 English, and about 100 Scotch, 100 Irish and 60 fusees; and there being in the town the council of that province, the Major-General, and other chief officers, the said colonel was put by his command by occasion of his opposition and protesting against the pacification with the Irish ; yet it pleased God to make him instrumental with others in reducing that garrison.

"And having some interest in the officers, who had been formerly under his command, he communicated this design only to three in command, and to Colonel Blunt, Lieutenant-Colonel Dowith, who had no command there, the officers, viz., Captain Myhill, Captain Cary, and Captain Burnell, and to some few townsmen whom he knew to be honest and faithful, viz., Colonel Hodder, Major Pierce, Mr. Boly, Mr. Cox, and some few others, holding it not safe to impart it to many, nor any long time before, lest it might be discovered.

"That night intelligence was given of divers Irish that were to be brought into that garrison, and there being 100 Scots, and but 18 English upon the guard, the business was so ordered that the captain that was to be on the guard that night exchanged with Captain Burnell, one of those who was privy to the design, who having privately removed the main guard with two companies, procured an order to be given to relieve the Scots at each post by small files at a time with English, by which means the English were able to overbalance them.

"Captain Myhill was employed in surprising the great fort,[2] he having formerly wrought with the ensign and corporal who managed the business, and prevailed with the English soldiers, who were very forward, that with forty men he surprised that fort and the guard in it. Which being done, and some signal of it given by four pieces of ordnance and proclamation "for the Protestant Religion," and "the English interest," and so went on to secure the rest of the town. In this action Colonel Gifford, Colonel Townsend, and Colonel Warden were released of imprisonment, being formerly committed for an attempt upon Youghal, in which they well behaved themselves. The soldiers were very nimble at it, and the townsmen, too, when they saw the great fort was taken, though till then they were not very forward, rather out of fear than wanting good affection.

"And having thus possessed themselves of all the guards and the town, they chose a committee of safety to order and dispose of all business. And it was strange to see how it pleased God to bring in the horse to them. They began in the morning with but six horse; within three days they had sixty; within little more than a week three hundred. When the Lord Broghill and Colonel Phayre came thither, they were near six hundred, and are now near a thousand, the horse getting

---

[1] *Crom. Sett.*, p. 192. On the 22d of September, Philip Mortell, one of the banished citizens of Cork, being just expelled, as he states, a second time by the revolt of the English garrison to Cromwell, sets forth for his petition, "that he and all those of his friends and nation were stripped and plundered of all they ever had, in so much as for the space of twenty-four hours one did not know the miseries of the other ; by which means the said poor inhabitants had a greater sense of the last than the former plundering"; i e., when driven out by Inchiquin in 1644. See *Account of the Carte MSS.*, p. 80.

[2] It stood on the site now occupied by the barracks in Cross's Green.

off from the enemy by 20, 30, 40, and 60 at a time, until almost all the English horse were come into them, and then none more eager than they to oppose the enemy.

"Before they had well settled Cork, Inchiquin, hearing what Cork had done, came down thither, and endeavored to cast in bones, and to make division among them; but that not prevailing, it was wrought about that, with the compliance of the soldiers, they had declared Inchiquin an enemy. He seeing himself disappointed of his stratagem, thought there was no other way but force, and so resolved to block up the town; and to that end he made four garrisons about it, viz., one at Ronon's house, another at Morrough's house, a third at the Blarney, and the fourth at Bally-graham, all at about three or four miles distance, to block them up; but it pleased God in a short space to remove them.

"The forces of the town with Colonel Gifford, beat up one of the garrisons at Ronon's house, and took it without the loss of one man, their powder being blown up, and so being disabled to hold out. Those at Morrough's and Blarney seeing that, deserted those two garrisons, and the fourth being English, were soon brought to a compliance, and upon our settling down before it did surrender upon articles; which was done colorably, having a design to march to Kinsale, and so to be a means to get that fort and the town; and were a means to draw them to declare for the same interest, and put the English in so good a condition there.

"These proceedings of Cork did also give encouragement to Youghal to declare for the Parliament, and it was observable that about the time that those proceed-ings were at Cork, Inchiquin, having seized upon the person of the mayor and some other honest men of Youghal, intended to hang them for their former action, but at that instant, hearing what Cork had done, was deterred from executing them. And after Cork and Youghal had thus declared, it was followed by divers other garrisons, viz., Bandonbridge, Baltimore, Castlehaven, Mallow, Mocollop, Cappoquin, Droma-nah, and Dungarvan.

"And thus in a short space that province, without bloodshed, was reduced, by which means the army hath had a great refreshing, by having all these places for their winter quarters, and the English interest is in a better condition in that prov-ince now than it was when the pacification was made with the Irish. . . . And truly this providence of God in delivering up Munster thus hath not only hindered the Irish from their winter quarters, and given them to the army plentifully supplied, but will in all probability save much blood and treasure, and quickly put a period to that war."

The Council of State ordered that Cornelius Glover, who brought the news of the rendition of Cork, should have £30 paid him.

The English garrison of Cork wisely determined to obtain some promise of security of their liberties from the Parliamentary party. The following were

The propositions sent in by the English Inhabitants of the city, suburbs and liberties of Cork, to his Excellency General Cromwell :—

1. The said inhabitants out of a sense of the former good service and tender care of the Lord Inchiquin to and for them, they desire that an act of oblivion pass for any act committed which might redound to the prejudice of his lordship or his heirs: and that he may quietly enjoy his own estate; and that satisfaction be made for what arrears are due to him until the perfection of the last peace.

2. The said inhabitants for themselves desire that an act of indemnity be passed for any former actions which they or any of them have done or might be supposed to have committed, whereby they and every of them may and shall as quietly pass and freely enjoy their liberty and estates which now they are possessed of, or shall be, in the same freedom as any of the people of England now do or shall do; and that all prize goods that have been bought by the said inhabitants, they may and shall enjoy them from any that might claim them.

3. The said inhabitants desire that whereas the charter of the city of Cork hath been forfeited by reason of non 'nadge, that there be a charter granted to the now inhabitants in as large and ample manner as the former.

4. They can make appear by ticket they have in any way lent, disbursed, or delivered for the use of the army before the late peace, and likewise for what they or any of them have or shall disburse, either in money or goods, since the time of their present declaration; and that one of the city be chosen to audity the said account on what debentures to issue for payment.

5. The said inhabitants desire that what they shall make appear is due unto them by speciality or otherwise, from any person or persons whatsoever, before or since the wars, satisfaction be made as to justice appertaineth.

6. That all English garrisons and persons that will come in and submit to these propositions shall have the benefit of the same.

7. That all lands, messuages, and tenements within the said city and county thereof that was held in burgage, to be totally confirmed on the now inhabitants of the said city; and that the inhabitants of the said city and suburbs be regulated into a regiment, under the command of Mr. John Hodder, as colonel, to be in pay when they pass on duty, not else."

To these demands Cromwell sent the following reply : —

By the Lord Lieutenant-General.

Answer to the several desires of the Inhabitants of Cork, sent by their Commissioners, received November, 1649.

1. I shall forbear to answer.

2. The inhabitants of the city of Cork that have joined in the late declaring of the parliament, shall be fully indemnified for anything that passed, as is desired, so as to restore them to the same condition of freedom, privileges and safety that they were in before the Lord of Inchiquin's defection; and as if the same, or anything that had ensued thereupon had never been.; and particularly shall enjoy the benefit of any prize goods they have bought, without being troubled or damnified for the same.

3 That the charter of the city of Cork shall be renewed as is desired, and no advantage taken of the forfeiture mentioned.

4. For what they have lent, disbursed, or delivered for the public service since this declaration, or hereafter shall lend or advance, it shall be satisfied with all speed out of the revenue or income of these ports out of which it may be best and safest done ; which I leave to themselves to think and dispose of ; and for anything so due to them from the public before the Lord Inchiquin's defection, they shall have the same right and be in the same capacity of satisfaction as before the said defection they were; and I shall endeavor it for them equally as to any others to whom such debts from the public are due, by all ways and means in my power: but for any thing lent, disbursed, or delivered as to the public use since the said defection and before the said declaration, it cannot be otherwise considered but as damage suffered by persons well-affected, living under the power of an enemy; and in that nature. so far as anything shall appear to have been forcibly taken from such persons, it shall be considered, examined, and represented to the parliament, to be satisfied according to the damage of any other well-affected person in Ireland.

5 For any debts due from any private persons, they shall be left to their full legal rights.

6. As all that is granted to the soldiers and inhabitants of Cork, Youghal, and other neighboring places that have already corresponded or joined with them in their late declarations, is most fully and heartily granted, because not bargained for before their declaring, and because to men's appearing by the carriage of the business to have done what they have done therein really from a recommended sense of an affection to the English Parliamentary and Protestant interests in this nation, so to any other places or persons that having been formerly of the Parliamentary party, shall so come in as it appears to be from the said sense and affection, and not from policy or necessity, I shall bear the same mind and have the same readiness to do them good and not hurt.

7. Not fully understanding the nature or extent of the thing desired, I can give no present full resolution, but shall be ready to do them full right in all things, and also to perform any such good office of respect within my power, unto the said

city of Cork, as may be a reward and memorial of their faithful and public office which in these late occurrences I really think they have deserved.

Lastly, as to their desiring other papers concerning the militia of the city of Cork, I am very willing that the inhabitants be formed into a regiment under the command of Mr. John Hodder as Colonel, Mr. Maurice Cuffe as lieutenant-colonel, Major Boreman, major; and the regiment, or any part thereof, when called on duty, to have the State's pay. For other officers of the regiment, I leave it to the said officers, or any two of them, to nominate, and to the Lord of Broghill, Sir William Fenton, Colonel Phayre, for approbation. to whom I refer it.

(Signed),

O. CROMWELL.

CHAPTER XVII.

REVOLT OF THE MUNSTER GARRISONS (*continued.*)

Revolt of Kinsale and Bandon — Propositions of the Governor of Bandon — Revolt of Youghal — Surrender of Cappoquin, Baltimore, Castlehaven and Mallow — Act of Indemnity — The Forty-nine Arrears — Privilege of Kinsale and Youghal — Consequences of the Revolt — The Royalist Fleet — Letter of Cromwell.

BEFORE Cork revolted, Colonel Crosby was sent by Lord Inchiquin with 500 Irish soldiers, to secure the town and fort of Kinsale for the King. The commonalty of the town shut the gates against him; but the sovereign and other chief men went out and agreed that he and his party should be admitted into the town. He stayed there about a week, and then retired to the fort. During that time he oppressed the town exceedingly; not only demanding gifts, but also exacting money and provisions from the inhabitants, which put the town upon "declaring." Some of the English inhabitants met, and asked some of the Irish, the sovereign in particular, to join them. At first he was unwilling, and wept; but he soon consented. They drew up a letter and addressed it to Lord Broghill and Colonel Phayre, acquainting them of their purpose to surrender the town, and asking some aid of horse and foot towards the taking of the fort. Captain Cuffe was sent with a troop of horse into the barony of Courcies, to the side of the town where the fort was. Colonel Gifford came soon after. The townspeople planted a gun on Compass Hill, over against the fort. After six or seven shots had been fired, the fort surrendered; soon after it was delivered on conditions to Lord Broghill.

Immediately after the declaration of Cork, Inchiquin, fearing that Bandon might follow the example set it, sent Captain Constantine with a troop of horse to take possession of the town and disarm all the inhabitants. Two companies of Irish soldiers were sent into the town at the same time. But seeing the disaffection of the townsmen to the Irish, he made Colonel Francis Courtenay governor, and bade him bring in his regiment of 500 foot and remove the Irish. The townsmen came together frequently, and expressed their readiness to attempt the seizure of the town, and the imprisonment of the officers and guards for the parliament and Cromwell. A day or two before Lord Broghill came, Captain Braly, Lieutenant Berry, and some others, succeeded in seizing on the western gate and disarming the guards. Those who had been appointed to seize on the two other guards were discovered and imprisoned. Braly and his companions were besieged in the guard by the soldiers and obliged to yield themselves prisoners. The same night the inhabitants dispatched a messenger to Lord Brog-

hill, informing him of the danger in which the prisoners were, and
asking him to come to their aid with some forces before the town ;
they engaged that if the governor did not deliver it up, they would
seize the sentinel, open the postern gate, and admit him. Two hundred of the garrison, under the command of Major Harden, with the
provost at their head, took possession of two houses near the sally-port
at the north side of the town ; they then surrounded the guard-house
where the governor had shut himself up, and forced him and those with
him to surrender themselves prisoners of war. They told him plainly
that it was useless for him to oppose them, as they were determined to
deliver up the town to Lord Broghill. The governor asked them not
to deliver him up, but to give him one hour's time to make conditions
for himself and his party. This was granted, and he departed with
his men the second next day and the day following.

*The Propositions sent from Colonel Francis Courtenay, Governor of Bandon,
to the Right Honorable the Lord of Broghill, for the delivery of the said town this
15th day of November, 1649:—*

   Imprimis, that Colonel Francis Courtenay shall, without any molestation,
march with his entire regiment, bag and baggage, drums beating, colors flying, matches
lighted, bullets in their mouths, to the Lord of Inchiquin's army or elsewhere where
they please, and that they may have one barrel of powder with bullets and match
proportionable.
   2. That all officers, soldiers, and townsmen, and any other person or persons
that will, may live quietly without any molestation, hindrance, or prejudice, either in
body, goods, estate, or any other thing else that to them or either of them belonged,
in any of the English garrisons or country, provided they act nothing against the
Lord of Broghill or his party, now under command of the Parliament of England.
   3. That Colonel Courtenay shall, with his entire regiment and all others that
will go with him, have two days' respite before they march, and in the meantime not
to receive any prejudice either for body, goods, or arms, by any of the Lord of
Broghill's party or his Lordship.
   4. That Captain Condon shall, with his horses, arms, bag and baggage, have the
benefit of the above articles.
   5. That if any horses, cows, garrans, or any other manner of goods have been
seized on by the Lord Broghill's party within one mile round his town belonging to
the above officers, townsmen, or any of them since his Lordship's coming before the
said town of Bandon, they shall be restored back to the owners.
   6. That the money due unto Colonel Francis Courtenay, his officers, and soldiers,
before these propositions by assignments from Sir Robert Coppinger by virtue of
the Lord of Inchiquin's warrant to Sir Robert, may be suffered to be levied by distress or otherwise, according to the tenor and meaning of the said assignment.
Provided it be not charged upon any place under the protection of the Parliament of
England.
   Upon the surrender of the within mentioned town of Bandon to me for the use
of Parliament of England, I do hereby promise and engage myself to make good and
perform the within Articles in every particular.

                                        Dated as aforesaid,

                                            BROGHILL.

   Mention has been already made of the unsuccessful attempt at
revolt of some of the Youghal garrison. Colonel Deane, in his letter,
speaks of " some officers who were imprisoned in Cork for that business." A fortnight after the revolt of Cork, hearing of the success of

his comrades there, Lieutenant-Colonel Widenham,[1] of the Youghal garrison, invited a party of cavalry under the command of Colonels Gifford and Warden to seize on the town. The Governor, Sir Piercy Smith, strove to prevent their entrance by drawing the chain of the iron gate; but Widenham called to Ensign Dashwood and Town-Major Smith, who were within, to seize the governor and open the gate. This they did, and Youghal, too, was given up to the Parliament. The reward of Widenham's treachery was Castletow Roche, the ancient seat of Lord Roche, who, with his four young daughters, for years after, "lived destitute of all kinds of subsistence except what alms some good Christians did in charity afford them."

The garrisons of the other walled towns in the south hastened to send in their submission; Timoleague, Cappoquin, Baltimore, Castlehaven, Mallow, "and some other places of hard names," all received garrisons of the Parliamentary army. As these soldiers, being under Inchiquin's command since 1642, had revolted with him from the King's service to the Parliament in 1644, and back again to the Royalists in 1648, they forfeited the arrears of pay due to them for their service from 1644 to 1648, even though they now submitted to Cromwell. Their temporary revolt from the Parliament barred their claim to the reward due to "constant good affection," and made them transplantable. An Act of indemnity, however, was, at the instance of Cromwell, passed five years later, on the 7th of June, 1654, on behalf of the officers and soldiers under Ormonde's and Inchiquin's command; and "in consideration of their voluntary rendition of Cork and the adjacent garrisons, and at a time," says the Act, "when the army under the command of his Highness, the Lord Protector, then Lord Lieutenant of Ireland, was at a great distance from them, and the winter season rendered his access to them improbable"; it was enacted that such of them as could prove themselves active in the rendition of these Munster garrisons should be allowed to state their arrears accrued due since June, 1644, and before June 5th, 1649, and received lands in satisfaction, as if they had never lapsed from their obedience to the parliament. These were called the "Forty-nine arrears." The rest of the army, much against their will, were obliged to assign or give up to them the three counties of Donegal, Longford, and Wicklow, to which Cromwell added Leitrim, taken from what had been previously allotted to the transplanted Irish, and so much within the mile line encircling Connaught as yet remained undisposed of. For the purpose of enabling them to prove their share in the rendition of these garrisons, a commission was issued by virtue of the Act of Indemnity to take their depositions. It was the aim of each of them to prove that he and his comrades had been active in the revolt. But before the lands were set out to them, the Restoration took place. The King returned from exile, and with him came many officers who had been driven out of Ireland by Cromwell for their loyalty; these were styled "the Protestant Royalist officers who had served the

---

[1] Widenham afterwards settled at Court, near Pallaskenry, in the county of Limerick: his grand-daughter and heiress married Valentine Quin, ancestor of the Earl of Dunraven. *Memorials of Adare*, p. 187.

King before June 5th, 1649," or "the '49 officers." By the Act of
Settlement they were granted the lands that had been assigned by
the Commonwealth for the '49 arrears of the Cromwellian officers and
soldiers. The above mentioned depositions were now used to bar the
Munster revolters of their claims.[1]

The ancient inhabitants of Cork, Youghal, and Kinsale, though
Catholics, as a reward for their loyalty to the English interest, had
this privilege granted them, that they were not forced to transplant
immediately like the rest of the Irish nation, but were permitted to
reside in the county of Cork until the Court of Commission should sit
at Mallow. Yet the Court, on the 29th of August, 1656, refused to
adjudge constant good affection to any of them, and declared them
by law transplantable.

This revolt was not merely a loss of the strong places and of men
to the Royalists in Ireland : it dissolved all their hopes and designs ;
it introduced a spirit of jealousy and distrust betwen the Irish and
the English in the Royalist army, which Ormonde tried in vain to
allay. It decided the fate of Ireland, for it gave to Cromwell's army,
without the loss of a drop of blood or the striking of a blow, excellent
winter quarters, and opened the means of holding direct communication at all times with England, just when his forces were reduced by
sickness and losses in the field from 12,000 to 6,000 men, and demoralized by the repulses they had met at Waterford and Duncannon.[2]

Three days after the revolt of Cork, Prince Rupert, whose fleet
had been blocked up by the Parliamentary ships in Kinsale harbor,
under the command of Admiral Blake, hearing of Cromwell's approach,
forced his way through the blockade with the loss of three of his ships,
and sailed for Lisbon.[3]

Cromwell hastened to communicate the news of his successes to
some of his friends. The following was addressed to his "beloved
brother Richard Mayor, Esquire, Hurstlye in the County of Hampton," from Ross, November 13th :

---

[1] *Account of the Carte MSS.*, p. 139. Though the Act of Settlement pretended to exclude the betrayers of the Munster garrisons, yet they were allowed to retain their debenture
lands, if they could prove that they made some reparation for their former faults by their
timely appearance for the King's restoration. *Crom. Sett.*, p. 194.

[2] Our great security, next to God's protection and the strength of our army, is the
approaching hard season of the year that will, in all likelihood, increase our advantages upon
passages, and, in so wasted a country as he must march through, expose his men to the endur-
ance of unusual hardships." Carte's *Collection*, &c., vol. ii. p. 399. The above mentioned
garrisons had been supplied by the Irish during the whole preceding summer to their excessive charge. *Ibid.*, vol. i. p. 419.

[3] Whitelocke, p. 413. There he was not only protected but caressed by the King of
Portugal ; which so much displeased Parliament, that they commenced a war with that
Prince, doing him great damages in the trade and navigation, wherein the riches of the
nation do consist. When he could neither by force nor entreaties be persuaded to cast off
Prince Rupert out of his protection, the English admirals resolved with patience to await his
coming out, and a long time they kept him in there, till at last want of provisions made them
retire, and give the Prince room, who immediately steered from thence to Malaga ; but in
the voyage, perplexed with extraordinary storms, he lost his brother Maurice, who, in the
Vice-Admiral, was never since heard of. Himself being again followed by the Parliament's
generals, lost all his ships but two, which his pursuers looking upon them as inconsiderable
and not worthy their time and pains to hunt after, returned and left him sea-room to come
with them into France. *Ibid.*, p. 414.

"It hath pleased God to give us since the taking of Wexford and Ross a good interest in Munster, by the access of Cork and Youghal, which are now both submitted. The Commissioners are now with me. Divers other lesser garrisons are come in also. The Lord is wonderful in all these things; it is His hand alone does them. Oh, that all the praise might be ascribed to Him! I have been crazy in my health, but the Lord is pleased to sustain me. I beg your prayers."

Some further details regarding the events spoken of in this and the preceding chapters, are given by Cromwell in his letter from Ross to the Speaker of the House of Commons, dated November 14th, 1649.

"About a fortnight since I had some good assurances that Cork may return to its obedience, and had refused Inchiquin, who did strongly endeavor to redintegrate himself there, but without success. I did hear also that Colonel Townsend was coming to me with their submission and desires, but was interrupted by a fort at the mouth of Cork harbor. But having sufficient grounds upon the former information, and other confirmation (out of the enemy's camp), that it was true, I desired General Blake, who was here with me, that he would repair thither in Captain Mildmay's frigate, called the Nonsuch, who, when they came thither, received such an entertainment as these enclosed will let you see.

"In the meantime, the Garland, one of your third-rate ships, coming happily into Waterford Bay, I ordered her and a great prize lately taken in that bay to transport Colonel Phayre[1] to Cork; witherward he went, having along with him near five hundred foot, which I spared him out of this poor army, and £1,500 in money; giving him such instructions as were proper for the promoting of your interests there. As they went with an intention for Cork, it pleased God, the wind coming across, they were forced to ride off from Dungarvan where they met Captain Mildmay returning with the Nonsuch frigate, with Colonel Townsend aboard, coming to me; who advertised them that Youghal had also declared for the Parliament of England. Whereupon they steered their course thither, and sent for Colonel Gifford, Colonel Warden, Major Purden (who with Colonel Townsend, have been very active instruments for the return both of Cork and Youghal to their obedience, having some of them ventured their lives twice or thrice to effect it), and the Mayor of Youghal aboard them; who, accordingly, immediately came and made tender of some propositions to be offered to me. But my Lord Broghill being on board the ship, assuring them that it would be more for their honor and advantage to desire no conditions, they said they would submit, whereupon my Lord Broghill, Sir William Fenton, and Colonel Phayre went to the town, and were received,— I shall give you my Lord Broghill's own words,— 'with all the real demonstrations of gladness an overjoyed people were capable of.'

"Not long after, Colonel Phayre landed his foot. And by the endeavors of the noble person aforementioned and the rest of the gentlemen, the garrison is put in good order; and the mounted officers and soldiers in that garrison in a way of settlement. Colonel Phayre intends, as I hear, to leave two hundred men there, and to march with the rest overland to Cork, I hear by Colonel Townsend and the rest of the gentlemen that were employed to me that Baltimore, Castlehaven, Cappoquin, and some other places of hard names are come in (I wish foot come over seasonably to man them), as also there are hopes of other places. We lie with the army at Ross, where we have been making a bridge over the Barrow, and hardly yet accomplished as we could wish. The enemy lies upon the Nore, on the land between the Barrow and it, having gathered together all the force they can get. Owen Roe's men, as they report them, are six thousand foot, and about four hundred horse, besides their own army. And they give out they will have a day for it: which we hope the Lord

---

[1] Phayre was one of those to whom the warrant for the execution of Charles I. was directed. He was governor of Cork from 1649 to 1660. On the 18th of July, 1660, he was arrested at Cork, and sent to London. By the interest of Donald M'Carthy, Lord Clancarty, whose life he had saved, he obtained pardon and returned to Cork. He was again arrested in 1666, for taking part in a plot to seize Dublin Castle and the other Irish garrisons; but peace being soon after proclaimed, the projectors were allowed to go unmolested. He died in Cork, and was buried in the Anabaptist burial ground there. Smith's *History of Cork*, vol. ii. p. 178.

in His Mercy, will enable us to give them in His own good time, in Whom we desire our only trust and confidence may be.

"Whilst we have lain here, we have not been without some sweet taste of the goodness of God. Your ships have taken some good prizes. The last one thus; There came in a Dunkirk man-of-war with thirty-two guns, who brought in a Turkish man-of war whom she had taken, and another ship of ten guns, laden with poor-john and oil. These two your ships took. But the man-of-war whose prizes these two were, put herself under the fort of Duncannon, so that your ships could not come near her. It pleased God we had two demi-cannon with the foot on the shore, which being planted raked her through, killing and wounding her men, so that after ten shots she weighed anchor, and ran into your fleet with a flag of submission, surrendering herself. She was well manned, the prisoners taken being two hundred and thirty. I doubt the taking prisoners of this sort will cause the wicked trade of piracy to be endless. They were landed here before I was aware; and a hundred of them, as I hear, are gotten into Duncannon, and have taken up arms there ; and I doubt the rest, that are gone to Waterford, will do us no good. The seamen being so full of prizes and unprovided of victual, know not how best otherwise to dispose of them.

"Sir, having given you this account, I shall not trouble you much with particular desires. These I shall humbly present to the Council of State. Only in the general, give me leave humbly to offer what in my judgment I conceive to be for your service, with a full submission to you.

"We desire recruits may be speeded to us. It is not fit to tell you how your garrisons will be unsupplied, and no field marching army considerable, if three garrisons more were in our hands.

"It is not good not to follow Providence. Your recruits and the forces desired will not raise your charge. If your assignments already for the forces here do come to our hands in time, I should not doubt, by the addition of assessments here, to have your charge in some reasonable measure borne, and the soldiers upheld, without much neglect or discouragement, which sickness in this country, so ill agreeing with their bodies, puts upon them : and this winter's action, I believe not heretofore known by English in this country, subjects them to. To the praise of God I speak it, I scarce know one officer of forty amongst us that has not been sick. And how many considerable ones we have lost is no little thought of heart to us.

"Wherefore I humbly beg that the moneys desired may be seasonably sent over, and those other necessaries, clothes, shoes, stockings formerly desired, that so poor creatures may be encouraged, and through the same blessed presence that has gone along with us, I hope, before it be long, to see Ireland no burden to England, but a profitable part of the Commonwealth. And certainly the extending your help in this way at this time is the most profitable means speedily to effect it. And if I did not think it your best thrift, I would not trouble you at all with it.

"I have sent Sir Arthur Loftus¹ with these letters. He hath gone along with us testifying a great deal of love to your service. I know his sufferings are very great ; for he hath lost near all : his regiment was reduced to save your charge, not out of any exception to his person. I humbly therefore present him to your consideration.

"Craving pardon for this trouble, I rest

"Your most humble and faithful servant,

"OLIVER CROMWELL."

_____

¹ Sir Arthur Loftus was the eldest son of Sir Adam Loftus of Rathfarnham, and great-grandson of Adam Loftus, Protestant Archbishop of Armagh from 1562 to 1567. Sir Arthur was the ancestor of that branch of the Loftus family which was afterwards ennobled under the title of Viscount Lisburn.

CHAPTER XVIII.

THE SIEGE OF WATERFORD.

CROMWELL remained for some time at Ross after the surrender of the town, "very sick and crazy in his health." While the siege was going on he had employed some of his troops in making a bridge of boats across the Barrow, to enable his army to pass into the county of Kilkenny. The Irish, it would seem, knew nothing of such bridges, for in the Jamestown "Declaration" it is spoken of as "a wonder to all men, but understood by no man." The bridge was almost com- pleted when the town surrendered. While this great work was carried on, Ormonde had 13,000 foot and 4,000 horse only one day's march off, yet he never offered the least interruption, though 1,000 musket- eers and two culverins might hinder the same in spite of all the enemy's forces. Later he sent Lord Taaffe[1] to destroy it, but the attempt proved a failure. As soon as he was reinforced by the arrival of Hugh O'Neill, who had come from Ulster with 1,500 foot, he sent orders to Inchiquin to make all possible haste to join him with the whole of his horse ; but these were so fatigued and disheartened after the late unfortunate expedition that they could do little for a time. His army was then at Innistiogue. From this place he intended to march the next day with his foot to fortify Rosbercan,[2] opposite Ross, and to hinder the passage of the river. On the arrival of the Ulster men, he asked them whether they were ready to fight. They replied that their object in coming to Leinster was to meet the enemy. They asked that the Irish should fight by themselves, and that Ormonde's and Inchiquin's men should form a division apart or merely look on ; Ormonde made no answer. But his plans were again frustrated by the activity of the enemy. When he was about to begin his march, he heard that a large body of Cromwell's horse had already crossed the

---

[1] Theobald, the second viscount. In the early part of this rebellion he was appointed General of the Province of Munster ; at the peace of 1646 he was deprived of this post, and remained without employment until April, 1649, when, on the death of Sir Thomas Lucas, he was made Master of the Ordnance. He was one of the ambassadors sent by the Confed- erates to solicit the protection and aid of the Duke of Lorraine ; hence he was excepted from pardon for life and estate by Cromwell. After the Restoration he got back his property. In 1661 he was created Earl of Carlingford. He died in 1677. Archdall's *Peerage*, vol. iv. p. 296.

[2] Rosbercan is so called from the territory of Iberean, in which it is situated. About the year 1300 it was incorporated, and granted all the liberties and free customs granted to the burgesses of Kilkenny by Gilbert de Clare, Earl of Gloucester.

river, seized on Rosbercan, and fortified it in such a way that the bridge was safe from any attack on that side. A few days after, he went to Thomastown,[1] intending to remain there until he should be joined by Inchiquin and the force under his command. Meantime the report reached him that the greater part of Cromwell's army, under the command of Ireton and Jones, had crossed the bridge and was in full march towards Kilkenny. Soon after he was told that the enemy had got as far as Bennett's bridge. Here he was joined by Lieutenant General Ferrall, with the rest of the Ulster forces which Owen O'Neill had sent on to his assistance. Taking with him seven days' provision he set out, determined to give Cromwell battle and to risk his fortunes on the issue.

Ireton despatched Colonel Abbot with a party of horse and dragoons in the dusk of the evening to seize on Innistiogue, a walled town on the Barrow, ten miles above Ross, where there was a garrison of three hundred men. "At first they vapoured over the wall; but when the assailants set fire to the gates, it so quashed them, that they took to flight and escaped in boats across the Nore, leaving the townsmen to be plundered and possessed by the plunderers." The heavy rains that had fallen the day before did not allow the army to cross the ford; they marched therefore to Thomastown, but on arriving there, they found the bridge broken down and a garrison left to defend the place.

"Whereupon, seeking God for direction, they took the road back to Ross." Their stock of provisions was exhausted. On their way they took the strong castle of Knocktopher,[2] and put into it twenty horse and thirty dragoons; but these were soon recalled, being too far into the enemy's country. Colonel Reynolds and Major Ponsonby were sent with twelve troops of horse and three of dragoons to attempt Carrick, in the hope of obtaining over the bridge there a passage into the county of Waterford. The town was garrisoned by a regiment of foot and two or three troops of horse. Ponsonby seized on some of the country people whom he met; these he induced by promises and threats to mount on horseback and advance in a body with the soldiers to the walls, and there proclaim to the townsmen in the Irish language that they were some of the Irish army sent by Ormonde to reinforce the garrison. The townsmen readily opened the gates.[3] As soon as the soldiers entered they took possession of the gates and walls. The garrison saw their mistake too late; some of

---

[1] Thomastown was called by the Irish Baile Mic Andaun, and in *The Itinerary of King John*, Boscus Terræ Filii Thomæ Filii Antonii. It was built by Thomas Fitz Anthony Den, who died in 1229. In 1346 Edward III. granted the customs for four years for the construction and repairs of the bridge. Lynch's *Feudal Dignities*, p. 232; London, 1830. In 1374 he made another grant of the tolls for twenty years for the walling of the town. See Morrin's *Patent and Close Rolls*, vol i. p. 78, note. The castle and some parts of the wall are still standing.

[2] Knocktopher is ten miles south of Kilkenny. The castle was the residence of the Earls of Ormonde. James, the second earl, founded a Carmelite monastary here in 1536.

[3] See Duffy's *Hibernian Magazine*, vol. iii. p. 17; Dublin, 1861. Ormonde said it was betrayed by the Protestant ward there. See his answer to the 9th Article of the "Declaration" of Jamestown, in Cox's *Hib. Angl.* vol. ii, appendix xlviii. There is, however, a tradition that the townspeople defended the wall bravely, and it was stormed after a breach had been made at the spot now known as the Red Gap. Some cannon-balls and pikeheads were lately found near the wall.

them fled in terror across the bridge to the county of Waterford, others were massacred without mercy. About a hundred of them shut themselves up in the castle, "a fair house of the Lord Ormonde's ;"[1] they surrendered, however, the following day, and were allowed to march away to the nearest garrison town in the possession of the Royalists ; eighty of them, who were Welshmen, joined the army of the parliament.

The news of Reynolds' success gave fresh courage to Cromwell. He was now quite recovered from his illness, and left Ross on the 21st of November at the head of his army, intending to cross the Suir at Carrick, to march on Waterford, and to lay seige to that city. On the 23d he entered Carrick ; there he met Ponsonby[2] and congratulated him on the successful issue of his stratagem. Reynolds was left behind as military governor of the town, to hold the bridge over the Suir. He had his own regiment of horse, a troop of dragoons, and two companies of foot. His first care was to put the place in a proper state of defence — a wise precaution, for it was attacked a few days after by a part of the Royalist army under Taaffe and Inchiquin, their object being to secure communication with Ormonde's army, which was advancing from Kilkenny to the support of Waterford. The Ulster troops undertook to storm the place, under Major Charles Geoghegan. For four hours they strove very resolutely to effect an entrance. They set fire to the gates and sprung a mine under the walls. But they were obliged to abandon the attempt after they had suffered considerable loss, for want of pickaxes and other implements to make a breech, and of ladders to scale the wall. Though the garrison was composed of only 150 foot, six troops of horse, and a troop of dragoons, and armed with swords and pistols, these did more execution with sticks and staves than with powder and bullets, as their ammunition was soon exhausted.[3] Want of provisions prevented the

---

[1] Carrick castle was supposed to be the finest specimen of an Elizabethan house in Ireland. An Irish poet of the sixteenth century, in a complimentary address to Thomas, tenth earl of Ormonde, says:

> " The court of Carrick is a court well fortified;
> A court to which numbers of nobility resort;
> A court noted for politeness; a court replete with pleasure;
> A court thronged with heroes;
> A court without torch-light, yet a court illumined;
> A court of the lights of wax tapers;
> A plentiful mansion, so artistically stuccoed,
> With sunlit gables, and embroidery-covered walls.

It was, with its demesne and park of 16,000 acres, given to Sir John Reynolds.

[2] Ponsonby, on the reduction of Ireland, received the honor of knighthood. His services were further awarded by the grant of a very considerable tract of land, including the estate of Kildalton, which he called Bessborough, in compliment, as Swift informs us, to his wife Bess, the daughter of Lord Ffolliott. Mr. Dalton, the original proprietor, died in his family mansion, after residing there for many years as the guest and companion of Sir John Ponsonby. Brewer's *Beauties of Ireland*, vol. i. p. 48 ; London, 1825. Tighe, in his *Survey of County of Kilkenny*, says that the present Bessborough estates were granted to Daniel Axtell, later governor of Kilkenny, and that Ballyragget was given to Ponsonby, but that they made an exchange. p. 372 ; Dublin, 1802. It is said that Axtell used the lime-tree still standing in the fair green of Ballyragget as a gallows.

[3] This will perhaps explain the finding of the cannon-balls and pikeheads mentioned above.

assailants from continuing the seige. Five hundred men and their brave commander fell in the storm ; the survivors retired to Clonmel.[1]

On his way to Carrick, Inchiquin summoned the garrison of a small castle on the Suir, about a mile from the town. Only six or seven dragoons had been left behind in it. None of them could either read the summons or write an answer to it. They learned its contents from the trumpter who had brought it. They returned their answer in plain phrase and without compliment, telling him "to bid Inchiquin go about his business and be hanged, for he had nothing to do with them." And thus, though they could not return an answer in writing, they did so in resolution.[2]

On the 24th, about noon, the army arrived before Waterford, having crossed the Suir at Carrick and marched along the southern bank of the river. They approached the town on the north-west ; Cromwell was deterred by the fort on Thomas' Hill from occupying the heights of Bilberry rock, a commanding position.[3] His army, according to Ormonde's estimate, numbered then but 4,000 foot, 2,000 horse, and 500 dragoons. He supposed that the city would surrender as soon as he appeared before it. Some of the more wealthy citizens wished to submit without awaiting the assault, in the hope of saving their property. The Mayor was so terrified, that he wrote to Ormonde asking what terms he should insist on when delivering up the city. But the greater number preferred to try the fortune of war, even though later they were offered liberal conditions, together with the privilege of the citizenship of London and the free exercise of their religion ; no doubt they were aware of the interpretation that had been put upon the latter article at the surrender of Ross, when Cromwell declared that it did not mean the open practice of the Catholic religion ; hence they resolved on resisting to the last.

Waterford had yielded to no other city in its devotion to religion and to the cause of the King.[4] It was there the Nuncio Rinuccini had intended to land before he was driven from his course by the renegade Plunkett, who pursued him and made him put into the bay of

---

[1] The repulse at Carrick was brought forward in the "Declaration" of Jamestown, as a proof of Ormonde's incapacity or treachery. " Our army appearing before the place, the soldiers were commanded to fight against the walls and armed men, without great guns, ladders, petards, shovels, spades, or other necessaries, there being killed about 500 soldiers valiantly fighting."

[2] Probably this was Dovehill castle.

[3] On the Kilkenny side of the river there is a spot called Cromwell's Fort ; but Cromwell did not take up his position there.

[4] " The citie of Waterford hath continued to the Crown of England so loyally, that it is not found registered since the Conquest to have been distained with the smallest spot, or dusted with the least freckle of treason, notwithstanding the sundrie assaults of traiturous attempts ; and therefore the citie arms are deckt with this golden word, *Intacta manet Waterfordia,* a posie as well to be heartily followed as greatly admired of all true and loyal towns " Holinshed's *Chronicles,* vol. ii. p. 13 ; London, 1577. *Secundas inter Hibernia urbes fert Waterfordia, imprimis honesta et officiis fidelis civitas.* Stainhurst *de Rebus Hib.,* p. 22. Some more substantial marks of royal favor were granted to the citizens of Waterford for their active opposition to Perkin Warbeck and his followers in 1497. Ryland's *History of Waterford,* p. 30 ; London, 1841. Henry VIII. sent William Wise with gracious letters and a cap of maintenance, an honorable gift, to be borne before the mayor when he walked in state. He had sent before by the same messenger a gilt sword for their renowned fidelity, to be also borne before the mayor.

Kenmare ;[1] and when the intrigues of Ormonde and his party forced him to leave Kilkenny and threatened his liberty, he was sure of a refuge in the fort of Duncannon. Patrick Comerford, the bishop, was ever the Nuncio's firm friend and the unyielding supporter of his policy, in spite of the threats which the Ormondists held out that they would deprive him of the temporalities of his see. To such threats he used to reply : "Though I were to be stripped of all that the world could give, for my submission to the decrees of Holy Church, I will, nevertheless, persevere in my obedience, nor will I cease to pray God, that He may guide faithfully the counsels of the Confederates of this kingdom."[1]

Strong defences and numerous batteries protected the city from assault. The only hope of taking it lay in the tedious process of investment. Ormonde had encouraged the citizens to a vigorous resistance ; he chid the cowards for their readiness to parley with an enemy before even the batteries were erected, and assured them that if they did their duty, Cromwell should be baffled before the place. Leaving his quarters at Kilkenny, he advanced at the head of his army to Carrick, in the hope of finding the enemy and giving him battle. There he learned that Cromwell had marched on Waterford and was investing it ; he determined to go forward and relieve the place. Some time before he had sent Lord Castlehaven to provide for the safety of the city and of the fort of Passage, which lay nearly opposite Duncannon on the Waterford side of the river. Now he sent him with 1,000 men to reinforce the garrison. But the citizens, through distrust of Ormonde, would not allow them to enter the town. "After several days' dispute" Castlehaven marched away. Alarmed at Cromwell's successes, they requested that 200 men, under the command of Major Cavenagh might be sent to their aid. A fortnight later, Ormonde sent them another reinforcement of 1,500 Ulstermen, a part of Owen Roe O'Neill's army. These they received. Their commander, Lieutenant-General Ferrall, who had been in the confidence of the Nuncio, was appointed military governor. The same night, Ormonde left the city, and crossing the Suir, marched till midnight with his life-guard to Dunkitt. The next day he set out for Carrick, sure of finding his army in possession of that place. When he came within a few miles of the town, he met Colonel Milo Power, who was sent by Lord Inchiquin to inform him of the failure of his attempt.

During the progress of the siege, Cromwell sent Ireton with a regiment of horse and three troops of dragoons towards the fort of Passage, six miles below Waterford. Its capture was of the greatest importance to him, as it commanded the entrance to Waterford harbor even better than Duncannon ; the possession of it would also enable him to reduce both the city and the fort by preventing supplies being brought to them by water. "The dragoons fell presently upon the storm, and in a short time set fire to the gate, whereupon the enemy

---

[1] Sir Richard Belling regretted that the Nuncio could not land at Waterford, where he would have been received " *con prepararte dimostrazioni e con sparamento di tutti le bombarde.*"

within called out for quarter; and upon assurance given by the Lord Lieutenant that they should have quarter for their lives and their wearing apparel, they surrendered the fort to him. Six pieces of ordnance were found in the fort." About 200 of the garrison were slain in the assault. One hundred men were left behind by the captors to garrison it.

At Faithlegg, in the neighborhood of Passage, there dwelt at that time a family named Aylward. Cromwell had known the proprietor in London, and now, in remembrance of their former friendship, was anxious to secure him in the possession of his property. He was aware that his friend was a Catholic, that he was opposed to the Parliamentary party, and he had resolved that such should be dispossessed. But in this particular instance he relaxed from his usual severity, and required what to him seemed an easy thing, that Aylward should conceal his faith. There was some hesitation between the love of religion and the attachment to worldly wealth. At length, owing in great measure to the advice of his wife, Aylward chose the better part, and prepared to defend his property, or to lose it and his life together. Irritated at what he considered foolish obstinacy, Cromwell resolved to punish his presumption, and sent some of his troops and a piece of ordnance, under the command of Captain Bolton, to take possession of the estate. The ruins of the castle, round which a moat can still be traced, mark the spot where the contest took place. The result is easily anticipated. Captain Bolton, was successful, and his descendants, up to a few years since, continued to enjoy the fruits of the conquest.

The citizens of Waterford were so affrighted at the loss of Passage, that they told the Commissioners of Trust they would surrender the city unless aid was sent to them immediately. In reply to their demand, Ormonde declared that his army could no longer be kept together for want of supplies; if these were procured, he would march without delay to their relief. But he found it impossible to procure them. He set out and marched all night along the northern bank of the Suir, conducting Brian O'Neill's horse and some foot to reinforce the garrison. Early the next day, he encamped on a hill opposite the town.

On arriving before the city, Cromwell had sent a trumpeter to summon the garrison to yield upon quarter. "Ferrall would give way to none to answer other than himself; he requested the trumpeter to return to his master with this result, that he was Lieutenant-General Ferrall, governor of that place, at present having 2,000 of his Ulster force there; that as long as any of them did survive, he would not yield the town." The sudden appearance of the reinforcements made Cromwell change his plans.

Having failed to corrupt the Governor, and being disheartened at the prospect of a tedious siege in midwinter, he thought his wisest course was to retire from before the place, and to seek winter-quarters elsewhere. He had already lost over 1,000 men by sickness during the short time the siege had lasted, among them his kinsmen, Major Cromwell. "Finding the indisposition in point of health increasing, and his foot falling sick near ten of a company every night they were on duty, and his numbers not above 3,000 healthful foot in the field, being necessitated to put so many into garrison, the enemy mustering about 12,000 horse and foot, having well near as many in the town as he without, bread and other necessaries not coming to them, and the dripping weather having made the ground so moist that it would not bear the guns, the council of war, in consequence, advised him to rise from before Waterford, and to retire into winter-quarters to refresh the sick and weak soldiers." Such was his haste that he left behind two large guns which he had brought with him. Ormonde besought the magistrates to supply him with boats to ferry his men over, that they might fall on the rear of the retreating army. But now that the danger was gone by, they feigned excuses for delay until the opportunity had passed ; they were afraid that the Royalist army, if once admitted within the walls, would take up its quarters permanently there. They would admit only a body of Ulster troops under Brian O'Neill ; even these they soon complained of as an intolerable grievance, urging their withdrawal in order to save the citizens from being starved. The same night Ormonde set off and joined the army at Clonmel.

A few days later an attempt was made to surprise Passage. Lieutenant-General Ferrall sallied out from Waterford. It was arranged that he should be joined by Colonel Wogan, the governor of Duncannon, who was to advance to the attack from the opposite side of the river. Cromwell had got information of the proposed attempt, and ordered Colonel Sankey,[1] who lay on the north side of the Blackwater, to march in haste with a regiment of horse, and two troops of dragoons, in all about 350 men, to the relief of the place. Ormonde, who was then in the neighborhood, sent for the Mayor, and, pointing out to him the exposed position of the assailants, besought him to supply boats to transport a regiment or two of horse from the north side of the river to their rescue. But the Corporation refused to allow any of his troops to march through the town. With fifty of his attendants he took horse, and went in haste towards Passage. Meantime Sankey, finding the fort closely invested by O'Neill and Wogan, resolved to attack them before they were reinforced by Ferrall's Ulstermen. O'Neill's men resisted bravely for a time, but the horse,

---

[1] Sankey (the name is also written Zanchy) had been a proctor in the University of Oxford. He came to Ireland with Henry Cromwell. Of him Taylor says, "that he seemed to revel in slaughter, and openly professed that no faith should be kept with the Papists." *Civil Wars*, vol. ii. p. 17. While he was military governor of the county of Tipperary, one of his soldiers was killed ; all efforts to find the murderer were in vain. He summoned to Fethard all the inhabitants of the parish in which the murder had taken place, and having compelled them to cast lots, hanged five of them on whom the lots fell. *Ibid*, vol. ii. p. 49. Though nobody exclaimed more against others, particularly against Sir William Petty, yet none had greater complaints made against them for ill treatment of their own men, for he got several of the lots that fell to his share to be left out of his patent, to oblige the Irish, who paid him well for it, and put in other lands which were not given them in satisfaction of their arrears. And thus he wronged many innocent Irish as well as his own people. He was reproached by Sir William Petty "for his unhandsome dealings with the soldiers in the matter of Lismalin Park," the estate of Lord Ikerrin, in south Tipperary. An account of the quarrel betwen Petty and Sankey is given in *The History of the Down Survey*, edited by Sir Thomas Larcom for the Irish Arch. Soc., p. 290 and 345 ; Dublin, 1851.

pressing on them, broke their lines. About 100 were killed, and 350 taken prisoners; among the latter were Wogan[1] and O'Neill. Ferrall came up soon after, but seeing his party utterly defeated, he retreated towards Waterford, hotly pursued by the enemy. Ormonde's numbers were too few to meet them. He drew up his men on the side of a hill in such a way that they seemed more numerous than they really were, and by this stratagem covered the retreat of the fugitives until they reached the town. The citizens were much disheartened at the failure of this attempt, for Passage was a constant danger to them. To protect the city, Ormonde again proposed to ferry his troops across the river, and to quarter them in huts outside the walls, where they should be in no way burdensome. But the citizens would not consent to this proposal; some of them even thought to seize on Ormonde and to fall on his followers as enemies. Irritated at what he conceived to be blind obstinacy on their part, he again withdrew to Clonmel, where the main body of his army lay.[2]

---

[1] February 22d. Letters from Ireland, that Wogan, that perfidious, revolted fellow, had escaped out of prison, and Colonel Phayre's marshal, in whose custody he was, being corrupted, fled with him. Whitelocke, p. 426. Cromwell would seem to have had a high opinion of Wogan, for in treating of an exchange of prisoners with Hugh O'Neill, he says: "In case you insist upon Wogan, I expect Captain Caulfield and his officers and soldiers for him." *Carte MSS.*, vol. xxvi. p. 510.

[2] Waterford surrendered to Ireton August 10th, 1650, and Duncannon four days after.

CHAPTER XIX.

THE MARCH TO YOUGHAL.

Capture of Butlerstown, Kilmeaden, Curraghmore, Granno, and Dunhill — Surrender of Dungarvan — Letter of Broghill — The Revolters — Cromwell enters Youghal — Sickness of the Troops — Death of Colonel Jones — His Character — Irish Army in Winter-Quarters — Ormonde asks Leave to Quit Ireland — Dean Boyle — Causes of Distrust.

CROMWELL's army began its march from Waterford towards Dungarvan on the 2d of December, "it being so terrible a day," says Cromwell, "as I never marched in all my life." Butlerstown castle,[1] outside the liberties of the city, was seized and blown up. Kilmeaden, on the Suir, was destroyed, and its owner, one of the Le Poer family, seized and hanged on a tree close by. His property, extending from Kilmeaden to Tramore, was afterwards confiscated.[2] A similar fate awaited Curraghmore. It chanced that the owner had a shrewd daughter, who knowing her father was a stanch Royalist, devised a plan to save him, and cleverly put it into execution. She contrived to entice the old man into one of the dungeons of the castle, and there she safely bolted and barred him in. She then received Cromwell at the door, and placed the keys of the castle in his hands. She assured him that, although her father had thought it prudent to remove for a time out of the way, he was not only well disposed towards the ruling powers, but willing to give any proof of his allegiance that might be required. The consequence was that Curraghmore remained in possession of its lord. The garrisons of Ballydoyne[3] and Granno[4] fled at the enemy's approach, leaving their arms behind. The castle of Dunhill,[5] situated on the sea-coast beyond Tramore,

---

[1] Butlerstown castle, three miles northwest of Waterford, belonged to Sir Thomas Sherlock. It was taken in 1644 by Lord Mountgarrett, then in command of the Irish forces. Sir Thomas was turned out of doors almost naked. He escaped to Dublin, and was there received by the English as their "constant friend." Yet neither Cromwell nor the King restored him to his estates. He died in 1663, worn out by poverty and despair. The Council granted the sum of £50 to bury him.

[2] It was purchased from the adventurers by John Ottrington. His granddaughter married into the St. Leger family, and brought the property to Viscount Doneraile. Archdall's *Peerage*, vol. vi. p. 121. Kilmeaden House is built on the spot where the castle stood.

[3] Four miles west of Carrick.

[4] Granno or Granny castle is on the Kilkenny side of the Suir, three miles above Waterford.

[5] Dunhill, i. e., the Port of the Cliff. In 1317 Arnold le Powere, Baron of Dunoile, with the Lord Justice, the Earl of Kildare, and Richard de Clare, furnished and armed thirty thousand men to oppose Robert and Edward Bruce. Campion's *History of Ireland*, p. 122; Dublin, 1809. In 1324 John le Poer of Dunoyle was one of the witnesses to the

was bravely defended by a lady. It was built on a rock almost inaccessible, and judging from the ruins still remaining, it must have been a place of prodigious strength. For a long time it resisted the attack, though artillery was used to make a breach in its outworks. At length it yielded. The Countess was the life and soul of the defenders. Day and night she was on the ramparts, animating by her presence and energy the spirits of the garrison. She had, it seems, a skilful engineer, who defeated all the plans of the besiegers. One day she retired to rest, but she neglected to provide for the wants of her weary soldiers. Her engineer sent to demand refreshment for himself and his comrades; he received in return the unwarlike meed of a drink of buttermilk. Irritated at the insult, he made signals to the foe, who actually had raised the siege and were marching off, and surrendered to them the castle. It was forthwith blown up with gunpowder. The Countess perished among the ruins.

The first day's march of the army was to Kilmacthomas. The whole of the next day was spent in crossing the river Mahon, which was swollen by a land-flood. During the night the soldiers were quartered in the neighboring villages. On the evening of the 4th the army reached Dungarvan,[1] and proceeded without delay to invest the town. It had submitted to Lord Broghill a few days before, as we learn from one of his letters, dated December 19th:

"The 2d of this month, with a party of 600 horse and 800 foot, I advanced to Dungarvan, where the Lord so ruled their hearts that on the 3d it was delivered up to me by Colonel Kinsale, who was in it with his regiment and troop, both which have since taken up arms with us. There was in the town six ordnance, sixteen barrels of powder, with bullet and match proportionable."

The townsmen would seem to have repented of their hasty submission to Lord Broghill; perhaps they were not satisfied with the conditions imposed on them. But now, terrified at the near approach of danger, they again surrendered at discretion. An order was issued to put the inhabitants to the sword, in punishment for their treachery. Cromwell rode into the town at the head of the troops. As they were about to execute the merciless command, tradition says a woman named Nagle forced her way through the crowd with a flagon of beer in her hand, and drank to the General's health, calling on him to pledge her in turn. It is added that Cromwell was so pleased with her courage and courtesy, that he accepted the pledge and permitted his soldiers to partake of the liquor, which they, thirsty and heated,

compact entered into between the King of England and the nobles of English descent for the capture of felons, robbers, and thieves of their family and sirname. Hardiman's *Statute of Kilkenny*, p. 66, note, published by the Irish Arch. Soc. in 1843. In 1328, on Sunday, the day after the feast of St. Agnes, died John le Poer, Baron of Dunhille. Clynn's *Annals*, p. 20; Dublin, 1849

[1] In 1643 the town of Dungarvan was incorporated by Act of Parliament, which recites that as the seignory of Dungarvan was the most great and ancient honor belonging to the King in Ireland, which through war was, for the most part, destroyed, it is provided that the Portreeve and commons of the said town, their heirs, &c., may enjoy all manner of free gifts and customs, as the inhabitants of the honorable manor of Clare in England have used and enjoyed, and as the mayor and commons of Bristol have done, the profits to go to the reparation of the walls under the survey of the Earls of Desmond. Ryland's *History of Waterford*, p. 23.

found very refreshing, and which the servants of the woman abundantly supplied. He revoked the order, and not only spared the lives of the people, but saved the town, the church and the castle excepted, from being plundered by the soldiers. Here he met Lord Broghill, to whose services he was so much indebted for his recent successes.

At Whitechurch, about five miles west of Dungarvan, he was met by 2,500 men of the southern garrisons that had lately revolted. They assured him that the towns throughout Munster, which had lately gone over to the parliament, would gladly receive garrisons and afford them winter quarters.

On the 5th he entered Youghal, where fresh supplies awaited him. Here he established himself and a part of his army in winter-quarters; the rest he distributed through the towns that had lately submitted to the parliament. Winter had set in, and sickness was beginning to spread. "I scarcely know an officer of forty amongst us," he writes, "that hath not been sick, and how many considerable ones we have lost is no little thought of heart to us. The noble Lieutenant-General (Jones), whose finger, to my knowledge, never ached in all these expeditions, fell sick, we doubt not, upon a cold taken upon our late wet march and ill accommodation. He went to Dungarvan, where, struggling for some four or five days with a fever, he died; having run his course with so much honor, courage, and fidelity, as his actions better speak than my pen. What England lost hereby, is above me to speak. I am sure I lost a noble friend and companion in labors." [1]

The news of Jones' death reached the House of Commons on the 5th of January, 1650, in a letter written by a Cromwellian soldier. "We had a very sore and stormy march hither; and that which added to the bitterness of it was the sickness of the truly noble and ever honored Lieutenant-General Jones. He was a gentleman very useful in the army, and was very much liked and lamented. His approved constancy and fidelity to the English interests was such as to manifest that he will very much shine and be famous for it to posterity. His straits, hazards, difficulties, and necessities were very many, and I might add, temptations, too. Yet he broke through all with unmoved gallantry, steadfastness, and resolution. His temper and disposition was very sweet and amiable, and obliging to all. And he had very much love and respect to all that came lately over." [2] His body was brought to Youghal, and buried with great solemnity in the chapel belonging to the Earl of Cork, in St. Mary's church.

[1] Letter to Lenthal from Cork, Dec. 19th, 1649. Cox says : "He was a man of clear valor, and excellent as well as fortunate conduct, and not inferior to anybody in a sincere passion for the good of his country." *Ibid.* Yet in spite of this panegyric, it is certain that great enmity and distrust existed between Jones and Cromwell. A strict surveillance was maintained by him and Ireton over Jones' movements, who, shortly before his death, was engaged in devising projects to beat Cromwell out of Ireland! Morrice's *Memoir of Lord Orrery*, p. 16. We are told also that one Mrs. Chaplain, daughter of the minister of Dungarvan under the Cromwellians, who lived in the house in which Jones died, often said that it was confidently believed that Cromwell had found means to poison Jones. Smith's *History of Waterford*, p. 65.

[2] Letter from Cork, in Whitelocke, p. 421. Ireton was appointed in his place. "Major General Ireton cannot well endure the yoke of his new honors, such is his modesty ;

Here also died two other persons eminently faithful, goodly, and true to the parliament, Lieutenant-Colonel Wolfe and Scoutmaster-General Rowe.[1]

Ormonde, too, was anxious to find winter-quarters for his army, whence it might be ready to issue forth without delay, to meet the enemy when he should take the field in spring. He had neither money to pay his men nor provisions to support them for twenty-four hours together. He suggested to the Commissioners of Trust that the troops should be distributed through the towns of Munster which still continued faithful to the king. Both Limerick and Waterford, the most important places now in the hands of the Royalists, persistently refused to receive them. To add to his mortification, his men began to desert in considerable numbers. He kept some of his forces together hovering between Clonmel and Waterford; the rest were obliged to scatter over the country and seek quarters where they could find them. Many of them never reassembled. He took up his own quarters at Kilkenny. Thence he wrote in disgust to the King, who was at Jersey, to acquaint his Majesty "how his authority was disputed by those great pretenders to royalty." About this time, he seems to have asked the King's permission to withdraw both himself and the King's authority from Ireland, should occasion require it. His friend Dean Boyle had even procured a pass for him from Cromwell. He was well aware of the people's distrust of himself and of their aversion to his government. Believing themselves betrayed by him, they could not be brought into a course of action that would put an end to all hope of obtaining favorable terms from the enemy. Besides, he was forced to confess that "it appeared every day more evidently than other, and would soon be visible to the shortest foresight, that upon anything that Ireland could afford, it would not be possible to make any resistance against the rebels, who had the whole coast towards England, Waterford excepted, ready to receive their forces, commodious harbors for their shipping, and garrisons from whence they could immediately be in the heart of his best countries and at the walls of his remaining towns. No supplies were arriving from abroad, no diversion was made by the Royalist Party in England, though Cromwell and Ireton, the supposed heads of the rebels, were removed from them."

Taaffe and the Connaught troops returned to their own province. Lord Dillon went to Westmeath, Major-General Hugh O'Neill, with 1,600 Ulster men was admitted into Clonmel, — the Mayor having asked that a considerable part of the army should be sent to garrison that town; that 300 men should march immediately into the town,

---

indeed he is a good soul." Letter from Pembroke, January 6th, in *Perf. Diurnal.* He was soon after appointed President of Munster.. "January 10th, 1650 — The Attorney-General was ordered by the House to prepare a patent to be passed under the Great Seal of England, appointing Major General Ireton to be President of Munster." Tonson's *Debates*, vol. xix. p. 46.

[1] Cromwell to Lenthal, February 16th, 1650, in *Aphor. Disc.*, vol. ii. p 468, Appendix 44: "Our condition for want of Physicians is sad, being fain to trust our lives in the Papist doctors' hands, when we fall sick, which is much, if not more, than our adventures in the field." Letter of W. A., in *Perfect Diurnal*, January 8th, 1650.

and that the rest might be in some garrisons near, to be brought in if necessity required it.

Inchiquin went towards Limerick ; with 400 horse he took pos-session of Kilmallock, against the will of the inhabitants. Daniel O'Neill, who as an Ulsterman and a nephew of Owen Roe, was accept-able to the gentlemen and officers of the North, and as a Protestant, was not objected to by the Scots, was sent with 2,000 Ulster foot, and Colonel Trevor with 400 horse, to assist Lord Montgomery of Ardes and Sir George Munroe, in recovering the places lost in the counties of Down and Antrim ; when, after a long and weary march, they arrived there, they found these commanders had been routed by Sir Charles Coote, at Lisburn. Carrickfergus surrendered a week after, " the town and castle being of the greatest importance of any place of the province ; " and thus all the North, except Charlemont and Enniskillen, was in the hands of the Parliamentary forces, while in the South, Broghill could boast that " there was no English garrison in Munster but was theirs."

CHAPTER XX.

IN WINTER-QUARTERS.

Head-Quarters at Youghal — Cromwell visits Cork and Kinsale — Stubber — Visits Bandon and Skibbereen — Cromwell's Bridge — His Recall — Sufferings of the People of Cork — Their Constancy — Bramhall — The Church Bells — Coppinger of Ballyvolane — The Clonmacnoise Decrees.

WHILE the army was enjoying its well-earned repose, Cromwell was busy making excursions from his head-quarters at Youghal.[1] About the middle of December, in company with Lord Broghill, who had joined him at Dungarvan, he went to Cork; as we learn from a letter of Thomas Herbert to an " Honorable Member of the Council," dated Cork, December 18th, 1649 : " Yesterday my Lord Lieutenant came from Youghal, the head-quarters, my Lord Broghill, Sir William Fenton,[2] and divers other gentlemen and commanders attending His Excellency, who has received here a very hearty and noble entertainment. The well-affected of the city entertained him with much heartiness and freeness. To-morrow the Major General (Ireton) is expected here ; both in good health, God be praised. This week, I believe, they will visit Kinsale, Bandonbridge, and other places in this province that have lately declared for us, and expect a return of his affection and presence, which joys many. Colonel Deane and Colonel Blake, our sea-generals, are both riding in Cork harbor."[3]

From Cork he went to Kinsale, to view the several forts there. He found it "ragged and without heat." The Mayor, as usual, came out to meet him, and delivered to him the town-mace and the keys of the gates. Instead of returning them, as was his practice, to the Chief Magistrate, he handed them over to the governor of the town, Colonel Stubber. He said he had been told that the Mayor was an Irishman and a Papist, and that he judged it inconvenient to entrust

---

[1] While at Youghal he is said to have lived in one of the old castles adjoining St. John's house of the Benedictines, in the Main Street. During the Protectorate it was known by the name of the Magazine. It was pulled down in 1835. The front room on the first floor was his council chamber. See *Kilk. Arch. Journal* for 1856, p. 15. " He lay at Lady Corke's house at the college ; he was about to take Mrs. Semmes' house to live in this winter, yet some say he will go to Cork." Letter in *Perf. Diurnal*, January 2d, 1650.

[2] His father, Sir Geoffrey, came to Ireland in 1579, as needy as his fellow-adventurer Boyle. Having obtained the place of Surveyor General, he helped Boyle, to whom he gave his daughter in marriage, in his extortions. In the course of one year he managed to amass a great fortune. Wallop spoke of him as "a most apparent bribe-taker." See *Flight of the Earls*, p 223. Sir William married Margaret, the daughter and heiress of Maurice Fitzgibbon, who inherited the estates of the White Knight ; their daughter and heiress married Sir John King, who was created Lord Kingston by Charles II. in 1660. See Archdall's *Peerage*, vol. iii. p. 228.

[3] Brief Relation, &c., January 1st to 8th, in *Cromwelliana*, p. 73. These, with Sir William Fenton and Colonel Phayre, were appointed temporary commissioners for the management of affairs in Cork. Cary's *Memorials*, &c., vol. ii. p. 188.

a place of such importance to one of that creed. It was whispered to
Cromwell that Stubber was not over strict in his religious duties.
"May be not," he replied; "but as he is a soldier he has honor, and
therefore we will let his religion alone this time." [1]

He visited Bandonbridge, too, and found there much heartiness,
"a fine sweet town, and an entire English plantation, without any ad-
mixture of Irish." He was greatly pleased with the strength of this
plantation and the devotion of the people to the cause of England ;
and speaking of the exertions of Richard Boyle, first Earl of Cork,
founder of the colony, he declared that if there were an Earl of Cork
in every province of Ireland, it would have been impossible for the
Irish to raise a rebellion.[2] Tradition says he went on to the west, by
Dunmanway and Skibbereen ; and that his army took up its quarters
for one night, at least, in the church of Abbey Strewry, on the northern bank of the river Ilen, about a mile to the west of the latter place.
The territory of the O'Donovans was wasted, the troops destroying
all that came in their way.[3] Two of their castles were blown up with
gunpowder. There is a bridge over the Glengariff river bearing
Cromwell's name, an ancient structure, shorn of its parapets and long
disused. It is said that, on Cromwell's approach, the natives broke
down this bridge, in order to hinder his advance ; but he forced them
to rebuild it, threatening to hang any who refused ; since then it has
borne his name, as also the ford, Ath Cromwell, over which the bridge
is erected.

On the 19th of December, Cromwell wrote from Cork to Lenthal,
giving an account of the attempt made by Ferrall and O'Neill to surprise the fort of Passage, and of the repulse they met with. This
letter did not reach the House of Commons until the 8th of January.
On that day a resolution was passed by the House, that the Lord
Lieutenant should be desired to come over and give his attendance
in parliament ; and the speaker was ordered to write to him to that
effect. A report had spread abroad that the King had left Jersey and
was gone to Scotland, and that he was raising forces there to invade
England. Some of the members proposed to muster an army in all
haste and send it across the border. But Fairfax, who then held the
supreme military command, did not seem willing to comply with their
wish ; by many he was said to be too favorably disposed to the Scotch,

---

[1] Wright's *History of Ireland*, vol. ii. p. 86 Stubber was afterwards governor of Galway. Under pretence of taking up vagrants and idle persons, he made frequent excursions
by night with armed troops into the country, and seized upwards of a thousand people, often
without discrimination of rank or condition, whom he transported to the West Indies, and
there had sold as slaves. Hardiman's *History of Galway*, p 134. It was suspected that
Stubber was the executioner of Charles I. *Ibid*, p. 12.

[2] Bennett's *Hist. of Bandon*, p. 154. He came to Bandon several times afterwards,
and always put up at a little two storied house that occupied the site on which the house of
Mr. F. Bennett now stands, in the South Main Street. About the beginning of this century
the house was taken down; but the boards of the bedroom occupied by Cromwell, in the
western end of the house, were carefully removed, and relaid in the new building. *Ibid.*

[3] Daniel O'Donovan, chief of Clancahill, in 1649, was reduced to great extremity by
Cromwell's forces, who seized all his estates, burning, killing, and destroying all that came
in their way. He surrendered his castle to the Commonwealth, Colonel Phayre, governor
of Cork, having engaged to him some satisfaction. *Annals of the Four Masters*, ad nn.
1600.

being influenced by his wife, who was a strict Presbyterian. As the Irish army was in winter-quarters, and the Parliamentary party was in possession of nearly all the strongholds, it was thought that the Lord Lieutenant's presence, so much needed elsewhere, might well be spared in Ireland. Cromwell at first showed a readiness to return to England and assume the chief command of the expedition ; but, on reflection, as the danger from the side of Scotland did not seem very urgent, he decided "to settle Ireland in a safe posture first." By another letter, written from Cork by Cromwell to his "dear friend Lord Wharton," we find that he had returned to Cork, and was staying there on the first of January.

A detailed account of the sufferings of the people of Cork about this time is fortunately preserved in the archives of the Irish College, Rome ; it bears the date of 1651, and was written by a Jesuit Father then on the Irish mission : —

"The hatred of the heretics towards our holy religion increasing every day, an order was published prohibiting the citizens to carry swords or to have in their houses any arms whatever. This order was carried out, and soon another proclamation was issued by the President of the Council of War, commanding all Catholics either to abjure their religion or to depart from the city without delay. Should they consent to embrace the religion of the Parliament, they were allowed to remain and keep their goods and property. Should they, however, adhere pertinaciously to popery, all, without exception, were to depart immediately from the city. Three cannon-shots were to be fired as signals at stated intervals before nightfall, and any Catholic found in the city after the third signal was to be massacred without mercy. Then it was that the constancy of the citizens in the faith was seen. There was not even one found in the city who would accept the impious conditions offered, or try to keep his property and goods with the loss of his faith. Before the third signal all went forth from the city walls, the men and women, yea, even the children and the infirm ; and it was a sight truly worthy of heaven to see so many thousands thus abandoning their homes, so many venerable matrons with their tender children wandering through the fields, or overcome with fatigue lying on the ground, in ditches, or on the highways ; so many aged men, some of whom had held high offices in the State and belonged to the nobility, with their wives and families, wandering to and fro, knowing not where to find a place of refuge ; so many merchants, who on that morning abounded in wealth, now without a home in which to rest their weary limbs. Yet all went forth with joy to their destruction, abandoning their houses and goods, their revenues and property and wealth, choosing rather to be afflicted with the people of God on the mountain-tops and in caverns, in hunger and thirst, in cold and nakedness, than to enjoy momentary pleasure and temporal prosperity with sin."

Bramhall, the Protestant bishop of Derry, happened to be in Cork about this time ; with difficulty he contrived to evade the Puritan spies. Cromwell was much displeased at his escape ; he declared that he would have given a good sum of money for that "Irish Canterbury," as he called him. Prelacy in any form was hateful to him. Ussher pleaded in vain with Cromwell for Bramhall and his brother-bishops of the Protestant church.[1]

---

[1] See Parr's *Life of Archbishop Ussher*, p. 75. He was afterwards declared incapable of pardon for life or estate, and banished. *Crom. Sett.* p. 97. He fled to the Continent, and remained there until the Restoration. In 1660 he was translated from Derry to Armagh. He died in 1663. Ussher was the head of the Puritan party among the Protestant clergy in Ireland. Leland's *History of Ireland*, vol. iii. p. 28.

Being very much in want of artillery, he had the bells of the Cork churches melted down. When remonstrated with for the sacrilege, he replied that as gunpowder was invented by a priest, he thought it not amiss to turn the bells into cannons.

During his stay in Cork he is said to have made the house of Mr. Coppinger, at Ballyvolane, his head-quarters, and to have passed the Christmas there.[1] The family tradition is, that Mr. Coppinger was travelling in Holland some years before, and was placed in circumstances in which he became security for a young Englishman, a brewer, for a debt, for which he was arrested. The bills, which were drawn in Mr. Coppinger's favor in liquidation upon England, were dishonored, and there the matter rested — Mr. Coppinger having to make good the payment. In 1649, at the Court of Claims in Cork, he was recognized by Cromwell, who sent a message to him that he could not decide about the forfeiture of his property without seeing him. Mr. Coppinger accordingly waited upon his Excellency, when Cromwell inquired, " Is not your name Coppinger?" " Yes." " Were you not at —— ?" mentioning the town and the year. " Yes." " Did you not become security for a young man whose bills were never honored, and you had to pay?" " Yes." " Then," said Cromwell, " I am that man, and you will receive your estate without further question, in compensation of these bills." [2]

On the 4th of December, the Irish prelates, to the number of twenty, met at Clonmacnoise. For nearly three weeks they sat in council, seeking some remedy for the dire evils that had fallen on the country. The task they set themselves was nearly a hopeless one: to unite the various discordant parties into which the country was split; to assemble an army scattered throughout the provinces, and demoralized by the treachery and incapacity of its leaders; to raise money for the public wants from a people that had been plundered by friend and foe alike; in a word, to make one last effort for their country and for their religion, both of which were now threatened with utter extinction. The result of their deliberations was embodied in an address to the clergy and the laity of Ireland, calling on them in the name of their country and of their faith, to forget their past feuds and join in resisting with all their might the new enemy that had invaded their native land. " The whole Irish party," says Leland, " was anxious for the event of this self-appointed council, and looked for nothing less important than a violent protestation against

---

[1] The house is still standing, between Mayfield and Dublin Hill, to the north east of the city.

[2] Wright, in his *Hist. of Ireland*, vol. ii. p. 86, gives the anecdote as communicated to him by Mr. Crofton Croker. " August 19th, 1841, Mr. Coppinger called on me at the Admiralty. He told me that his property at Dodge's Glynn, near Cork, was a forfeiture of King William's time, the possessor having been killed in the battle under Sir James Cotter, . . . He further says that Cromwell took up his residence there while at Cork," &c. Another version, which we have from a member of the Coppinger family, says that Cromwell gave the owner a protection, which saved the property from confiscation, and that he wrote it on the pommel of his saddle, seated on horseback, before the door. This is more probable, for the Court of Claims was not established until 1651; its first sittings at Mallow, where the cases of the inhabitants of Cork were heard, took place in July, 1656, *Crom. Sett.*, p. 61.

the government of Ormonde. Happily the temper of one of their bishops, Heber McMahon, bishop of Clogher, disappointed their expectations. From the time of the accommodation between Ormonde and O'Neill, in which MacMahon had been instrumental, the Marquis frequently conversed with him on public affairs, and inspired him with a high opinion of his talents for government and his zeal for the interests of religion. With these sentiments he entered the assembly of his brethren, where he had the consequence naturally derived from superior abilities. He silenced the factious, encouraged the moderate ; he defeated all the practices of Antrim, and, at length, with difficulty prevailed on the prelates to declare, by a formal instrument, that no security for life, fortune, or religion, could be expected from Cromwell ; to express their detestation of all odious distinctions and animosities between old Irish, English, and Scottish Royalists, and their resolution of punishing all the clergy who should be found to encourage them."[1]

"It cannot be denied," says Borlase, repeating the words of Clarendon, "that the conclusions which were then made were full of respect to the King's service and of wholesome advice and counsel to the people." Even Ormonde admitted that "in the assembly there were divers speeches made, tending to the satisfaction of the people, and to incline them to obedience to his Majesty and unity among themselves, in opposition to the rebels."

It is not easy to see what there is in these decrees to excite the anger of Mr. Carlyle, or to make him descend to the use of hard names. Can it be that it was a great crime on their part not to accept with gladness "the true message brought them," not to recognize in his hero, "the veritable heaven's messenger clad in thunder"? He admits, indeed, that there was "some glow of Irish patriotism, some light of real human valor in those old hearts ; though it had parted company with facts, and came forth in a huge embodiment of headlong ferocity and general unveracity." How far this latter statement is borne out by history, our readers know from the results of a recent controversy.

Immediately after the publication of the bishops' decrees, Cromwell published a reply to them under the title : "A Declaration of the Lord Lieutenant of Ireland for the undeceiving of deluded and seduced people, which may be satisfactory to all that do not shut their eyes against the light : In answer to certain late Declarations and Acts, framed by the Irish Popish Prelates and Clergy in a Conventicle at Clonmacnoise." This Mr. Carlyle styles "the remarkablest state paper ever issued by any Lord Lieutenant." Though it is by no means so rare as the Declarations of the Bishops, it may be new to some of our readers.

---

[1] *History of Ireland*, vol. iii. p. 359. The Declarations and Decrees of the Bishops made at Clonmacnoise December 4th and 13th, 1649, will be found in Appendix viii. to this work. They are taken from *Spicil. Ossor.*, vol ii. p. 38, &c.

CHAPTER XXI.

OPENING OF THE SPRING CAMPAIGN.

IMPATIENT of all delay, Cromwell took the field once more on the 29th of January, the weather being unusually favorable for his purposes.[1] Hitherto his course had been along the coast ; now he would venture inland, and try whether fortune would favor him there as it had done elsewhere.[2] His forces were considerably less in number than when he had landed in Dublin six months before, though they were largely recruited from the garrisons that had revolted to the parliament, and from the English that were made prisoners in the captured fortresses. They had profited of the rest afforded them in their winter quarters ; for, in his letter to the House of Commons from Cork, dated December 20th, he says : " The army is in so good health, that regiments which lately had marched only 400 men, now march 800 or 900." From England he had received plentiful supplies of men and provisions. And so he found himself at the head of " a healthy and gallant army, full longing to be abroad against the enemy, all new-clothed and money in their pockets." His friends, too, gave him the help of their pious prayers, for " the officers of the army kept the 16th of February a day of humiliation, grounded on the dealings of God with their brethren in Ireland, Who, though He had made them a glorious testimony against the bloody enemies, yet had afflicted them by the death of many worthies ; which chastening of the Lord they did desire to lay to heart, as also that affliction in the miscarriage of some vessels sailing from Minehead."[3]

Ormonde, with a portion of the Confederate army, was in winter-quarters at Kilkenny. If he could be taken unawares, before he had time to get his scattered forces together and make the necessary preparations for the siege, the war would be at an end. Besides, Kilkenny and its inhabitants were special objects of dislike to the Puritans, for it was the nursery of the late rebellion, and the headquarters of the Supreme Council of the Confederate Catholics. Towards Kilkenny, therefore, Cromwell led his army with all speed.

---

[1] The winter had proved fairer than in man's memory any winter hath been.

[2] " Though God hath blessed you with a great longitude of land alongst the shore, yet it hath but little depth into the country." Cromwell to Lenthal, Dec. 19th, 1649.

[3] February 8th — Letters received from Cork, that five ships with soldiers were all cast away coming from Linehead for Ireland — only 20 or 30 swam on shore — 80 horse and 150 foot, and all the seamen except 20 or 80.

The history of this part of the spring campaign is given in such graphic detail in one of 'his letters to the Speaker of the House of Commons that we cannot do better than set it before our readers, supplementing it, when possible, from other sources. It was written from Castletown,[1] which was a seat of the Archbishop of Cashel, and dated February 11th, 1650:

> " Having refreshed our men for some short time in our winter-quarters, and health being pretty well recovered, we thought fit to take the field, and to attempt such things as God by His providence should lead us to upon the enemy. Our resolution was to fall upon the enemy's quarters two ways. The one party, being about fifteen or sixteen troops of horse and dragoons and about two thousand foot, were ordered to go up, by way of Carrick, into the county of Kilkenny, under the command of Colonel Reynolds, whom Major-General Ireton was to follow with a reserve. I myself was to go by the way of Mallow, over the Blackwater, towards the county Limerick and the county Tipperary, with about twelve troops of horse and three troops of dragoons, and between two and three hundred foot. I began my march upon Tuesday, the nine-and-twentieth of January, from Youghal."

Lord Broghill was left with a flying camp in South Munster. Colonel Ingoldsby was sent towards Limerick.

He passed by Conna, five miles north-west of Tallow. To the west of the castle[2] is Gallows Hill. Here he is said to have halted with his army, and held council about executing the garrison. From this point he battered the castle with his guns, but apparently with little effect. He sent out parties which captured the castles of Mocollop, Cappoquin and Dromanah.

Castletown Roche was heroically defended for some days by Lady Roche against a detachment of the army. She was at length forced to surrender by the heavy fire from a battery erected in a field on the opposite side of the river Awbeg, Spencer's ".Gentle Mulla," which is still called " the camp."[3]

> " On Thursday, the one-and-thirtieth, I possessed a castle called Kilbenny,[4] upon the edge of the county Limerick, where I left thirty foot. From thence I marched to a strong house called Clogheen,[5] belonging to Sir Richard Everard, who is one of the Supreme Council, where I left a troop of horse and some dragoons. From thence I marched to Roghill castle,[6] which was possessed by some Ulster foot and a party of the enemy's horse; which upon summons, I having taken the captain of the horse prisoner before, was rendered to me. These places being thus

---

[1] Four miles north of Carrick.

[2] A large, square tower, built on a steep hill on the south side of the river Bride; it was the residence of Thomas Fitzgerald, elder brother of Gerald, the great Earl of Desmond, and father of the famous Sugan Earl.

[3] In *The Cromwellian Settlement* it said that Cromwell passed it by, not caring to assault a place so well fortified; p. 183. Lady Roche was hanged four years after in Cork, having been falsely accused of murder by a certain ungrateful English maid-servant, whom she had taken into her house. Morison's *Threnodia*, p. 72.

[4] Kilbenny, midway between Mitchelstown and Clogheen.

[5] Twelve miles south west of Clonmel. The Everards were owners of large estates near Fethard. The barrack in that town was formerly their residence. Sir Richard played an important part in the rebellion of 1641. When Limerick surrendered in 1651 his life and estates were declared forfeited, because he was " one of those who opposed and restrained the deluded people from accepting the conditions offered to them." Lenihan's *History of Limerick*, p. 183; Dublin, 1866.

[6] Now Rehill, nine miles south-west of Cahir.

possessed gave us much command, together with some other strongholds we have of the White Knight,[1] and Roche's country,[2] and of all the land from Mallow to the Suir side, especially by another old castle, taken by my Lord of Broghill, called Old Castletown,[3] since my march, which I sent his lordship to endeavor."

When Castletown was captured, Broghill "gave quarter for life and their wearing apparel to the private soldiers, and the officers to be at his discretion, Thereupon, by advice, he caused all these to be shot to death, to affright those little castles for so persistently holding out."

"Also a castle of Sir Edward Fitzharris,[4] over the mountains in the county of Limerick; I having left his lordship at Mallow with about six or seven hundred horse, and four or five hundred foot to protect these parts and your interest in Munster, lest while we were abroad, Inchiquin, whose forces lay about Limerick and the county Kerry, should fall in behind us. His lordship drew two cannon to the foresaid castle, which having summoned they refused. His lordship having bestowed upon it about ten shot made their stomachs come down, He gave all the soldiers quarter for life, and shot all the officers being six in number. Since the taking of these garrisons the Irish have sent their commissioners to compound for their contributions as far as the walls of Limerick."

He sent a detachment to Newcastle, a stronghold on the southern bank of the Suir, the seat of the Prendergasts. The castle was surrendered by the owner ; but it was immediately restored to him on condition that the defences should be taken down. A few soldiers were left to see the order carried out. The rest of the detachment had not proceeded far when they heard confused noises behind ; they hurried back, thinking that the tenants of the castle were murdering their comrades. It was only the noise of a pack of buck-hounds kept in the bawn. The owner and his hounds were led off to Cromwell. The dogs seem to have been successful mediators for their master, for he obtained the General's favor. There is a letter of Cromwell's still extant requesting that this gentleman and his family might be spared from transplantation. The request, however, was not complied with ; his estates passed to the Adventurers, and his children became exiles.[5]

He crossed the Suir at Rochestown, three miles south of Cahir.

"From thence," he continues, "we marched to Fethard, almost in the heart of the county Tipperary, where was a garrison of the enemy. The town is most pleasantly seated, having a very good wall with round and square bulwarks, after

---

[1] John Fitzgerald, called John of Callan, because he was slain there by the M'Carthys in 1261, was married twice. By his first marriage he had a son Maurice, the ancestor of the Kildare Fitzgeralds ; by the second he had four sons, on whom, as Count Palatine, he conferred knighthood ; these were the ancestors of the Munster Fitzgeralds. The eldest was Gilbert or Gibbon ; hence his descendants were called the Clan Gibbon. The two last who bore the title of White Knight, made themselves infamous by their treachery towards their kinsmen, the great Earl of Desmond and the Sugan Earl. Their territory lay about Mitchelstown, in the county of Cork. An interesting account of the fate and fortunes of the last of this family who was owner of the castle, is given in Mr. A. M. Sullivan's *New Ireland*, p. 129 ; London, 1878.

[2] The district about Fermoy.

[3] Near Kildorrery, in the county of Cork ; it belonged to the Fitzgibbons.

[4] Castlehaven speaks of "Cloughnosty, a house of Sir Edward Fitzharris, seated in the mountains between the counties of Cork and Limerick."

[5] *Crom. Sett.*, Introd. xxv., and *Kilk. Arch. Journal* for 1876, p. 51. Only a scanty remnant of the castle is standing. It is about seven miles south of Clonmel.

the old manner of fortifications. We came thither in the night, and indeed were very much distressed by sore and tempestuous wind and rain. After a long march we knew not well how to dispose of ourselves; but finding an old abbey in the suburbs, and some cabins and poor houses, we got into them, and had opportunity to send the garrison a summons. They shot at my trumpet, and would not listen to him for an hour's space. But having some officers in our party whom they knew, I sent them to let them know I was there with a good part of the army. We shot not a shot at them; but they were very angry, and fired very earnestly on us, telling us it was not a time of night to send a summons. But yet in the end the governor was willing to send out two commissioners; I think rather to see whether there was a force sufficient to force him than to any other end. After almost a whole night spent in treaty, the town was delivered to me the next morning, upon terms which we usually call honorable, which I was the more willing to give, because I had little above two hundred foot, and neither ladders, nor guns, nor anything else to force them."

In *The Irish Monthly Mercury,* a newspaper of the time, a ludicrous account is given by one of Cromwell's soldiers of the terror of the town authorities when called on to surrender :

"From Rahill his Excellency went to Rochestown, where he got over the river Suir in such a nick of time that the least protraction had metamorphosed the ford into a ferry. The same night, in a hideous tempest, he came late before the town of Fethard, where the governor, little dreaming of any storm but that of the weather, was summoned by his Excellency. The gentleman at first thought it was in jest; but the corporation swearing and trembling it was in earnest, he concluded from the last as much as from the first, that it was so; and by the same action evidencing he was of the same faith, like one well versed in his trade, called a council of Shakers to know whether it was consonant to the rules of war to summon a town by candle-light? After a small debate, either for the time or for the sense, they concluded that whether it were or no — for the thing was left amphibious — it was consonant to the rules of safety to surrender the place; which he did, modestly saying that he had lost his government in a storm and not tamely, as other governors had done, and that by his then surrendering he had satisfied his engagement to the Supreme Council, which was that none of them should live to see the day in which he should lose Fethard; no, nor the sun neither, though it shine on all the world but Wood Street. We were more troubled to come to than to come by this town, which my Lord Lieutenant entered the same light in which he had summoned it, the late Governor entertaining him with a file of health; but sure he had so much care of his own that he did not drink it, so that his modesty or circumspection lessened him of one cup, but he had drunk of another had he wanted the latter."

Ludlow, whose account of all that took place before his arrival in Ireland, is singularly inaccurate, says the Corporation of Fethard sent deputies to surrender the town before Cromwell thought of approaching it. The towns-people, with a pardonable vanity, believe that the town was surrendered only after an obstinate resistance. Both these statements are false, as may be seen from the following document. Cromwell arrived before the town late at night, and on his arrival sent a trumpeter with a summons, calling on the garrison to surrender. To this summons he received the following reply : —

For Oliver Cromwell, General of the Parliament forces now in Ireland :

MAY IT PLEASE YOUR LORDSHIP, —

           I have received your letter about nine of the clock this night, which hour I conceive unreasonable for me to treat with you. Yet if your Lordship pleases to send sufficient hostages in for such as I will employ to treat with you, I will be ready to entrust some in that business. Having no more at present,

I remain,

Your honor's friend and servant,

PIERCE BUTLER.

From the Garrison at Fethard, Feb. 2d, 1650,
half an hour of nine o'clock of the night.

The following articles of surrender were signed the next morning before six o'clock ; the Parliamentary garrison was admitted before eight :

Articles of agreement made and concluded on the 3d day of February, 1650, between the Most Hon. Oliver Cromwell, Lord Lieutenant-General of Ireland, and Lieutenant-Colonel Pierce Butler, Governor of the Town of Fethard, concerning the surrender of the said town, as follows :.

1. That all the officers and soldiers shall march freely with their horses and arms and all other goods, bag and baggage, colors flying, matches lighted, ball in bouche, into any place within his Majesty's quarters or garrisons, except such as are now besieged, safely conveyed thither, free from violence from any of the Parliament's party.

2. That all the country families and inhabitants, as also any of the officers may freely live and enjoy their goods either in town or abroad; if they or any of them be disposed to betake themselves to their former habitations in the country, that they have respite of time for that, and admittance to enjoy their holdings, paying contribution, as others in the country do, and carry with them safely such goods as they have within this garrison.

3. That all clergymen and captains of the soldiers, both town and county now in this garrison, may freely march bag and baggage without any annoyance or prejudice in body or goods.

4. That all and every the inhabitants of the said town, and their wives, children and servants, with all their goods and chattels, both within the town and abroad in the country, shall be protected from time to time, and at all times; and shall quietly and peaceably enjoy their estates, both real and personal, in as free and good condition as any English or Irish shall hold his or their estates in this kingdom, they and every of them paying such contribution as the rest of the inhabitants of the county of Tipperary pay proportionably to their estates, and no more.

In consideration whereof the said Governor doth hereby engage himself that he will deliver up the said town with all things therein, except such things as are before agreed upon, to be taken away with them by eight of the o'clock this morning.

(Signed),

O. CROMWELL.[1]

By reason of their timely surrender, not only the people but even the priests were then spared, and allowed to enjoy their liberties and properties in security ; and later they escaped, being transplanted to Connaught. On the 26th of October, 1653, in reply to their petition to be secured in the possession of their lands, the Standing Committee of Officers for References were ordered by the Commissioners of the Commonwealth of England for the affairs of Ireland, to consider of their petition and the articles annexed, and to testify their opinion therein to the said Commissioners of the Commonwealth. To which they sent in the following answer, Nov. 2d, 1653 :

---

[1] MS. in the Royal Irish Academy. In Hall's *Ireland*, vol. i. p. 231, there is mention of a certain gate of the town through which no corpse was ever carried, because it was by it that Cromwell entered the town. This gate was taken down about ten years since.

" In obedience to your Honor's reference, having taken into consideration the Articles of Fethard, and the testimony of the good affection of the inhabitants of the said town to the English interest in the beginning of the rebellion, and the constant manifestation of their good affection since the said Articles, and the several expressions of the Lord Lieutenant and the late Lord Deputy upon consideration of their Articles, that they were a people to be differenced from the rest of the whole nation ; we humbly offer that the said inhabitants may enjoy the benefit of their Articles in the place where they now live, and not be transplanted into Connaught or elsewhere.

" Signed in the name and by appointment of the said Committee.

" CHARLES COOTE."

When the Royalist officers, after the restoration of Charles II., who were to divide between them all the houses of the Irish in the towns as not yet set out to the Adventurers or soldiers, sent surveyors there, as to all other towns, to measure and value the houses, the Sovereign and Commons of·the town opposed them, and prevented them by force from so doing.

" The night we entered Fethard," continues Cromwell, " there being about seventeen companies of the Ulster foot in Cashel, about twenty-five miles from thence, they quit it in some disorder. The Sovereign and aldermen since sent to me a petition that I would protect them ; which I have also made a quarter."

Hearing the favorable conditions which their neighbors at Fethard had received, they hastened to offer the keys of the town to Cromwell and to throw themselves on his mercy. They too were promised, at least such of them as were not in the rebel army, and were actually inhabiting the town at the time of the surrender, that they should be dispensed from transplanting.[1] Such mercy was not acceptable to those who, four years later, laid claim to the town ;[2] any delay allowed they thought displeasing to God : and when on the 23d of May, 1654, the whole town, except some few houses that the English lived in, was burnt to the ground in little more than a quarter of an hour, the disaster was attributed to the wrath of God against the iniquity of the people, not the least of their crimes being their unwillingness to depart from their homes and transplant to Connaught.

A regiment was sent from Fethard to garrison Thurles, which some of the Royalists threatened. In a " Letter of the Commissioners to the Lord Deputy and Council of Ireland, from Mallow, August 13th, 1656, on behalf of Lady Thurles,[3] the daughter of Sir John Poyntz, of Acton, in Gloucestershire, who sought to be excused from

---

[1] *Ibid.* p. 114. In reply to their petition, an order was issued dispensing them from transplanting till May 1st, 1655.

[2] These were called the 'forty-nine officers ; they had been in the standing army of Charles I. in Ireland before June 5th, 1649 ; as these got no lands from Cromwell, there was granted to them at the Restoration all that portion of the forfeited property of the Irish which had not been given already to the Adventurers and soldiers, viz , the houses in the corporate towns and the mortgaged lands. The distribution was intrusted to a body of trustees, sitting in the Green Chamber in the Custom House, Dublin. See *The Calendar of State Papers* (1603–1606), edited by Rev. C. W. Russell and J. P. Prendergast, Esq., preface lxxxiii. ; London, 1872.

[3] She was the mother of the Marquis of Ormonde, and wife of Thomas, eldest son of Walter Butler of Kilcash, who by courtesy was styled during his grandfather's life-time Lord Thurles. After his death she married George Mathews of Thurles, founder of the Llandaff

transplanting, on the ground of constant good affection to the English Government," it is stated that —

"When his Highness sat before Fethard, Lieutenant-Colonel Brian O'Neill, with about 1,500 of the Irish army well appointed, came to Lady Thurles' town of Thurles, and desired admission with his party, to garrison her house, which she refused: and immediately sent advertisement to his Highness thereof, and prayed he would be pleased to send a garrison of his army. Whereupon Major Bolton, with a regiment of horse and foot, was immediately commanded away to her house. A certificate of Major Bolton's was produced declaring the same, and likewise that the said lady was instrumental in the rendition of Cahir."

family. She was "a Popish recusant," and, as such, transplantable, though she had advanced considerable sums of money towards the relief of the English army, and entertained at her house for many weeks Major Peisley and some of his company, who were wounded at the capture of Archerstown by the Irish. From time to time she was dispensed from transplanting, and dwelt, perhaps, with the Countess of Ormonde (who retained her own property, though the estates of the Earl, her husband, were confiscated), till her son returned with increased honors and power at the Restoration. *Crom. Sett.* p. 245, and the *Kilk. Arch. Journal* for 1863, p. 282.

CHAPTER XXII

March on Callan — Fanning of Ballingarry — " A Country worth fighting for " — Defence of Callen — The Assault — Geoghegan of Frevanagh — Skerry's Castle — Butler's Castle — Return to Cashel — Ardfinan — Cost of the War in Ireland — Thanks of the House — The Cockpit.

FROM Fethard, where some of the sick were left behind, the army took the road towards Callan. Fanning, who had a strong castle near the village of Ballingarry, visited Cromwell on his way. He represented himself as the constant friend of the Parliamentary party, and in consequence hated by the peasantry. He invited the General to his house. On their way a blaze appeared in the distance. Fanning declared that his enemies had set fire to his castle. A huge heap of furze had been gathered together by his order, and fired at their approach. The trick succeeded for a while; Fanning was assured that he should be left in full possession of his property. But it was soon found out, and he was put to death.

Somewhere here Cromwell is said to have stood on a hill, and gazing on the country that lay at his feet, to have exclaimed, " This, indeed, is a country well worth fighting for."[1] Perhaps it was the sight that made him " set apart a good and great part of Tipperary for himself as a demesne, as he called it, for the State, in which no adventurer or soldier should demand his lot to be assigned, and no doubt intended both the State and it for the making great his own family."

Tradition says that Cromwell came to Callen by way of Kells, and that as he was passing Castle Eve, then belonging to the Sweetman family,[2] a shot was fired at him from one of the windows. He continued his march, merely remarking that it was not worth while losing precious time to look after the person who was silly enough to fire the shot. The family had abandoned the place, leaving behind a simpleton ; he had fired the shot. When Cromwell was passing by soon after, he plundered the castle, and compelled the simpleton, a man of prodigious strength, to take to the highroad a curiously wrought gate with brass fittings. His life was spared, and he lived for many years after.

---

[1] William of Orange is said to have uttered the same exclamation when, on his march to Carrick, he gained the summit of a hill overlooking Tipperary, and beheld the Golden Vale for the first time.

[2] The Sweetman arms are still to be seen at Newtown on the tomb of Walter Sweetman, Baron of Erly, which bears the date of 1553. In the neighboring church yard of Kells is buried Milo Sweetman, who was archbishop of Armagh from 1361 to 1380.

Callan had been appointed the rendezvous for Reynolds, Ireton and Sankey. This was then a place of considerable strength; it was surrounded by a strong wall and defended by three castles.[1] Cromwell, in order to batter down the gate and wall, planted his cannon on a hill at the southern end of the fair green, afterwards called Cromwell's Moat, which stood about two hundred yards south of the gate or fosse. In this place soon after he erected a gallows to hang his prisoners. Here probably suffered "my Lord of Ossory's captain-lieutenant of horse." Some years ago the remains of weapons, and the bones of horses and men were found in this fosse. The mound was removed about thirty-five years since by order of the Sovereign of Callan, when the fair-green was levelled.

The author of the *Aphorismal Discovery* gives the following account of the capture of this town:

"In this time Ormonde did appoint a garrison in Callan, 1,500 men in the great castle, an impregnant piece of work, under the command of Sir Robert Talbot. Among the rest was one Captain Geoghegan, of Frevanagh, in the barony of Moycashel, with his company, in a petty castle, a kind of gate-house, thatched with straw. The enemy marching home, Captain Geoghegan advising with Sir Robert Talbot, that they were best to demolish the said petty castle, as not defensible, and he and his company to come to the great castle, and did undertake to defend the same. Though this motion was so reasonable that no true-hearted martialist in such an extremity could ever deny it; notwithstanding, Talbot would not admit it, as not suiting to his former treachery. The Captain's motion rejected, must now stick to his gate-house for proper security or perish; whereupon (he) did resolve either to die or make good the place. The enemy now approaching thought all to be safe; but, contrary to his expectation, was opposed at the said gate-house with a bloody volley of shot, laying down dead at least a dozen. The enemy observing that fatal beginning, did march in a full body towards the said gate. The assault was mighty fierce and bloody, the defence extraordinary; the enemy was three several times repulsed and beaten back, with mighty great loss, and the defendants lost many of their men; quarter they would not accept, though several times offered; the Governor never yet relieved them with one man. The enemy now marched with main force, the defendants (though the best they could be), now by the multitude overswayed, were all to the last man put to the sword; never a man escaped the fury, and none killed but in action and who well deserved death. Three hundred at least of the enemy was killed in the same place, and many deadly wounded. Captain Geoghegan was killed, and was truly reported by the very enemy that he never saw such feats done by one man as was acted by the Captain. Twenty at least he killed with his proper sword; nay, his wife and the rest that survived him, and the rest during the assault, did kill eight men with stones and other weapons that fell from the perishing soldiers, as was given out; who was tyrannically butchered, and left for dead among her comrades, though now living. My Lord Cromwell's party, since he came to Ireland, never received such a fire and by so weak an instrument.

"The Governor observing all the former passages, capable to relieve the one and highly annoy the other, did neither of both, his castle being impregnable against any running army. The enemy . . . having now gone so far as to possess themselves of the gate, marched towards the great castle, who without one shot in opposition, presently embraced a parly for surrender which out of hand they did, upon quarter only of their lives which granted, the Governor did yield this brave castle to the enemy."[2]

---

[1] Callan received a charter, with very extensive privileges, from William, Earl Marshal, in 1217.

[2] *Aphor. Disc.*, vol. ii. p. 64. Talbot was a partisan of Ormonde's. After the loss of Callan he got the command of Kilkea castle, in the county of Kildare, and later of Tecroghan, both of which he surrendered in an equally cowardly way.

In the West Street there is an old building still standing, called in ancient documents Skerry's Castle. It is said that after the surrender of the town this castle still held out, and that it was reduced by scalding to death the soldiers who defended it. Some of the towns-people who took refuge in the lower rooms perished in the same way. This tradition seems to be confirmed by the fact that in 1830, when the castle was undergoing some alterations, the workmen engaged in levelling the garden at the rear came on an immense quantity of bones a little below the surface, which were estimated to be the remains of over one hundred and fifty human beings.[1] A woman named Kate Haherney threw herself from one of the windows, to escape punishment for refusing to give some secret information. The garrison of Butler's castle, a short distance from the town, were so terrified at the fate that had befallen those who had offered any resistance, that they surrendered at the first summons, and asked permission to go to Kilkenny, which was given them by Cromwell.

Cromwell's account of the capture of Callan is as follows :

" From thence (Fethard) I marched to Callan, hearing that Colonel Reynolds was there with the party before mentioned. When I came hither, I found he had fallen on the enemy's horse, and routed them, being about a hundred, with his forlorn ; he took my Lord of Ossory's captain-lieutenant and another lieutenant of horse prisoners ; and one of those who betrayed our garrison of Enniscorthy, whom we hanged. The enemy had possessed three castles in the town, one of them, belonging to one Butler, very considerable ; the other two had about a hundred or a hundred and twenty men in them, which he attempted ; and they refusing conditions, reasonably offered, were put all to the sword. Indeed, some of your soldiers did attempt very notably in this service. I do not hear there was six men of ours lost. Butler's castle was delivered upon conditions for all to march away, leaving their arms behind them, wherein I have placed a company of foot and a troop of horse, under the command of my Lord Colvill, the place being six miles from Kilkenny. From thence Colonel Reynolds was sent with his regiment to remove a garrison of the enemy's from Knocktopher,[2] being the way of our communication with Ross, which accordingly he did. We marched back with the rest of the body to Fethard and Cashel, where we are now quartered, having good plenty both of horse meat and men's meat for a time, and being indeed, as we may say, even almost in the heart and bowels of the enemy, ready to attempt what God shall next direct. And blessed be His name only for this good success ; and for this that we do not find our men are at all considerably sick upon this expedition, though indeed it hath been very blustering weather."

At Cashel he established his head-quarters, and from thence sent detachments to reduce the chief garrisons in the surrounding country. While here, he levied monthly contributions on the counties of Tipperary and Limerick.

" I had almost forgot one business. The Major-General (Ireton) was very desirous to gain a pass over the Suir, where indeed we had none but by boat, or when the weather served. Wherefore, on Saturday, in the evening, he marched with

---

[1] Callan held out but one day, and paid dear for that short resistance, all persons there being put to the sword except Butler's troops, which surrendered before the town was fired. Echard's *History of England*, p. 667. Braudin says Cromwell ordered all the citizens to be put to death : *Cives omnes ad unum . . . trucidari jussit.*

[2] Mention has been made already of the capture of this castle.

a party of horse and foot to Arsinom.[1] where was a bridge, and at the foot of it a strong castle, which he about four o'clock the next morning attempted, killed about thirteen of the enemy's outguard, lost but two men, and eight or ten wounded. The enemy yielded the place to him, and we are possessed of it, being a very considerable pass, and nearest to our pass at Cappoquin over the Blackwater, whither we can bring guns, ammunition, or other things from Youghal by water, and then over this pass to the army. The county of Tipperary have submitted to £1,500 a month contribution, although they have six or seven of the enemy's garrisons still upon them.

" Sir, I desire the charge of England as to this war may be abated as much as may be, and as we know you do desire, out of your care to the Commonwealth. But if you expect your work to be done, if the marching army be not constantly paid, and the course taken that hath been constantly represented, indeed it will not be for the thrift of England, as far as England is concerned, in the speedy reduction of Ireland. The money we raise upon the counties maintains the garrison forces, and hardly that. If the active force be not maintained, and all contingencies defrayed, how can you expect but to have a lingering business of it? Surely we desire not to spend a shilling of your treasury wherein our consciences do not prompt us to serve you. We are willing to be out of our trade of war, and shall hasten (by God's assistance and grace) to the end of our work, as the laborer doth to be at his rest. This makes us bold to be in earnest with you for the necessary supplies; that of money is one.[2] And there be some other things which indeed I do not think for your service to speak of publicly, which I shall humbly represent to the Council of State, wherewith I desire we may be accommodated.

" Sir, the Lord, who doth all these things, gives hopes of a speedy issue to this business, and, I am persuaded, will graciously appear in it. And truly there is no fear of the strength and combination of enemies round about, nor of slanderous tongues at home. God hath hitherto fenced you against all those, to wonder and amazement; they are tokens of your prosperity and success; only it will be good for you and us that serve you to fear the Lord; to fear unbelief, self-seeking, confidence in an arm of flesh, and opinion of any instruments that they are other than as dry bones.

" That God be merciful in these things, and bless you, is the humble prayer of,

" Sir,

"Your most humble servant,

" O. CROMWELL."

The Commons' Journals, under the date of February 25th, state that " A letter from the Lord Lieutenant of Ireland, from Castletown, dated February 15th, was this day read, and ordered to be forthwith printed and published. Ordered, that a letter of thanks be sent to the Lord Lieutenant of Ireland; and that the speaker do sign the

---

[1] The strong castle of Ardfinan was taken, well victualled and manned; it yielded after about eight or nine shots had been fired, upon condition to march to Limerick. *Perfect Diurnal*, February 5th. This castle is on the Suir, seven miles south-west of Clonmel. A round tower at the north-west angle, a gateway, and a square tower at the south-west angle, and the remains of the connecting walls, constitute all that is left of this celebrated fortress. Hemphill's *Illustrations of Clonmel*, p. 52; Dublin, 1860.

[2] It appears from an entry in " *A Booke conteyning the Chardge of the Commonwealth of England for the Warre of Ireland, and other Disbursements depending thereupon*," that from the 1st of March, 1649, to the 16th of February, 1650, the sum of £535,590 7s. 8d. was paid out. Of this sum £100,128 1s. 5½d. was for arrears due, besides meal, beeves, wheat, winter-quarters, King's customs, and enemies' estates.

same.   Resolved, that the Lord Lieutenant of Ireland should have the
use of the lodgings named the Cockpit,[1] of the Spring Garden, and
St. James's House, and the command of St. James's Park."

[1] Henry VIII. added the Cockpit to Whitehall Palace.   Hatton describes it as "between the gate into King's Street, Westminster, and the gate by the Banqueting House";
the former was known as Cockpit Gate.   James I. went there twice a week to see the sport
of cockfighting.   At this time, and long after, it was a sumptuous royal dwelling.   Monk,
duke of Albemarle, died there in 1670.   After the fire of 1697 it was altered into the Privy
Council Office.   It retained its original name long after the change in its uses.   The Treasury minutes, so late as 1780, were headed "The Cockpit."   Its site is occupied by the present Privy Council Office.   Even in 1830 the place where the Court of Appeal of the Privy
Council sat was commonly spoken of as the Cockpit, because it set on the site of the old
cockpit at Whitehall.

CHAPTER XXIII.

THE CAPTURE OF CAHIR CASTLE.

On the 24th of February the army appeared before Cahir. Hugh O'Neill had been ordered by Ormonde to proceed to Clonmel with 1,500 Ulster men, and to act as governor of the town and the surrounding country. He took care to strengthen not only Clonmel but the neighboring towns of Cahir and Fethard, as he knew the enemy purposed marching on Kilkenny as soon as he could take the field in spring. Cahir Castle[1] was secured with strong gates and a drawbridge; and the court-yard was surrounded by a high wall. It was well supplied with provisions and ammunition of every kind. Mr. Mathews, a uterine brother of Lord Ormonde, was the governor; he welcomed the reinforcement, 80 in number, and set about the preparations necessary for a vigorous defence. He ordered the Ulster troops to defend the court-yard, promising at the same time to admit them within the castle walls in case they were overpowered by superior numbers, or the works could be held no longer. Cromwell, as was his custom, sent forward a messenger calling on the Governor to surrender:

For the Governor of Cahir Castle. These:

SIR, *Before Cahir*, 24th February, 1650.

Having brought the army and my cannon near this place, according to my usual manner in summoning places, I thought fit to offer you terms honorable for soldiers: That you may march away with your baggage, arms, and colors, free from injury or violence. But if I be, notwithstanding, necessitated to bend my cannon upon you, you must expect the extremity usual in such cases. To avoid blood, this is offered to you by

Your servant

OLIVER CROMWELL.

Very soon Cromwell's army came up and strove to scale the outer wall; they were gallantly repulsed by the Ulstermen, who bravely held their ground until they saw the heavy ordnance planted against the walls. Knowing that certain death awaited them if they

---

[1] The Earl of Essex, at his being with the army in Ireland (1599), made a journey into Munster, in the hope to compose the troubles; all that he performed at the time was the taking of Cahir castle. It was retaken almost immediately after by James Butler, brother of the Earl of Cahir; but he gave it up within a short time to the President of Munster.

remained any longer in the courtyard, their officer went to Mathews and asked him to admit the men within the castle, as he had promised. Mathews refused. On his return to his men the officer found a trumpeter from Cromwell demanding a parley; this was granted. A capitulation followed, Mathews stipulating for the security of his wife's jointure and of his own private property. The garrison was allowed to march out with banners displayed in body and posture of fight, with all their arms, bag and baggage. A pass was given to the Ulstermen to continue in the English quarters for a month, if they pleased; this they accepted, and they marched towards Clonmel. Cromwell made much of them, and told the captain that if he would continue with them in his army, he would use him well and give him a month's pay before hand. The captain gallantly answered, to Cromwell's admiration, that for a world he would not change places, but he would rather undergo any penalty, nay, the basest death that could be invented, rather than give a stroke against his religion or swerve from his principles. He and his party went to join their countrymen who were garrisoned at Clonmel.

Articles made and agreed on the 24th day of February, 1650, between his Excellency the Lord Lieutenant of Ireland on the one part, and Captain George Mathews, Governor of Cahir Castle of the other part, concerning the surrender of the same Castle, viz.:

Imprimis, that the Governor and all the officers, soldiers, and clergymen, and servants may march out with their horses, and arms, and bag and baggage. The English soldiers willing to serve his Excellency may be entertained. Those that will not, either English or Irish, to have liberty to live quietly in the country, laying down their arms, or passes to go elsewhere.

That the Governor may enjoy his estate which he hath, as his wife's jointure or wardship of the heiress of Cahir.

That he may have his goods and chattels, and liberty for a week to carry them away; and have the possession of the castle of Roghill for his habitation, and his corn yet remaining there, his Excellency keeping two files of musketeers there.

That the goods he hath in the castle belonging to others may be delivered to the several proprietors.

That in consideration hereof, the Governor is to deliver up the same castle to his Excellency upon signing these Articles.

                                     O. CROMWELL.

February 24th, 1650.

Kiltenan,[1] "a very large and strong castle of Lord Dunboyne's," was next captured "with the cannon without the loss of one man." Dundrum was taken by a detachment sent to seize it under the command of Colonel Sankey, though it was well provisioned for a siege and manned by two troops of horse and some foot. Sankey's horse attacked the outer wall, while his foot stormed the town; the defenders were soon driven into the castle. Seeing that resistance was hopeless, they made terms with the assailants and delivered up the town and castle, leaving their arms and horses behind. During the

---

[1] Six miles north of Clonmel. Three of the four round towers at the angles of the bawn are standing; the breaches made in them by Cromwell's cannon are still visible. Hemphill's *Clonmel.* &c., p 116.

assault, Sankey received a wound in the right hand. Goldenbridge[1] and Ballynakill[2] were also taken ; in the latter a strong garrison was left. "We have also divers garrisons in the locality of Limerick," wrote Cromwell, "and by these we take away the enemy's subsistence and diminish their contributions, by which in time I hope they will sink."

The Commissioners of Trust, with Ormonde's consent, issued circular letters asking deputies from all parts of the kingdom to come in and represent the grievances of which the people complained, "that by their joint advice and assistance, life might be conserved in this gasping kingdom, the only means to attain to that end being for them to remove such causeless distrust, which, being maliciously infused into the people's minds, did slacken, if not wholly withdraw, their obedience from his Majesty's authority, rendering it impossible with honor or hope of success to contend against a powerful, absolutely obeyed, and plentifully supplied enemy." About the end of January they assembled at Kilkenny ; but being alarmed at Cromwell's approach, they adjourned to Ennis, the capital of Clare. The sole result of their conference was, that they seemed to be only more confirmed in their distrust of Ormonde and of his policy.

Ormonde left to Castlehaven the government of Kilkenny, and went to Limerick, in the hope of obtaining contributions towards the raising and support of an army. On the 27th of February, he issued letters of invitation to the archbishops, bishops, and other persons of quality of the kingdom, to repair to Limerick, and meet him there on the 8th of March, "that by their advice and assistance, the best and speediest way of advancement of his Majesty's service and preservation of his people may be resolved upon." They came at the appointed time. Ormonde told them that "unless the people were brought to have full confidence in him, and yield him perfect obedience ; and unless the city of Limerick, in particular, would receive a garrison and obey orders, there was no hope of making any considerable opposition to the enemy ; and desired them to deal freely, if they had any mistrust of him or dislike of his government, since he was ready to do anything for the people's preservation that was consistent with his honor and his duty to the King. And since it was manifest that the name without the power of Lord Lieutenant could bring nothing but ruin upon the nation and dishonor upon him, they should either procure entire obedience to his authority or propose how the kingdom might be preserved by quitting it." To all which they answered with many expressions of respect and affection. They presented the following considerations to his Excellency :

1. That a privy council should be appointed of the peers spiritual and temporal and other natives of the country, to sit with his Excellency daily, and determine all weighty affairs of the country by their counsel, the Commissioners of Trust being only charged with the care of the due observation of the Articles of Peace. 2. That an exact establishment of the forces forthwith be agreed on, directing what should

---

[1] Five miles west of Cashel. This castle is still standing.
[2] In the Queen's County, five miles south-east of Abbeyleix. A part of this castle is still standing.

be the number of horse and foot; no payments to be made except for the forces ready for service; care to be taken to avoid the burdening of the people with free quarters. 3. That care be taken in the enrolling of the army and in the garrisoning of the places, that none who could not be confided in should be in the number of the forces or continue in garrison. 4. That the forces be withdrawn from the several places already garrisoned without the concurrence of the Commissioners of Trust, and these not again garrisoned without the consent of the Commissioners. 5. That great mistrust and jealousy having arisen on account of Catholics having been removed from some of the greatest employments of trust in the army, those so removed to be forthwith restored. 6. That for the satisfaction of the people, who, in the many disorders of the times, saw no face of justice among them, judges be appointed to go circuit twice a year, and justices of the peace in quarter sessions, to whom the people might apply for redress against oppression and extortion. 7. That an account be taken of all the moneys received since the signing of the peace, that due satisfaction may be given to the people in the knowledge of the right disposal thereof; in future all payments of public moneys to be made only with the consent of the Commissioners of Trust. 8. That any oppressions or extortions of any of the officers or others of the army hitherto, or the surrender of castles or towns to the enemy, be strictly examined and punished by the lord lieutenant, the Privy Council, and a council of war. 9. That all acts and orders be recalled whereby any public revenue was in any way diminished; and those profiting thereby to account in full for the profits that accrued to them. 10. That no charge be imposed on the people by appointment, free quarters, or otherwise, but by the Commissioners of Trust.

To these demands Ormonde replied that the appointment of Privy Councillors was reserved exclusively to the King; but if those formerly in power had abused their trust, he would appoint in their place others free from all just exception. The second point he would immediately put in execution, reserving, however, to himself the right of nominating such officers as he should think suited to the posts. The other recommendations he promised to carry out to the best of his power, pleading as an excuse for the violations of the terms of the peace, the straits to which he had been reduced in his efforts to keep the army on foot. To many his answers seemed unsatisfactory, leaving him means of escape when it suited his purposes. But the chief reason of their suspicion was owing to the particular favor and friendship which he showed to his partisans. The bishops seemed satisfied with his answer, and soon after presented him with the following Declaration, in which they vindicated their conduct in the past, and set before him their plans for the welfare of the country in the future:

The Declaration of the undernamed Bishops, in the name of themselves and the rest of the Bishops convoked at Limerick, as deputed by them, presented to the Lord Marquis of Ormonde, Lord Lieutenant for his Majesty, etc.

May it please your Excellency to be informed that we are very sensible of the jealousies and suspicions conceived of us (as was intimated unto us), that we believe arising from some disaffected and misunderstanding persons that spare not to give ill characters of us; as if in these deplorable times, wherein our religion, king, and country are come to the vertical point of their total ruin and destruction, it should be imagined by any that we behave ourselves like sleeping pastors, in no ways contributing our best endeavors for the preservation of the people, which ought to be more dear unto us than any worldly thing that may be thought of. Wherefore as well for the just vindication of our own reputation against such undeserved aspersions, as for future testimony of our sincerity and integrity to endeavor always the safety of the people and to manifest to your Excellency, as the King's Majesty's lieutenant and chief governor of this kingdom, that no labor or care of ours hath been, or shall be wanting to proceed effectually to any proposals you will please to make known unto us that may conduce to those ends : we thought it therefore fit to present this Declaration of our real intentions, in the name of ourselves and the rest of our Brethren, the Archbishops and Bishops of this kingdom, whereby we avow, testify, declare and protest before God and the world, that since our annual meeting at Clonmacnoise or here, we have omitted nothing that did occur unto us, tending to the advancement of his Majesty's interest and the good of the kingdom generally; but have there and then ordered and decreed all unto us appertaining, or which was in our power, necessarily conducting to the public conservation of his Majesty and his subjects' interests. And also do, and have endeavored to root out of men's hearts all jealousies and sinister opinions, conceived either against your Excellency or the present Government, as by our acts then conceived may appear; and after our parting from thence, in pursuance of our unanimous resolution taken in that place, we have accordingly declared to our respective flocks our happy agreement amongst ourselves, and our earnest desire to labor with them to those ends, and made use of our best persuasions for the purchasing of their alacrity and cheerful concurrence to the advantage of that service; so that if anything was wanting of due correspondence sought by your Excellency, we conceive it cannot be attributed to any want of care or diligence in us.

And for further intimation of our hearty desires on all occasions to serve our king and country, we declare that we are not yet deterred for want of good success in the affairs of the kingdom, but rather animated to give further onsets and try all other possible ways. Wherefore we most humbly entreat your Excellency to give us some particular instructions, and to prescribe some remedies for and touching the grievances presented by us to your Excellency for pacifying of discontented minds, and put us in a way how to labor further in so good a cause. And we do faithfully promise that no industry or care shall be wanting in us to receive and execute your conditions.

And in conclusion, we leave to all impartial, judicious persons sad and serious considerations to think how incredible it is, that we should fail to oppose, to the uttermost of our power, the fearful and increasing potency of a rebellious and malignant murderer of our late Sovereign King Charles ; to which enemy also nothing seemeth more odious than the names of Kings and Bishops, and who aims at nothing so much as the dethroning our now gracious King Charles the Second, and the final extirpation of our natives, in case (as God forbid) events and successes would fall suitable to his most wicked designs. So far we thought necessary to declare to your Excellency from ourselves, as the sense likewise and true meaning of the rest of our brethren, other Bishops of this kingdom.

Dated at Loughrea the 28th of March, Anno Domini, 1650.

  Jo. Archiepiscopus Tuamensis.
  Wal. Episcopus Clonfert.
  Franc. Allad.
  Rob. Corcag. et Cluanensis.
  Fr. Hugo Episcopus Duacensis.

"Some of the principal persons among the confederates," says Cox, "and with them some of the bishops, under show of great confidence and trust, repaired to the Lord Lieutenant at Limerick, and declared unto him, that all the waywardness and indisposition of the people proceeded from the prejudice they had against Lord Inchiquin, who had always, they said, prosecuted the war against them with the utmost rigor and animosity ; and the places and persons which had been most at his devotion having treacherously revolted to the Parliament, the people were not too confident of him, and jealous that the Marquis had too great confidence in him ; so that, if he would dismiss that Lord and discharge the troops that yet remained under his command, of which some frequently ran away to the Parliament, not only that city (Limerick) but the whole nation, as one man would be at his

disposal."[1]   Other leading men of the city came to Inchiquin and
assured him that they expected no success under Ormonde, because
he was not of their nation, and was so indulgent to English interests
and Englishmen, that he regarded little them or theirs.   But if his
Lordship, who was of the most ancient and noble extraction of Ireland, had the supreme command, then all would be well.

From this time forward Ormonde had so small hopes of the Irish,
that he employed Bramhall, bishop of Derry, to treat with some foreign prince about transporting five or six thousand men and employ-
ing them in his service.   The Commissioners of Trust, about the end
of March, issued a manifesto, declaring that their fellow-countrymen,
the Irish, had been very jealous of the English regiments associated
with them under Ormonde's command, since the betrayal by their
comrades of the garrisons of Cork, Youghal, Kinsale, and Bandon to
Cromwell.   They now found those that remained praising Cromwell ;
and they reminded Ormonde that Inchiquin had admitted in his presence, that the men under his command were not to be trusted.
Accordingly they requested his Excellency to dismiss his English
forces.   The earnest wish of these was to obtain liberty, if possible,
to lay down their arms and retire to their homes.   They sent commissioners to Cromwell, then at Fethard ; and by articles signed there,
April 26th, 1650, by Sir Robert Sterling, Michael Boyle, and Colonel
John Daniel, as agents for Ormonde's Protestant forces, to such of
these officers and soldiers, and gentlemen and clergymen, being English or Scotch and Protestants, as desired to come off from the Irish
Popish party, protection would be given for six months, to dispose of
their goods ; and on giving in such engagement of fidelity as should
be required, and submitting to such fine and composition as parliament might impose on them, they should be allowed their estates as
other people not obnoxious to any delinquency, until the pleasure of
the parliament should be known ; all others willing to give such engagements should have passes given them to transport themselves
and their families beyond the seas : the benefit of these conditions
extending, however, to such only as should come in within thirty days.
Vice-Admiral Penn, who had command of the Irish Sea, was ordered
to allow them a passage over the Shannon, where his ships then rode,
and to offer them what countenance and assistance they needed for
the furthering of their purpose.   Those of Colonel Daniel's party
were to present themselves at Doneraile, Lord Montgomery of Ardes
at Enniskillen, and Sir Thomas Armstrong at Trim.   Inchiquin's
forces too disbanded, except Colonel Butler's regiment, which went
towards Galway.[2]

----

[1] I confess the Lord Lieutenant had his faction at Limerick, though the major and
honester part were against him

[2] Cromwell's Articles for the Protestant party of Ireland are given in full in *Aphor.
Disc.*, vol. ii. p. 393, appendix clxxxv.   Dean Boyle obtained a pass from Cromwell for
Ormonde ; this Ormonde indignantly rejected.   In a letter to Cromwell he says : " I had no
intention to treat with you for a pass or any other thing.   I have by this trumpeter returned
you your paper ; and for your unsought courtesy do assure you, when you shall desire a pass
from me, I shall not make use of it to corrupt any that commands under you."

.The conduct of the people of Limerick would seem to have irri
tated Ormonde very much. They did not show him any of that
outward respect which was due to his exalted position. No one had
access to him without the special permission of the mayor, and this
was given very unwillingly. Lord Kilmallock, who had quartered a
troop of horse within the liberties by his Excellency's order, was cast
into prison. Unwilling to bear such affronts any longer, he went to
Loughrea, in the county of Galway, and there issued his reply to the
demands of the Commissioners already mentioned.

Of the Parliamentary army, on the other hand, a letter from
Cork reported, " Our foot are in gallant posture, well armed, well
clothed ; and for bread, corn, and other things, by the State plentifully
provided for. The army's diligence, courage, thankfulness, and behavior is such, through the strict care and providence of our General
and chief officers, that never did men obey orders more cheerfully, nor
go upon all duty more courageously ; never did greater harmony
appear, or resolution to prosecute this cause of God than in this army,
such a consent of hearts and hands, such a sympathy of affection not
only in a carnal but spiritual bond, which lies faster than chains of
adamant. I have often observed, especially in that time and those
actions, a wonderful consent of the officers and soldiers, and indeed
of all the parliamentary forces, upon the ground of doing service for
God, and how miraculously they were in all their actions successful.
The mind of man being satisfied and fixed upon God, and that his
undertaking is for God's glory, it gives the greatest courage to these
men and prosperity to their actions. Our musters are strict ; here is
no free quarter allowed or practised ; either they pay or give ticket,
which being demanded by the poorest Irish is not, durst not be denied
by any officer. Our horse have in many places wanted hay, but by
the supply of oats from England have made good shift with straw.
We have 7,000 horse, and our foot trebles that number, yet are English recruits of moneys and necessaries to be continued."

CHAPTER XXIV

HEWSON JOINS CROMWELL.

Hewson advances from Dublin — Takes castles in Co. Kildare — Siege and Surrender of Ballysonan — Harristown, Lea, and Dunamaise taken — Massacre at Timahoe — Capture of Castledermot — Surrender of Leighlin — Castlehaven takes Athy — Rendezvous at Gowran.

EVERY place of importance was now subdued except Waterford, Limerick, Clonmel, Galway, and Kilkenny, all towns of considerable strength and needing much time to take. Cromwell, who had just captured Cahir, determined to make a more formidable demonstration against Kilkenny. But fearing that he had not a sufficient force to carry out his purpose, he despatched orders to Colonel Hewson, Governor of Dublin, to join him at Gowran with all the troops he could draw off out of that and the other lesser garrisons on the way. Hewson had not been idle during the winter. He had made frequent incursions into the county of Kildare, and reduced several of the strong places there ; by this means he had kept the line of communication with the capital open, and rendered his advance to Kilkenny a comparatively easy matter. The following letter gives an account of these excursions ; it is dated Dublin, January 10th.

> " I sent a party three weeks ago to quarter at the Naas, and from thence to take in Ballysonan or the Black Ditch[1] by surprise, which by storm was unfeasible. The latter was effected upon a stormy night, a place that twenty men might easily keep against twenty thousand. I have placed twenty-four of my men there under Lieutenant Moore ; and the same party took Castlemartin,[2] a considerable place. Also last week I marched into the Island of Allen[3] with one hundred horse and six hundred foot, summoned the castle of Kilmore,[4] but found it unseasonable to take by storm without artillery ; marched over at Black Ditch, and took Rathdred[5] and Panser's Grange,[6] two garrisons beyond the Liffey, in the Co. Kildare. I have placed one hundred foot and twenty horse there ; and as soon as the weather will permit artillery to march, I shall be ready to prosecute what is begun in order to the reducement of the Bog of Allen and the county of Kildare.

---

[1] Probably Nurney, near Black Ditch, 4 miles south of the town of Kildare.

[2] Castlemartin, on the southern bank of the Liffey, belonged to the Fitz-Eustaces. Different branches of this family were ennobled, having the titles of Portlester, Harristown, and Baltinglass. Five of the name were chancellors. A great part of the family estates was confiscated in consequence of James, third Viscount Baltinglass, having taken a leading part in the rebellion of Gerald, Earl of Desmond. D'Alton's *Army List*, vol. ii. p. 444.

[3] The district about the Hill of Allen, being then entirely surrounded by bogs and marshes, was called the Island.

[4] Kilmeague, six miles north of Kildare.

[5] Rathbride, three miles north-east of Kildare. It belonged to a junior branch of the Fitzgeralds.

[6] i. e., Punch's Grange, five miles north of the town of Kildare.

On the 24th of February Hewson marched out of Dublin with 2,000 foot and 1,000 horse, and two small field-pieces. Among his men were some whom Cromwell had left behind when going to Wexford. The next day he reached Naas, which had been fortified a year before by the party of Owen Roe O'Neill. The day following he came before the strong fort of Ballysonan [1] We have Hewson's own despatch, giving full details of the siege and capture of this important place : —

"To the Honorable William Lenthal, Esq., Speaker of the Parliament of England.

SIR,

When his Excellency marched from Dublin towards Munster, he left me entrusted with the garrison, myself and those left with me at that time being sick. The first party that recovered were sent after the army, to wit, about 800 foot and 200 horse, which fought and beat the enemy upon their march. Some more of those sick men that were left recovering, and some recruits coming over, after I had surprised the strong fort upon the Bog of Allen and taken Castlemartin, in the county of Kildare, and placed a garrison therein, about the latter end of December, marched with a party of 1,000 horse and foot into the Island of Allen, and summoned Kilmagog therein ; but finding it not feasible to storm without guns, I marched to Rathbride and Ponser's Grange, and took them, and placed two strong garrisons there. which did give me good footing in the county of Kildare. Then sent a party and took Kildare, Hertwell,[2] and Cotlingstowne,[3] three useful garrisons in the said county ; and provisions being spent, returned back to Dublin, there endeavoring to get guns, mortar-pieces, and other necessaries, ready to draw forth again with all possible speed. In the interim I received propositions from the governor and officers in the strong garrison and fort of Ballysonan, the original whereof I here enclosed present you withal under their own hands.

"Which being by me utterly rejected, I marched upon Tuesday, the 26th of February, with a party of 2,000 foot and 1,000 horse, towards the county of Kildare, and took with me one culverin, and one demi-culverin, and one mortar-piece. The enemy fired their garrison of Lease,[4] Blackreath,[5] and the forementioned Kilmagog, in the Island of Allen ; but I shall easily make it tenable again, it being very useful for your service. They did also blow up the castle of Athy, where they had a strong garrison, and broke up the bridge.

"Upon the 28th February I marched from the Naas, and about four o'clock with the van of the party, I came to Bellisonan, a strong garrison, double works, and double-moated, full of water, one within another, and a mount with a fort upon it. Most of the officers with me esteeming the taking of it to be unfeasible, it being late, and I unwilling to lose time, did send in a summons, a copy whereof is here enclosed, and the enclosed answer under the Governor's hand, was presently returned, and the town, which was without his works, by him burned that night. I

---

[1] Now Ballyshannon, four miles south-west of Kilcullenbridge. It belonged at this time to Pierce Fitzgerald, descended from the Kildare family. He took a leading part in the Catholic Confederation. He was Colonel of a regiment, and later sergeant-major of the Leinster horse. See *The Earls of Kildare*, by the Marquis of Kildare, p. 257 ; Dublin, 1864. In 1642 he was declared a rebel and an outlaw by the Lords Justices ; any one bringing in his head would receive a reward of £400 Borlase's *Rebellion*, Appendix, p. 31. Ballysonan castle was pulled down a few years ago by the Annesly family, to build a castellated mansion close by.

[2] Rev. J. Graves says Hertwell still exhibits the remains of a strong fortress ; but he does not give its site.

[3] Now Cotlandstown, in the barony of Naas, between Kilcullenbridge and Ballymore Eustace.

[4] Maryborough, in the Queen's County, where the castle is still standing.

[5] Blackrath, on the old coach-road between old Kilcullen and Castledermot, five miles south of Kilcullen.

caused a battery to be made, and planted the artillery, and made a fort for the security thereof, having intelligence that the Lord of Castlehaven, with 4,000 horse and foot, would come to raise me within two days, in which fort I could secure the guns and batter their works, whilst I drew off to fight the enemy, if need were. We played our guns and mortar-piece at the fort upon the mount, intending before night to storm it, having ladders and all the necessaries ready. But before any breach was made, the Governor did send me a paper, which is here enclosed, whereunto the enclosed answer was returned, and he treated with me about the surrender, which was concluded accordingly. The Articles signed with both our hands herewith is represented unto you.

"And now, sir, you have without the loss of one man this strong place, and thereby most of the county of Kildare. Those garrisons in this county yet remaining, as Castle Dormount [1] and Kilkenny, with others, I hope you shall have a good account thereof speedily from

"Your humble servant,

"JOH. HEWSON.

    "*Ballysonan, March 3rd, 1650.*"

[ENCLOSURES.]

SIR,

    I am now marching the army to reduce the place you possess unto the obedience of the Parliament of England, and it being apparent to the world that God is making inquisition in Ireland for innocent blood, how far you and those with you may be concerned therein, I shall observe by your answer hereunto.

These are to require you to deliver the place that you now possess unto me for the end aforesaid; whatsoever your return hereunto may be, and the effect thereof, my summons will justify the future proceedings of

Your servant,

    28*th Feb.,* 1650.   J. HEWSON.

For the Governor of Bellisonan.

SIR,

    I am now in possession in this place by authority from my King; how you may demand it by authority from the Parliament of England I know not. England denying their King, therefore your power I disobey. And for God, my King, and country, will defend this place to the uttermost of my power.

Sir, your servant,

    28*th Feb.,* 1650.   DONNO KELLY.

For Colonel Hewson, Commander-in-Chief of the Parliamentary Party now in the field of Ballysonan.

Propositions made by the Garrison, which were rejected.

We do hereby employ Governor Donno O'Kelly for the delivery of the hereunder propositions to the General of the Parliament's forces in Ireland : —

Imprimis. That the party commanding this garrison and fort of Ballysonan, and all other that will adhere to them, are really and willingly to join to the Parliament forces, upon such terms as are hereunder written.

2d. That a colonel, lieutenant-colonel, and a major, besides captains and under-officers, be employed of the said party constantly in the standing army of the Parliament's forces in this kingdom.

---

[1] Castledermot, called in ancient times Diseart Dhiarmuda and Tristle Dermot, a walled town, seven miles south-east of Athy. It was the chief residence of the O'Tooles. After the English invasion it was held by de Riddlesford, who erected the castle and a monastary for Crouched Friars, the tower of which is still standing close to the town. In 1302 a Franciscan monastery was founded here by Thomas Lord Offaly. Parliaments were held here at different times.

3d. That in case any such officers do come in, that they may have free liberty of their religion, and two priests admitted and employed for to serve the said regiment now intended.

4th. That neither Taaffe nor Dillon shall be accepted of in the parliament's party.

5th. That their estates, wrongfully detained and enjoyed by the said Dillon, Browne, and Taaffe, may be allowed unto them by the State of Parliament.

6th. That their arrears since May last may be allowed to them. This and aforesaid propositions may be granted by the General, Lieutenant-General, Major General, and Commissioners-General of the Parliament forces of this kingdom, that what those countries assigned to them for their pay are in arrear since their coming to Ballysonan, may be forthwith caused to be paid.

7th. That this granted, they shall obey any deriving power from the State of Parliament.

J. GORDON,   CONNOR KELLY,
CH. KELLY,   M. DONNOGH.

Colonel Hewson's last summons.

SIR,

     Blood I do not thirst after ; yet so far a soldier as not to neglect present opportunity, I shall, for the end in your letter mentioned, send Captain Hewson, according to your desire, provided you send one or two fully authorized to treat and conclude, and all to be concluded within half an hour, provided also you do not work at all to repair what my guns and mortar-pieces have demolished ; and to that end that Captain Hewson may remain in the Mount during that half-hour. Sir, I shall be glad if your wisdom prevent what otherwise unavoidably will fall out, though not desired by

Your servant,

March 1st, 1650.   J. HEWSON.

SIR,

     To avoid the confusion of Christian blood, we sent out a drum to demand a parley. My desire, for the reasons aforesaid, is that you send in a captain of yours to treat with us, and we will send forth a captain of ours, who shall demand no more but what is honorable and just ; and so, sir, I conclude,

Your servant,

DONNO KELLY.

March 1st, 1650.

Articles agreed upon between the Hon. Colonel John Hewson of the one part, and Captain Donnogh Kelly, Governor of Ballysonan, in the county of Kildare, on the other part, 1st March, 1650.

Imprimis. That the said garrison and fort of Ballysonan shall be immediately delivered, with all the ammunition and provisions therein, except as in the ensuing article is agreed upon.

2d. That the said Governor, officers, and soldiers shall continue in the castle until to-morrow morning at ten of the clock, if they please ; and then they are to march out of the said castle and fort with a trumpeter for convoy ten miles, if they desire it, and to any of the next Irish garrisons within ten miles, as aforesaid, the trumpeter returning without any prejudice. And the said officers are to march with their horses and pistols, and with their colors flying and drums beating, and the soldiers with their arms and matches lighted, and each musketeer one pound of powder with bullet and match proportionable.

. 3d. Whatsoever oats and pease shall appear in the castle belonging to Mis[tress] Fitzgerald shall be restored to her.

And lastly, for the due performance of the aforesaid articles, we do hereunto set our hands the day and year first above written.

JOHN HEWSON,
DONNO KELLY.

The taking of Ballysonan had a most important effect on the campaign. "In Leinster," says Carte, "there was scarce a castle or strong house which the husband or wife were not for giving up and receiving conditions from the enemy. Thus Ballysonan and other castles were delivered up to Hewson, who was thereby enabled to march with a party from Dublin into the county of Kilkenny. . . . These successes encouraged Cromwell to lay seige to Kilkenny."

From Ballysonan Hewson took the road to Castledermot. Diverging somewhat from the straight road, he took Harristown, lying between Naas and Kilcullenbridge. Then Lea, near Portarlington, was dismantled. The confused masses of towers and broken arches show the merciless havoc then made. Dunamaise [1] was next taken and blown up. Tradition points out the site of the old cornmill, at the corner of the mill-field, as the spot where the battery was erected. The monastery of Timahoe was seized, and the friars found there massacred. The place where they were put to death is still called "the road of murder." [2] When he reached Castledermot he found his provisions exhausted, and was obliged to return to Dublin.

After three days' rest, he set out again for Castledermot and Kilkea,[3] taking with him provisions for fourteen days. When he came before the former place, he found that the enemy had burnt down a great part of the town, pulled down the walls, and betaken themselves to a strong tower. He caused a great quantity of straw and other combustible materials to be put to the door and set on fire, which forced those within to cry out for mercy. In the tower were taken Captain Shirlock, "a bloody Tory," [4] three friars, and divers others. Shirlock had received a shot through the breast with a brace of bullets before he yielded. Shirlock and the friars were taken prisoners ; the others were saved or executed as was thought fit.

Lord Castlehaven, who a short time before had been appointed to the chief command in the province of Leinster, was ordered by Ormonde to take the field. After providing as best he could for the safety of Kilkenny, he set out for Carlow, hoping to meet there the troops he had ordered to assemble from all parts of the province.

---

[1] Dunamaise was the residence of the chief of the O'Mores before the English invasion. In 1325 it was retaken by Lysagh O'More. For the next two centuries it changed hands frequently. Some parts of the castle and walls are still standing. See *The Irish Penny Magazine*, p. 18.

[2] *Notes on Irish Architecture*, by the Earl of Dunraven, vol. ii. p. 33; London, 1875. From the Ordnance Survey letters, Queen's County. Timahoe, i. e., Teach Mochoe, St. Mochua's house. A round tower and an ancient door-way of singular beauty are still remaining. It is four miles south-west of Stradbally.

[3] Kilkea castle is two miles north-west of Athy. It was built in 1180 by Walter De Lacy ; the greater part of the present building dates from 1426. It passed into the hands of the Fitzgerald family by the marriage of Maurice, third Baron of Offaly, with Emelina, daughter of Sir Stephen de Longespée by his marriage with the only daughter and heiress of Walter de Riddlesford, Baron of Bray, to whom O'Murthy, in which Kilkea and Castledermot are situated, was granted by King John. See *The Earls of Kildare*, by the Marquis of Kildare, p. 17. In 1634 Elizabeth, daughter of the second Lord Delvin and widow of Gerald, fourteenth Earl of Kildare, bequeathed Kilkea to her cousin, Father Nugent, S. J., for a novitiate of the order. Rinuccini and his suit were entertained there for twenty days, when he was on his way to besiege Dublin.

[4] Borlase says Captain Shirlock was the head of the Waterford rebels in 1642.

Lord Dillon's division of 3,000 men did not come. Castlehaven put himself at the head of a force of 3,000 men, 800 from Leinster, an Ulster regiment, and Sir Thomas Armstrong's and Ormonde's horse. But not finding his numbers at all equal to those of the enemy, he could do no more than watch their movements.

"Upon my march," says Hewson, "I received a letter from my Lord President of Munster to haste up and join unto Colonel Reynolds near Leighlinbridge, and either to take in some passage over the Barrow or prosecute Castlehaven. The latter was prevented by the enemy's withdrawal. The former (to wit, Leighlinbridge) I attempted, and I obtained it without the loss of one man. The Articles on surrender thereof is herewith presented to you. This garrison gave a pass over the Barrow, and indeed the benefit you have thereby is very great, and the time about the taking of it was one day. When I came hither, my Lord President was gone back to my Lord-Lieutenant about Thomastown, whither I despatched a letter to his Excellency, intimating the taking of Leighlinbridge and my purpose to march towards him next morning and to stay at Gowran, except I received other command from his Excellency, after I had settled the garrison of Leighlinbridge, where I found 800 bushels of corn and 200 arms."

Articles agreed on, between the Honorable John Hewson, Governor of Dublin, of the one party, and Lieut. Laurence Dempsey and Lieut. William Brereton, Commissioners appointed and authorized by Captain Piercy Brereton, Commander of the Castle and Garrison of Leighlinbridge, for the surrendering of the said Castle and Garrison of Leighlinbridge,[1] of the other party, this 19th of March, 1650.

1. The said Captain Brereton is to deliver the castle and garrison of Leighlinbridge unto the Honorable Colonel John Hewson for the use of the Parliament of England by three of the clock this afternoon, and all ammunition and provisions therein, without any embezzlement, except what is hereafter excepted.
2. The said Captain Brereton, with all the officers and soldiers within the said garrison, are to march away with their arms, muskets laden, bandoleers filled, drums beating, and matches lighted, and bag and baggage which is to them belonging, which they can carry away on their backs.
3. The said Captain Brereton, with all the officers and soldiers within the said garrison, shall have free liberty to march to Kilkenny, and shall have a safe-conduct to that effect.
4. The full benefit of the aforesaid articles is to extend to all and every the officers and soldiers in the said garrison without exception.

Lastly, for the full performance of all and singular the premises, the parties hereunto have to these presents interchangeably put their hands the day and year first above written.

J. HEWSON, LAURENCE DEMPSEY, WILL. BRERETON.

Confirmed by PIERCE BRERETON.

[1] This bridge was built by Maurice Jakes, canon of Kildare, in 1320. See Ware's *Annals*, ad ann. It was for a long time the only passage over the Barrow to the south. In "A Note for the Winning of Leinster," A. D. 1536, the O'Tooles, Byrnes, and Kavanaghs are said to have exiled the King's law from Munster by preventing the judges from riding circuit past Leighlinbridge. See *State Papers*, Henry VIII. (Ireland), vol. i. p. 411; London, 1825. Hence the by word used by the Irish, "they dwelt by west the law, which dwelt beyond the river Barrow." *True Causes Why Ireland Was Never Subdued*, by Sir John Davis, p. 50; Dublin, 1704. About 1250 a Carmelite monastery was founded here by one of the Carews; it stood near the Black Castle, on the eastern bank of the river. Archdall's *Monasticon*, p. 38. In consideration of the great labor, burthen, and expense which the friars of Leighlin did sustain in supporting their house and the bridge contiguous thereunto against the King's enemies, Richard II. gave them an annual pension of 80 marks. Ryan's *History of Carlow*, p. 84; Dublin, 1833.

Castlehaven succeeded in taking Athy by storm, where Hewson had a magazine.   The garrison, 700 in number, were taken prisoners at discretion.   " Not knowing what to do with my prisoners," says Castlehaven, " I made a present of them to Cromwell, desiring him by letter to do the like to me, if any of mine should fall into his power. But he little valued my civility, for he caused Hammond, with some English officers, to be shot to death."

Cromwell and Ireton met at Thomastown.

"Our men," says Cromwell, "attempting to take the town, the enemy made no great resistance ; but by the advantage of the bridge quitted the town, and fled to a castle about half a mile distant off,[1] which they had formerly possessed.   That night the President of Munster and myself came up to the party.   We summoned the castle, and after two days it was surrendered to us, the enemy leaving their arms, drums, colors, and ammunition behind them, and engaging never to bear arms more against the Parliament of England."

Cromwell remained at Thomastown for three days.   He sent Ireton back to Fethard to bring up some large guns, which were wanted for the attack on Granny and some other castles thereabouts, for the better blocking up of Waterford.   The general rendezvous was Gowran,[2] seven miles south-east of Kilkenny.

" We met," continues Cromwell, " near by Gowran, a populous town, where the enemy had a very strong castle,[3] under the command of Colonel Hammond, a Kentish man, who was a principal actor in the Kentish insurrection and did manage the Lord Capel's business at his trial.[4]   I sent him a civil invitation to deliver up the castle unto me, to which he returned to me a very resolute answer and full of height.   We planted our artillery, and before we had made a breach considerable, the enemy beat a parley for a treaty, which I, having offered so fairly to him, refused ; but sent him in positive conditions that the soldiers should have their lives, and the commissioned officers to be disposed of as should be thought fit, which in the end was submitted to.

" The next day the colonel, the major, and the rest of commissioned officers, were shot to death, all but one, who being a very earnest instrument to have the castle delivered, was pardoned.   In the same castle also we took a Popish priest, who was chaplain to the Catholics in this regiment, who was caused to be hanged.[5] I trouble you with this the rather because the regiment was the Lord of Ormonde's own regiment.   In this castle was a good store of provisions for the army."

---

[1] Probably Grenan castle ; this is still standing.
[2] In 1414 a grant of tolls was made to Ballygaveran for 40 years, to enable the burgesses to pave and wall the town, which had been lately burned and the lieges there destroyed by the Irish enemy, by whom it was surrounded, and who threatened to do it again.
[3] Gowran castle was built by James, third Earl of Ormonde, in 1392.   It was his chief residence after he was driven from Nenagh by the O'Kennedys, who rooted out all the English Gentlemen and freeholders that dwelt in Ormonde, and razed the town of Nenagh, except the castle.   MSS. in Kilkenny castle, quoted in *Kilk. Arch. Journal*, vol. i. p. 392. Gowran castle was rebuilt by Margaret, the great Countess of Ormonde, about 1500   Archdall's *Peerage*, vol. iv. p. 21.   No trace remains of it now ; it was razed to the ground within the present century by the Viscount Clifden of the day.   It was outside the townwall, near where Clifden House now stands.
[4] Lord Capel was executed in March, 1649.   An account of his trial is given in Clarendon's *History of the Rebellion*, vol. iii. p. 272.
[5] The common soldiers delivered up their officers that they might have quarter themselves, viz., Colonel Hammond, Major Townley, two captains, Lieutenant Donnella, a quartermaster, and a Popish priest ; all which officers were shot to death the next day, save only the lieutenant, who was spared, because he complied with the soldiers for delivering up their officers ; and the priest was hanged.

CROMWELL IN IRELAND.

CHAPTER XXV.

THE SIEGE OF KILKENNY.

Cromwell returns to Cashel — Tickle's Treachery — The Garrison of Kilkenny — The Plague — Castel Howel — Summons to Surrender — The Batteries — Capture of St. Canice's and of the Irishtown — Repulse at the Breach — The Mayor's Letter — Proposals of the Governor — Cromwell's Answer — Breach in the Wall — Surrender — The Articles — Want of Supplies.

OUR readers will remember that after the capture of Cashel Cromwell marched on Kilkenny,[1] and that when he had got within a few miles of the city, he returned once more to Cashel and fixed his headquarters there. The causes of his hurried retreat were these. He had advanced on Kilkenny without any of the materials necessary for a siege, relying on the promises of Tickle, an officer of the garrison, whom he had gained over, to secure a gate or two of the city and to betray the Lord Lieutenant (Ormonde) and some others whom he should think fit. "If your Excellency," wrote Tickle to him, "will draw before this town, I shall send a messenger unto you upon your first approach, and shall give you an account of the weakest part of the town and the force within exactly, and what else I shall find, or you may direct me to be most necessary for you."[2] Some of Tickle's letters were intercepted, and though written in cipher, fully revealed his treachery. The plot was thus discovered in time, and the traitor executed. Ormonde, too, who had established his headquarters in Kilkenny during the winter, hearing of the rapid approach of the Puritan army, got together about 700 foot and 100 horse ; with these and some of the townsmen, who seemed eager to aid him, he presented such a formidable appearance, that Cromwell thought it wiser to retire and wait for the arrival of the other corps which he had ordered to come to his assistance. Ormonde was well aware that the advance would not be long delayed ; he prepared for the attack by stengthening the defences as well as circumstances would permit. Giving the chief command of Leinster to Lord Castlehaven, he went to Clare with the Commissioners of Trust, to raise an army there and in the adjoining counties, that would offer some resistance to Cromwell's progress. Castlehaven appointed James Walsh governor of the castle, and Sir Walter Butler governor of the city.

---

[1] "Kilkenny, the seat of the Supreme Council, the spring-head of an execrable rebellion, the centre from which all the treasons and damnable counsels against the king, country, and religion were so many lines drawn."

[2] *Carte MSS.*, vol. xxvi. The bribe offered to him was £4,000, a high command in Cromwell's army, and the governorship of Kilkenny: a fact beyond all doubt, since Tickle confessed it.

Yet in spite of the measures taken for its safety, Kilkenny was but ill fitted to resist the attack of a well-disciplined army, or to sustain the hardships of a siege. A plague, which had appeared a few months before in Galway — brought, it was said, by a Spanish ship that had put in there — and had spread with amazing rapidity throughout the country, was then raging within the walls. "A small party of ours," says a Cromwellian soldier, " by way of affront, went to the gates of Kilkenny to ask who was there ; where they learned, since the plague of the Supreme Council was gone, that the sickness supplied their room. And truly it is so briskly there, that what is their danger is their security, and what fortifies besieges them. So that his Excellency, thinking he ought not to meddle with what the Lord has so visibly taken into his hands, has declined taking Kilkenny into his own."[1] Castlehaven had sent a force of 1,000 foot and 200 horse to garrison the city. In a short time their number was so reduced by disease that their effective strength did not exceed 300 men.[2] He had ordered Lord Dillon, with the forces under his command, amounting to 2,500 foot and 600 horse, to meet him at Carlow, that they might combine and march towards Kilkenny. Lord Dillon's men refused to go to the aid of the doomed city; they marched away to their own country, declaring that they were ready to fight against men but not against God. Sir Walter Butler urged the garrison of Cantwell Castle[3] to abandon that place and to come in all haste to his aid. But the officers, being English, Welsh, and Scotch, sent some of their number to Cromwell, offering him possession of the castle, and asking money and passes to go beyond the sea to serve in the armies of foreign states. He accepted their terms, " on condition that they should do nothing to the prejudice of the Parliament of England."

From Gowran Cromwell and his army advanced on Kilkenny by Bennett's bridge. On the way he took Castle Howel, between Ballyhale and Castlemorris, belonging to the Walshes. Some of the family had taken up arms in self-defence ; a detachment was sent against them, which totally defeated them. The inhabitants of the castle were all slaughtered ; their bodies were thrown into a hole at the foot of the hill on which the castle stood.[4]

He approached the city by the old road still known by the name of Boher na thoundish.[5] He halted about a mile outside the city,

---

[1] *Irish Penny Magazine,* p. 114. Borlase says 17,000 persons died of it during the summer of 1650 in Dublin. *Rebellion,* p. 282. During the three years it lasted, it is reckoned that 30,000 perished of it in that city alone. See O'Connell's *Memoir of Ireland,* p. 329. It abated in the winter of 1651.

[2] Cox says the garrison consisted of 600 foot and 50 horse.

[3] Now Sandfort's Court, near Kilkenny.

[4] A large quantity of bones was found there about the end of last century, when the road was making from Castlemorris to Kilmaganny. See Tighe's *Survey of Kilkenny,* p. 334, and *Kilk. Arch. Journal* for 1881, p. 380.

[5] The Road of the Infirm or Aged. The old road ran parallel with the city-wall. The present Upper Patrick Street is a modern entrance, at which the ancient road was turned from its original course and led into the High Town through St. Patrick's gate, the direct continuation of the old way being through New Street, Flood Street, and Blackmill Street. *Kilk. Arch. Journal* for 1861, p. 366.

near the Black Quarry, and planted his guns on a neighboring hill, still known by the name of "Cromwell's Hill." [1] From there he sent forward a troop of cavalry to reconnoiter the defences.

On Friday, March 22d, he appeared at the head of his army before the walls. In the evening he sent the following summons : —

(1.) To the Governor, Mayor, and Aldermen of the City of Kilkenny.
These :

Before Kilkenny, 22d March, 1650.

GENTLEMEN,

My coming hither is to endeavor, if God so please to bless me, the reduction of the city of Kilkenny to their obedience to the State of England, from which, by an unheard-of massacre of the innocent English, you have endeavored to rend yourselves; and as God hath begun to judge you with His sore plagues, so will He follow you until He hath destroyed you if you repent not. Your cause hath been already judged in England upon them who did abet your evils; what may the principals then expect?

By this free dealing you see I entice you not to a compliance. You may have terms such as may save you in your lives, liberties, and estates, according to what will be fitting for me to grant and you to receive. If you choose for the worst, blame yourselves. In confidence of the gracious blessing and presence of God with His own cause, which by many testimonies this is, I shall hope for a good issue upon my endeavors. Expecting a return from you, I rest

Your servant,

OLIVER CROMWELL.

Immediately after the governor, Sir Walter Butler, sent the following reply :

(2.) For General Cromwell.

Kilkenny, 22d March, 1650.

Sir,

Your letter I have received : and in answer thereof, I am commanded to maintain this city for his Majesty, which, by the power of God, I am resolved to do. So I rest, Sir,

Your servant,

WALTER BUTLER.

Early the next day he invested the place, and planted the batteries. In the evening he attempted to possess himself of the Irish-town ; but he was repulsed. He seized on St. Patrick's church,[2] and planted on the tower three pieces of ordnance, two demi-cannon and one culverin. Again he wrote to the governor, asking him to treat about terms of surrender. The letter has been lost, but we have the Governor's answer :

(3.) For General Cromwell.

Kilkenny, March 25th, 1650.

Sir,

Your last letter I received, and in answer, I have such confidence to maintain

---

[1] Such is the tradition ; but the battery could hardly have been planted here, the distance being too great for the guns to act from it on any part of the town.

[2] It was outside the walls, on the brow of the Boher na thoundish, near its modern entrance through St. Patrick's gate into the High Town.

this place as I will not lose it upon such terms as you offer, but will sooner lose my life and the lives of all that are here, rather than submit to such dishonorable conditions. So I rest, Sir,

Your servant,

WALTER BUTLER.

Between five and six, on the morning of the 25th, the battery began to play on the town-wall, beneath the Marquis of Ormonde's stables, which lay between the castle gate and the rampart. The firing continued till noon. By this time a breach was made in the town-wall. But the governor erected two works within the walls with palisadoes ; he had engines also laid in the way to hinder an entry. The soldiers were posted behind in full body to receive the enemy if they attempted to enter. Lieutenant-Colonel Axtell had the command of the storming party ; Colonel Hewson led on the reserve very gallantly. St. Canice's church being observed to command the town in some parts, Colonel Evers, with a party of 1,000 foot, was sent to storm and take possession of it. The attack was made in both places simultaneously, to distract the attention of the garrison. The Irish-town [1] had been entrusted to the keeping of the townsmen, the garrison being employed in defending the portions of the town-wall that were assailed, and in securing the breach against another attack. The townsmen, at the first onset of the enemy, deserted their post almost without striking a blow,[2] and allowed the assailants to enter through the Dean's gate, and take possession of the cathedral and of the Irishtown. Twice the storming party at the breach strove to enter ; each time they were repulsed ; they lost Captain Higly and thirty or forty men.[3] Hewson was slightly wounded : he received a shot in the back, which " penetrated his buff coat, and a little bruised the flesh." Each time the breach was immediately repaired by the garrison. A third time the assailants were ordered to advance, but they would not obey. They saw that an entrance could not be effected there, as the counter-works raised within the walls were strongly palisadoed and commanded the breach. "It was a mercy to us," says Cromwell, " that we did not further contend for an entrance there, it being probable if we had, it would have cost us very dear." [4]

---

[1] The inland-walled towns were so strictly English that the Irish could not lawfully dwell therein. Sir Henry Sidney considered them "the Queen's unpaid garrisons." Outside the principal gate there was commonly a suburb inhabited by the Irish, who supplied the townsmen with provisions, or worked for them as tradesmen, laborers, &c. *Crom. Sett.*, p 295. In Dublin, Limerick, Kilkenny, Clonmel, Bandon, and New Ross there is a district still called by this name.

[2] However, in " The Petition sent to the Marquis of Ormonde by the Irish inhabitants Kilkenny, June 18th, 1661, asking to be restored to their homes," they say, " The siege of Kilkenny having endured for six or seven days, your petitioners having not sufficient forces to defend the same nor hope of relief, by reason of the plague and great sickness then raging in the same city, after suffering in a high degree all the extremities of the plague, fire and sword, and four several storms in several parts of the city, which were repulsed, and after a great breach made in the walls by cannon-shot of above fifty great bullets ; at last, by direction or allowance of Sir Walter Butler, governor of the city and castle, yielded upon quarter."

[3] Bruodin says 600 of the assailants fell at the breach. *Propug.*, p. 684. The more probable accounts represent the garrison as fighting with all the energy of despair.

[4] Cromwell to Lenthal, from Carrick, April 2d, in Carlyle's *Letters*, &c.

Another letter from Cromwell followed on the same day, there being no cessation during the correspondence in reference to the surrender.

(4.) For the Governor of Kilkenny.

Before Kilkenny, 25th March, 1650.

Sir,

If you had been as clear as I was in my last, I might, perhaps, have understood you so as to give you some further answer. But you expressing nothing particularly what you have to expect against mine, I have nothing more to return save this — that for some reasons I cannot let your trumpeter suddenly come back, but have sent you this by a drummer of my own. I rest

Your servant,

OLIVER CROMWELL.

And this reply from the Governor : —

(5.) For General Cromwell.

Kilkenny, 25th March, 1650.

Sir,

Yours of this instant I received: the particulars you would have me express are these : —

That the Mayor and citizens, and all the other inhabitants, and others now resident in the city and the liberties thereof, with their servants, shall be secured of their lives, liberties, estates, and goods, and live in their own habitations with all freedom. And that our clergymen and all others here residing, of what degree, condition, or quality soever, that shall be minded to depart, shall be permitted to depart safely hence, with their goods and whatever they have, to what place soever they please with this realm, and in their departure shall be safely conveyed. And that the said inhabitants shall have free trade and traffic with all places under the parliament of England's command and elsewhere; and that the aforesaid inhabitants shall have their arms, ammunition, and artillery for their own defence, the town and liberties thereof paying such reasonable contribution as shall be agreed on, and not to be otherwise charged. And that the governors, commanders, officers, and soldiers, both horse and foot, now garrisoned as well in the castle as in the city, without exception of any of them, shall safely march hence, whither they list, with their arms, ammunition, artillery, bag and baggage, and whatsoever else belongs to them, with their drums beating, colors flying, matches burning, and bullet in bouche; and that they shall have a competent time for their departure and carrying away their goods, with a sufficient and safe convey; and that Major Nicholas Walt, and all other commanders, officers, and soldiers, who came out of the English quarters, now residing here, shall have the benefit of this agreement. Without which, I am resolved to maintain the place, with God's help.

Thus expecting your answer to this letter, and that during this treaty there shall be a cessation of arms and all other acts of hostility on both sides, I rest, Sir,

Your servant,

WALTER BUTLER.

Cromwell was on the point of raising the siege when the Mayor and townsmen invited him to stay, promising to obtain admittance for his forces into the city. The conditions are set down in the following letter of the Mayor :

(6.)   For the Right Honorable the Lord Cromwell.

RIGHT HONORABLE,

   We know by experience, and have it by your Honor's letters, that you desire not the spilling of blood nor the spoiling of cities and towns; and though I doubt not but your Honor would easily agree to good and profitable conditions for the city and citizens, yet we having a Governor of the city, and another of the castle, who commands us also, if befitting honorable conditions be not given unto the military part, the city and citizens do stand in danger of ruin as well from our own party as that of your Honor's.   This, in the name of the city, and citizens, I humbly offer to your Honor's gracious, wise consideration, and desire your favorable remedy therein, and rest, Sir,

Your servant,

JAMES ARCHDAKIN,

Mayor of Kilkenny.

To which Cromwell sent the following answer :

(7.)   For the Mayor of Kilkenny.

26th March, 1650.

Sir,

   Though I could have wished you and the citizens had been indeed more sensible of your own interest and concernments, yet, since you are minded to involve it so much with that of the soldiers, I am glad to understand you, which will be some direction to me what to think and what to do.   I rest

Your friend,

O. CROMWELL.

The Mayor replied :

(8.)   For the Right Honorable General Cromwell.

Kilkenny, 26th March, 1650.

RIGHT HONORABLE,

   I received your Honor's letter in answer to mine, which I wrote unto your Honor in pursuance of the propositions sent by our Governor unto your Honor for obtaining of the said conditions, which seemed unto us almost befitting to be granted, the military part having exposed themselves for our defence; which obligeth us not to accept of any conditions but such as may be befitting to them.   I desire your Honor to grant a cessation of arms, and that hostages on both sides be sent, and commissioners appointed to treat of the conditions.   I rest

Your Honor's servant,

JAMES ARCHDAKIN,

Mayor of Kilkenny.

  Cromwell, in consequence of his success, partial though it was, could now insist upon conditions more favorable to himself.   What these were we learn from the following letters : —

(9.)   For the Mayor of Kilkenny.

Before Kilkenny, 26th March, 1650.

Sir,

   Those whom God hath brought to a sense of His hand upon them and to amend, submitting themselves thereto and to the power to which He hath subjected them, I cannot but pity and tender, and so far as that effect appears in you and your fellow-citizens, I shall be ready, without capitulation, to do more and better for you and them upon that ground, than upon the high demands of your Governor or his capitulations for you.

I suppose he hath acquainted you with what I briefly offered yesterday in relation to yourself and the inhabitants; otherwise he hath done you the more to answer for to God and man. And notwithstanding the advantages, as to the commanding and entering the town, which God had given us since that offer, more than we were possessed of before, yet I am still willing, upon surrender, to make good the same to the city, and that with advantage.

Now, in regard of that temper which appears among you by your letter, though I shall not engage for more upon the Governor's demands for you, whose power, I conceive, is now greater to prejudice and endanger the city than to protect it; to save it from plunder and pillage, I have promised the soldiery that, if we should take it by storm, the inhabitants shall give them a reasonable gratuity in money, in lieu of the pillages; and so made it death for any man to plunder. Which I shall still keep them to, by God's help, although we should be put to make an entry by force, unless I shall find the inhabitants engaging still with the Governor and soldiery to make resistance. You may see, also, the way I chose for reducing the place was such as tended most to save the inhabitants from pillage, and from perishing promiscuously, the innocent with the guilty: to wit, by attempting places which being possessed might bring it to a surrender, rather than enter the city itself by force.

If what is here expressed may beget resolution in you, which would occasion your safety and be consistent with the end of my coming hither, I shall be glad, and rest

Your friend,

OLIVER CROMWELL.

(10.) For the Governor of Kilkenny.

Before Kilkenny, 26th March, 1650.

Sir,

Except the conditions were much bettered, and we in a worse posture and capacity to reduce you than before the last letters I sent you, I cannot imagine whence these high demands of yours arise. I hope in God, before it be long you may have occasion to think other thoughts; to which I leave you.

I shall not so much as treat with you on those propositions. You desire some articles for honor's sake; which out of honesty I do deny, viz.: that of marching in the equipage you mention, "muskets loaded, matches burning," &c. I tell you my business is to reduce you from arms, and the country to quietness and due subjection; to put an end to the war, and not to lengthen it; wishing, if it may stand with the will of God, this people may live as happily as they did before the bloody massacre, and better, too. If you and the company with you be of those who resolve to continue to hinder this, we know who is able to reach you, and, I believe, will.

For the inhabitants of the town, of whom you seem to have a care, you know your retreat to be better than theirs; and, therefore, it is not impolitically done to speak for them, and to engage them to keep us as long from you as they can. If they be willing to expose themselves to ruin for you, you are much beholding unto them.

As for your "clergymen," as you call them, in case you agree for a surrender, they shall march safely away, with their goods and what belongs to them; but if they fall otherwise into my hands, I believe they know what to expect from me. If upon what I proposed formerly, with this addition concerning them, you expect things to be cleared, I am content to have Commissioners for that purpose. I rest. Sir,

Your servant,

OLIVER CROMWELL.

The Governor seeing the temper of the townsmen, and well aware of the weakness of the force under his command, knew that t resistance he could offer would be worse than useless. The example of Drogheda and Wexford taught him "what to expect" if the city was taken by assault. On the receipt of the above he wrote to propose a conference. It was readily accepted by Cromwell.

(11.) For General Cromwell.

Kilkenny, 26th March, 1650.

SIR,

In answer of your letter, if you be pleased to appoint officers for a treaty for the surrender of the castle and city upon soldier-like conditions, I will also appoint officers of such quality as are in the garrison, provided that hostages of equality be sent on both sides, and a cessation of arms be also granted during the treaty. Assuring a performance, on my side, of all that will be agreed upon, I rest, Sir,

Your servant,

WALTER BUTLER.

P. S. — I desire to know what's become of my trumpeter whom I employed two days ago.   W. B.

(12.) To the Governor of Kilkenny.

Before Kilkenny, 26th March, 1650.

SIR,

That no extremity may happen for want of a right understanding, I am content that commissioners on each side do meet in the leaguer at the south side of the city, authorized to treat and conclude. For which purpose, if you shall speedily send me the names and qualities of the commissioners you will send out, I shall appoint the like number on my part, authorized as aforesaid, to meet with them; and shall send in a safe-conduct for the coming out and return of yours. As for hostages, I conceive it needless and dilatory. I expect that the treaty will begin by eight of the clock this evening and end by twelve; during which time only will I grant a cessation. Expecting your speedy answer, I rest

Your servant,

OLIVER CROMWELL.

The trumpeter by whom the message was sent was at first refused admittance; it was nine o'clock when the despatch reached the Governor. His reply was given immediately.

(13.) For General Cromwell.

Kilkenny, 26th March, 1650.

SIR,

Yours of this instant I received, and do hold the time appointed for the treaty and cessation of arms to be too short. Major John Comerford, Capt. David Turnball, James Cowley, Esq., Recorder of this city, and Edward Rothe, Merchant, are the commissioners appointed by me, who will meet such commissioners as you fix on at the place by you appointed by six of the clock to-morrow morning, or sooner, if you please, so as hostages be sent to me for their safe return; for without hostages the gentlemen will not go. The reason that I conceive the time to be short is because your trumpeter came not hither till nine of the clock this night; so, as I conceive, the business cannot be ended in so short a time. I have commanded mine to forbear acts of hostility during this treaty, and I desire that you do the like. I rest, Sir,   Your servant,

WALTER BUTLER.

(14.) To the Governor of Kilkenny.

27th March, 1650.

Sir,

The reason of the so late coming of my answer to you was because my trumpet was refused to be received at the north end of the town; and where he was admitted, was kept long upon the guard.

I have sent you a safe-conduct for the four commissioners named by you: and if they be such as are unwilling to take my word, I shall not, to humor them, agree to hostages. I am willing to a treaty for four hours, provided it begin by twelve of the clock this morning; but for a cessation, the time last appointed being past, I shall not agree unto it to hinder my own proceedings.

Your servant,

O. CROMWELL.

The Commissioners were sent out soon after from the city, with a warrant for a treaty, signed by both the governors of the city and castle of Kilkenny, "appointing and authorizing Major John Comerford, Captain David Turnball, James Cowley, Recorder of Kilkenny, and Edward Rothe, Merchant, to treat and agree with the Lord General Cromwell, or such as he shall appoint, touching the yielding up to the said Lord General the city and castle of Kilkenny, and the conditions whereupon they shall be given up." [1]

The same day, March 27th, a breach was made with the pickaxes, in the wall adjoining the Franciscan monastery, to make a way for the horse and foot to enter. There is a piece of comparatively modern work in the old town-wall, at the angle where the Bregagh joins the Nore; probably this was the spot where the breach was affected. The townsmen, who were guarding this part of the city, also began to forsake their posts. Fortunately the governor at the head of a troop of horse, came up, and beat off the enemy, killing most of those that were near the spot.

That night a party, consisting of eight companies of foot under Colonel Gifford, was sent across the river to take possession of that part of the town. The attempt proved successful. They next tried to cross St. John's bridge, fire the gate, and thus effect an entrance into the city. Though they advanced resolutely, yet they lay so open to the enemy's shot that they were repulsed, with the loss of forty or fifty men.

Cromwell, in the meantime, was preparing to erect a second battery. The governor, seeing the weakness of the garrison, few in number, and exhausted by continual watching at their posts, and despairing of further aid, determined to carry out Lord Castlehaven's orders, viz:—That if he was not relieved by seven o'clock on the evening of the 27th inst., he should not, through any false notion of honor, expose the inhabitants to be massacred, but rather make as good conditions as he could by a timely surrender. A parley was beaten, a cessation of hostilities was agreed on, and at noon next day, March 28th, the town and castle were delivered up. The same day, Ireton arrived with 1,500 men to aid the besiegers. The following were the conditions of surrender:—

---

[1] Captain Frewen was unhappily killed during the treaty, there being no cessation.

Articles of agreement between the Commissioners appointed by his Excellency, Lord Cromwell, Lord Lieutenant General of Ireland, for and on behalf of his Excellency, of the one part, and those appointed Commissioners by the respective Governors of the City and Castle of Kilkenny, of the other party. March 27th, 1650.

1. That the respective Governors of the city and castle of Kilkenny shall deliver to his Excellency, the Lord Cromwell, the Lord Lieutenant General of Ireland, for the use of the State of England, the said city and castle, with all arms, ammunition, and provisions of public stores therein, without embezzlement, except what is hereafter excepted, at or before nine of the clock to-morrow morning.

2. That all the inhabitants of the said city of Kilkenny, and all others therein, shall be defended in their persons, goods, and estates, from the violence of the soldiery, and that such as shall desire to remove thence elsewhere, none excepted, shall have liberty so to do, with their goods, within three months after the date of these articles.

3. That the said Governors, with all the officers and soldiers under their respective commands in the said city and castle, and all others who shall be so pleased, shall march away at or before nine of the clock to-morrow morning, with their bag and baggage; the officers with their attendants, their arms, and with their horses not exceeding the number of one hundred and fifty horses; and their foot soldiers to march out of the town, two miles distant, with their arms, and with drums beating, colors flying, matches lighted, and ball in bouche; and then and there to deliver up the said arms to such as shall be appointed for receiving them, excepting one hundred muskets and a hundred pikes allowed them for their defence against the Tories.[1]

4. That the said officers and soldiers shall have from his Excellency a safe-conduct six miles from the city of Kilkenny; and from thenceforward a pass for their security out of his Excellency's quarters; the said pass to be in force for six days from the date of these presents, they marching, at least, ten miles each day, and doing no prejudice to quarters.

5. That the city of Kilkenny shall pay £2,000 as a gratuity to his Excellency's army; whereof £1,000 to be paid on the 30th of this month, and the other on the first day of May next following, to such as shall be by his Excellency hereunto appointed.

6. That Major John Comerford and Mr. Edward Rothe shall remain hostages, under the power of his Excellency, for the performance of the said articles, on the part of said city and garrison of Kilkenny.

7. Lastly, for the performance of all and singular the premises the parties have hereunto interchangeably put their hands, the day and year first above written.

JAMES COWLEY,   JOHN CUMERFORD,   O. CROMWELL.
EDWARD ROTHE,   DAVID TURNBALL,

The author of the *Aphorismal Discovery* says, " The surrender was entirely owing to the conduct of the citizens; if the governor were pleased, and the citizens loyal, he might have kept the town for

---

[1] During the rebellion of 1641 the name of Tories was given to such persons as at first preferred to remain neutral, but who ultimately — perhaps urged by their loss of property and consequent distress — took up arms with a view of reprisal or revenge on those by whom they had been reduced to absolute ruin. English and Irish, Protestant and Catholic, Republican and Royalist, were alike their common enemies; and, being joined by men of desperate fortunes, they united themselves in bodies and became formidable gangs of free-booters, who harassed the regular troops of all parties without distinction. Croker's *Hist. Researches*, p. 52; London, 1824. It was applied by the opponents of Charles I. to his party, under the idea that he favored the Irish rebels. By an easy transition it became the distinctive appellation of the party who wished for the widest extension of the royal prerogative. Some derive it from *Tar a Righ*, Come, O King, a cry used by the Irish adherents of Charles I. Titus Oates used to call any one who opposed him a Tory.

a twelvemonth, if a straiter siege were not laid unto. But the base cowardice and disloyal townsmen betrayed both the gentlemen and the city, and did capitulate with the enemy. Which agreed upon, the gates were opened for him, and all unknown to the governor. No mention made in the said capitulation either of him or any of his party, all his now remedy was, seeing the enemy had the city, to defend the castle, thereby to force a quarter for himself and his soldiers, which being put in execution until the enemy thought the last of evils to grant him and his an honorable quarter of both lives and arms; which projected, both city and castle were yielded."

Cromwell found "the castle exceedingly well fortified by the industry of the enemy; being also very capacious, so that if we had taken the town, we must have had a new work for the castle, which might have caused much blood and time."

After describing his successes in detail, he concludes his letter by a demand for supplies : —

"I may not be wanting to tell you, as to renew it again, that our hardships are not a few; that I think in my conscience, if moneys be not supplied, we shall not be able to carry on your work. I would not say this to you if I did not reckon it my duty so to do. But if it be supplied, and that speedily, I hope, through the good hand of the Lord, it will not be long before England will be at an end of this charge; for the saving of which I beseech you help as soon as you can. Sir, our horse have not had one month's pay of five. We strain what we can, that the foot may be paid, or else they would starve. Those towns that are to be reduced, especially one or two of them, if we should proceed by the rules of other states, would cost you more money than this army hath had since we came over. I hope, through the blessing of God, they will come cheaper to you; but how we should be able to proceed in our attempts without reasonable supply, is humbly submitted and represented to you. I think I need not say that a speedy period put to this work will break the expectation of all your enemies. And, seeing the Lord is not wanting to you, I most humbly beg it, that you would not be wanting to yourselves.

"In the last place, it cannot be thought but the taking of these places, and the keeping but what is necessary of them, it must needs swallow up our foot; and I may humbly repeat it again, that I do not know of much above two thousand of your five thousand recruits come to us."

CHAPTER XXVI

SURRENDER OF KILKENNY.

Bravery of the Garrison — Dr. Rothe — Churches profaned — Ecclesiatics put to death —
The Market Cross — St. Canice's Cathedral — The Windows — The Ormonde Monument — F. Lea, S. J. — Ormonde and the Bishop of Clogher.

KILKENNY surrendered on the 28th of March, 1650. As the
garrison marched out of the town, with their commander, Sir Walter
Butler, at their head, they were complimented by Cromwell for their
bravery : he said that they were gallant fellows ; that he had lost
more men storming that place than at Drogheda, and that he should
have gone without it were it not for the treachery of the townsmen.
Writing from Carrick, April 2d, he expresses "to his loving brother,
Richard Mayor, Esquire," his great satisfaction at the success of his
arms. "The taking of the city of Kilkenny hath been one of our
last works ; which indeed, I believe, hath been a great decomposing of
the enemy ; it's so much into their bowels."

The inhabitants who remained behind, owing to the timely
surrender, escaped many of the calamities that befell the other places
captured by the Puritan army, though "for the securing of their lives,
estates, and goods from the violence of the soldiery, they were forced
to pay £2,000 to Cromwell for the making good of that quarter."[1]
Dr. Rothe,[2] the bishop, availing himself of the terms of the treaty,
that the clergy should have liberty to go elsewhere, quitted the city
with the garrison. Not that he feared danger or cared for his own
life — he had often given proof of his readiness to run any risk for
the welfare of the flock.[3] When the plague appeared in the city, he
rose from his bed, to which he had been confined for more than a
year by excruciating pains, and he had himself borne on a litter from
door to door, in order to minister with his own hands the consolations
of religion to those of his flock who stood in need of them. He had
not gone more than a mile outside the walls, when he was seized by
some stragglers from the victorious army and robbed of all he possessed. The news of Rothe's capture was at once despatched to

[1] Petition of the Irish inhabitants of Kilkenny ; see p. 306, antea.

[2] An interesting account of the Rothe family, by the Rev. J. F. Shearman, is given in
The Confederation of Kilkenny, p. 330. At Jenkinstown there is a portrait of Dr. Rothe,
and also some vestments which belonged to him. The Bishop of Ossory has a monstrance
made by his order ; of this there is a drawing in the *History of St. Canice's Cathedral*, p. 40 ;
Dublin, 1857.

[3] Messingham says he was well versed in all sorts of learning, an eloquent orator, a
subtle philosopher, a profound divine, an eminent historian, and a sharp reprover of vice.
Florilegium Insulæ Sanctorum, p. 87 ; Paris, 1624. A list of his works is given in Ware's
Writers of Ireland, p. 122.

Cromwell. He gave permission to have the aged prelate[1] brought back to the city and handed over to his kinsfolk, that he might pass the brief remainder of his life among them.[2] Another and a more probable account is that given by Dr. Fleming, then archbishop of Dublin, when announcing Rothe's death officially a few months later. He says that he was dragged from the carriage in which he sat, a tattered cloak covered with vermin was given him, and he was cast into a loathsome dungeon, where he expired after a prolonged martyrdom.[3] He died on the 20th of April, in the seventy-eighth year of his age and the thirty-second of his episcopate.[4] His remains were laid in the family vault in St. Mary's church, after the usual obsequies had been performed without any hindrance. Some years before, in more peaceful times, he had erected a tomb in the cathedral of St. Canice, where he hoped his bones might be laid after his course was run;[5] here his friends strove hard to have him interred; but owing very probably to the fact that Colonel Axtell's regiment was quartered in the sacred edifice, they could not carry out their pious intentions. Strange to say, this monument escaped the fury of the Puritans, though they destroyed the sumptuous tomb of the Ormondes. It was partly demolished later by the ill-judged zeal of John Parry, the Protestant bishop of Ossory.[6]

Catholicity was flourishing in the city of Kilkenny, when the Puritan army, like a devastating torrent, overturning everything in its course, appeared before the walls. As soon as they got possession of the city, they impiously profaned the churches, overthrew the altars, destroyed the paintings and crosses, and showed their contempt for everything sacred. The vestments, which had been for the most part concealed, were discovered and plundered by the soldiery. The books and paintings were cast into the streets, and either burnt or taken away as booty. Dr. Patrick Lynch, of Galway, writing on the 1st of May, 1650, to the Secretary of the Congregation of the Propaganda, says that a report had reached him of cruelties that had taken place in the city of Kilkenny, and of a number of priests, religious, nobles, and merchants, who had been put to death there.[7]

There is a tradition still current in Kilkenny, that after the surrender of the town, some distinguished ecclesiastics took refuge

---

[1] In his "Petition to the Confederate Council," August 1st, 1649, he speaks of himself as "old and bedrid." See *Account of the Carte MSS*, p. 83.

[2] The family mansion of the Rothes was in the Coal Market, Kilkenny; the entrance to it was by Wolf's Arch. *Kilk. Arch. Journal* for 1849, pp. 45 and 133.

[3] In *Spicil. Ossory*, vol. i. p. 340. Dr. Fleming's letter is dated June 5th, 1650.

[4] He was promoted to the see of Kilkenny in 1618, in his forty-fifth year. For many years previous he had been Vicar-General of Armagh. His name appears in a list of students at Douay, in 1613. See *Calendar of the Carew MSS.* (1603-24), p. 286; London, 1873.

[5] Robert Rothe in his will, executed in 1619, directs that he should be buried "in ye Chapel of the B. V. Mary and St. Michael, Kilkenny, where his father and grandfather are interred."

[6] He held the see from 1672 to 1677. He was succeeded by his brother, Benjamin Parry, who held it only nine months. See Ware's *Antiquities*, vol. i. p. 429.

[7] The ecclesiastics who survived were banished, for in the *Langton Memorials* it is said: "Bishop Phelan was our first Catholic bishop in the diocese of Ossory since the year 1540; at which time all our clergy were expelled by the Parliament and the usurper Cromwell."

from the violence of the soldiery in a secret chamber of the Dominican friary attached to the Black Abbey. None knew of their place of concealment except a few trusted friends, among whom was a woman named Thornton, who engaged to supply them every night with milk. This woman, for a bribe, betrayed the secret, and indicated to the Cromwellian soldiers where their victims could be found by spilling the milk along the road from the outer gate to the spot where the entrance to the secret chamber should be sought. The consequence was that the ecclesiastics were dragged from their concealment and put to death. Their betrayer received a grant of land as her reward.[1]

F. Archdeacon, S. J.,[2] in his *Theologia Tripartita*, a work published in 1678, describes the manner in which the soldiers displayed their fanaticism : " There. stood, and still stands, in the market-place of Kilkenny,[3] a magnificent structure of stone, of elegant workmanship, rising aloft after the manner of an obelisk. It is supported by four lofty columns, which bear the weight of the whole superstructure. You ascend it on the four sides by flights of stone steps ; and above all, on the highest point, was placed a sculptured figure of the Crucifixion.[4] After the occupation of the city by Cromwell's soldiers, some of them, who were particularly remarkable for their impiety, assembled in the market-place, armed with their muskets, and directed many shots against the symbol of the Crucifixion, in order that they might fully complete their irreligious triumph ; this their persecuting fury at length accomplished. But behold ! the wrath of an avenging God quickly pursued the authors of this sacrilege. A mysterious malady seized on them, and effected them so, that none survived beyond a few days." Another writer, whose name has not come down to us, says, " Seven soldiers of the Parliamentary army, like seven unclean spirits, set on it. After firing at it for some time, they broke off the higher portion of it, and returned in triumph to their dwellings. But behold ! of the number, six died immediately after, three on that same day, and three on the day following. The seventh was on the point of death ; I know not whether he escaped. These facts became known to the whole city, and served to confirm the Catholics in their veneration for the cross, and to terrify, in no small degree, the heretics, its enemies."

The church of St. Canice was the special object of their pious

[1] A family named Thornton still resides within a few miles of the city, and to this day they are frequently upbraided with the alleged treachery of their ancestors.

[2] He was born in Kilkenny, in 1619. At the age of twenty-three he entered the Jesuit novitiate at Mechlin. For many years he taught philosophy, theology and Scripture at Louvain and Antwerp. He died in the latter place in 1690. Besides the above work, which has been frequently reprinted, he wrote a *Treatise on Miracles* and an *Epitome of the Life of St. Patrick.*

[3] Between the Butter Slip and the Tholsel, in the middle of High Street, and in the centre of the market. It was erected in 1335.

[4] A drawing of this cross is given in the *Dublin Penny Journal*, vol. i. p. 92 ; and in the *Kilk. Arch. Journal* for 1853, p. 219, the latter taken from an old drawing in the collection of the late W. Robertson, Esq. Here, in 1335, many were marked on the naked flesh in the sign of the cross with a red-hot iron, that they might go to the Holy Land. Clyun's *Annals ad ann.* Rinuccini, too, speaks of it in his *Nunziatura*, p. 82. An address in Latin was read to him by a youth in front of it as he was entering the city. It was taken down by order of the Corporation in 1771.

wrath. We have already seen that, in the earlier part of the siege, the assailants had attacked the quarter of the city where it was situated, and had succeeded in effecting an entrance there and establishing themselves within its walls. After the surrender, the aisles were converted into stabling for the troopers' horses. Colonel Axtell's[1] regiment was quartered in it for a considerable time. Eight years before it had been taken possession of by the Catholics, Dr. Griffith Williams,[2] the Protestant bishop, having fled at the breaking out of the rebellion. It was then solemnly reconciled for the Catholic service by Dr. Rothe, in presence of the members of the Supreme Council and of the prelates assembled in the city. Bale, whom Rothe calls "an image-breaking debauchee "[3] (*iconoclastes ganeo*), had sold the gold and silver vessels, and demolished the altars and statues of the saints. Rothe devoted all his energies to repair these injuries, and succeeded so well that he merited the eulogy of the legate Rinuccini. An inscription still extant in the cathedral records the gratitude of the people for his zeal.[4] Williams thus laments over the disasters that had befallen the noble edifice: "The great and famous and most beautiful cathedral church of St. Keney (Canice) they have utterly defaced and ruined. They have thrown down the great roof of it, taken away five great and goodly bells, broken down all the windows, and carried away every bit of glass, which, they say, was worth a very great deal; and all the doors of it, that hogs might come and root, and the dogs gnaw the bones of the dead; and they broke down a most exquisite marble font, wherein the Christians' children were regenerated, all to pieces, and threw down many goodly marble monuments that were therein, and especially that stately and costly monument of the most honorable and noble family of the House of Ormonde,[5] and divers others of most rare and excellent work, not much inferior, if I be not much mistaken, to most of the best, excepting the Kings', that are in St. Paul's Church or the Abbey of Westminster. Rothe says of the painted glass, put up by Bishop Ledrede:[6] "The choir of the cathedral of St. Canice is ornamented with colored glass, in which the whole life, passion, ressurection, and ascension of our Lord are most skilfully depicted. Such is its beauty

---

[1] Axtell was one of those who signed the warrent for the King's death. Cromwell made him governor of Wexford, and later of Kilkenny. In 1660 he was condemned to death with the other regicides still surviving, "for being commander of that black guard, that cruel and bloody guard, as the Attorney-General called it, that surrounded the High Court of Injustice which condemned the King to die." See the *Indictment of the Regicides*, p. 181. London, 1724.

[2] Williams was Protestant Bishop of Ossory from 1641 to 1672.

[3] An interesting account of Bale's "godly career" in Ireland is given in the *Irish Ecclesiastical Record*, vol. i. p. 569; Dublin, 1865.

[4] The inscription is given in Graves' *History of St. Canice's Cathedral*, p. 293; it is set on an elaborate Renaissance monument, bearing the arms of the Rothe family, or a stag tripp nt gules, by an oak tree vert, with the motto, "*Virtuti non audacia.*"

[5] It was erected in memory of Thomas Butler, surnamed the Black, tenth Earl of Ormonde, who died in 1614. He was buried in the choir of St. Canice's cathedral.

[6] Clynn (*Annals*, p. 13) says he was consecrated on the 8th of the kelands of May, A. D., at Avignon, where the Pope then dwelt. About 1334 he began the repairs of the cathedral, which had been much injured by the falling in of the belfry in 1322. He died in 1360.

and splendor, that when the iconoclasts of modern times, in the reigns
of Edward and Elizabeth, destroyed the sacred pictures, and though
that unclean drunkard, Bale, broke and profaned all the statues of the
saints which he could lay hands on, yet neither he nor the two other
intruding bishops who succeeded him touched these windows." Yet
these, too, were demolished by the bigots.

In the account of the Jesuit Mission from 1641 to 1650, some
further details are given of the state of the city during the siege : —

"Father Patrick Lea, a man held to be a saint by all who knew him, was employed in the service of those who were struck down by the plague. He was well
versed in all kinds of learning, even in the knowledge of medicine; for this reason
he was asked by the citizens to undertake that duty. But owing to his ardent tem-
perament and his zeal for the salvation of souls, his life was not a long one. Not
only did he continuously hear the confessions of the plague-stricken, give them Holy
Communion and Extreme Unction, and bestow on them all the spiritual aid they
needed, but, besides, he was unceasing in attending to their bodily wants, supplying
them with medicines and food and cleansing their sores. It happened that a poor
man, whom he was attending, died. The body was spreading contagion all around.
Father Lea took up the corpse in his arms and carried it to a neighboring cemetery,
and, making a grave, buried it there. Owing to the heated state in which he was,
and to the contact with the corpse, he was stricken down by the fatal disease on the
24th of March, 1650, to the great grief of the cititens.

"A few days after his death the city was taken. Our Fathers sought to avoid
the danger in various ways. One of them took up a weapon, and passed out with
the soldiers who were leaving the town. Another acted as servant in the house of a
certain nobleman, and when waiting at table, often poured out wine and ale to the
enemy. A third, in the disguise of a merchant, remained behind in the city, and employed himself in consoling the Catholics.

"Meantime the army of the heretics entering the town, overturned the altars
and profaned the images, crosses, and all the other sacred things. They destroyed
our house and oratory, sparing nothing that they believed belonged to a Jesuit. The
sacred furniture had been hidden away ; yet it was found and plundered. The books
were thrown out into the street and burned. The soldiers who were struck down by
the plague were put into our house, which was turned into a hospital, and profaned
everything."

After the capture of Kilkenny, Ormonde, Castlehaven, and the
Bishop of Clogher met in Westmeath to consult with the gentleman
of that county about the King's interests. Ormonde set before them
the following queries : 1st. Whether they were able to raise such
forces as would be sufficient to engage Cromwell ? 2d. In case they
were not able to fight, whether it were not necessary with all the force
they could muster to fall on the English quarters, and there burn and
destroy all they could, that the enemy might not be able to subsist?
3d. If this was not feasible, whether it was not most convenient for
them to join in some proposals of peace for the whole kingdom, or
every one for himself, to make his own particular application ? The
last expedient was much approved by some ; but most of them,
knowing they had little claim to good conditions, preferred to attack
the English in their quarters, and thus protract time until they should
have an opportunity of escaping.

CROMWELL IN IRELAND.

CHAPTER XXVII.

THE BATTLE OF MACROOM.

Sadlier's successes — Ennisnag, Pulkerry, Ballydoine, Granny, and Dunkill taken — Henry Cromwell arrives in Ireland — Defeat of Inchiquin — The Munster Army — Confederate Standards — Battle of Macroom — The Bishop of Ross hanged — Surrender of Carrigadrohid — Broghill's Account.

THE main body of Cromwell's army remained but a short time at Kilkenny, perhaps through fear of the plague. Within a week after the surrender he set out for Carrick, as is shown by a letter of his written from there to his friend Richard Mayor. The headquarters were at Burntchurch, four miles south-west of Kilkenny.

Parties were sent out to seize on the various strongholds in the neighborhood. "Colonel Abbot attempted Ennisnag,[1] where were gotten a company of rogues, which revolted from Colonel Jones. The soldiers capitulated for life, and their two officers were hanged for revolting. Adjutant-General Sadlier was commanded, with two guns, to attempt some castles in the counties of Tipperary and Kilkenny, which being reduced would exceedingly tend to the blocking up two considerable towns. He summoned Pulkerry,[2] a garrison under Clonmel, and battered it. They refusing to come out, he stormed it, put thirty or forty of them to the sword, and the rest, remaining obstinate, were fired in the castle. He took Ballopoin,[3] the enemy marching away, leaving their arms behind them He took also the Granny and Donhill,[4] two very considerable places to Waterford, upon the same terms.

A month before, Henry Cromwell[5] had arrived at Youghal from England with a regiment of foot and about two hundred horse. He and Lord Broghill, having united their forces, defeated Lord Inchiquin in the neighborhood of Limerick, killing 160 of his men, and taking over 100 prisoners. Among those captured were three officers. They were tried by court-martial for betraying their trust, having been formerly in the service of the Parliament. They were sentenced to

---

[1] In the county of Kilkenny, between Kells and Gowran ; the castle is in ruins, only some parts of the east and south walls remaining.

[2] In the county of Tipperary, five miles east of Clonmel.

[3] Ballydoine, midway between Carrick and Clonmel.

[4] Four miles north of Waterford, on the Thomastown road.

[5] Another of the name, Thomas Cromwell, a descendant of "the destroyer of monasteries," under Henry VIII, came to Ireland in the reign of James I., and, in exchange for an estate in Devonshire, got from Lord Mountjoy the abbey lands of Down, Innis, and Saul, granted to that nobleman for his services to the Crown. He was governor of Lecale. His son Thomas became Viscount Lecale and Earl of Ardglas.

die. Two of them were shot; the third, Colonel Claydon, was pardoned. The country people were so terrified that they fled with their goods and cattle across the Shannon into Clare, having first set fire to their houses and castles, that the enemy might not find shelter. This success kept in check those who might have fallen on Cromwell's rear. Broghill, on his way to join the main body of the army, received urgent orders from Cromwell to hasten to Clonmel. But meantime he had secret information from his brother, who was then at Castlelyons, that David Roche had got together a body of 700 men in Kerry with the design of relieving that town. With him was Boetius Egan,[1] who had been consecrated bishop of Ross the year before. He had been obliged to fly from his diocese and take refuge in the fastnesses of Kerry. Broghill took horse and posted in all haste to Clonmel. Having obtained from Cromwell some reinforcements, at the head of 1,600 foot and 200 horse, he set off for Cork, which he reached on the 8th of April.[2] There he learned that the rendezvous of the enemy was at Macroom. The next day he reached Kilcrea. On the morning of the 10th he came before the castle of Carrigadrohid,[3] about three miles from Macroom. He found it garrisoned by some of Roche's troops. Leaving his foot behind to keep the garrison in check, he hurried with his horse to Macroom. At his approach the garrison set fire to the castle and joined the main body, which lay encamped in the park. Broghill immediately charged them. Surprised by the suddenness of the attack, they gave way and fled, leaving many of their number on the field. According to Whitelocke, the loss amounted to 700 slain; many prisoners were taken, among them 20 captains, lieutenants, and other officers of the army; the standard of the church [4] of Munster was also captured, it

---

[1] He was a native of Duhallow, county Cork. He entered the Franciscan Order, and studied at Louvain with Colgan and Fleming. On the recommendation of Rinuccini he was appointed to the see of Ross. The Ormondists strove to exclude him from the assembly of the Confederates. But Rinuccini and the other bishops supported his claim and obtained his admission. See *The Franciscan Monasteries*, p. 228.

[2] Ware gives May 10th as the date of the battle of Macroom. From Broghill's letter it is clear that the battle took place April 10th.

[3] Carrigadrohid castle is built on a steep rock jutting out into the river Lee. This romantic site was the choice of the wife of M'Carthy, by whom it was built.

[4] The Christian symbols which the Catholic soldiers use on their military standards are — 1st. On the white banners flecked with drops of blood, the image of Christ crucified; motto : "Æquum est pro Christo mori" (It is right to die for Christ). 2d. On the green banners, an image of our Saviour bearing the cross; motto : "Patior ut vincam" (I suffer that I may conquer). 3d. On the cloth of gold banners, Christ rising from the tomb; motto, "Exsurgat Deus et dissipentur inimici ejus" (let God arise and his enemies be scattered). 4th. On the red banners, the name of Jesus; motto : "In nomine Jesu omne genu flectatur" ("In the name of Jesus every knee shall bend). 5th. On the sky-blue banners, the image of the B. V. Mary, bearing in her arms the child Jesus, and crushing with her foot the serpent's head ; motto : "Solvit vincula Deus" (God hath broken our chains). 6th. On the crimson banners, an arm argent, armoured, issuing from a cloud, holding a lance of the same color; motto : "Fortitudo mea desuper" (my strength is from above). 7th. On the banners of the cloth-of-silver, a knight armed cap-à-pie, setting fire to the *Institutes* of Calvin ; motto : "So may all heresies perish." 8th. On the purple banners, an image of our Saviour delivering the souls of the fathers from Limbo; motto : "Victor redit de barathro" (he returns victorious from hell); or, the image of Judith, holding a golden-hilted sword, and dealing Holofernes the fatal blow; motto : "Dominus vindicat populum suum" (the Lord avengeth his people). On the dexter side of each of the above banners there was an Irish cross within a red circle on a green field. Under the cross the motto : "Vivat Carol

being a church army. The Bishop of Ross, the High Sheriff of Kerry, and several other persons of distinction were taken prisoners.[1] The High Sheriff was condemned to be shot. Broghill ordered the Bishop to be led to the castle of Carrigadrohid, and offered him pardon if he would use his efforts to make the garrison surrender. When he was brought within hearing of those within, instead of urging them to yield, he exhorted them to maintain their post resolutely against the enemies of their religion and country. A true soldier would have honored such heroism, even in an enemy. But not so Broghill; by his order the brave Bishop was abandoned to the fury of the soldiers. His arms were first severed from his body; he was then dragged along the ground to a tree close by, and hanged from one of its branches with the reins of his own horse.[2] Roche's men had meanwhile fled into the woods; he tried to rally them about Killarney, and sent to Inchiquin for a reinforcement of horse from Clare, in order to make a second attempt to relieve Clonmel. But Broghill advancing to Drishane, near Millstreet, prevented their uniting. The castle was afterwards taken by a silly stratagem. The assailants yoked teams of oxen to large beams of timber. The garrison supposed these were cannon, and thought it better to make terms than to continue a resistance that would certainly end in their destruction. They surrendered on articles, by which they were allowed to march out without arms, the Governor being "allowed sixteen arms to defend his soldiers from the Tories."

A letter from the Lord Broghill, dated at Cork the 16th of April, 1650, was this day read, wherein was the enclosed relation:

"My Lord Lieutenant understanding by several ways that the enemy was gathering a considerable body of an army in the county of Kerry, which, by its advancing into these parts, was like to put them into arms, also, sent me back from the army before Clonmel to draw together 14 troops of horse and dragoons and 12 foot companies; and with these forces to take all advantages upon the enemy.

"On my arrival in this town, the 8th of this inst., I found they had prevented our expectation, and were come within twelve miles of it to Macroom, a town and castle of the Lord Muskerry, where their army daily increased, and was like to do so, unless immediately defeated. This pressing necessity made me draw out Captain Deane's and Captain Jenning's troops, newly landed, my own, Colonel Warden's, Major Powel's, and Captain Bishop's troop, all mine own regiment, to which I added about 800 foot of Sir Hardress Waller's, Colonel Phayre's, and Colonel Ryves' regiment, with his party. The 9th instant, I advanced seven miles towards the rebels, and the 10th, learning they still kept their ground, we resolved, by the help of the Lord, to engage them; but one of the carriages with ammunition breaking, I was

et Rex" (long live King Charles), and over it the letters C. R. and a regal crown. A portion of one of these banners is in the possession of the Dominicans at Tallaght, in the county of Dublin.

[1] The Brief Chronicle says between 500 and 600 were slain, whereof some of good quality; and almost 1,000 arms, and good store of rich plunder was taken.

[2] De Burgo gives a list of the Irish bishops residing in their sees in 1649, which Dr. French, bishop of Ferns, presented to Clement IX, in 1667. Dr. Egan is set down among those who were slain through hatred of the faith, "interfecti in odium fidei." Hib. Dom., p. 489. The Louvain Record of the Franciscan Order says he was a zealous champion and apostle of the faith, and that he crowned his life by the glorious death of a martyr. Ortho doxæ fidei strenuus defensor et asserto, pro qua glorioso martyrio vitæ finem et coronidem imposuit." He was buried in the cemetery of Aghina. See The Franciscan Monasteries, p. 228, and O'Reilly's Sufferers for the Faith in Ireland, p. 228.

resolved to leave a good part of the foot and some horse with it, and to advance with all the rest of our horse to engage them till our foot came up.

" Thus it pleased God we did, and after a third rallying of their foot, gave them a total rout, though in a place, the worst for horse ever I saw, and where one hundred musketeers might have kept off all the horse of Ireland. By our most moderate computation we killed between five and six hundred on the place, whereof some of good quality. Our prisoners, which are but few, because I gave orders to knock all on the head, were the bishop of Ross, their general, though he tells me but a joint commissioner with my Lord Roche's son, the High Sheriff of the county Kerry, with about twenty captains, lieutenants, and other officers, and gentlemen.

" Amongst other colors that were taken, there fell into our hands the standard of the church of Munster (as I am informed), for this was a clergy army.

" Our men got in the camp and in the pursuit good store of rich plunder, and I verily believe the enemy carried not away with him 300 arms. Had it been possible for our foot to come up, in human probability there had not escaped 100 of the rebels ; but I hope they are so well dispersed that it will not be in any man's power to call them together a good while, especially if some new commands hinder us from prosecuting the success. I found some papers of singular consequence in the bishop's pocket, which, I hope, shall not want improving.

" The night after we received this mercy, which, if any longer protracted, had I find, cast all these countries into arms, I sent Major Nelson with 200 foot and 70 horse to summon Carrigadrohid castle, a place the enemy had surprised in our quarters, and of great consequence for the strength and situation of it. I gave orders that if the garrison in it delivered it not up, we should hang the bishop before it. The former not being done, the latter was ; and 'tis observable that immediately after the bishop was hanged, I came up and persuaded ·the governor after the execution to surrender me the castle almost upon the same terms he had refused to save the bishop's life, the only difference being that I gave him 16 arms to defend his soldiers from the Tories.

" The bishop was wont to say there was no way to secure the English but by hanging them. That which was his cruelty became his justice.

" This is the exactest account I can give of the late mercy, wherein the Lord was as visible as the mercy itself." ·

CHAPTER XXVIII.

THE SIEGE OF CLONMEL.

Conduct of the Inhabitants — The Garrison — Summons to Surrender — O'Neill's Answer — Fennell's Treachery — Broghill's Arrival — The Assault — Langley of the Iron Hand — Want of Ammunition — Surrender — Account by an Eye-Witness — Letter of S. Dillingham — The Articles of Surrender — FF. O'Reilly and Magrath, O P.

On the 27th of April[1] Cromwell came before Clonmel. This town was one of the first places seized on by the Lords of the Pale when they resolved on making common cause with the Ulster Irish. The citizens strongly insisted on their allegiance to the King, averring that their purpose was to defend themselves against a parliament equally hostile to the sovereign and to themselves. They granted a safe-conduct to those Protestants who were unwilling to join their side ; and when the Commissioners subsequently made inquisition into the Irish massacres, they found that no murder had been perpetrated in its vicinity.

Hugh O'Neill,[2] the nephew of Owen Roe, had been sent in the month of December preceding with 1,500 foot under Colonel Turlogh Oge O'Neill MacHenry of the Fews, and about 100 horse under Major Fennell, to garrison the town.[3] It was well protected on the south side by the Suir. The other parts were surrounded by a wall. But even during the first days of the siege the garrison was in want of provisions. "O'Neill and the mayor had joined by a solemn protestation and oath in union for God, king, and country, and defence of the town to the uttermost of their power." They told Ormonde that "the garrison was of good courage and resolution, and that on Clonmel the safety of the kingdom chiefly depended. They besought him to prevent any bloody tragedy to be acted there as in other places, for want of timely relief ; that the army should march night and day to their succor, and, in the mean time, that the promised relief might

---

[1] "Mr. Lloyd, chaplain to the Lord Lieutenant of Ireland, came to London with letters from his lordship. He informs that on Saturday seven-night the Lord Lieutenant came before Clonmel, and the Tuesday following the great guns were brought before it." *Perfect Diurnal*, May 6th to 13th. The army must have marched to Clonmel immediately after the surrender of Kilkenny ; otherwise how could it be said that the siege lasted for two months? *The War of Ireland* says, "Cromwell sent two or three regiments of horse before him to block up Clonmel at distance.

[2] M'Geoghegan says he had served under his uncle in foreign countries, and was deemed an able captain and proved himself such at Clonmel and Limerick. *Hist. of Ireland*, p. 574.

[3] The muster-roll of the Ulster horse and foot at Clonmel in January, 1650, is given in the *Aph. Disc.*, vol. ii. p. 502, Appendix "Military List"; from which it appears that the foot numbered about 1,200, and the horse about 50, but a small handful in comparison with the multitude of horse and foot under Cromwell, who was supported by heavy artillery. *Ibid.*, p. 78.

be sent them, accommodated with provisions for themselves and the garrison." Ormonde directed Lord Castleconnell and the sheriff to raise the county of Limerick. They met, and agreed to provide 1,000 foot and 300 horse; but the Commissioners of Trust declared such a proceeding contrary to etiquette. Lord Castleconnell appointed another day for the meeting, and wrote to the Commissioners for instructions; they did not even vouchsafe an answer. The gentlemen of Limerick, not knowing how to proceed, separated, and Clonmel was left to its fate. Here, too, the plague was raging; "it was reported to be very hot in the Irish quarters."

On arriving before the town, Cromwell sent a summons to O'Neill to surrender, offering him favorable terms. "He answered that he was of another resolution than to give up the town on quarters and conditions, till he was reduced to a lower station, and so wished him to do his best." Cromwell then fell to his work and planted his cannon.[1] He sent Colonel Reynolds and Sir Theophilus Jones, with a detachment of 2,500 horse and dragoons, to prevent Ormonde's design of falling on the Parliamentary quarters. During all this time several sallies were made out, sometimes with good success, sometimes without. "O'Neill," says the author of the *Aporismal Discovery*, "always behaved himself both wise, courageous, and fortunate against Cromwell and his party, not only in a defensive but offensive way, with many valiant sallies and martial stratagems, to the enemy's mighty prejudice, who did lose some days 200, and other days 300, other 400, other 500 men; this loss was so often and so common, that my Lord Cromwell was weary of the place, that if his honor did not impede, his lordship would quit the place and raise the siege; resolving this and many other things in his breast, and among the rest that he was confident of no relief to come to this town, and therefore a strain in his honor to quit such a place, being for the conquest of a whole kingdom, having men enough at a call, after so much loss to raise the siege would discourage his own and alien men joining with him, thought by these and other such motives to tire this brave warrior, losing daily men and ammunition, without the least expectation to be either supplied, though all this while severally promised by Preston from Waterford : notwithstanding that my Lord Cromwell observed these conceptions to be sufficient ground to wear out the invincible courage of Major O'Neill, nevertheless was most desirous to know some other stratagem to abbreviate the business. Studying all devices, none came to any purpose, the dexterity and vigilance of the Major was such, crossing each of his attempts. At length, by the information of some of Inchiquin's party or other proper surmises, he lighted upon a fit instrument of treachery."

Among the defenders of the town there was a major of horse named Fennell, with whom Cromwell contrived to enter into a secret correspondence. Tempted by an offer of £500 and of full pardon for the crime of taking up arms against the parliament, he promised to open one of the gates on the north side of the town the next night,

---

[1] "This relation," says the author, "I had not only from some of the officers and soldiers of the besieged, but also from the besieged themselves."

at twelve o'clock, and to allow five hundred of the besieging force to enter by it. A party of Ulster men were on guard there; these he drew off, and in their place he put some men of his own regiment; as he knew they would not offer such a stubborn resistance as the brave men of the north. It so happened that, on the same night, Hugh O'Neill went to visit the post and see with his own eyes how they were kept. He was told that Fennell was more busy than usual. When he reached the gate, he found it guarded by Fennell's men only, though he had given the strictest orders, shortly before, that two-thirds, at least, of the number who watched the gates should be Ulster men. Suspecting that treachery was at work, he called for the officer in command, and having questioned him and found his answers unsatisfactory, he had him taken into custody. Fennell could not conceal his guilt; he promised to reveal the conspiracy in all its details on condition that he should receive a full pardon for his crime. As soon as O'Neill was made aware of the plot, he secured the various posts by means of strong reinforcements. In addition to the ordinary guard, he placed a body of five hundred men at the gate by which the enemy would be admitted. All this was done so noiselessly that no suspicion was excited of the discovery just made. "Advising with the rest what was best to do in that extremity, they resolved to open the gate, according to the former covenant. The enemy was watching his opportunity, and observing the signal, marched towards the gate; five hundred did enter, the rest *nolens volens* were kept out; all that entered were put to the sword."

This was not the first time Fennell had played false. At the battle of Portlester, in May, 1643, when serving under Lord Castlehaven, he showed great inactivity while some of O'Neill's kinsmen were cut down before his face, though he had a strong brigade of horse under his command at the time. O'Neill, who had been ill during the battle, on learning how his men had been sacrificed, called Castlehaven's officers cowards. And when their commander resented bitterly the charge, O'Neill replied: "I must confess, gentlemen, I did say so to a gentleman here, Lieutenant-Colonel Fennell, with the feather, a cowardly cock, for seeing my kinsmen overpowered by some of the enemy, and some of them hacked to pieces before his face, he never offered to relieve them. To the Supreme Council, who employed us both, he shall answer for this." Unhappily, in spite of his cowardice and treachery, he seems to have been allowed to continue in positions of trust. He surrendered Cappoquin without striking a blow. He abandoned the pass at Killaloe, and allowed Ireton to cross the Shannon there and invest Limerick from the Clare side. During the siege of that city he conspired with some of the officers, and seizing on St. John's gate, threatened to admit the enemy unless the garrison capitulated.[1]

---

[1] The author of the *Aph. Disc.* throws the whole blame of the surrender of Limerick on him. Castlehaven says he was hanged in Limerick soon after, by Ireton's order, "with more than ordinary justice." *Memoirs*, p. 128. Others say he was taken to Cork and executed there, though he pleaded in defence his services in betraying not only the garrison of Limerick, but also Lord Castlehaven before Youghal. Lenihan's *History of Limerick*, p. 181. The Fennell family seem to have been dependents of the Ormondes.

"My Lord Cromwell certified of the preposterous issue of his late bargain with Fennell, was mighty troubled in mind, and therefore did send for other armies and great ordnance" He despatched messengers to Lord Broghill, informing him that his army was in a pitiable condition, suffering much from disease, and sorely distressed at the many repulses it had met with, and that he must raise the siege and retire with disgrace, if not immediately relieved ; he conjured him, by all the ties of duty and friendship, to desist from all further designs in that quarter, and to come without delay to his assistance. The message reached Broghill after he had defeated Roche, and while he was putting the country under contribution and taking measures to prevent any muster of forces there. So urgent an order could not be disregarded ; he immediately despatched a messenger to tell Cromwell that, by the blessing of God, he had just defeated the enemy, and would not fail to join him on the evening of the third day following. Cromwell was delighted at the news of his successes and of his speedy arrival, as his army was greatly reduced in numbers and enfeebled by sickness. The author of the *Memoir of Lord Orrery* says that he was transported with joy at Broghill's arrival ; that he embraced him and congratulated him on his bravery, and that the whole army cried — a Broghill ! a Broghill !

But Broghill's force was composed mainly of Protestant gentlemen, whose fathers had come over fifty years before, to take possession of the confiscated estates of the Earl of Desmond. These were all favorable to the royal interests. Hence they could not be induced to return the greeting and to cry out : a Cromwell ! a Cromwell ! This circumstance, trifling as it may seem, made a deep impression on Cromwell's mind.

As soon as his additional force came up, Cromwell renewed the siege with increased vigor and industry. At length " with continual thunderings a long breach was made near one of the gates, but it proved not level enough when night fell." The spot where this breach was made is near the west wall, about twenty yards south of the tower called the magazine, where a portion of the wall is still standing. From Ludlow's description of the place, it would seem that houses abutted on that part of the wall, and that it was not far from the church.

"Within two hours after, the Major-General sent two hundred chosen men and officers, with a good guide, through by-ways from a place at the wall next the river that was neglected by the besiegers, and fell on the backs of those in a fort not fully finished behind them, and cut them off before any relief came. On which immediately the next gate was opened for them, and they got in safe, with the loss of half-a-dozen. The number killed in the fort was about sixty, being one of their companies."

O'Neill was not idle within the town. "He did set all men and maids to work, townsmen and soldiers (only those on duty attending the breach and the walls) to draw dunghills, mortar, stones, and timber, and make a long lane a man's height and about eighty yards length, on both sides up from the breach, with a foot bank at the back of it ; and he caused to be placed engines on both sides of the lane, and two guns at the end of it invisible, opposite to the breach, and so ordered all things against a storm." He entrusted the defence of this to a body of volunteers, armed with swords, scythes and pikes. In the adjoining houses he placed a picked body of musketeers, and ordered them to keep up a steady fire on all approaching the breach.

The storm began about eight o'clock in the morning.[1] The Puritans advanced to the assault singing one of their Scripture hymns. "They entered without any opposition ; and but few were to be seen in the town till they so entered that the lane was crammed full with horsemen, armed with helmets, backs, breasts, swords, musquetoons, and pistols, on which those in the front, seeing themselves in a pound, and could not make their way further, cried out, 'Halt! Halt!' On which those entering behind at the breach, thought by those words that all those of the garrison were running away, and cried out, 'Advance! Advance!' as fast as those before cried, 'Halt! Halt!' and so advanced till they thrust forward those before them, till that pound or lane was full and could hold no more. Then suddenly rushes a resolute party of pikes and musketeers to the breach, and scoured off and knocked back those entering. At which instance Hugh Duff's men within fell on those in the pound with shots, pikes, scythes, stones, and casting of great long pieces of timber with the engines amongst them ; and then two guns firing at them from the end of the pound, slaughtering them by the middle or knees with chained bullets, that in less than an hour's time about a thousand men were killed in that pound, being a top one another. About this time Cromwell was on horseback at the gate, with his guard, expecting the gates to be opened by those entered, until he saw those in the breach beaten back and heard the cannons going off within. Then he fell off, as much vexed as ever he was since he first put on a helmet against the King, for such a repulse he did not usually meet with."

So great was the slaughter that the infantry refused to advance a second time. Cromwell appealed to the cavalry. Amongst the first who responded to his call was Lieutenant Charles Langley. He was followed by Colonel Sankey, and one of the sons of John Cooke, whose services in pleading against Charles I. had been rewarded with the chief justiceship of Munster. The troopers imitated the conduct of their officers, and in this way a second storming party was formed, under the command of Colonel Culin. Langley put himself at the head of the dismounted cavalry. Sankey seems to have directed the assault. Cromwell's soldiers displayed an energy and bravery worthy of their former fame. Their onset was so fierce that the Irish were driven from the breach. The assailants made their way to the eastern breastwork, opposite the breach ; but there they were exposed to the galling cross-fire from the neighboring houses. Colonel Culin and several of his officers fell. Langley strove to mount the wall. His left hand was cut off by a blow of a scythe.[2] Determined at all

---

[1] Lingard says the storming took place May 9th.

[2] Hall's *Ireland*, vol. ii. p. 90 ; Taylor's *Civil Wars*, vol. ii. p. 38. He had afterwards an iron hand made, into which he used to thrust the stump to hold the bridle. Hence the

hazards to gain the place, Cromwell continued to pour masses of troops into the breach, the hinder ranks pushing on those before them. For four hours the slaughter continued. By that time the greater part of the assailants were killed or wounded. The survivors were forced to retreat, leaving 2,000 of their companions dead.[1] Of the officers Colonel Culham, Captains Jordan and Humphries, and some others were slain; Lieutenant-Colonels Grey and Lee, and many more wounded. With much entreaty he persuaded them to lodge that night under the walls, that the siege might be believed not absolutely to be quitted. Their seconds and comrades, seeing what happened, retired; neither the threats of the General nor the bloody sword of the inferior officers was sufficient to keep them from turning tail to the assault. Unable to conceal his admiration of the defenders' gallant conduct, he declared they were invincible. Knowing that any further attempt would so weaken his army that it might be annihilated by a sally of the garrison, he ordered a retreat to be sounded, and withdrew to his camp, leaving O'Neill in full possession of the breach. It is even said that he had ordered the army to march away and abandon the place, when he espied something in the grass, which he took up and found to be a silver bullet. This incident suggested to him the straits to which the garrison was reduced. He determined to return and call in the detachments of his army from the neighboring garrisons, though a reinforcement had just reached him from England of a regiment of foot and 260 horse, and by changing the siege into a blockade to try what famine could do.

Ormonde was much delighted at the news of O'Neill's successful defence. Fortune seemed, at length, inclined to favor the royal cause. But a message soon after reached him that the ammunition of the garrison was nearly spent. In truth O'Neill could resist no longer. For nearly two months he had held out. His provisions were now exhausted; his ammunition was now failing.[2] "The siege at distance and close being about five or six weeks, and by several sallies out and on the walls several of these within were lost, but many wounded and sick; on which the Major-General consulted with his officers; and seeing that their ammunition was gone, concluded to leave the town without Cromwell's leave. And so at nightfall he imparted the same to the mayor, one White, and advised him, after he was gone half a dozen miles off, as he might guess, to send privately out to Cromwell for leave to speak to him about conditions for the town, but not to make mention of himself on any account till he had done. After

---

sobriquet given him of "Langley of the Iron Hand." It is said that a silver hand was buried with him. The iron hand is still in the possession of George Langley, Esq., of Coalbrook, county Tipperary. He has also the *jeu d'esprit* given in Appendix x. The author is not known; from the style of the handwriting it must be at least a century old.

[1] According to M'Geoghegan's *Hist. of Ireland*, p. 574, and Borlase's *Rebellion*, p. 240, his losses amounted to 2,500. Carte gives 2,000 of his best men as the number slain at the storming. *Life of Ormonde*, vol. ii. p. 115. Ware gives the same number. *Antiq., Gest. Hib.*, p. 183. The "Relatio" says "he lost more than 2,000 men before Clonmel, a greater number than he had lost by all the towns which he had stormed and taken since he came to Ireland.

[2] Preston, who commanded at Waterford, had promised to send him ammunition, but had failed to do so.

which advice to the mayor, he marches away with his men, about two hours after nightfall, and passed over the river undiscovered by the guard of horse that lay at the other side of the bridge; and he made no great halt till he reached to a town called Ballynasack, twelve miles from Clonmel, where he refreshed his men.

Then the Mayor, according as he was advised, about twelve o'clock at night sent out to Cromwell, very privately for a conduct to wait upon his Excellency; which forthwith was sent to him, and an officer to conduct him from the wall to Cromwell's tent; who, after some compliments, was not long capitulating, when he got good conditions for the town: such, in a manner as they desired.

After which Cromwell asked him if Hugh O'Neill knew of his coming out; to which he answered he did not, for that he was gone two hours after nightfall with all his men, at which Cromwell stared and frowned at him, and said: "You knave, have you served me so, and did not tell me so before?" To which the Mayor replied: "If his Excellency had demanded the question, he would tell him." Then he asked him what that Duff O'Neill was; to which the mayor answered, that he was an over-the-sea soldier, born in Spain. On which Cromwell said, "G—d d—n you and your over-sea!" and desired the Mayor to give the paper back again. To which the other answered, that he hoped his Excellency would not break his conditions or take them from him, which was not the repute his Excellency had, but to perform whatsoever he had promised. On which Cromwell was somewhat calm, but said in a fury, "By G—— above, he would follow that Hugh Duff O'Neill wheresoever he went."

Then the Mayor delivered the keys of the gates to Cromwell, who immediately commanded guards on them, and next morning himself entered, where he saw his men killed in the pound; notwithstanding which and his fury that Hugh Duff went off as he did, he kept his conditions with the town." [1]

Some of his officers strove to persuade him that O'Neill's escape was a breach of the articles; and that being overreached he was not bound to grant such favorable terms to the town. Cromwell rebuked them and declared the townsmen deserved to be highly commended for their gallantry. Other writers, however, say that Cromwell discovering the trick in the morning, was vexed, and sent some troops to pursue the garrison in the rear. They had got out of reach, having in the night passed the hills and most difficult ways; but the Cromwellians overtaking many straggling, who, by reason of their wounds and other hindrances, stayed behind, among whom there were not a few women, put them all without mercy to the sword.[2] "They had like to bring my nobles to nine pence," he exclaimed.[3] "Cromwell,'

[1] *The War of Ireland*, p. 109. The author of the *Apher. Disc.*, however, says "the inhabitants were rifled, pillaged and plundered without respect of persons or mercy of degree."

[2] Bate's *Elenchus, &c.*, vol. ii. p. 38. "After the signing of the conditions we discovered the enemy to be gone, and very early the next morning pursued them and fell upon their rear of stragglers, and killed about two hundred of them." Letter of an eye-witness and hand-actor from Clonmel. May 10th, 1650, in *Cromwelliana*, p. 81.

[3] This proverb owes its existence in great part to its alliteration. Some coins of these denominations were struck during the Usurpation, but long before the base testoons of

says Whitelocke, "found at Clonmel the stoutest enemy his army had ever met with in Ireland; and never was seen so hot a storm of so long continuance and so gallantly defended, neither in England nor in Ireland." From thence O'Neill and his party marched to Waterford, hoping to obtain admittance there; but Preston, who had command of that city, refused them permission. Besides, the plague was within the town. He remained in the neighborhood for some time; but the plague having shown itself among his men, and his forces decreasing daily, he advised his foot to look to themselves as best they could. He and Major Fennell took the shortest route they could to Limerick.[1]

Some further details are given in a letter of S. Dillingham to Mr. Sancroft.

"In the taking of Clonmel you may think we paid dear. Having lain long before it, and in the meantime taken Kilkenny, much loss by sallies being sustained, an onslaught was resolved. It was done with much loss and the town carried. But the inner intrenchments, devised by the governor, a kinsman of O'Neill's, cost far dearer gaining. After all which, they were by main force cast out of all, and with much entreaty of Cromwell, persuaded to lodge that night under the walls, that their siege might be believed not absolutely to be quitted. In the night, little powder left to defend, all was drawn away, persons and things worth anything.

"Cromwell himself says he doubted of getting on the soldiers next day to a fresh assault. Towards morning a parley beat, and was gladly received; so that conditions were granted to their desires, not being above eighty defendants in all, of two thousand five hundred. They were mad when they came in, and sending to pursue, cut off two hundred women and children. Since a review of their force, which consisted of all the strength they could make, their troopers dismounted to foot, near all the officers of Ireton's regiment are wanting; and you may guess shrewdly at Hercules by his foot; and the business is at this pass, that he that undertook to have Ireland at his command so by last Michaelmas as a child should keep it under with a rod, can't now assure his soldiers two miles from home and promise them a safe return.

The Articles made between the Lord Lieutenant and the inhabitants of Clonmel touching the rendition thereof, May 18th, 1650.

It is granted and agreed by and betwixt the Lord Lieutenant, General Cromwell, on the one part, and Mr. Michael White and Mr. Nicholas Betts, Commissioners entrusted in the behalf of the town and garrison of Clonmel, on the other part, as follows: —

1st. The said town and garrison of Clonmel, with the arms, ammunition, and other furniture of war that are now therein, shall be surrendered and delivered up into the hands of his Excellency, the Lord Lieutenant, by eight of the clock this morning.

2d. That, in consideration thereof, the inhabitants of the said town shall be protected, their lives and estates, from all plunder and violence of the soldiery, and shall have the same right, liberty, and protection as other subjects, under the authority of the Parliament of England, have, or ought to have, and enjoy within the dominion of Ireland.

O. CROMWELL.

Henry VIII. and Edward VI., by proclamation of July 9th, 1551, were made to pass for nine pence, their original value being twelve pence.

[1] The soldiers who were in Clonmel fled to Waterford, and were there denied admittance. Only Hugh Duff O'Neill and two or three other commanders were admitted.

The townsmen strove to make conditions for Ormonde and Inchiquin, but they were refused. Passes, however, were offered them to go beyond the sea, which they would not take; but the Lord of Ardes and others of quality took them.[1] Sankey was made governor of the town and of the county of Tipperary.

Details are wanting of the events that followed the surrender. The history of the preceding sieges will help our readers to fill up the void without much difficulty, and to conjecture what took place. The learned author of *Hibernia Dominicana* gives the following account of the death of two holy priests of the order at this time.

" Father James O'Reilly was a learned theologian, an eloquent preacher, and a famous poet. He had been sent a short time before from Waterford to Clonmel, to train the youth of the town in polite learning and in the Christian doctrine. When the garrison abandoned the town, he, too, sought safety in flight. Not knowing whither the road led, he wandered about and fell in with a troop of Puritan cavalry. They asked him who he was. He replied fearlessly: 'I am a priest and a religieux, albeit an unworthy one, of the Order of St. Dominic. I have lost my way, and while trying to escape you, I have fallen into your hands. I am a member of the Roman Catholic Apostolic Church. So have I lived, and so will I die. May God's will be done." The soldiers fell on him and covered him with wounds. For a whole hour he lay weltering in his blood; he did not cease to invoke the holy names of Jesus and Mary, and to beseech his patron saints to aid him in his last struggle. At length, exhausted by his numerous wounds, the holy martyr gave up his soul."

" Father Myler Magrath was put to death after the capture of the town. He came to Clonmel to give the consolations of religion to those who should need them. He was seized, while engaged in his holy work, by the bedside of a sick man. The Governor's satellites hurried him off to their master's presence. His trial was a brief one. He was condemned to death, and hanged immediately after."

During the siege F. Nicholas Mulcahy, Parish Priest of. Ardfinan, in the county of Tipperary, was seized by a troop of Cromwell's cavalry, that had been sent out to reconnoitre. Immediately on his arrest he was put in irons, conveyed to the camp of the besiegers and offered his pardon, if he would only consent to use his influence with the inhabitants of Clonmel and induce them to give up the town. But he steadily refused, and was, in consequence, led out in view of the besieged city, and there beheaded whilst he knelt in prayer for his faithful people, and asked forgiveness for his enemies.

About this time Richard Magner, who had joined the party of the Catholic Confederates, went to Clonmel to make his submission to the Parliament. Cromwell had been duly informed of his previous conduct; yet he received him with much kindness, and promising him protection, gave him a letter to Colonel Phayre, the governor of Cork. The letter contained an order to execute the bearer. Magner, distrusting this show of friendship, opened the letter. As soon as he had read it, he closed it and sealed it carefully. He set off to Mallow without delay and handed it to the governor of the town, against whom he bore a grudge, informing him that Cromwell wished

---

[1] Whitelocke, p. 439. In April the Lord of Ardes, Lord Moore, and Colonel Trevor, came from the Irish quarters to Cromwell at Clonmel, soon after he had taken that town, to render themselves to him, as being persons of great note and eminence in the kingdom, and the front of quality of all the Protestant party that came from the Irish army unto them.

him to be the bearer of the letter to Phayre. Not suspecting any deceit, this officer presented the letter in due time. He was saved from death, however, Phayre having made the facts known to Cromwell before carrying out the order. Magner's lands were given to Bretridge, and from him they passed through the Hartstonges into the possession of the present Earl of Limerick. The ruins of the old family residence are still to be seen about six miles to the west of Mallow.

CROMWELL LEAVES IRELAND.

His last Public Act in Ireland — Pass to Lord Moore — Recall of Cromwell — Troubles in Scotland — Fairfax — Cromwell Sails from Youghal — Reception in London — His Speech in Parliament.

CHAPTER XXIX

THE last public act of Cromwell, of which an account has reached us, was the indicting of the following letter of protection to the Governor of Dublin. It was dated May 22d :[1]

The Lord Viscount Moore [2] having had passes from me to repair to Mellifont, in the county of Louth, and there to reside during the space of six months next ensuing, I desire you that the said Lord Moore, during his stay at Mellifont, and if he shall during the said time have occasion to repair to Dublin to the Commission there, may be fairly and civilly treated, and that no incivility or abuse be offered unto him by any of the soldiery, either by restraining of his liberty or otherwise, it being a thing which I altogether disapprove and dislike that the soldiers should intermeddle in civil affairs farther than they are lawfully called upon. Your care herein will oblige the said Lord, in relation to his present condition, and will be accepted by

Your loving friend,

O. CROMWELL.

The danger on the side of Scotland was growing greater each day, and the demands of the Parliament for Cromwell's return became more urgent. His successes in Ireland pointed him out as the one man who could meet the enemy in the field and crush every attempt at rebellion. On the 8th of January preceding, the Parliament had ordered "that the Lord Lieutenant of Ireland be desired to come over and give his attendance, and that the Council of State prepare a letter, to be signed by the Speaker and sent to the Lord Lieutenant for that purpose, as also to thank him for his great services and faithfulness to the Commonwealth." "The ground of this resolution was," adds Whitelocke, "that the news of the King's coming to Scotland became more probable than formerly, and the Scots' proceedings in the rising of new forces gave an alarm to the parliament ; and some

---

[1] This letter was formerly in the possession of Dean Swift.

[2] This was Henry, third Viscount Drogheda. His father, Charles, the second Viscount, took a leading part in raising forces to oppose the Irish in 1641, and had the command of the horse when Drogheda was besieged by Sir Phelim O'Neill. He was killed by a cannon-shot at Portlester, in 1643 ; his death gave rise to the following jeu d'esprit :

Contra Romanos mores, res mira, dynasta
Morus ab Eugenio canonisatus erat.

His son Henry took the King's side in the Civil War ; but in 1647, on the surrender of the government by Ormonde, he left the Royalists and got the command of a regiment from the parliament. For two years he continued in the service of this party; but immediately before Cromwell's arrival he "ran off to the enemy." *Perfect Diurnal*, July 6th, 1649. In April he surrendered to Cromwell. He was restored to his estate in 1653. After the Restoration he was was made an earl.

of their members who had discoursed with the late General (Fairfax) on these matters, and argued how requisite it would be to send an army into Scotland, found the General wholly averse to any such thing; and, by the means of his lady, a strict Presbyterian, to be more a friend to the Scots than they; that, therefore, they thought this a fitting time to send for the Lord Lieutenant of Ireland, and the rather, his army being now drawn into winter quarters."

In a letter to the Speaker of the parliament from Carrick, dated April 2d, he says:— "I have received divers private intimations of your pleasure to have me come in person to wait on you in England; as also copies of the votes of parliament to that purpose. But, considering the way they came to me was but by private intimations, and the votes did refer to a letter to be signed by the Speaker, I thought it would have been too much forwardness in me to have left my charge here until the said letter came, it being not fit for me to prophesy whether the letter would be an absolute command, or having limitations with a liberty left by the parliament to me to consider in what way to yield my obedience. Your letter came to my hands upon the 22d of March, the same day that I came before the city of Kilkenny, and when I was near the same. And I understood by Dr. Cartwright, who delivered it to me, that reason of cross-winds and the want of shipping in the West of England, where he was, hindered him from coming with it sooner, it bearing date the 8th of January, and not coming to my hands till the 22d of March. The letter supposed your army in winter quarters and the time of year not suitable for present action; making this as the reason for your command. And your forces have been in action ever since the 29th of January; and your letter, which was to be the rule of my obedience, coming to my hands after our having been so long in action, with respects had to the reasons you were pleased to use therein, I knew not what to do. And having received a letter signed by yourself of the 26th of February, which mentions not a word of the continuance of your pleasure concerning my coming over, I did humbly conceive it much consisting with my duty, humbly to beg a positive signification what your will is, professing (as before the Lord) that I am most ready to obey your commands herein with all alacrity, rejoicing only to be about that work which I am called to by those whom God hath set over me, which I acknowledge you to be, and fearing only in obeying you to disobey you. I most humbly and earnestly beseech you to judge for me, whether your letter doth not naturally allow me the liberty of begging a more clear expression of your command and pleasure, which, when vouchsafed unto me, will find most ready acceptance and cheerful observance."

On the 21st of April, Hugh Peters wrote from Pembroke: "Yesternight the President frigate set sail from Milford towards Ireland, to attend his Excellency's pleasure, being sent to fetch the Lord Lieutenant Cromwell over unto England, if he thinks fit to come. The letters from the Council of State were carried over in her, directed to his Excellency, with Mr. Jenkin Loyd, his chaplain. God send them a safe arrival. Captain Evans went over from hence last

night, and about thirty horse with him for Ireland. Waterford, Limerick and Galway were still in the hands of the Irish rebels ; and he
would fain try whether the same good luck that had accompanied
him hitherto might not attend him for a few months more. But the
affairs of Scotland had become more pressing, and the new letters
from the parliament left no room now to doubt what was its supreme
will. He surrendered the command of the army to Ireton, his major-
general, who already held the appointment of President of Munster,
and on the 29th of May he set sail from Youghal to England.[1] He
had been little more than nine months in Ireland, having landed in
Dublin on the 15th of August.

He landed at Bristol after a boisterous voyage. "There he was
received with all honors and acclamations, the great guns firing
thrice." On the 31st he reached London. As soon as it was known
that he was approaching, the Lord General Fairfax, many members
of parliament and officers of the army, and a multitude of people
went out to Hounslow Heath to meet him, and to see him who had
made himself so famous and acquired such high renown by his great
and valorous actions. As he approached the city, the whole of the
inhabitants turned out to give him a hearty welcome. At Hyde Park
the Lord Mayor and the train-bands were waiting for him. He was
saluted with great guns and a volley of shot from Colonel Barkstead's
regiment, which was drawn up for the purpose. As he was passing
by Tyburn, some sycophant near having said, "What a crowd has
come out to see your Lordship's triumph !" "Yes," he replied, with
a smile, "but if it were to see me hanged, how many more would
there come ?"[2] From thence to St. James's Palace, where he was
to lodge. Being conducted to the Cockpit, which had been prepared
for his reception, the Lord Mayor and aldermen of London visited
him and complimented him ; most of the persons of quality, the
members of parliament, and officers of the army about the town paid
their visits to him, and congratulated him on his safe arrival, after so
many dangers by sea and by land, wherein God had preserved him,
and the wonderful successes He had given him.[3]

In the record of the proceedings of parliament, under the date
of June 4th, we read: "This day Cromwell, the parliamentary victorious General and Lord Lieutenant of Ireland, took his seat in the
House, when the Speaker did, by order of the House, give thanks in
an eloquent oration for his great and faithful services unto the parliament and commonwealth, setting forth the great providence of God in

---

[1] The author of the *Aphor. Disc.* says that after putting a garrison to hold Clonmel,
he marched with all expedition to Waterford, to recover there what by Hugh O'Neill he
had lost at Clonmel. On arriving there he encamped before the town ; but he had scarce
encamped there when he received commands from England to appear there on sight. Vol.
ii. p. 79.

[2] On Cromwell's expedition to Scotland, when followed by the acclamations of the
assembled populace, Lambert turned to him and expressed his gratification that the nation
was so evidently on their side. "Don't trust them," said Cromwell ; "these very persons
would shout as much if we were going to be hanged."

[3] Cromwell returned to London in the month of May, and was received by the parliament and the people, as a soldier who had gained more laurels, and done more wonders, in
nine months than any age of history could parallel.

those great and strange works which God had wrought by him as the instrument." After which the Lord Lieutenant gave them a full and particular account of the present state and condition of the kingdom. And on the 11th of June: "All the members of the House having been required to give their attendance this day by nine in the morning, General Cromwell, standing up in his place in the House, made a narrative of the state of the garrisons and forces of the enemy in Ireland and their interest there, and likewise of the parliament's forces in garrison and in the field and their condition; in what employment they were, and under what commands; at the end of which it was resolved — That it be referred to the Council of State to take care of sending such speedy supplies of money for Ireland as shall be necessary for the carrying out of that work, and to see what money there is in the present view that can be made effectual for that service, and how the obstructions against bringing it may be removed; also to consider by what means the reduction and settlement of Ireland may be perfected to the best advantage and the futurage of the charge of this commonwealth."

CROMWELL IN IRELAND.

Meeting of the Officers of the Ulster Army—Heber McMahon General—March north-
wards—Plan of the Campaign—Coote and Venables—The Battle—Defeat of the
Irish—Bravery of Henry O'Neill—Flight of McMahon—His Death—Death of
Henry and Colonel Phelim O'Neill.

OWEN ROE O'NEILL died November 6th, 1649. On the 8th of
March following, the officers of the Ulster army and the nobility and
gentry of Ulster, " mourning the death of their General, feeling his
now want, and not to be as a flock without a pastor, their dispersed
soldiers and commanders flocking home by degrees," met at Belturbet
to elect a commander in his place. In the articles of the treaty made
between him and Ormonde it was provided that, in case of O'Neill's
death or removal by advancement or otherwise before any settlement
in parliament, the nobility and gentry of the Province of Ulster
should have power to name to the Lord Lieutenant, and the command
was to be given according to the person so named.

The candidates for the post were the Marquis of Antrim, Sir
Phelim O'Neill, Lieutenant-General Ferrall, Owen Roe's son Henry,
and Heber Mac Mahon, bishop of Clogher. Ormonde, from whom
the person elected should receive his commission, protested against
Antrim, as being known to favor Cromwell. The nobility and
gentry, as well as Ormonde, favored Daniel O'Neill ; but he, considering himself disqualified from the fact of his being a Protestant, had
gone a short time before to Kilkenny, and expressed a wish that the
choice might fall on Major-General Hugh O'Neill, then absent in
Clonmel, as " being a man who knew the ways Owen Roe O'Neill
took to manage the people, and one not unacceptable to the Scots, and
who would do nothing contrary to Ormonde's command." The Bishop
of Kilmore presided. He had the articles of the treaty between
Ormonde and Owen Roe read over. " Many competitors did appear,"
says the author of the *Aphorismal Discovery;* " every one thought
himself worthy of that place. The Marquis of Antrim was an earnest
suitor in proper behalf. The O'Neills thought their claims for the
chiefry and command of Ulster to be hereditary. Lieutenant-General
Ferrall, by the law of arms, was confident of his title, as next in command to the defunct ; Hugh O'Neill, as of that sept and Major-General,
and the better soldier of both name and province ; Sir Phelim
O'Neill, by the numerosity of his followers, and with pregnant hopes
of being seconded by the Leinster Ormondian faction ; Con Mac
Cormac O'Neill, heretofore lieutenant-general for the same province,

and of the oldest descent of that family; and Philip MacHugh
O'Reilly, a good Commonwealth's man, of great respect, and by the
plurality of his name and followers was thought to carry a main stroke
on the election. The assembly, wisely considering the danger that
vas likely to ensue by the choosing any of the former (nor the late
general's son, Henry Roe O'Neill), though each worthy of honor and of
better hopes to be so promoted than any other not here specified, unanimously chose Heber Mac Mahon for the post." [1] Though not deficient
in personal courage or in zeal for the cause of his country, Mac
Mahon was not equal to the heavy burden laid on him. The training
of a churchman is hardly a fit school in which to learn the science of
war; yet, on the whole, perhaps no better choice could be made.
Jealousy and intrigue were at work, and it was hoped that these
would cease, and that all would follow the leadership of one who was
known to have had the confidence of O'Neill[2] and to be heart and
soul devoted to the good cause. The appointment was sanctioned by
Ormonde, who issued a commission " nominating and appointing his
trusty and well-beloved Bishop Heber MacMahon General of all his
Majesty's forces of horse and foot of the Province of Ulster."   " It
must be acknowledged," says Borlase, " that MacMahon performed
the agreement made with the Marquis and observed it very justly."
Ferrall was at the same time confirmed as lieutenant-general. Soon
after Mac Mahon put himself at the head of his troops, numbering
about 5,000 foot and 600 horse. Recruits flocked to his standard;
and in a short time, owing to Ferrall's exertions, the whole army was
disciplined and ready to take the field. The plan of the campaign
was communicated to Ormonde and Clanrickarde. They promised to
raise forces in Connaught, and to send a plentiful supply of artillery
and provisions; " they would give him all possible assistance, and if
he brought his army towards Tyrconnell they would send a considerable army, both of horse and foot, with ordnance and other engines
fit for the winning of a town or fort."   Relying on these promises,
the army set out from Monaghan and marched to Charlemont; there
the Commander issued a manifesto, inviting the Scots, who were serving under Coote and Venables, to make common cause with the Irish
and enroll themselves under the royal standard. His appeal brought
over only a few; the majority preferred to adhere to their old commanders, though these refused to acknowledge the newly proclaimed
King. Mac Mahon knew that the Irish army was more than a match
for either Coote's or Venable's forces; he determined, therefore, to
prevent their union and to crush them in detail. Some time was
spent in skirmishing and in the taking of the strongholds garrisoned
by Coote. Marching northwards along the Bann, he crossed the
Foyle near Lifford, in order to keep open the communication through

---

[1] As for the bishop, though a good politician, he was no more a soldier fit to be a general than one of Rome's cardinals. He had been Vicar Apostolic of Clogher for four
years; in 1642 he was appointed to the united sees of Down and Connor; a year after he
was transferred to Clogher, to enable him to take part in the important business concerning
the kingdom of Ireland with the other prelates and lords.

[2] The Bishop of Clogher, Owen Roe's great counsellor. Borlase says he was Owen
Roe's chief confident.

Ballyshannon with Connaught for the supplies promised by Ormonde. This fatal movement allowed Coote and Venables to unite their forces near Letterkenny. Mac Mahon, contrary to the advice of his officers, resolved to risk a battle. In vain their spokesman, young Henry O'Neill, who seemed to have inherited not only the bravery but the prudence of his father Owen Roe, pointed out to him that the Irish troops, owing to the nature of the ground, were unfavorably placed, and that they were weakened by the absence of a large body that had been detached to seize Castle Doe; a few days delay would ensure their return, and oblige the enemy to retire from their position, as provisions were already beginning to fail them. Mac Mahon replied by taunts, telling them that such arguments were not suited to brave soldiers, but rather to dastards who feared the sight of their own or of others' blood. The ill-merited rebuke had the fate which he desired. "His language did so distemper the warlike deportment of these heroes that, beyond the limits of reason transported, oblivious of all military advantage and indifference of either ground or elements, putting themselves in a distracted posture of battle, where horse could scare relieve the foot, both wind and weather not their friends, they bade their men prepare for battle."

Early the next day, June 21st, the fight began. The fierce onset of the Irish at first produced a panic among the enemy. Unhappily, owing to the rugged nature of the ground, they could not advance in compact masses, nor be supported by the cavalry. The enemy were, therefore, able to recover from their terror; a charge of their cavalry drove back the Irish and restored confidence to their whole army. The battle continued until mid-day, when a combined attack, made by the whole of Coote's forces on flank and rear, obliged Mac Mahon to retreat. The infantry, led by Ferrall, fought with great bravery. Henry O'Neill won the admiration even of the enemy, "dashing among them like a merlin hawk among a multitude of sparrows." Before sunset the Irish were utterly defeated. "This was," says Borlase, "a most happy victory for the parliament; in that three thousand of the rebels were there slain, all mere Irish; out of an opinion they could not prosper as long as they had any English joined with them, and for that end had thoroughly purged their army, which was styled by them the confident, victorious army of the North." The *Brief Chronicle* gives the following list of those killed, and of the prisoners : —

"In this fight was taken the Bishop of Clogher, General. Killed — The Lord of Enniskillen, Colonel ; the Bishop of Down, Shane O'Cane, Major-General Henry Roe O'Neill, General O'Neill's son, Colonel of the Horse ; Nice MacCollckelagh, Colonel ; Hugh Mac Guier, Colonel ; Phelim MacTool O'Neill, Colonel ; Hugh MacHahan, Colonel ; Lieutenant-Colonels Torlogh O'Boyle, Shane MacDonnell, James O'Donnelly, Phelemy O'Neal, Adjutant-General ; Torlogh O'Neill, Adjutant-General. Taken prisoners — Shane O'Haggan, Henry O'Neill, Quarter-Master-General Saxton. Majors killed — Phelemy O'Neal, Don O'Neal, Emer MacQuillan, John MacGuier, Captain of Horse ; Art Oge O'Neal, Colonel ; MacMaghan, Mull

Holland O'Quine, Ferrall, Captain of Foot; Stewart, Fergus Farrell, Bryan O'Neal, Owen O'Quine, George Russell, James MacCartain, Patrick O'Connally, Donnel MacGuier Gollagher, Bryan MacGil, Tiege O'MacHugh, MacOge O'Quine, Cormache O'Mullen, Hen. Kannalds, Conagher. Three priests and friars are killed; 3,000 slain in all."

Only a few were made prisoners, those taken being for the most part put to the sword, even after quarter was promised them. Major-General O'Cahan, Colonels Maguire and MacMahon, Art Oge O'Neill, and Colonel Phelim O'Neill perished on the field. The Bishop fled with a party of horse, "going night and day for twenty-four hours, without meat, drink or rest." Information of his movements having been given to Major King, governor of Enniskillen, a party of horse was despatched from that garrison to capture him and his companions. The party was too strong for the Bishop, who, however, defended himself with notable courage; but, after he-had received many wounds, he was forced to become prisoner, upon promise first that he should have fair quarter; contrary to which Sir Charles Coote, as soon as he knew he was prisoner, caused him to be hanged, with all the circumstances of contumely, reproach and cruelty he could devise. And thus, in less than a year after he had brought Owen O'Neill to relieve Sir Charles Coote in Derry, who must otherwise in a few days have delivered it up to the King, his army was defeated by the same Sir Charles Coote, and himself, after quarter and life promised, executed two months after, by the positive order and command of him whom he had thus preserved.[1] His head was set over the gate of Derry. Ferrall and a few more who survived sought safety in flight, and hid themselves in the mountains and woods, to avoid the certain death that awaited them if they were taken.

Henry Tully O'Neill describes the death of young Henry:—"Quarter had been given to several of the Irish officers, and in particular to Colonel Phelim O'Neill,[2] for which he agreed to give one hundred beeves to Sir Charles Coote. Whilst the articles were drawing, the day after the action, a sergeant came into Coote's tent with the news that he had brought in Colonel Henry Roe O'Neill, General Owen O'Neill's son, prisoner. Without more ado, Coote reprimanded the sergeant for not bringing his head, and commanded him to go and despatch him immediately. Colonel Phelim pleaded on behalf of his relative, that he was a Spaniard born, and that he had come to Ireland as a soldier of fortune. The order, however, was executed;[3] he

---

[1] Nor is it amiss to observe the variety and vicissitude of Irish affairs; for this very bishop and those officers, whose heads were now placed on the walls of Derry, were, within less than a year before, confederate with Sir Charles Coote, and raised the siege of that city, and were jovially merry at his table, in the quality of friends. The author of the Memoir of Owen Roe says Mac Mahon was executed at Enniskillen.

[2] He was the grandfather of Colonel Henry, the author of the "Relation." He was lieutenant-colonel of General O'Neill's regiment, in the Ulster army, in 1645, and commanded a party of horse and musketeers at the battle of Benburb. In 1649 he was appointed colonel, and in the ensuing year he defeated a party of the troops of Coote and Venables in Ulster. The author of the Aphor. Disc. speaks of him as a courageous humane and successful commander.

[3] Morison says a promise had been made to Colonel Henry that his life would be

was beheaded by the unchristian and tigrish doom of the thrice-cruel butcher and human blood-sucker, Sir Charles Coote." Colonel Phelim was told that if he began to prate he should be served the same way. He replied that he would rather be served so than owe his life to such a monstrous villain as he was. Whereupon he was carried out and knocked on the head with tent-poles by Coote's men. This being observed by one of Coote's officers, he asked what they meant by using the gentleman so. They replied it was by the General's orders. The officer, in compassion and to put him out of pain, drew his sword and ran him through the heart. Sir Phelim, who acted as the Bishop's lieutenant-general, escaped from the battle-field. He was arrested in Roughan Island by one of the Caulfields, tried at the High Court of Justice before Judge Lowther, and hanged, drawn and quartered.

And so perished at the pass of Scariffhollis the Ulster army which had so often followed Owen Roe to victory.

---

spared. *Threnodia*, p. 66. It was reputed that for a certain sum of money he would be ransomed. His wife made herself ready, having the said sum, to go and ransom her beloved husband. But alas! he was, notwithstanding his quarter, beheaded, and the rest of his companions executed, in disrespect of all human and divine law. She was the daughter of Sir Luke Fitzgerald.

Appendix.

I.

THE GREAT DUKE OF ORMONDE.

THEOBALD FITZWALTER, the founder of the Butler family, came to Ireland with Henry II. in 1171. Large estates were granted to him as a reward for his services. His chief seat was Arklow castle. In 1177 he was made Chief Butler of Ireland, Pincerna Regis, with a perquisite of two tuns of wine out of every cargo of eighteen tuns or upwards, a right repurchased by the Crown from the Ormonde family in 1810 for £216,000. Hence the family name of Butler, and the addition of the three cups or to the original arms, topaz, a chief indented, sapphire. James, the 1st Earl, who married Eleanor de Bohun, grand-daughter of Edward I., in consideration of his valuable services, as also of the consanguinity existing between him and his Majesty, obtained a grant of the regalities, liberties, and other royal privileges of the county of Tipperary, and the rights of a palatine in that county for life; these privileges were afterwards granted to his heirs male and continued to be enjoyed by them up to the year 1716. He built the castle of Nenagh; but the English power having fallen very low in Ireland during the Wars of the Roses, the O'Carrolls, O'Kennedys, and other tribes of North Munster, rose in arms and drove out the English settlers. James, the 3d Earl, built the castle of Gowran, and resided there for some time. In 1391 he purchased the estates of le Despenser in the county of Kilkenny, derived from the heirs of William Earl Marshal; the castle became henceforth the chief seat of the family. The Butlers at all times adhered faithfully to the English interest in Ireland, and, as a consequence, were well rewarded by the ruling powers. James, the 4th Earl, was one of those "who engaged to resist the usurpations of the bishop of Rome," and in return he received vast grants of ecclesiastical property through-out Ireland. At the end of his life, indeed, he lamented the part he had taken against his religion and country. But the spoils of the church were not restored to their rightful owners. His son Thomas, surnamed the Black, was closely connected with the royal family by blood, Margaret, the daughter of the 7th Earl, being the grandmother of Anne Boleyn. He was brought up with "the royal imp," Edward VI., and such was the regard shown him by Elizabeth, that he incurred the lasting jealousy of the Earl of Leicester. He was succeeded by his nephew, Sir Walter Butler of Kilcash. This branch of the family had continued to adhere to the Catholic faith; Sir Walter was known by the sobriquet of "Walter of the Beads." His eldest son, Viscount Thurles, was drowned while on his way to England. The care of his son, then only twelve years of age, later the Great Duke of Ormonde, devolved on his mother, the daughter of Sir John Poyntz, of Acton, in the county of Gloucester. By her he was placed at a school kept by a Catholic at Barnet, near London. But James I. soon interposed. He was bent on effecting the reform of religion in Ireland through the leading families. By the manœuvres of Sir William Parsons, the Crown obtained the wardship of the young nobleman, though he inherited no lands the tenure of which involved any such consequence. His grandfather was cast into prison, and the boy was handed over to the care of Abbot, archbishop of Canterbury, and brought up a Protestant. During life he adhered to that creed. In a letter to Sir Robert Southwell he says he is the only Protestant of his family. There is a curious letter of Father Peter Walsh addressed to him a few months previous to the death of both, in which the fidelity of the Ormonde family to the Catholic Church is strongly urged as a motive to induce him to return to the faith of his fathers. He anticipates the grace of conversion for him through the daily prayers poured out for him by an infinite number of his Roman Catholic friends and relations, amongst which he has had and still has advocates which, like shining stars of the greatest magnitude, are admired in the brightness and lustre of the pious and virtuous, Colonel Butler of Kilcash, his brother, and Lady Thurles, his mother. Ormonde replies that he is "surprised a friend so zealous as Walsh should have delayed to the very close of life an exhortation of such vital import." By his marriage with his cousin, Elizabeth, daughter and heiress of Sir Richard Preston, he got back the estates of which his grandfather had been deprived by James I., to enrich that royal favorite.

At the breaking out of the rebellion of 1641 he was appointed Lieutenant-General of the English army, and two years later Lord Lieutenant. Though at the head of the Royalist army, he was little inferior to Inchiquin in cruelty to his countrymen. His conduct is described at length in the works of his contemporary, Dr. French, bishop of Ferns, especially in his *Unkinde Deserter of Loyal Men.* The author of *The Aphorismal Discovery* says of him: "What hath been the cause of the now destruction of Ireland other than the arbitrary covetousness, treason, and faction of Ormonde and his accomplices, a man of small deserving in martial affairs, weak in his directions, cold in his resolutions, and unfortunate in his actions, in whom nothing was great or noble but his blood?" Dr. O'Conor, who wrote under the pseudonym of Columbanus, is almost the only Irish writer who has attempted a defence of his conduct, in his strictures on Plowden's *Historical Review of the State of Ireland.* To these strictures Plowden replied at some length in his *Historical Letter to Columbanus.*

The surrender of Dublin and the other strong places to the parliament in June, 1647, is perhaps the greatest stain on his character as a public man. Carte, his biographer, defends his conduct in this matter, and says he had received private instructions from Charles I. to make this surrender. But Ormonde's own letters state that he did it "on the presumption that it was more for his Majesty's honor and service, and consequently more agreeable to his pleasure, which he had neither the means nor the time to consult." Even his apologists admit that the possession of these strongholds paved the way not only for the complete conquest of Ireland, but even for the murder of the

King. It must be borne in mind that he got, in return for his treachery, the sum of £5,000 in hand, a promise of £2,000 a year, and a complete release from all debts which encumbered his estates before the breaking out of the rebellion. After the Restoration he received vast grants of lands, not only getting back all his own estates which were leased or mortgaged, but other men's estates too, most of these belonging to persons of his own name. A list of these grants with the names of the original owners will be found in Plowden's *Historical Letter* and in Carte's *Life of Ormonde.* The annual rents of his estates before the rebellion amounted to £40,000, but they were reduced by annuities and leases to £7,000. In 1674 they amounted to £80,000. The Earl of Anglesey says Ormonde and his family were the greatest gainers of the kingdom, and had added to their inheritance vast scopes of land, a revenue three times greater than what his paternal estate was, and most of his increase was out of the estates of those who adhered to the peace of 1646 and 1648, or served under his Majesty's ensigns abroad. Petty sets down at 130,000 acres the lands he got by the Act of Settlement and the Court of Claims.

His hatred to the Catholic Church was almost that of a renegade. As early as 1646 Rinuccini writing to Rome, said of him that all the broils arose from one source alone, the faction of the Marquis of Ormonde. We have already spoken of the charge made against him of showing too much kindness to the Catholics. His answer was that "his object was to work division among the Romish clergy, and he believed he had compassed it, to the great security of government and Protestants and against the opposition of the Pope and his creatures, and Nuncio, if he had not been removed from the government. Some ascribed his opposition to the clergy and Irish party who countenanced them, to the fact that he feared the church-lands which his ancestors had got, should, in part at least, be restored. His brother-in-law, Lord Muskerry, declared on his death-bed that the heaviest fear that possessed his soul, then going into eternity, was for having confided so much to his Grace, who had deceived them all, and ruined his poor country and countrymen.

A list of the honors which he received from Charles II. after the Restoration, will be found in Archdall's *Peerage.* He died in 1688, at the age of 77.

II.

MORROUGH O'BRIEN, LORD INCHIQUIN.

THE O'Briens were among the first of the Irish chiefs who submitted to Henry II. Donald surrended Limerick to the English, but he soon threw off the yoke, and burnt the city, "lest it should become a nest for foreigners." His descendant, Morrough, offered to support Henry VIII. in his contest with the Pope, provided his estates were confirmed to him. The King accepted his offer. He should utterly forsake and refuse the name of O'Brien, and use such name only as it should please the King to give him, adopt the English habit and language, and bring up his children in the same. In return for his submission he was created Earl of Thomond for life, and Baron of Inchiquin; the latter title to pass to his heirs male. His nephew Donogh was created Baron of Ibrickan with remainder to his male issue, and Earl of Thomond after his uncle's death. The latter title was conferred on him and his heirs male by Edward VI.

Morrough was born about 1618. His career was one of the strangest adventure. In early life he was a soldier of fortune: he went to Italy, and served in the Spanish army there. Soon after we find him one of the most zealous supporters of Strafford in his attempt to rob the Anglo-Irish and Irish alike, and to establish in the south and west of Ireland such a "plantation" as Chichester, in the time of James I., had established in the north.

Some years later he was appointed Vice-President of Munster, under Sir William St. Leger, whose daughter he had married. On the breaking out of the rebellion he took the side of the King, and afforded valuable aid in opposing the rebels in the counties of Cork and Waterford. At the death of St. Leger he was appointed to the chief military command in the province of Munster, and soon after the whole civil administration of that province was entrusted to him. Offended at the cold reception he met with from the King at Oxford, and at the refusal to grant him the presidentship of Munster, he joined the party of the Parliament, and for some years continued to devote his great military skill and bravery to the service of the Puritans. Again he changed sides, but his zeal was not so active on behalf of the King as on that of his former friends. In fact both he and Ormonde were distrusted by the people, and to that well-founded distrust were due in a great measure the rapidity and completeness of Cromwell's successes in his Irish campaign. One thing only Inchiquin was constant in, his hatred of his countrymen — his fierce and unrelenting enmity towards the Catholic Church. His cruelties have earned for him the sobriquet of Morrough of the Burnings, and are not yet forgotten, for even to this day throughout the whole of Munster there is a saying applied to one who looks frightened: "He has seen Morrough or some of his companions." Ludlow, the Cromwellian general, in his *Memoirs*, says that he did not spare even his own kindred; but if he found them faulty, hanged them up without distinction. The massacre of Cashel is one of the saddest pages of Irish history; and that was only one of his many cruel deeds — Cork and Kilmallock could tell tales of woe almost as pitiful.

After the surrender of the strong places in Ireland he went to France, where he was advanced to the rank of lieutenant-general. On the conquest of Catalonia he was made viceroy there. He continued for many years in the French service in Spain and the Netherlands. On one occasion he and his family were taken by Algerine corsairs. They were set free on payment of a large sum.

After the Restoration he came to England. By the Act of Settlement he was restored to his estate, and a sum of £8,000 was granted him as a compensation for the losses he had sustained. Towards the end of his life he seems to have returned to the Catholic faith. He did not revisit Ireland; Charles II. feared that his excessive zeal on behalf of Catholics would cause commotions among the new settlers there. He lived in London, and there, it would seem, devoted himself to the practice of religion. In the Memoirs written by F. Gamache, one of the French Capuchin priests who came to England with Henrietta Maria, queen of Charles I., mention is made of the conversion of a Monsieur Inchiquin, and of the penitential practices which he followed; and of the sufferings he endured at the hands of his wife, a Dutch Calvinist, "who kep her husband in a state of continual penance." He died in 1674, at the age of 56. By his will he left £20 to the Franciscan monastery of Ennis, also a sum of money "for the performance of the usual duties of the Roman Catholic clergy, and for other pious uses." There is a tradition current in Limerick that he was buried in St

Mary's Cathedral. Certain it is that in his will he ordered that his body should be buried there. Some years ago, while repairs were going on, and a part of the floor in the north aisle was ripped up, a coffin was found covered with Irish freize. The covering was quite fresh, the coffin sound, but on opening it no remains were found within. Tradition further says, that though the burial took place, the people of Limerick, indignant that the old church should be profaned by the presence of the bones of one who during life was the enemy of their country and their faith, took up the corpse during the night and threw it into the Shannon. Morrough, too, was one of those who were brought up as king's wards, and well did he repay the price of his nurture.

At the death of James, third marquis, seventh earl, and twelfth baron, in 1855, the earldom became extinct; but the barony of Inchiquin devolved on Sir Lucius O'Brien of Dromoland, descended from a younger son of the first baron.

III.

SUPPLIES SENT TO CROMWELL DURING THE IRISH CAMPAIGN.

1649, Sept. 15th. An order of the Council of State for supplies of horse-saddles, &c , for the Lord Lieutenant, Oct. 16th, Captain Long, of Colonel Venables' regiment, was sent to recruit 200 men. The Council of State promised him sixpence a day for each man not exceeding that number he should bring on board, for their marching money. They were to be transported to Ireland at the charge of the state. An agreement was made between the Council of State and Richard Downes, for furnishing 16,000 coats and breeches for the soldiers in Ireland, the coats to be made of Gloucester or Coventry cloth of Venice, color red, shrunk ; the breeches to be made of gray or other good colors, of Reading or good cloth ; 2,500 of each to be delivered within a fortnight, and 2,500 more every week after, until the 16,000 are delivered; and that 17s. be paid for each coat and breeches. The 16,000 cassocks and breeches were not sufficient for the foot forces. 1,900 in the Tower to be sent to Sir Charles Coote for his own and Colonel Venables' men. 19th. The Council of State ordered 5,000 recruits to be raised, and to be divided into five regiments, and a sum of £6,939 to be given to the officers that raised and conducted the men, for the payment of quarters' victuals,

&c., on board ship, and for transplantation 30th. Contract of the Irish Committee with Richard Thorowgood for 16,000 shirts approved ; with John Harvey and Thomas Hayes for 16,000 pairs of stockings ; with James Graves and others for 16,000 pairs of shoes. Nov. 2d. Contract for 15,000 yards of broadcloth for the horsemen in Ireland, at 1s. 3d. per yard. 9th. The general officers of the army met this day, with a committee of the Council of State, about the raising of 800 horse out of the army for recruits for Ireland, which, with the 5,000 foot volunteers, will be very considerable for that service. 15th. Report of the Irish Committee approved by the Council of State as to sending recruits of horse to Ireland 20 out of each troop of 10 regiments. ships are to be provided and pressed at the several ports for their transport ; to land at Wexford, unless prevented by contrary winds, in which case they are to land at any safe port they can make in Ireland. 20th. The Council is satisfied with Sir Hardress Waller's acceptance of the employment in Ireland; he is to use all speed in raising his men. 26th. Order given to Colonel Fleetwood and Colonel Whalley to march 1,000 recruits of foot raised by them to Chester. Colonel Henry Cromwell's men are to have their entertainment during their stay for a wind and until they are shipped for Ireland, and also one month's pay in advance when they ship for Ireland. Dec. 7th. Sir Hardress Waller and his company ready to go to Ireland. 10th. Last week there was shipped at Liverpool and Chester 500 men of Colonel Pride's party, 557 of Major Pitson's, 366 of Colonel Massey's, of Colonel Fenwick's 220. In November there were transported 8 companies consisting of 700 men; in all of late, 2,708 14th. About 7,000 soldiers shipped from Liverpool for Ireland. About this time 1,500 recruits landed at Dublin from Chester and Liverpool. Dec. 15th. Sir Hardress Waller, with his five companies viz: the Colonel's, Lieutenant Colonel Smyth's, Captains Smyth's, Hodden's, and Wilson's, took shipping at Plymouth, and 200 recruits besides. 18th. Letters from York, that there was a rendezvous of Colonel Lilbourne's party that are marching for Ireland — about 100 old blades stout men, and ready for service. 19th. From Chester, an account of soldiers to be shipped there for Ireland. From Plymouth, an account of recruits to be shipped for Ireland. Letters from Duncaster Castle, that recruits were raising there for Ireland. 21st. Letters from Pymouth, an account of the shipping there of Sir Hardress Waller with his company and other recruits for Ireland, all which go with great willingness. 24th. From Portland, that Colonel Cox and his men sail for Ireland with a fair wind. 1650, Jan. 4th. An account of recruits for Ireland. 5th. Captain Barrington's troop of Colonel Oky's regiment, designed for Ireland, are marched towards the sea-side. 8th. Several orders and references to the Council of State and the Committee of the Army concerning recruits, and for supplies of provisions, ammunition, and money for the forces in Ireland. This day a gallant troop of 80 horse, commanded by Captain Theophilus Sandford, set sail from Liverpool for Wexford. 12th. About 140 foot under Captain Whiting, and about 20 recruits under Captain Owen. 15th. Some of Colonel Desborough's men shipped for Ireland. From Liverpool : There is now shipping here a troop of Major-General Lambert's. 19th. Account of recruits for Ireland. 23d. A ship with 30 horse and 120 foot, bound for Ireland, was cast away, and all drowned. Feb. 4th. Mr. Whalley is preparing shipping to transport three troops of horse for Ireland about Chester and Liverpool. Captain Crofton, with the horse drawn out of Colonel Riche's regiment and 80 foot, are ready in the west to be joined with Colonel Desborough's recruits for Ireland. Mr. Peters' 1,000 foot are near ready at Milford, were the wind seasonable. 6th. Account of troops and recruits marching towards Chester for Ireland. 8th. Account of recruits for Ireland. Letters from Cork, that five ships with soldiers were all cast away coming from Minehead for Ireland; only twenty or thirty men swam ashore. Captain Ensor, Captain Whiting, with 80 horse and 150 foot, and all the seamen drowned except 20 or 30. An account from Chester, that, after too long a stay, ships are at length ready to carry the money ordered by the Council of state to Leinster and the north of Ireland. 23d. Letters from Milford, that there were 400 horse of Colonel Cromwell's, the Lord Lieutenant's son, to be transported to Ireland. 27th. Letters from Pembroke, that Colonel Cromwell and Colonel Venables were there waiting for a wind for Ireland. March 1st. Divers ships gone from Liverpool with supplies for Ireland. 6th. Letters from Chester, that £11,000 was put on board for Dublin, and £6,000 for Carrickfergus. 9th. Several

orders conveying supplies of money, provisions, and recruits for Ireland. 16th. Twelve ships or barks from Milford laden with oats, beans, and pease, and several sorts of grain. 22d. Account of forces supplied for Ireland. 27th. Colonel Henry Cromwell arrived at Youghal from Milford Haven with a regiment of foot and about 200 horse. April 5th. That eight ships were come in from England and Wales, laden with oats, and 1,500 yards of cloth, and 200 pairs of boots. There came from Milford Haven to Youghal 13 ships laden with oats, beans, and pease for the supply of the army. 6th. Account of the shipping of some troops for Ireland. 10th. Account of the transporting of forces for Ireland. Clothes, monies, and necessary recruits came to Sir Charles Coote for his army in the north of Ireland. May 6th. From Taunton, many volunteers listed for Ireland. Colonel Reeves' recruits landed safe at Cork.

IV.

GENEALOGY OF OWEN ROE O'NEILL.

ACCORDING to O'Donovan, the Ui Neill, or descendants of King Nial of the Nine Hostages, were divided into two great branches, the northern and the southern. The latter were kings of Meath, and many of them were monarchs of Ireland also. The northern branch, too, produced many monarchs. Of this branch there were two great families.—the race of Eoghan, princes of Tyron, and the race of Conell, princes of Tyrconnell. The descendants of Eoghan were the most celebrated of all the Milesian clans. These took the name of O'Neill in the 10th century from Nial Glan Dubh (Black Knee), who was slain by the Danes in battle in 919. The elder branch took the name of O'Lochlainn and MacLoughlin, from one of their chiefs. The O'Neills had their chief seat at Duncannon, and were inaugurated as chieftains at Tullahogue. Con O'Neill, surnamed Bocagh (the Lame), head of his clan, accepted the title of Earl of Tyrone, from Henry VIII. in 1542, renouncing at the same time the name of O'Neill, and engaging that himself and his heirs should adopt the English dress and language, obey the King's laws, assist the Deputy in his hostings, and refuse all succor to any of the King's enemies. It is obvious that though Con could accept for himself any title from the King of England, he, acting as chief of his

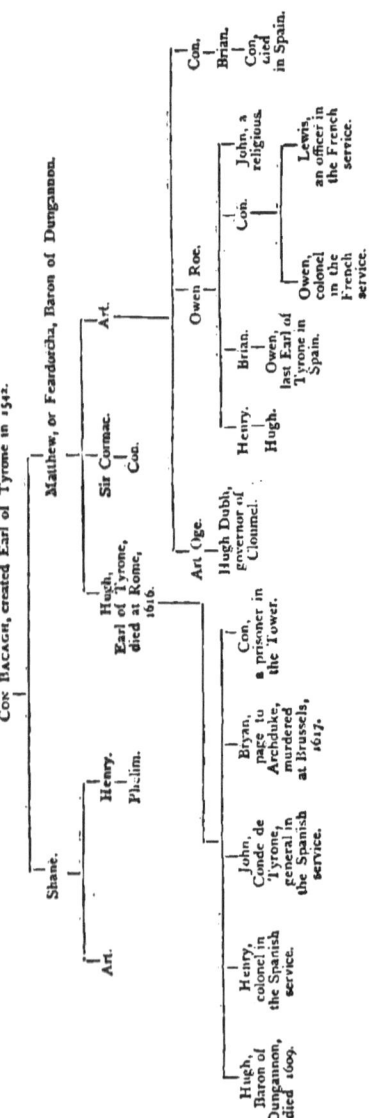

THE GENEALOGY OF O'NEILL.

tribe, had no shadow of right to take upon himself to give away all the tribal lands. In the eyes of his clan such a grant was simply a nullity. He had soon good reason to regret his submission, and cursed any of his posterity who should learn to speak English, sow wheat, or build castles. On the death of his eldest son Shane, in 1567, than whom none of the Irish chiefs during the 15th century was more feared or hated by the English, an Act of Parliament was passed for "the extinguishment of the name O'Neill, and the entitling of the Queen of England, her heirs and successors to the county of Tyrone and two other counties and territories in Ulster." "The name of O'Neill," says the Act, "in the judgments of the universal people of this realm doth carry in itself so great a sovereignty, as they suppose that all the lords and people of Ulster should rather live in servitude to that name than in subjection to the Crown of England.

Matthew, surnamed Feardorcha (the Swarthy), an illegitimate son of Con, was created Baron of Dungannon at the same time that his father was made Earl of Tyrone. His second son, Hugh, was perhaps the ablest of the Irish chieftains, either in the council or the field. In his youth he was taken to the court, to be taught English manners. But the rapacity of the English adventurers soon roused him to resistance. At the head of the Ulster chieftains, he carried on a war for eight years. The defeat which he inflicted on Bagnall at the Yellow Ford was admitted by their own historians to have been the greatest which the English ever received since their arrival in Ireland. Through want of supplies he was at length obliged to submit. But even after his submission he was looked on as one whom it would be dangerous to provoke. A conspiracy was set on foot to bring about his ruin. With O'Donnell he sailed from Lough Swilly, Sept. 14th, 1607. "Woe to the heart that meditated, to the mind that conceived, to the council that decided on the project of their setting out on this voyage without knowing whether they should ever return to their native principalities, to the end of the world. Both died soon afterward in exile. They are buried side by side in front of the high altar, in the church of San Pietro in Montorio, Rome.

Matthew's third son was Art M'Baron. In his old age he removed from his own territory of O'Neilan and got in exchange an estate of 2,000 acres during the lives of himself and his wife. Art's second son was Owen Roe.

It is said that F. Wadding sent to Owen Roe the two-handed sword of the great Earl of Tyrone. Massari, dean of Fermo, who brought it to Ireland in 1647, writing to Rinuccini, says: "Recuperavi illius celebris bellatoris Tyroniæ Comitis Ultoniensis ex O'Neillorum familia gladium duarum manuum, quem Generali Don Eugenio destinavi." One of O'Neill's enemies vented his spleen in the following verses:—

"The sanguine hands of the O'Neillian sept,
Have now received the papal gifts long kept,
Earl Hugh, to whom the phœnix plume was sent,
Among the birds on earth most eminent;
And to his nephew Owen a sword is come,
That Hercules of both the world and Rome.
And now expect a further present!—
What?
The imperial sceptre of O'Neill's lost state
Left with the Pope to keep;—with reason, then,
The Pope should not restore the same again."

Rancati, the Cistercian abbot of Santa Croce in Rome, sent him a cross made of the wood of the True Cross, as "a protection to body and soul against even invisible enemies." "Receive this," he adds, "from a poor monk, and in this sign conquer, and give back Ireland to God."

The following Indult was given by Urban VIII. to "Owen O'Neill, that very brave and noble Irish chieftain, and to the other Catholics who would stir up and carry on the war in Ireland against the English heretics;" it is dated October 8th, 1642:—

Dilecto Filio Eugenio O'Neillo.

Dilecte fili salutem. Nullam prætermittere soles occasionem, qua non majorum tuorum vestigiis insistens eximium zelum et propagandæ ecclesiæ studium perspectum facis, idque luculenter in præsentia præstitisti in Hiberniam proficisci cogitans, ut Catholicorum rationibus præsto sis. Quam ob rem pergratæ nobis advenerunt literæ quibus hujusmodi itineris deliberationem declaras et rei feliciter gerendæ principium a cœlesti ope auspicatus, non minus humiliter quam religiose Apostolicam benedictionem a nobis postulas. Præclarum hunc in te ardorem et constaniam adversus hæreticos et veræ fidei animum non parum laudamus, tuæque jam pridem pietatis conscii a te expectamus in hac opportunitate strenui atque excelsi roboris documenta quæ antehac singularem nominis famam tibi compararunt. Illorum pariter commendamus consilium quos tu excitans exemplo significasti. Speramus autem fore ut Altissimus tuæ causæ præsto sit, ut notam faciat populis virtutem suam. Interim, ut confidentius cuncta aggrediamini, nos divinam clementiam indesinenter orantes, ut adversariorum conatus in nihil redigat, tibi ceterisque Catholicorum rem in prædicto regno curaturis nostram libenter impertimur benedictionem, universisque et singulis, si vere pœnitentes confessi fuerint, et sacra communione (si fieri possit) debite refecti, plenariam suorum peccatorum veniam et remissionem, atque in mortis articulo indulgentiam etiam plenariam elargimur. Datum Romæ sub Annulo Piscatoris die 8 octobris, 1642, Pontificatus nostri anno 20.

The following is the "Lament" of O'Neill's secretary.

I lament the death of a brave warrior, the choice champion of his Holiness, Urban VIII., requiring his repair into Ireland, chief commander, immediately from himself for the Catholic war, as having pregnant testimonies of his fidelity and uberant fortune in such affairs. A soldier since a boy in the only martial academy of Christendom, Flanders; never drew his sword unto his dying day otherwise than in Catholic religion's defence, as witness Bohemia, Sweden, Norway, Denmark, and now Ireland. This bulwark of holy religion and Pope's Scanderberg, Don Eugenius O'Neill, severally impeded in this his godly design by factious and treacherous members of this same kingdom, as a tall cedar, placed on the mountain-top of fame and reputation, was terribly shaken, and overturned by the lofty blasts and thundering winds of emulation and self-envy. Ireland's fortune in his time was favorable; the Church of God flourished; the militia, in emulation of his virtues, warlike; the enemy weak and declining; the country plentiful. But now by his death the enemy is grown strong and cruel; no city, fort, or town to oppose him; no church, monastery, or religious house inhabited; the militia discouraged, disheartened, and grown coward;

none to show his face in the field, for now the enemy doth not fear the naming of General Owen O'Neill, which not long before did sound like a thunderbolt in his ears. This it is that I lament the death of so well deserving a man, whose now want is the cause of all the woe and evil happening unto us, whose only name (if but like an echo uttered, and, his corpse in a cradle or chariot carried) would keep life and breath in the decayed affairs of Ireland. What will the poor northern people do now? Your father, your general, your ruler, your steerer is now wanting!

Lament for the Death of Eoghan Ruadh O'Neill.

I.

"Did they dare, did they dare, to slay Owen Roe O'Neill?"
"Yes they slew with poison him they feared to meet with steel."
"May God wither up their hearts! may their blood cease to flow!
May they walk in living death, who poisoned Owen Roe!

II.

"Though it break my heart to hear, say again the bitter words!"
"From Derry against Cromwell he marched, to measure swords;
But the weapon of the Sacsanach met him on his way,
And he died at Clogh Uachtair, upon St. Leonard's Day."

III.

"Wail, wail ye for the mighty one! Wail, wail ye for the dead!
Quench the hearth, and hold the breath—with ashes strew the head!
How tenderly we loved him! How deeply we deplore!
Holy Saviour! but to think we shall never see him more!

IV.

Sagest in the council was he, kindest in the hall;
Sure we never won a battle—'twas Owen won them all.
Had he lived, had he lived, our dear country had been free;
But he's dead, but he's dead, and 'tis slaves we'll ever be.

V.

O'Farrell and Clanricarde, Preston and
Red Hugh,
Audley and MacMahon, ye are valiant,
wise, and true;
But what, what are ye all to our darling
who is gone ?
The rudder of our ship was he — our cas-
tle's corner-stone.

VI.

Wail, wail hi n through the island ! Weep
for our pride !
Would that on the battle-field our gallant
chief had died !
Weep the victor of Bein-Burb ! Weep him,
young men and old !
Weep for him, ye women—your Beautiful
· lies cold !

VII.

We thought you would not die — we were
sure you would not go,
And leave us in our inmost need to Cromwell's cruel blow,
Sheep without a shepherd, when the
snow shuts out the sky —
Oh ! why did you leave us, Owen ? why did
you die ?

VIII.

Soft as woman's was your voice, O'Neill !
Bright was your eye !
Oh ! why did you leave us, Owen ? why did
you die ?
Your troubles are all over — your're at
with God on high ;
But we're slaves, and we're orphans,
Owen—why did you die?

EPITAPH OF OWEN ROE O'NEILL.

Eugenii O'Nelli, copiarum ultoniensium
prœfecti generalis, epitaphium.

Hic jacet ille ingens patriæ defensor
O'Nellus,
Nobilis ingenio, sanguine. Marte, fide.
Qui genus et magni mensuram stemmatis
implens,
Per sua Catholicos arma probavit avos.
Quem neque vis dubii potuit perfringere
belli,
Nec mutare boni spesve timorve mali.
Quem tria conjuncto petierunt agmine
regna,
In caput unius tot coiere manus.
Celsus in immota mentis sed constitit
arce,
Et cœptum in fracto pectore duxit iter,

Spem contra humanam, cœlum tamen
adfuit ausis,
Cumque suo Christus milite miles
erat.
Impia Catholicorum seu strinxit in
agmina ferrum,
Discolor hæretica cæde madebat hu-
mus.
Sive fugam simulat, simulando com-
primit hostem,
Nec minus arma viri quam metuenda
fuga.
Hoc tamen, hoc urgens et inexpugnabile
Marti,
Pectus humi positum spicula mortis
habent.
Æmula nam crebris Parca invidiosa
triumphis,
Vincendi et vitæ sit tibi finis, ait.
Fata sed Eugenium nequeunt ita sternere
servent
Postuma Romanam quominus arma
fidem.
Hanc lapis et cineres, sed et ipsa cadavera
spirant,
Et Petrum litui, tela, tubæque so-
nant.
Magna viri merces, tot palmas astra coro-
nant,
Sic præstant meritum terra polusque
decus.

Hugh O'Neill was born in the Spanish
Netherlands. He was the son of Art
Oge, brother of Owen Roe, whence he
was called Hugh MacArt Oge. He went
by the name of Hugh Dubh or Buidhe,
epithets used by the Irish to designate
persons of swarthy or sallow complexion.
He is mentioned as one of the "brave
warriors and prime captains who, out of
the martial theatre of Flanders, enlisted
under the banner of Owen O'Neill,
and came to Ireland in 1642." He was
taken prisoner at the battle of Clones in
1643, and did not regain his liberty till
released by exchange after the battle of
Benburb in 1646. In that year he was appointed major-general of the Ulster army.
The author of the *Aphorismal Dis-*
covery speaks of him as a tried, wise,
faithful, successful officer, unsurpassed
in courage, vigilant, industrious, zealous,
for religion, loyal to the king, faithful to
his country, constant in his principles.
During the illness of his uncle, Owen
Roe, he commanded the Ulster army, and
was with Ferrall despatched in October,
1649, to the Marquis of Ormonde with a
body of 2,000 men. After Owen Roe's
death, he was anxious to succeed him as
commander of the Ulster army. His

qualifications were strongly urged by Daniel O'Neill, as being a "man who knew the ways Owen Roe O'Neill took to manage the people, and one not unacceptable to the Scots, and one who would do nothing contrary to Ormonde's commands."

We have already given an account of his successful defence of Clonmel. After retiring from that place, he was appointed to act as military governor of Limerick by Ormonde, and to defend that city against the Parliamentarians. In reply to the demand of Sir Hardress Waller to surrender the city, September, 1650, he declared "he was determined to maintain it for the use of his Majesty Charles II., even to the effusion of the last drop of his blood." The author of the *Aphorismal Discovery* states that Ireton made him offers of great preferment, to induce him to surrender; but he would not betray the trust reposed in him. In his reply he is stated to have said that he had promised to hold Limerick for a year, and that period having expired, he intended to hold it, even without assistance, for another year. At the surrender, finding that his name was not included in the treaty, "he rode up to encounter Deputy Ireton, and offered him the pommel of his sword. Ireton receiving the same, asked him who he was, who answered that he was Hugh O'Neill, and desired the benefit of the law of arms in the behalf of a soldier of fortune, voluntarily yielding himself and 'the lives of other such soldiers as served under his command to his lordship's mercy and favor. Ireton embraced him gently, and bad him be of good cheer, and that he would receive no prejudice. Commanding his men to ride forward, he was alone and in private discourse with O'Neill, which one of his chief commanders perceiving, turned his horse in a fury, telling him it was now no time for such business. Notwithstanding all which Ireton was so tender of O'Neill's safety, that before he parted him he did command his own guard under pain of death to attend only that gentleman and bring him to a place of safety, where he did not receive the least prejudice."

"A few days after the taking of the city Ireton was infected and died, and at the point of his death was so nobly minded that he commanded his lieutenant-general, Edmund Ludlow and the rest of his officers to use all good behavior towards O'Neill, and to send him with his own corpse into England, and bestow on him three horses, one for himself and two for two servants, and means to defray their charges. He also wrote a letter to the parliament, humbly desiring to use that brave warrior with all civility and humanity, all which was actually performed.

Another account says that "a court-martial was held, in which the Governor (O'Neill) having been condemned to die, the Deputy (Ireton) asked what he had to say for himself. He replied that the war had been long on foot before he came over, that he had been guilty of no base or dishonorable act, having only discharged the duty of a soldier as became a man subject to a superior power, to which he must be accountable. But the blood formerly shed at Clonmel, where O'Neill had been governor, made such an impression on the Deputy, that his judgment, which was of great weight with the court, moved them a second time to vote him to die, though some of the court earnestly opposed it, for the reason he had mentioned himself, and because whatever he had been guilty of before had no relation to these articles. The Deputy, finding some of the officers to be unsatisfied with the judgment, referred it again to the consideration of the court, who by their vote consented to save his life." It would seem that Ireton had persuaded the court to pronounce the sentence of death; but Ludlow and some other officers interfered, representing to him the odium which such an execution would bring on the English name abroad, where O'Neill was well known.

On O'Neill's arrival in London, January 10th, 1652, he was committed a close prisoner to the Tower, for being in arms against the Parliament. Twenty shillings a week was allowed for his support. Don Alonzo Cardeñas, the Spanish Ambassador, proposed to the Council of State in July, 1650, to give permission to the Irish troops to pass into Spain, especially to Don Hugo O'Neill, since he was born in Flanders, and consequently a Spanish subject, having besides borne no part in the first insurrection in Ireland, nor in the excesses which took place there. He seems to have gone to Spain, for there is a letter of his to Charles II., dated from Madrid, October 27th, 1660, in which he solicits the restoration of his family to the royal favor. He assumed there the title of Earl of Tyrone.

The name of Daniel O'Neill occurs frequently in this work. He, too, was a nephew of Owen Roe. From a petition which he presented to the House of Lords, in 1641, we learn that his grand-father and father were owners of all the Upper Clandeboys 'and Great Ardes, in the province of Ulster, and had served the English in the war against their own kindred, and that his father had been in-duced by undue influence to transfer these lands, amounting to 66,000 acres, to Sir Hugh Montgomery and James Hamilton for the sum of £60 and a yearly rent of £160. He spent his early life in Holland, in the army of the Prince of Orange. Later he entered the English service, and was known as an officer of name and repute. At the beginning of the Irish rebellion he was accused of high treason, and imprisoned in the Tower. He escaped in disguise after a confinement of six months. Soon after we find him lieutenant-general of Prince Rupert's horse. Clarendon says of him that "in subtlety and understanding he was much superior to the whole nation of the old Irish, a great discoverer of men's talents and humors, of good experience in the most active armies of that time, and of a courage very notorious, and that Ormonde loved him very much, and had much esteem for him." One of the charges brought against Ormonde in the "Declaration" of Jamestown was his too great partiality for Daniel O'Neill, shown by his giving him a command of which he had deprived Major-General Purcell. Ormonde's answer was: "The manner of Daniel O'Neill's coming into the com-mand was this: he had taken great pains in bringing his uncle General Owen O'Neill to submit to the peace and his Majesty's government, and he did effectu-ally labor after that work was effected to bring the Ulster army to his assistance, when Cromwell was on his march from Dublin to Wexford. Owen O'Neill being sick, the army was conducted by Lieutenant-General Ferrall and Major-General Hugh O'Neill. But when it joined with the Leinster, Munster, and Connaught forces, and some English and Scotch horse and foot, he found great difficulty how to distribute orders with satisfaction to all these parties, the Ulster party being unwilling to receive these from Major-General Hugh O'Neill. But all parties were content to receive them from Daniel O'Neill, and by him they were distributed; and Major-General Ferrall was sent into Munster, where he had and exercised a command-in-chief in the absence of superior officers. Nor was his commission annulled, nor any

new place given to any other to this day." He was sent by Ormonde to make pro-posals to Owen Roe, and it was mainly owing to his exertions that the treaty was brought about between them. Ormonde was anxious that he should be appointed to the chief command of the Ulster army after Owen Roe's death. But his religion stood in the way, for, strange to say, he was a Protestant. In 1650 he left Ire-land, having obtained permission from Ireton to transport 5,000 men for service to Spain or Holland. On the Continent he was one of the most active partisans of Charles II. After the Restoration he was made Postmaster-General. He died in 1664. On the occasion of his death, Charles II. wrote to the Duchess of Orleans, "This morning poor O'Neill died of an ulcer in his guts. He was as honest a man as ever lived. I am sure I have lost a good servant by it."

V.

THE SACK OF CASHEL BY INCHIQUIN, SEPTEMBER 13TH, 1647.

Narrative by Father Andrew Sall in a Letter to Father John Young.

THE year 1647 was a disastrous one for the whole of Ireland, and the times fell most heavily on Cashel, the Metro-politan see of the province of Munster. Lord Inchiquin, who was rightly called the scourge of God, after reducing and burning nearly the whole of this district, moved his Parliamentary army upon Cashel. The garrison of the city num-bered only four hundred men, and the citizens were thrown into the utmost con-fusion by the difficulties of their situation and the sudden approach of the enemy. The garrison deserted the walls, and re-tired to St. Patrick's Rock, while a great part of the inhabitants, taking with them a supply of provisions and most of their household effects, followed the soldiers thither. The remainder, not trusting to the protection of the rock, concealed themselves in the outlying country, just in time to escape the fast advancing enemy. The Puritan troops entered the city without resistance, and after making merry on the food and drink left behind by the citizens, lay down to sleep. The next day, which was the feast of the Ex-altation of the Holy Cross, the enemy re-connoitred the rock and its defences for the space of an hour, although information about its state had already been given by some traitors, Catholics only in name, who, after having lived on our bounty for a long time, were terror-stricken at the enemy's ravages, and had disappeared. We believe that God appointed that day to be the witness, not indeed of our destruction, but of our glory, and it was meet that those who wished to taste the delight of the Cross must first share its ignominy. When the reconnoitring was over, the hostile army divided into three parties, whose points of attack were the three weaker portions of our fortifications. Before attacking, a messenger left their lines and came up to the rock to treat about a surrender on these terms: that the garrison should be allowed to depart with their muskets and with bullets in bouche, but that the clergy and citizens should be left to the mercy of their commander. Here the bravery of the Catholic soldiers shone out, and they replied that they would risk their lives in defence of those whom they had vowed to protect rather than break their word, and that they preferred to dye with their hearts' blood that holy ground to allowing it to be desecrated by heretical miscreants. The Puritan leader was stung to the quick by this generous answer, and ordered the charge to be sounded. On they come with lightning speed, at the same time throwing fire-brands into the air, one of which, happening to fall into the vestibule of the monastery of the Friars Minor, set the hall on fire, and burned it to the ground. They slack not their speed until under cover of the walls, where they are safe out of range, for the turrets and embrasures were too high to admit of aim being taken at the enemy as they lay at close quarters. The beseiged, therefore, throw away their guns, and climbing up the steep bastions, hurl down the foe as they appear above the scaling-ladders, until overcome by the numbers that swarmed up the north wall, the least defensible portion of the fort, they fall back slowly, intending to take up a position in the church. Scarcely have they begun to retreat when the enemy press round them on all sides with renewed energy. The very cemetery itself is disputed inch by inch, and of those that remained outside the church not one survived. The issue of the day depends on the capture of the main building, which therefore the enemy make the centre of attack. They charge the north and south doors, but are driven back with no less determination by our sol-

diers. Unable to effect an entrance in this direction, the Puritans plant their ladders against the walls of the church, and leap through the windows. Hemmed in on all sides, nevertheless our brave defenders fight with the energy of despair, and nothing could be heard in that vast edifice but the clash of arms and the shouts of the combatants. For upwards of half an hour the contest raged in the very nave of the cathedral with equal valor on both sides, but unequal forces, the fanatical enemy polluting the very sanctuary, and dyeing its stones with blood consecrated to God and His Church. At length our defenders, now reduced to sixty, turn and ascend the steps of the bell-tower, followed by the enemy, who call on them to surrender. With the alternative before them of death by starvation or by the enemy's sword, they give themselves up on condition of their lives being spared. The deceitful commander gave his word, but as soon as their swords were collected he gave the order to kill all without exception. Many are at once cut down, some of the richer citizens are spared in hope of ransom, others run to hide themselves in the crypts and vaults, of which there was a great number about. All, however, with the exception of one or two, are either dispatched by the sword or retained as prisoners. The Bishop, together with the Mayor and his son, and a few others, conceal themselves in a more secure and secret hiding-place, but do not stir therefrom until assured of their safety.

Thus ended that cruel butchery and the most disgraceful sacrilege that was ever seen in Ireland. We lost about one thousand men, the enemy at least five hundred. Of these latter twelve, or as some say sixteen, were descendants of the same family, and bore about them the marks of that disgrace which had befallen their ancestors on account of the injury done to the horses of St. Thomas of Canterbury. Three of the secular clergy, the Prior of the Dominicans, and one of our Society, fell in the performance of their sacred duties. Old men on the verge of the grave, whose weapons were their rosaries, defenceless women and children, were struck at the very altars without regard to age or sex. Women, whom the sword had spared, were stripped and sent away, yet not daring to expose their nakedness to the light of day, slunk into the corners of the temple and covered themselves with blood. The mind sickens at the thought; but what was more horrible than the desecration of the sacred objects! In one word, the enemy, exulting over their prey, hew in pieces and burn all the statues, overthrow the altars, and pollute the sacred vessels. The large crucifix that towered above the entrance to the choir had its head, hands, and feet struck off, the organ was broken, and the bells, whose chimes cheered our soldiers as they fought, were deprived of their clappers and their beautiful tone. Nothing escaped the ruthless hand of the spoiler. The Puritans load themselves with the goods of the citizens, with which the church was filled; they excavate the very crypts, and break open the marble tombs in hope of plunder. To gain credit for the story that was afterwards circulated, that only six or seven of their own soldiers were slain, they strip the clothing off their dead, and drag them into the church and cemetery, that they may not be distinguished from our own people. All the passages, even the altars, chapels, sacristies, bell-tower steps, and seats were so thickly covered with corpses, that one could not walk a step without treading on a dead body. Those who remember the splendor of the cathedral in the celebration of the sacred ceremonies on holidays and feast days, and the sumptuous workmanship of the altars and monuments, could not bring themselves to view the scene of horror, or, if they did look upon it, they shed abundant tears the while. Here the course of cruelty and sacrilege did not end, but rather increased in fury. The soldiers sold the property of the citizens, the church furniture, and the sacred vessels to the people of the neighboring villages, who came flocking together as if to a fair. What they cannot sell is either torn in pieces or thrown into the dung-pits. Some dress themselves in the precious vestments, and with birrettas on their heads invite the rest to Mass. Others dash the holy images against the walls, and others again bear aloft in solemn procession a headless statue of the Immaculate Virgin, exquisitely wrought with golden tracery. The pictures of St. Patrick and St. Ignatius, together with those of other saints, deaf and dumb idols as they called them, were turned into horse-cloths or used as sacks. One man there was, who on catching sight of the smaller statue of the Blessed Virgin at our house, scoffed at it, saying: "How now, Mary of Ireland, how now? Eat some peas." But his mockery was the cause of his death, for for a little time after, while he was re-moving the iron bars from the window of a house, a stone dropped from the topmost story, and falling on his head broke in his skull. Lord Inchiquin himself put on the Archbishop's mitre, boasting aloud that he was the Governor of Munster and the Mayor and Archbishop of Cashel. Not only the goods of the citizens and the church ornaments suffered from the ravages of the soldiers, but also the dwellings in the city and the houses consecrated to God. Already the burning brands were applied to the wooden partitions, when some of the chief men stepped forward, and by the promise of a large sum of money, to be contributed by all the citizens, saved the city from a deluge of fire. Yet the conflagration could not be got under, and the most ancient city of Cashel, that had seen so long a succession of kings and archbishops, was burnt to the ground. That city, I say, which because it had received the light of the faith from Patrick, suffered it never to be extinguished or obscured, endured such a change that for a long time no priest or sacred rite was seen there. Graced by the trophies of so many victories for the faith, strengthened by the protection of so many patron saints, the city contains a Puritan enemy in its midst. Hallowed by the presence of so many religious orders, the home of so many families that worshipped God in fear and love, in one hour the devoted city pays the penalty of the sins of Ireland. And the cause of wonder to all is, that heaven looks upon it and is silent, and does not yet avenge the death of its saints. Has the confidence of the people been a vain one? Truly we should rather admire than question the judgments of God; we should rather weep for our sins than besiege heaven to turn aside its wrath. What we hope for is that Cashel will not become a by-word among men, and will acquire greater glory by its losses for the faith than by its triumphs. While we mourn that loved ones are no more, we rejoice that they are crowned with the martyr's crown above, and it is not wrong to think that their souls are in bliss. For on the nights preceding the destruction of the city, when we went to the soldiers of the garrison and exhorted them to abstain from swearing and other practices of the camp, we found them compliant beyond measure, and prepared to shed their blood for the faith. Before they engaged the enemy most of them several times, all at least once, cleansed their consciences by confession, and received the Bread of Life. But if they are detained in the cleansing fire of purgatory, I recommend them most earnestly to the sacrifices and prayers of your Reverence and the rest of the Fathers on this day, the Commemoration of the Souls of the Faithful Departed.

VI.

THE WALLING OF ROSS.

NEW ROSS was formerly styled Nova Villa Pontis Wilelmi Marescalli, having been built by William Earl Marshal, who married the grand-daughter of Dermot McMorrogh, near the monastery of Ross-mic-truin, founded in the sixth century by St. Abban. Holinshed says, " It was also called Rosse Nova or Rosse Ponte, by reason of the bridge, that which they call old Ross bearing east three miles into the countrie of Wexford." The same author gives the following curious account of the building of the walls; "The towne is builded in a barren soyle, and planted among a crew of naughtie and prowlyng neighbours. And in olde tyme when it flourished, albeit the towne were sufficiently peopled, yet as long as it was not compassed with walles, they were formed with watche and warde, to keep it from the greedy snatchyng of the Irishe enemies. With whome as they were generally molested, so the privat consenyng of one peasaunt on a sodayne incensed them to inviron their towne with strong and substantial walls. There repayred one of the Irishe to this towne on horsebacke, and espying a piece of clothe on a merchant's stall, tooke hold thereof, and bet the clothe to the lowest pryce he could. As the merchant and he stood dodging one wyth the other in cheaping the ware, the horseman considering that he was well-mounted, and that the merchant and he had growen to a pryce, made wyse as though he woulde have drawen to his purse to have defrayed the money. The clothe in the meane while being tuckte up and placed before him, he gave the spurre to his horsse, and ranne away with the cloth, being not imbard from his posting pase, by reason the towne was not perclosed eyther wyth ditch or wall. The townesmen being pincht at the heart that one rascall in such scornful wise should give them the stampaine, not so much weighing the sclendernesse of the losse as the shamefulnesse of the foyle, they put their heads together, consulting how to prevent eyther the sudden rushing or the posthast flying of any such adven-turous rakehell hereafter. In which consultation a famous Dido, a chaste wydowe, a politike dame, a bountiful woman called Rose, who representing in sinceritie of life the sweetnesse of that herbe whose name she bore, unfolded the devise how any such future mischaunce shoulde be prevented; and withall opened her coffers liberally to have it furthered, two good properties in a counsaylour. Her devise was, that the towne shoulde incontinently be inclosed with walles, and therewythal promised to discharge the charges, so that they would not sticke to finde out labourers. The devise of this worthie matrone being wise, and the offer liberall, the townesmen agreed to follow the one and to put their helping handes to the achieving of the other. The worke was begunne, which through the multitude of handes seemed light. For the whole towne was assembled tagge and ragge, cutte and long tayle ; none exempted except such as were bedrid and impotent. Some were tasked to delve, others appointed with mattockes to digge, divers allotted to the unheaping of rubbishe, many bestowed to the caryage of stones, sundry occupied in tempering of morter, the better sort busied in overseeing the workemen, eche one according to hys vocation employed, as though the citie of Carthage were a freshe in building, as it is featlye verified by the golden Poet Virgil. The laberours were so many, the worke, by reason of round and exchequer payment, so well applyed, the quary of fayre marble so neere at hand, that these walles with diverse brave turrets were sodainly mounted, and in manner sooner finished than to the Irishe enemies notified. These walles in circuit are equal to London walles. It hath three gorgious gates, Bishop his gate, on the east side ; Allegate, on the east-south-east side ; and South gate, on the south porte."

This bountiful gentlewoman was probably the widow of Sir Ralph Meyler, who obtained a grant of freedom for the port from Edward III. But an Anglo-Norman poem, "Rithmus facture ville de Rosse," an old manuscript copy of which, supposed to be in the handwriting of the author, Friar Michael Bernard of Kildare, now among the Harleian MSS. in the British Museum, says Ross was fortified in 1265, in consequence of the feud then existing between Maurice Fitzgerald, Baron of Offaly, and Walter de Burgo, Earl of Ulster, " whose deadly wars wrought bloodshed and trouble throughout the realm of Ireland." The citizens, fearing they should suffer in consequence, enclosed the town. This old poem was inserted by Sir Frederick Madden, in vol. xxii. of the *Archæologia.* The spirited translation which we give is by L. E. L. (Mrs. Mac Lean) : it is taken from Crofton Croker's *Popular Songs of Ireland,* who gives the original side by side with it. This ballad is the basis of Sir S. Ferguson's " Rosabel of Ross " in the *Dublin University Magazine :—"*

I have a whim to speak in verse,
If you will list what I rehearse,
For an unheeded tale, I wisse,
Not worth a clove of garlic is.
Please you, then, to understand,
'Tis of a town in Ireland;
For its size the one most fair
That I know of anywhere.
But the town had cause of dread
In the feud two barons spread;
Sir Maurice — and Sir Walter, see,
Here their names shall written be;
Also that fair city's name —
Ross they then did call the same.
'Tis the new bridge-town of Ross,
Which no walls did then enclose :
It therefore feared a stranger's blows.
Commons both, and leading men,
Gathered in the Council then,
What for safety to devise,
In shortest time and lowest price :
'Twas that round the town be thrown
Walls of mortar and of stone.
For this war filled them with fear;
Much they dreaded broil so near.
Candlemas, it was the day
They began to delve in clay,
Marking out a foss, to show
Where the future wall should go.
Soon 'twas traced, and then were hired
Workmen; all the task desired.
More than a hundred workmen ply
Daily 'neath the townsmen's eye;
Yet small advance these fellows made,
Though to labor they were paid.
So the Council met again ;
Such a law as they passed then !
Such a law might not be found,
Nor on French nor English ground.
Next day a summons read aloud,
Gathered speedily a crowd ;
When the law proclaimed they hear,
'Twas received with many a cheer.
Then a good man did advance,
And explained the ordinance ;
Vintners, drapers, merchants, all
Were to labor at the wall,
From the early morning time,
Till the day was in its prime.
More than a thousand men, I say,
Went to the goodly work each day.

Monday they began their labors,
Gay with banners, flutes and tabours;
Soon as the noon hour was come,
These good people hastened home,
With their banners proudly borne.
Then the youth advanced in turn,
And the town they made it ring
With their merry carrolling;
Singing loud and full of mirth,
Away they go to shovel earth.
And the priests, when Mass was chanted,
In the foss they dug and panted :
Quicker, harder, worked each brother.
Harder far than any other;
For both old and young did feel
Great and strong with holy zeal.
Mariners came next, and they
Pass'd along in fair array,
With their banner borne before,
Which a painted vessel bore.
Full six hundred were they then ;
But full eleven hundred men
Would have gathered by the wall,
If they had attended all.

Tuesday came — coatmakers, tailors,
Fullers, cloth-dyers, and "sellers; "
Right good hands, these jolly blades,
Were they counted at their trades.
Away they worked like those before,
Though the others numbered more;
Scarce four hundred did they stand,
But they were a worthy band.

Wednesday following down there came
Other bands who worked the same;
Butchers, cordwainers, and tanners,
Bearing each their separate banners.
Painted as might appertain
To their craft, and, 'mid the train
Many a brave bachelor;
Small and great were numbered o'er,
Singing, as they worked, their song,
Just three hundred were they strong.

Thursday came, the fishermen
And the hucksters followed then,
Who sell corn and fish : they bear
Divers banners, for they were
Full four hundred; and the crowd
Carrollèd and sung aloud ;
And the wainwrights, they came too —
They were only thirty-two ;
A single banner went before,
Which a fish and platter bore.

But on Saturday the stir
Of blacksmith, mason, carpenter,
Hundreds three with fifty told,
Many were they, true and bold ;
And they toiled with main and might
Needful knew they 'twas and right.

Then on Sunday there came down
All the dames of that brave town ;
Know, good laborers were they,
But their numbers none may say.
On the ramparts there were thrown
By their fair hands many a stone ;
Who had there a gazer been,
Many a beauty might have seen.
Many a scarlet mantle too,
Or of green or russet hue ;
Many a fair cloak had they,
And robes dight with colors gay.
In all lands where I have been,
Such fair dames working, I've not seen.
He who had to choose the power,
Had been born in lucky hour.
Many a banner was displayed,
While the work the ladies aid ;
When their gentle hands had done
Piling up rude heaps of stone,
Then they walked the foss-along,
Singing sweet a cheerful song ;
And returning to the town
All these rich dames there sat down ;
Where, with mirth and wine and song,
Passed the pleasant hours along.
Then they said a gate they'd make,
Called the Ladies', for their sake,
And their prison there should be ;
Whoso entered, straightway he
Should forgo his liberty.
Lucky doom, I ween, is his
Who a lady's prisoner is ;
Light the fetters are to wear
Of a lady kind and fair ;
But of them enough is said,
Turn we to the foss instead.

Twenty feet that foss is deep,
And a league in length doth creep,
When the noble work is done,
Watchmen then there needeth none ;
All may sleep in peace and quiet
Without fear of evil riot.
Fifty thousand might attack,
And yet turn them bootless back.
Warlike stores there are enough,
Bold assailant to rebuff.
We have hauberks many a one,
Savage, garcon, haubergeon ;
Doublets too, and coats of mail,
Yew bows good withouten fail.
In no city have I seen
So many good glaives, I ween.
Crossbows hanging on the wall,
Arrows too, to shoot withal ;
Every house is full of maces,
And good shields and talevaces.
Crossbow men, when numbered o'er,
Are three hundred and three score ;
And three hundred archers show,
Ready with a gallant bow ;

And three thousand men advance,
Armed with battle axe and lance ;
Above a hundred knights who wield
Arms aye ready for the field.
I warrant you the town's prepared
'Gainst all enemies to guard.
Here I deem it meet to say,
No desire for war have they,
But to keep their city free,
Blamed of no man can they be.
When the wall is carried round,
None in Ireland will be found
Bold enough to dare to fight.
Let a foeman come in sight,
If the city horn twice sound,
Every burgess will be found
Eager in the warlike labor,
Striving to outdo his neighbor ;
God give them the victory ;
Say amen for charity.
In no other isle is known
Such a hospitable town ;
Joyously the people greet
Every stranger in their street.
Free is he to sell and buy,
And sustain no tax thereby.
Town and people once again
I commend to God. Amen.

VII.

REVOLT OF THE MUNSTER GARRISONS TO CROMWELL.

THE following are the depositions made by the leading "Revolters" in each of the garrisons.

CORK.

Colonel Richard Townsend, now resident in Castlehaven, English Protestant, at the declaring of Cork for the Parliament of England, October 16th, 1649, a prisoner in said city, being duly sworn, saith : That about three days before the declaring of Cork, Captain Robert Myhill came to this Examinant's chambers where he was committed, and informed him that Colonel Sterling, then governor of Cork, commanded him to acquaint this E. that the Lord Inchiquin had ordered Colonel Jefford should be sent to Bandon Bridge, and Colonel Warden, to the fort of Cork, and this E. to the fort of Kinsale the next morning : upon which tidings the E. with his partners were very much troubled, and did believe their separation was with intent to have them speedily executed. Whereupon Captain Myhill took E. aside, and advised him to endeavor their continuance in the place where they were, and he did believe it would be much to their security, and thereupon acquainted him of an intention of several persons to secure the city and fort of Cork and castle of Shandon for the Parliament of England and the then Lord Lieutenant of Ireland. He well remembered that the same night of the declaring he saw Colone John Jefford, William Warden, Charles Blunt, John Hodder, Lieutenant-Colonels William Reeves and Thomas Dowdridge, Captains Robert Myhill, Peter Carew, George Bell, Captain-Lieutenant Richard Burnell, Lieutenants Thomas Hewett and John Thomas, Ensigns Roland Langford, Samuel Pomeroy, Thomas Benger, Capt. Thomas Dethick, Thomas Powell, Captain Henry Rogers, and Thomas Boles, to be very active in securing said city, fort, and castle for the English interest.

Colonel Charles Blunt, now resident at Clonmel, English Protestant, at the declaring of Cork commanding a regiment of foot in Lord Inchiquin's army. That night he saw Jefford, Townsend, and Warden at first drawing of the men together at the mainguard, very active in promoting said work; and particularly that Colonel Jefford secured Colonel Sterling, then governor of Cork.

Captain Peter Carew,[1] now resident at Rosscarbery, at the declaring of Cork, a captain of foot in that city. Two months before the declaring of the city, E. and Captain Myhill had several meetings to contrive the surrender of Cork, which, by the blessing of God, was effected with the assistance of Colonels Townsend, Gifford, and Warden, then imprisoned for Inchiquin; and also one sergeant Hugh Buckland, then in the fort of Cork, under the command of Colonel Agmondisham Muschamp, then governor thereof, was of the council four days before, and did assist by removing a sentinel and giving an opportunity by placing of a ladder and entrance by a port-hole which was effected by the industry of Captain Robert Myhill, with a small party of men, said Muschamp being absent, who took the lieutenant, ensign, and about twenty more that kept the same.

Captain Robert Myhill, a captain in Colonel Sterling's regiment. About six weeks before the declaring of Cork, considering with himself the sad condition the

---

[1] The name is written, Carew, Cary, and Carey; the latter is the form used in the signature. His widow and son obtained a grant under the Act of Settlement of lands in the county of Cork, on the Blackwater, two miles east of Fermoy, where his descendants still reside.

English interest was then brought into, he cast about in his own thoughts what was best for him and the other English Protestants to do, in order to freeing himself and them. So went into the shop of one Captain Thomas Bowles, to whom he opened his mind, and told Bowles he thought it advisable to use some means for delivering himself and others from the bondage they were in (the Lord Inchiquin having joined with the Irish); and thus having a great influence on him, told him that he had about eight good men of his own company who, he was sure, would stand by him.

Bowles promised to influence the townspeople also. When several officers had secured the mainguard, the two ports of the city, and placed a guard upon Colonel Sterling and others whom they durst not trust, E. with fourteen private soldiers, about twelve o'clock the same night, went to surprise the fort, which he soon effected by going in at a port-hole where a sentinel was wont to be set, one Sergeant Buckland being promised £50 to remove said sentinel, and also he surprised in the fort a lieutenant and thirty-four soldiers, the governor Muschamp being that night at his farm, and having no knowledge of his design. Nor durst they inform him, being looked upon as a great enemy to the English interest.

William Sexton, mason, now resident at Cork, saw Thomas Hooper, and others, about eleven o'clock, making barricadoes at the mainguard with butcher's blocks and other materials, for better securing the same in case any rising should be in the town.

Colonel Robert Phayre, now governor of Cork, about the end of August, 1649, knew divers persons of his old acquaintance who were in Lord Inchiquin's army, and taken at the rout before Dublin, which he knew to be honest-hearted toward the English interests; and some of these stayed by his advice in Inchiquin's army to serve said interest; and therefore E. made it his request to Lord-Lieutenant Cromwell and Lord Ireton that such of said persons as he might choose might have paroles to come down to Munster, to procure their ransom and exchange, which was only a disguise for their employment thither in the county of Cork, and had instructions to several well-affected persons to inform them of the Lord Lieutenant's design to redeem the English inhabitants, and said county and the ports adjacent, from the bondage Inchiquin had brought them under.

YOUGHAL.

Ensign Nicholas Monkton, English Protestant, now resident at Ballingarry — in the county of Limerick, at the securing of Youghal for the parliament, an ensign in the town. A few days before the first declaring of Youghal, Captain Henry Smithick, acquainted E. with a resolution of several officers in Youghal to secure the town for the Parliament of England.

The same night on which they did declare, Captain John Widenham and others did meet to consider the best way for the prosecuting of the design, and to inform themselves what their expectations might be of Colonel Warden, who had promised to come with a party of horse to their assistance. Notwithstanding they had certain information that Colonel Warden, with others, were taken prisoners by the Lord of Inchiquin, yet they prosecuted their former resolution. The next morning after the declaring, the Lord of Inchiquin came before the town with a party of horse, and sent a messenger to desire that some might be sent to treat with him; and both Captain Widenham and Captain Thomas Graham went forth, and on the second and third day after there were conditions made between them; but what they were E. knoweth not, only that Sir Piercy Smyth, formerly governor by the Lord Inchiquin's appointment, was then restored to his command. And about a fortnight after Cork had declared for the English interest, Colonels Gifford and Warden came with a party of horse to secure the garrison of Youghal for the Parliament of England. About seven o'clock at night E. and others were drinking a pint of wine at the White Hart. There came in a little boy or maid and told them that Colonels Warden and Gifford were come with a party of horse. Whereupon they immediately ran down to the iron gate, where they found Sir Piercy Smyth, then governor, and Colonel Manhood, with some of their servants, having drawn the chain of the iron gate with an intent, as he conceives, to secure it till they had made some conditions. But E. with Dashwood and Smyth, observing Captain Widenham to be come with his company to the other side of the gate and calling to have the gate open, sent away Sir Piercy Smyth and Colonel Manhood to their homes (where they were secured), and immediately opened the gate.

Major Jasper Farmer, English Protestant, then resident at Garmore, in the county of Cork, was told by Major Foulke that his brother Lieutenant Foulke was sent by Colonel Phayre from Dublin to him, that he might engage as many English then of Inchiquin's army to do their utmost in securing the chief garrisons of Munster for the then Parliament. And among the rest Foulke engaged him to use his endeavors in the work. Whereupon he acquainted Colonel Richard Townsend and several others, who were ready to yield their assistance. Major Foulke told him that he would go to Youghal to engage the officers there, which he did; and some small time after there was a day appointed by Major Foulke, Colonels Townsend, Warden, and himself, to meet at Tallow, and there to make what party of horse they could, and intended from thence to have marched to Youghal, in order to have joined themselves with those who had engaged to secure the town. But so it was that one Johnson, who had taken his oath to be faithful in the business, discovered the same to the Lord of Inchiquin, and by that means Inchiquin sent a party to Tallow and apprehended Colonels Warden and Gifford, and so prevented the bringing of the horse to Youghal. Townsend made his escape into the country; but the next morning he was apprehended in his own house. But by this time the town of Youghal had actually declared for the Parliament, which he and Major Foulke hearing of, took a cott and went down by water to Youghal, and having joined themselves with the officers there, at a council of war resolved to maintain the town for the English interest. The next day after the town declared, Inchiquin came with force and encamped before the town, and it was by the council resolved that the town should be defended against him. The soldiers upon the walls cried out that the town might be defended against Inchiquin and the Irish; but after some jealousy of Captains Widenham and Graham, articles were agreed upon by consent of the officers for the redelivering of the said garrison to Inchiquin, upon conditions that none of the English might be drawn out of the said town nor Irish put in.

Colonel John Widenham, English Protestant, now residing at Adare, in the county of Limerick, and at the time of securing of Youghal for the Parliament of England and the Lord Lieutenant of Ireland a captain in the said town. At the first declaring of Youghal he and Captain Smithick had frequent consultations about the securing of the town; and that which moved the discourse and action was the sense that Captain S. had of the danger the town was then in, and the English interest, for that the Lord Inchiquin had not only joined with the Irish, but also intended to place an Irish garrison in the town and to draw out the English then in the town. Ensign Nicholas Monkton was within the iron gate when the gate was opened to let him in with his company, and some of the party of horse that came from Cork.

KINSALE.

Mr. Robert Southwell, at the rendition of Kinsale to the Parliament, Nov. 12th, 1649, an inhabitant of Kinsale, remembers that a few days before, Major Woodliff came to Kinsale with about 60 soldiers, who were received into the town, being reputed a friend; being Englishmen made them to be joyfully received. They maintained the guard of the Englishtown. Near 100 of the Irish soldiers that came into the town from the fort were taken, disarmed, and secured in the magazine. At the time of Cork's declaring for the Parliament, the town of Kinsale was secured by the English and Irish inhabitants of the same, and not by the soldiers of the army in pay; and before the declaring of Cork Colonel Crosby, with about 500 men, was sent by Lord Inchiquin to secure the fort and town for the King, which it could not oppose, though very fearful to receive them being Irish. About a fortnight before the town declared, Crosby drew all his soldiers out of the town into the fort. About Nov. 12th, 1649, the inhabitants convened themselves together, viz., the chief of both Irish and English, and agreed to declare for the Commonwealth, in order to which they drew up a letter, which they subscribed, and directed to Lord Broghill and Colonel Phayre, acquainting them, and desiring some assistance of horse and foot for the taking of the fort, to which work the inhabitants did yield their best endeavors. An answer was returned with assurance that said inhabitants should be reckoned under the same care with their own party, and promised assistance, which was sent next day; and Captain Cuffe was sent with a troop of horse into the barony of Coursies, on the fort side, to besiege it; and Colonel Gifford with some others came to Kinsale, where the towns-people planted a gun upon Compass Hill over against the fort, from whence were made about six or seven shot, and soon after it was delivered to Lord Broghill upon conditions.

William Wolf, of Cork, at the rendition of Cork an inhabitant of the town. At the

time of Cork's declaring, the town of Kinsale was wholly secured by the English and Irish inhabitants for Lord Inchiquin; and at the arrival of Colonel Crosby with about 600 men, the commonalty of the town shut the gates against him; but the sovereign and other chief men of the town went out to Crosby and agreed that he and his party should come into the town, where he stayed about a week, and then drew into the fort. He did exceedingly oppress the town, demanding not only cadows, but also exacting money, from the inhabitants and meat from several merchants, which did put the town upon declaring, and which he believes was the only reason for so doing. On Tuesday night being resolved to declare, they sent for some of the Irish inhabitants, in particular the sovereign, to come and join with them; but at first he was unwilling and wept, but at length consented, and sent a letter to Cork to Lord Broghill.

TIMOLEAGUE.

John Godfrey, minister of Timoleague, at the time of the rendition of Timoleague castle for the Parliament, November, 1649, an inhabitant of Timoleague. Remembers that Captain Swete acquainted him of his purpose to secure the castle for the English interest, and that he had despatched letters into England intimating so much, and likewise for the coming of shipping into the bay. That afterwards Swete acquainted him that he had received orders from Lord Inchiquin to march with his company from the castle, and desired E. to frame a petition in the name of the gentlemen and other inhabitants of the country and present it to Lieutenant General Barry, that Swete and his company might be continued among them.

John Barnes, of Clonakilty, English Protestant, at the rendition of the castle of Timoleague sergeant in the castle. Remembers Captain Swete, then governor and captain of the castle, did acquaint him of his intention of securing the castle for Parliament, and willed deponent to discourse his company, which consisted of about 32 men in the castle, and try whether they would join in the design. He did discourse with them, and finding them ready to join, acquainted Swete, who directed E. to bring them two or three, at a time to himself, which was done. E. was sent to Bandon to inform Lord Broghill that they had secured the castle for the Parliament, and had seven Irish prisoners. He found Lord Broghill had marched from Bandon, and left Colonel

Warden governor, who ordered the prisoners to be brought to Bandon.

BANDONBRIDGE.

Abraham Savage, now resident at Bandonbridge and at the time of the rendition. Suddenly after the declaration of Cork for the Parliament, Lord Inchiquin, being jealous of the town following the example of Cork, ordered Captain Constantine with a troop of horse to possess himself of said town, and disarm all townsmen; and Inchiquin ordered a company or two of Irish into the town, but soon after observing the disaffection of the town towards the Irish soldiers, ordered one Colonel Francis Courtenay to be governor, who brought in his own company, and soon after all the Irish were removed; and the townsmen came several times to E., expressing their readiness to attempt the seizing of the governor, officers, and guards then in the town, and secure it for the Parliament, but could not effect their purpose; and also Captain Braly and some others, a day or two before Broghill came with a force against the town, secured the west guard of the town, and disarmed the soldiers, turning them out; but it being so sudden a business, such as were appointed to seize on the other guards were prevented, the design being discovered. And so those persons were besieged in the said guard by the soldiers then in town, and several shots made at them, so they were constrained to yield themselves prisoners; and that night the inhabitants dispatched William Bull to Lord Broghill, informing him of the danger of the persons taken prisoners, and desiring him with some forces to come before the town, the inhabitants engaging that if the governor did not deliver up the town, they having his countenance would open the postern gate by seizing on the sentinel, and receive them into the town; but when Lord Broghill came, hostages were sent forth, and the town suddenly delivered by the Governor on conditions only made for himself and his soldiers.

Nathaniel Cleere, of Bandonbridge, merchant. Remembers the inhabitants of the town, about Nov. 16th, in the forenoon, did endeavor to surprise the guard of the west gate, at which time other persons were appointed to surprise two other guards, but were discovered and imprisoned. Next day Lord Broghill came against the town with a party of horse and foot, when those persons told the governor, Colonel Courtenay, that it was in vain for him to oppose them, for they were resolved to deliver up said town to Lord Broghill; thereupon Colonel Courtenay desired them not to deliver him up before he had one hour's time to make conditions for himself and party, which was granted; and that time expired, Mr. Savage and an officer belonging to the said colonel were sent forth to treat with Lord Broghill, to whose pleasure the town wholly referred itself. And there was only one gun fired from a flanker by one of Courtenay's gunners, who with his men departed second next day, and some the day following; and the inhabitants live since quietly without giving any assistance to the Irish or other enemies of the Commonwealth.

HALLBOWLINE.

Edward Holwell, in October, 1649, a sergeant employed in the fort. The second day after the rendition of Cork, being in the fort, and having with him Thomas Davis, Sergeant Richard Estcourt, gunner, and some private soldiers, said Davis and E. conferred, and speedily resolved to deliver the fort, and thereupon called the gunner, captain, and soldiers, and acquainted them with their resolution, who were ready and gave their assistance, first in securing Captain Whitcraft, governor there, and his lieutenant, and setting the guards for keeping said fort for the Commonwealth, and sent away the captain and lieutenant prisoners to Cork.

Richard Estcourt, gunner. Two days after the declaring of Cork, the governor sent his lieutenant to Lord Inchiquin, to obtain more forces for securing of Hallbowline. The next morning Sergeant Davis came to E. and consulted how they might secure the governor and deliver up the garrison for the use of the Parliament, which was done. And the same boat which carried up the captain to Cork brought down relief both of men and provisions for the garrison, and the day following more relief was sent from Cork.

VIII

THE CLONMACNOISE DECREES.

Declaration of the Bishops and Clergy assembled at Clonmacnoise, 4th December, 1649.

By the Ecclesiastical Congregation of the Kingdom of Ireland, we, the Archbishops, Bishops, and other Ordinaries and Prelates of this Kingdom of Ireland, having met at Clonmacnoise *proprio motu* on the 4th day of December in the year of our Lord God, 1649, taking into our consideration among other the affairs then agitated and determinated for the preservation of the Kingdom, that many of our flock are misled with a vain opinion of hopes that the Commander-in-chief of the rebel forces, commonly called Parliamentarians, would afford them good conditions, and that relying thereon, they suffer utter destruction of religion, lives, and fortunes, if not prevented. To undeceive them in this their ungrounded expectation, we do hereby declare as a most certain truth that the enemy's resolution is to extirpate the Catholic religion out of all his Majesty's dominions, as by their several covenants doth appear, and the practice wherever their power doth extend, as is manifested by Cromwell's letter of the 19th of October, 1649, to the then Governor of Ross; his words are: " for that which you mention concerning liberty of religion, I meddle not with any man's conscience; but if by liberty of conscience you mean a liberty to exercise the Mass, I judge it best to use plain dealing and to let you know, where the Parliament have power, that will not be allowed of." This tyrannical resolution they have put in execution in Wexford, Drogheda, Ross, and elsewhere; and it is notoriously known that by the Acts of Parliament called the Acts of Subscription, the estates of the inhabitants of this Kingdom are sold, so there remaineth now no more but to put the purchasers in possession by the power of forces drawn out of England. And for the common sort of people, towards whom if they show any more moderate usage at the present, it is to no other end but for their private advantage and for the better support of their army, intending at the close of their conquest (if they can effect the same, as God forbid) to root out the commons also, and plant this land with colonies to be brought hither out of England, as witness the number they have already sent hence for the Tobacco Island, and put enemies in their places.

And in effect, this banishment and other destructions of the common people must follow the resolution of extirpating the Catholic religion, which is not to be effected without the massacring or banishment of the Catholic inhabitants.

We cannot, therefore, in our duty to God and in discharge of the care we are obliged to have for the preservation of our flocks, but admonish them not to delude and lose themselves with the vain expectation of conditions to be had from that merciless enemy. And, consequently, we beseech the gentry and inhabitants, for God's glory and their own safety, to the uttermost of their power to contribute with patience to the support of the war against that enemy, in hope that by the blessing of God they may be rescued from the threatened evils, and in time be permitted to serve God in their native country, and enjoy their estates and the fruits of their labors, free from such heavy levies or any other such taxes as they bear at present; admonishing also those that are enlisted of the army to prosecute constantly, according to each man's charge, the trust reposed in them, the opposition of the common enemy in so just a war as is that they have undertaken for their religion, king, and country, as they expect the blessing of God to fall on their actions. And that to avoid God's heavy judgment and the indignation of their native country, they neither plunder nor oppress the people, nor suffer any under their charge to commit any extortion or oppression, so far as they shall lie in their power to prevent.

Declaration of the Bishops and others assembled at Clonmacnoise, 13th December, 1649.

Whereas heretofore many of the clergy and laity did in their actions and proceedings express much discontent and divisions of mind, grounding the same on the late difference of opinion which happened amongst the prelates and the laity, by which the nation was not so well united as was necessary in this time of great danger, wherein all as with one heart and hand ought to oppose the common enemy. We, the Archbishops, Bishops, and Prelates of this Kingdom met, *motu proprio*, at Clonmacnoise, 4th December, 1649, having removed all difference among us, not entering into the merits of diversities of former opinions, thought good for the removing of all jealousies from our own thoughts, hearts, and resolutions, and from others who had relation or were adherent to the former diversity of opinion, to manifest hereby to all the world that the said divisions and jealousies grounded thereupon are now forgotten and forgiven among us on all sides as aforesaid. And that all and every of us, the above Archbishops, Bishops, and Prelates, are now by the blessing of God as one body united, and that we will, as becometh charity and our pastoral charge, stand all of us as one entire body, for the interest and immunities of the Church, and of every the Prelates and Bishops thereof, and for the honor and dignity, estate, right, and possession of all and every the said Archbishops, Bishops, and other Prelates. And we will, as one entire and united body, forward by our counsel, action, and devices, the advancement of his Majesty's rights and the good of this nation in general and in particular occasions according to our power, and that none of us, in any occasion whatsoever concerning the Catholic religion or the good of this Kingdom of Ireland, will in any respect single himself, or be, or seem opposite to the rest of us, but will hold firm and entire in one sense, as aforesaid, hereby detesting the actions, thoughts, and discourses of any that shall renew the least memory of the differences past, or give any ground of future differences among us, and do in the name of Jesus Christ exhort all our flock to the like brotherly affection and union, and to the like detestation of all past differences or jealousies as aforesaid, arising hitherto among them. And we desire that this our declaration be printed and published in each parish, by command of the respective Ordinaries, ut videant opera vestra bona et glorificent Patrem vestrum qui in cœlis est.

Datum apud Clonmacnoise, 13 Decembris, 1649.

HUGO, Ardmachanus.
FR. THOMAS, Dubliniensis.
THOMAS, Casselensis.
JOANNES, Archiep. Tuamensis.
FR. BOETIUS, Elphinensis.
FR. EDMUNDUS, Laghlinensis et Procurator Waterfordiensis.
EMERUS, Clogherensis.
ROBERTUS, Corcagiensis et Cluanensis.
NICOLAUS, Fernensis.
EDMUNDUS, Lymericen. et Procurator Episcopi Ossorien.
FRANCISCUS, Aladensis.
ANDREAS, Fenaborensis.
JOANNES, Laonensis.
FR. OLIVERIUS, Dromorensis.
FR. ANTONIUS, Clonmacnoisensis.
FR. HUGO, Duacensis.
Fr. ARTHURUS, Dunensis et Connorensis.
FR. TERENTIUS, Imolacensis.
FR. PATRITIUS, Ardachadensis.
OLIVERIUS DEISE, Procurator Episcopi Midensis.
DR. JOANNES HUSSEI, Procurator Ep. Ardfertensis.

FR. JOANNES CANTWELL, Abbas S. Crucis.
DR. THADEUS CLERY, Procurator Episcopi Rapotensis.
FR. GREGORIUS O'FERRALL, Provincialis fratrum min.
WALTERUS, Ep. Clonfertensis, Congregationis Secretarius.

Decrees of the Bishops, &c., assembled at Clonmacnoise, 13th December, 1649.

We, the Archbishops, Bishops, and other Ordinaries and Prelates of the Kingdom of Ireland, having met at Clonmacnoise, *proprio motu*, the 4th day of December, in the year of our Lord 1649, to consider of the best means to unite our flocks for averting God's wrath fallen on this nation, now bleeding under the evils that famine, plague, and war bring after them, for effecting a present union, decreed the ensuing acts :—

1. We order and decree as an Act of this Congregation, that all Archbishops and other Ordinaries within their respective dioceses shall enjoin public prayers, fasting, general confessions, and receiving, and other works of piety, *toties quoties*, to withdraw from this nation God's anger and to render them capable of his mercies.

2. We order and decree as an Act of this Congregation, that a Declaration be issued from us, letting the people know how vain it is for them to expect from the common enemy commanded by Cromwell, by authority from the rebels of England, any assurance of their religion, lives, or fortunes.

3. We order, and decree as an Act of this Congregation, that all the pastors and preachers be enjoined to preach unity. And for inducing the people thereunto, to declare unto them the absolute necessity that is for the same, and as the chief means to preserve the nation against the extirpation and destruction of their religion and fortunes resolved on by the Enemy. And we hereby do manifest our detestation against all such divisions between either provinces or families, or between old English and old Irish, or any of the English or Scots adhering to his Majesty. And we decree and order, that all ecclesiastical persons fomenting such dissensions or unnatural divisions be punished by their respective prelates and superiors, juxta gravitatem excessus, et (si opus fuerit) suspendantur beneficiati et pastores a beneficio et officio ad certum tempus, religiosi autem a divinis juxta circumstantias delicti. Leaving the laity offending in this kind to be corrected by

the civil magistrate by imprisonment, fine, banishment, or otherwise, as to them shall seem best for plucking by the roots so odious a crime; the execution whereof we most earnestly recommend to all those having power and that are concerned therein, as they will answer to God for the evils that thereout may ensue.

4. We decree and declare excommunicated those highway robbers commonly called the Idle Boys, that take away the goods of honest men or force men to pay them contribution; and we likewise declare excommunicated all such as succour or harbor them, or bestow or sell any victualling, or buy cattle or any other thing else wittingly from them; likewise all ecclesiastical persons ministering sacraments to such robbers or Idle Boys, or burying them in holy grave, to be suspended ab officio et beneficio si quod habent, by their respective superiors juxta gravitatem delicti. This our decree is to oblige within fifteen days after the publication thereof in the respective dioceses.

Datum apud Clonmacnoise, 13 Decembris, 1649. (Here follow the same signatures as before.)

IX.

A Declaration of the Lord Lieutenant of Ireland. For the Undeceiving of Deluded and Seduced People: which may be satisfactory to all that do not shut their eyes against the light: In answer to certain late Declarations and Acts framed by the Irish Popish Prelates and Clergy in a Conventicle at Clonmacnoise. [1]

Having lately perused a Book printed at Kilkenny in the year 1649, containing divers Declarations and Acts of the Popish Prelates and Clergy framed in a late Conventicle at Clonmacnoise, the 4th day of December, in the year aforesaid, I thought fit to give a brief Answer unto the same.

<hr>

[1] Carlyle's *Letters*, &c., vol. ii. p. 130, &c. We give this "Declaration" in full, as it contains a complete statement of the policy, civil and religious, pursued by Cromwell and his party in dealing with Ireland. We beg to refer the reader who wishes to see how that policy was carried out, to Mr. Prendergast's work, *The Cromwellian Settlement of Ireland*, which John Mitchel, no mean authority on such a matter, has declared to be "the most perfect monograph of one special and cardinal point of our Irish history." *Reply to Froude*, p. 21.

And first to the first;— which is a Declaration wherein (having premised the reconciliation of some differences among themselves), they come to state their War, upon the interest of their Church, of his Majesty, and the Nation, and their resolution to prosecute the same with unity. All which will deserve a particular survey.

The Meeting of the Archbishops, Bishops, and other Prelates at Clonmacnoise is by them said to be *proprio motu*. By which term they would have the world believe that the Secular Power hath nothing to do to appoint or superintend their spiritual Conventions, as they call them ;— although in the said meetings they take upon them to intermeddle in all secular affairs; as by the sequel appears. But first for their "Union" they so much boast of. If any wise man shall seriously consider what they pretend the grounds of their "differences" to have been, and the way and course they have taken to reconcile the same; and their expressions thereabout, and the ends for which, and their resolutions how. to carry on their great design declared for; he must needs think slightly of their said union. And also for this, That they resolve all other men's consent into their own, without consulting them at all !

The subject of this reconciliation was, as they say, "the Clergy and Laity." The discontent and division itself was grounded on the late difference of opinion, happening amongst the "Prelates and Laity." I wonder not at differences of opinion, at discontents and divisions, where so Antichristian and dividing a term as "Clergy and Laity" is given and received. A term unknown to any save the Antichristian Church, and such as derive themselves from her : *ab initio non fuit sic.* The most pure and primitive times, as they best know what true *union* was, so in all addresses to the several churches they wrote unto, not one word of this. The members of the Church are styled "Brethren and Saints of the same household of Faith ;" although they had orders and distinctions among them for administration of ordinances — of a far different use and character from yours,— yet it no where occasioned them to say, *contemptim* and by way of lessening in contradistinguishing "Laity and Clergy." It was your pride that begat this expression. And it is for filthy lucre's sake that you keep it up, that by making the people believe that they are not so holy as yourselves, they might for their penny purchase some sanctity from you, and that you might bridle, saddle, and ride them at your pleasure; and do, as is most true of you, as the Scribes and Pharisees of old did by their Laity,—keep the knowledge of the law from them, and then be able in all their pride to say, "This people, that know not the Law, are cursed."

And no wonder,—to speak more nearly to your "differences" and "union,"—if it lie in the Prelates' power to make the Clergy and Laity go together by the ears when they please, but that they may as easily make a simple and senseless reconciliation! Which will last until the next Nuncio comes from Rome with supermandatory advices, and then this Gordian knot must be cut, and the poor Laity forced to dance to a new tune.

I say not this as being troubled at your "union." By the grace of God, we fear not, we care not for it. Your covenant is with Death and Hell; your union is like that of Simeon and Levi: "Associate yourselves, and ye shall be broken in pieces; take counsel together, and it shall come to naught!" For, though it becomes us to be humble in respect of ourselves, yet we can say to you: God is not with you. You say, your union is "against a common enemy;" and to this if you will be talking, of "union," I will give you some wormwood to bite on, by which it will appear God is not with you.

Who was it that created this "common enemy" (I suppose you mean Englishmen)? The English? Remember, ye hypocrites, Ireland was once united to England. Englishmen had good inheritances which many of them purchased with their money, they and their ancestors, from you and your ancestors. They had good Leases from Irishmen, for long times to come; great stocks thereupon; houses and plantations erected at their own cost and charge. They lived peaceably and honestly amongst you. You had generally equal benefit of the protection of England with them; and equal justice from the Laws, saving what was necessary for the State, out of reasons of State, to put upon some few people, apt to rebel upon the instigation of such as you. You broke this "union." You, unprovoked, put the English to the most unheard-of and most barbarous Massacre (without respect of age or sex), that the sun ever beheld; and at a time when Ireland was in perfect Peace. And when, through the example of English Industry, through commerce and traffic, that which was in the Natives' hands was better to them than if all Ireland had been in their possession, and not an Englishman in it. And yet then, I say, was this unheard-of villainy perpetrated,—by your instigation, who boast of "peace-making" and "union against this common enemy." What think you: by this time, is not my assertion true? Is God, will God, be with you?

I am confident He will not! And though you will comprehend Old English, New English, Scotch or whom else you will, in the bosom of your Catholic charity, yet shall not this save you from breaking. I tell you and them, you will fare the worse for their sakes. Because I cannot but believe some of them go against, some stifle, their consciences. And it is not the fig-leaf of pretence that "they fight for their King," will serve their turn: when really they fight in protection of men of so much prodigious of blood; and with men who have declared the ground of their "union" and fighting, as you have stated it in this your Declaration, to be *Bellum Prælaticum et Religiosum*, in the first and primary intention of it. Especially when they shall consider your principles: that except what fear makes you comply with, viz., that alone without their concurrence you are not able to carry on your work of War,—you are ready, whenever you shall get the power into your hands, to kick them off, too, as some late experiences have sufficiently manifested! And thus we come to the Design, you being thus wholesomely "united," which is intended to be prosecuted by you.

Your words are these: "That all and every of us, the above Archbishops, Bishops, and Prelates, are now, by the blessing of God, as one body united. And that we will, as becometh charity and our pastoral charge, stand all of us, as one entire body, for the interest and immunities of our Church and of every the Bishops and Prelates thereof; and for the honor, dignity, estate, right, and possessions of all and every of the said Archbishops, Bishops, and other Prelates. And we will, as one entire and united body, forward by our counsels, actions, and devices the advancement of his Majesty's rights and the good of this Nation, in general and in particular occasions, to our power. And that none of us in any occasion whatsoever concerning the Catholic religion or the good of this Kingdom of Ireland, will in any respect single himself; or be or seem opposite to the rest of us; but will hold firm and entire in one sense, as aforesaid, &c."

And now, if there were no other quarrel

against you but this, which you make to be the principal and first ground of your Quarrel ; to wit, As so standing for the rights of your "Church," falsely so called, and for the rights of your "Archbishops, Bishops, and Prelates," as to engage People and Nations into blood therefor :— this alone would be your confusion. I ask you, Is it for the "lay-fee," as you call it, or for the Revenue belonging to your Church, that you will after this manner contend? Or is it your jurisdiction, or the exercise of your Ecclesiastical Authority? Or is it the Faith of your Church? Let me tell you, Not for all or any of these is it lawful for the ministers of Christ, as you would be thought to be, thus to contend. And therefore we will consider them apart.

For the first, if it were "St. Peter's Patrimony," as you term it, that would be somewhat that you lawfully came by! But I must tell you. Your predecessors cheated poor seduced men in their weakness on their death-beds ; or otherwise unlawfully came by most of this you pretend to. And Peter, though he was somewhat too forward to draw the sword in a better cause, yet if that weapon, not being proper to the business on hands, was to be put up in the case, he must not, or would he, have drawn it in this. And that blessed Apostle Paul, who said, "the laborer was worthy of his hire," chose rather to make tents than be burthensome to the Churches. I would you had either of these Good Men's spirits ; on condition your Revenues were doubled to what the best times ever made them to your predecessors! The same answer may be given to that of your "Power and Jurisdiction," and to that pre-eminence of Prelacy you so dearly love. Only consider what the Master of these same Apostles said to them : "So it shall not be amongst you. Whoever will be chief shall be servant of all." For He Himself came not to be ministered unto, but to minister. And by this he that runs may read of what tribe you are.

And surely if these, that are outward things, may not thus be contended for, how much less may the doctrines of Faith, which are the works of Grace and the Spirit, be endeavoured by so unsuitable means! He that bids us "contend for the Faith once delivered to the Saints," tells us that we should do it by "avoiding the spirit of Cain, Corah, and Balaam ;" and by "building up ourselves in the most holy Faith," not pinning it

upon other men's sleeves. Praying "in the Holy Ghost ;" not mumbling over Matins. Keeping "ourselves in the love of God ;" not destroying men because they will not be of our Faith. "Waiting for the mercy of Jesus Christ ;" not cruel, but merciful! But, alas, why is this said? Why are these pearls cast before you? You are resolved not to be charmed from "using the instrument of a foolish shepherd." You are a part of Anti-Christ," whose Kingdom the Scripture so expressly says should be "laid in blood ;" yea, "in the blood of the Saints." You have shed great store of that already; and ere it be long, you must all of you have blood to drink, "even the dregs of the fury and the wrath of God, which will be poured out unto you."

In the next place, you state the "interest of his Majesty," as you say. And this you hope will draw some English and Scotch to your party. But what "Majesty" is it you mean? Is it France, or Spain, or Scotland? Speak plainly You have, some of you lately, been harping, or else we are misinformed, upon his Majesty of Spain to be your Protector. Was it because his Majesty of Scotland was too little a Majesty for your purpose? We know you love great Majesties. Or is it because he is not fully come over to you in point of religion? If he be short in that, you will quickly find out, upon that score, another "Majesty." His Father, who complied with you too much, you rejected ; and now you would make the world believe that you make the Son's interest a great part of your Quarrel.

How can we but think there is some reserve in this? And that the Son has agreed to do somewhat more for you than ever his Father did? Or else tell us : Whence this new zeal is? That the Father did too much for you, in all Protestant judgments, instead of many instanced let this be considered : What one of your own Doctors, Dr. Enos, of Dublin, who writing against the Agreement made between the Lord of Ormonde and the Irish Catholics, finds fault with it and says it was "nothing so good as that the Earl of Glamorgan had warrant from the King to make ; but exceeding far short of what Lord George Digby had warrant to agree with the Pope himself at Rome, in favour of the Irish Catholics." I intend not this to you : but to such Protestants as may incline to you, and to join with you upon this single account, which is the only appearing inducement to them ; seeing there is so much probability of ill in this abstracted. And so much certainty of ill in fighting for the Romish Religion against the Protestant; and fighting with men under the guilt of so horrid a Massacre. From participating in which Guilt, whilst they take part with them, they will never be able to assoil themselves, either before God or good men.

In the last place, you are pleased, having, after your usual manner, remembered yourselves first and "his Majesty," as you call him, next, like a man of your tribe, with his *Ego et Rex meus*, you are pleased to take the people into consideration. Lest they should seem to be forgotten: or rather you would make me believe they are much in your thoughts. Indeed I think they are! Alas, poor "Laity!" That you and your King might ride them and jade them, as your Church hath done, and as your King hath done by your means, almost in all ages! But it would not be hard to prophesy, That the beasts being stung and kicking, this world will not last always. Arbitrary power men begin to be weary of in Kings and Churchmen; their juggle between them materially to uphold Civil and Ecclesiastical Tyranny begins to be transparent. Some have cast off both, and hope by the grace of God to keep so. Others are at it! Many thoughts are laid about it, which will have their issue and vent. This principle, That People are for Kings and Churches, and Saints are for the Pope or Churchmen, as you call them, begins to be exploded: and therefore I wonder not to see the Fraternity so much enraged. I wish "the People" wiser than to be troubled at you; or solicitous for what you say or do.

But it seems, notwithstanding all this, you would fain have them believe it is their good you seek. And to cozen them, in deed and in truth, is the scope of your whole Declaration, and of your Acts and Decrees in your foresaid Printed Book. Therefore to discover and unveil those falsities, and to let them know what they are to trust to, from me, is the principal end of this my Declaration. That if I be not able to do good upon them, which I most desire,— and yet in that I shall not seek to gain them by flattery: but tell them the worst, in plainness, and that which I am sure will not be acceptable to you, and if I cannot gain them, I shall have comfort in this, that I have freed my own soul from the guilt of the evil that shall ensue, and on this subject I hope to leave nothing unanswered in your said Declarations and Decrees, at Clonmacnoise.

And because you carry on your matter somewhat confusedly, I shall therefore bring all that you have said into some order; that so we may the better discern what every thing signifies, and give answer thereunto.

You forewarn the People of their danger, which you make to consist : First, "in the extirpation of the Catholic Religion ; " Secondly, " in the destruction of their lives ; " Thirdly, " in the ruin of their Fortunes," to avoid all which you forewarn them; First, that they be not deceived by the Commander-in-Chief of the Parliament Forces; and in the next place, having stated your War, as aforesaid, you give them your positive advice and counsel to engage in blood. And lastly, bestow upon them a collation in Four Ecclesiastical Decrees or Orders, which will signify as little, being performed by your spirit, as if you had said nothing. And the obligation to all this you make to be your Pastoral relation to them, " over your Flocks."

To which last a word or two. I wonder how this relation was brought about! If they be Flocks, and you ambitious of the relative term? You are Pastors; but it is by an antiphrasis, a *minime pascendo!* You either teach the People not at all; or else you do it, as some of you came to this Conventicle who were sent by others, *tanquam Procuratores*, as your manner is, by sending a company of silly, ignorant Priests, who can but say the Mass, and scarcely that intelligibly: or with such stuff as these your senseless Declarations and Edicts! But how dare you assume to call these men your "Flocks," whom you have plunged into so horrid a Rebellion, by which you have made them and their country almost a ruinous heap? And whom you have fleeced, and polled, and peeled hitherto, and make it quite your business to do so still. You cannot feed them! You poison them with your false, abominable, and Antichristian doctrine and practices. You keep the Word of God from them; and instead thereof give them your senseless Orders and Traditions. You teach them " implicit belief ; " he that goes amongst them may find many that do not understand anything in the matters of your Religion. I have had few better answers from any since I came into Ireland that are of your Flocks than this, " That indeed they did not trouble themselves about matters of religion, but left that to the Church." Thus are your "Flocks" fed; and such credit have you of them. But they must take heed of "losing their religion." Alas! poor creatures, what have they to lose?

Concerning this is your grand caveat. And to back this, you tell them of " Resolutions and Covenants to extirpate the Catholic Religion out of all his Majesty's Dominions." And you instance in " Cromwell's Letter of the 19th of October, 1649, to the then Governor of Ross," repeating his words, which are as follows, viz : " For that which you mention concerning liberty of conscience, I meddle not with any man's conscience. But if by liberty of conscience you mean a liberty to exercise the Mass, I judge it best to use plain dealing, and to let you know, Where the Parliament of England have power, that will not be allowed of.' And this you call a " tyrannical Resolution : " which you say hath been put in execution in Wexford, Ross, and Tredah.

Now let us consider. First, you say, The design is, to extirpate the Catholic Religion. Let us see your honesty herein. Your word "extirpate " is as ill-collected from these grounds, and as senseless as the word " Catholic," ordinarily used by you when you mention the Roman Catholic Church. The word " extirpate " means a thing already rooted and established ; which word is made good by the proof of " Covenants," by that Letter expressing the non-toleration of the Mass (wherein, it seems; you place all the " Catholic Religion," and there you show some ingenuity), and your instance of what was practiced in the three Towns afore-mentioned : do these prove, either considered apart or all together, the "extirpation of the Catholic Religion? "

By what law was the Mass exercised in these places, or in any of the Dominions of England or Ireland, or Kingdom of Scotland? You were *intruders* herein : you were open violators of the known Laws! And yet you call the " Covenant," and that in the Letter, and these practices " Extirpation " of the Catholic Religion — thus again set on foot by you by the advantage of your Rebellion and shaking off the just Authority of the State of England over you ! Whereas, I dare be confident to you, you durst not own the saying of one Mass above these eighty years in Ireland. And through the troubles you made, and through the

miseries you brought on this Nation and the poor People thereof, your numbers, which is very ominous, increasing with the *wolves*, through the desolations you made in the Country, did you recover again the exercise of your Mass ? And for the maintenance of this, thus gained, you would make the poor People believe that it is ghostly counsel, and given in love to them as your " Flocks," That they should run into Wars, and venture lives, and all upon such a ground as this ! But if God be pleased to unveil you of your sheep's-clothing, that they may see how they have been deluded, and by whom, I shall exceedingly rejoice ; and indeed, for their sakes only have I given you these competent characters, for *their* good, if God shall so bless it.

And now for them, I do particularly declare what they may expect at my hands in this point. Wherein you will easily perceive that, as I neither have, nor shall flatter you, so neither shall I go about to delude them with specious pretences, as you have ever done.

First, therefore : I shall not, where I have power, and the Lord is pleased to bless me, suffer the exercise of the Mass where I can take notice of it. Nor suffer you that are Papists, where I can find you seducing the People, or by any overt act violating the Laws that are established ; but if you come into my hands, I shall cause to be inflicted the punishments appointed by the Laws, to use your own term, " *secundum gravitatem delicti*," upon you ; and to reduce things to their former state on this behalf. As for the People, what thoughts they have in the matter of Religion in their own breasts I cannot reach : but shall think it my duty, if they walk honestly and peaceably, Not to cause them in the least to suffer for the same. And shall endeavor to walk patiently and in love towards them, to see if at any time it shall please God to give them another or a better mind. And all men under the power of England, within this Dominion, are hereby required and enjoined strictly and religiously to do the same.

To the *second*, which is " the destruction of the Lives of the Inhabitants of this Nation :" to make it good that this is designed, they give not one reason. Which is either because they have none to give ; or else for that they believe the People will receive everything for truth they say ; which they have too well taught them, and God knows the People are too apt, to do.

But I will a little help them. They speak, indeed, of "rooting out the common People;" and also, by way of consequent, that the extirpating the Catholic Religion is not to be effected without the "massacring, destroying, or banishing the Catholic Inhabitants." Which how analogical an argument this is, I shall easily make appear by and by.

Alas ! the generality of "the Inhabitants" are poor " Laity," as you call them, and ignorant of the grounds of the "Catholic Religion." Are they then so interwoven with your Church Interest as that the absence of *them* makes your Catholic Religion fall to the ground ? We know you think not so. You reckon yourselves, and yourselves only, the pillars and supporters thereof ; and the Common People, as far as they have the exercise of the club-law, and like the ass you ride on, obey your commands. But concerning these relations of your Religion, enough has been spoken in another place; only you love to mix things for your advantage.

But to your logic. Here is your argument: The design is to extirpate the Catholic Religion ; but this is not to be done but by the massacring, banishing, or otherwise destroying the Catholic Inhabitants: *ergo*, it is designed to massacre, banish, and destroy the Catholic Inhabitants. To try this no-concluding argument, but yet well enough agreeing with your learning, I give you this dilemma ; by which it will appear that whether your religion be true or false, this will not follow : If your Religion be the true Religion, yet if a Nation may degenerate from the true Religion and apostatise, as too many have done (through the seducements of your Roman Church), then it will not follow that men must be " massacred, banished, or otherwise destroyed," necessarily ; no, not as to the change of the *true* Religion in a Nation or Country ! Only the argument doth wonderfully well agree with your principles and practice, you having chiefly made use of fire and sword, in all the changes in Religion that you have made in the world. If it be change of your Catholic Religion so-called, it will not follow, because there may be found out another means than "massacring, destruction, and banishing," to wit, the Word of God ; which is able to convert. A means which you as little know as practise, which, indeed, you deprive the People of ! Together with humanity, good life, equal and honest dealing with men of a different opinion ; which we desire to exercise

towards this poor People, if you, by your wicked counsel, make them not incapable to receive it, by putting them into blood !

And therefore, by this also, your false and twisted dealing may be a little discovered. Well, your words are, " Massacre, destroy, and banish." Good now. Give us an instance of one man since my coming into Ireland, not in arms, massacred, destroyed, or banished ; concerning the massacre or the destruction of whom justice hath not been done, or endeavored to be done. And as for the other of banishment, I must now speak unto the People, whom you would delude, and whom this most concerns; that they may know in this also what to expect at my hands.

The question is of the destruction of life ; or of that which is little inferior to it, to wit, of banishment. I shall not willingly take, or suffer to be taken away, the life of any man not in arms, but by the trial to which the People of this Nation are subject by Law, for offences against the same. And as for the banishment, it hath not hitherto been inflicted upon any but such who, being in arms, might justly, upon the terms they were taken, and put to death : as those who are instanced in your Declaration to be "sent to the Tobacco Islands." And, therefore, I do declare, That if the People be ready to run to arms by the instigation of their Clergy or otherwise, such as God by His providence shall give into my hands may expect that or worse measure from me ; but not otherwise.

Thirdly, as to that of "the ruin of their fortune." You instance the Act of Subscription, " whereby the estates of the Inhabitants of this Nation are sold, so as there remaineth now no more but to put the Purchasers in possession ; and that for this cause are the Forces drawn out of England." And that you might carry the Interest far, to engage the Common sort of People with you, you further say to them, That " the moderate usage exercised to them is to no other end but to our private advantage, and for the better support of our Army ; intending at the close of our conquest, as you term it, to root out the Common People also, and to plant the land with Colonies to be brought hither out of England." This, consisting of divers parts, will ask distinct answers. And first, to the Act of Subscription. It's true there is such an Act ; and it was a just one. For when, by your execrable Massacre and Rebellion, you had not only raised a bloody War to justify the same ; and thereby occasioned the exhausting the Treasury of England in the prosecution of so just a War against you, was it not a wise and just act in the State to raise money by escheating the Lands of those who had a hand in the Rebellion ? Was it not fit to make their Estates defray the charge, who had caused the trouble? The best, therefore, that lies in the argument is this, and that only reaching to them who have been in arms, for further it goes not : " You have forfeited your Estates, and it is likely they will be escheated to make satisfaction ; and therefore you had better fight it out than repent or give off now; or see what mercy you may find from the State of England. And seeing holy Church is engaged in it, we will, by one means or another, hook in the Commons, and make them sensible that they are as much concerned as you, though they were never in arms, or came quickly off!" And for this cause doubtless are these two coupled together; by which your honest dealing is manifest enough.

But what? Was the English Army brought over for this purpose, as you allege? Do you think that the State of England will be at five or six Millions charge merely to procure Purchasers to be invested in that for which they did disburse little above a Quarter of a Million ? Although there be a justice in that also, which ought, and, I trust, will, be seasonably performed towards them. No, I can give you a better reason for the Army coming over than this. England hath had experience of the blessing of God in prosecuting just and righteous Causes, whatever the cost and hazard be ! And if ever men were engaged in a righteous Cause in the world, this will scarce be a second to it. We are come to ask an account of the innocent blood that hath been shed, and to endeavor to bring to an account, by the blessing and presence of the Almighty, in whom alone is our hope and strength, all who, by appearing in arms, seek to justify the same. We come to break the power of lawless rebels, who having cast off the authority of England, live as enemies to Human Society; whose principles, the world hath experience, are, To destroy and subjugate all men not complying with them. We come by the assistance of God, to hold forth, and maintain the lustre and glory of English Liberty in a Nation where we have an undoubted right to do it ; wherein the People of Ireland (if they listen not to such seducers as you are), may equally participate in all benefits ; to use liberty and fortune equally with Englishmen, if they keep out of arms.

And now, having said this to you, I have a word to them ; that in this point, which concerns them in their estates and fortunes, they may know what to trust to. Such as have formerly been in arms, may, submitting themselves, have their cases presented to the State of England; where, no doubt, the State will be ready to take into consideration the nature and quality of their actings, and deal mercifully with them. And as for those now in arms, who shall come in and submit, and give engagements for their future quiet and honest carriage and submission to the State of England, I doubt not but they will find like merciful consideration, excepting only the Leading persons and Principal Contrivers of this Rebellion, whom I am confident they will reserve to make examples of Justice, whatever hazards they incur thereby. And as for such Private Soldiers as lay down their arms, and shall live peaceably and honestly at their several homes, they shall be permitted so to do. And, for the first two sorts, I shall humbly and effectually represent their cases to the Parliament, as far as becomes the duty and place I bear. But as for those who, notwithstanding this, persist and continue in arms, they must expect what the Providence of God in that which is falsely called the Chance of War, will cast upon them.

For such of the Nobility, Gentry, and Commons of Ireland, as have not been actors in this Rebellion, they shall and may expect the protection on their Goods, Liberties, and Lives which the Law gives them ; and in their husbandry, merchandising, manufactures, and other trading whatsoever, the same. They behaving themselves as becomes honest and peaceable men ; testifying their good affections, upon all occasions, to the service of the State of England, equal justice shall be done them with the English. They shall bear proportionately with them in taxes. And if the soldiery be insolent upon them, upon complaint and proof, it shall be punished with utmost severity, and they protected equally with Englishmen.

And having said this, and purposing honestly to perform it, if this People shall headily run on after the counsels of their Prelates and Clergy and other Leaders, I hope to be free from the misery and desolation, blood and ruin, that shall befall them ; and shall rejoice to exercise utmost severity against them.

OLIVER CROMWELL.

Given at Youghal, January, 1650.

X.

LANGLEY OF THE IRON HAND.

WHEN Erin before Clonmel fell,
  A man of whom I'll tell you
As they advanced to storm Clonmel
  Was foremost in the melee.

Charles Langley hight, a man of power,
  Of all the troops the best,
For when they stormed the western
    tower,
  He towered above the rest.

A mower standing in the breach,
  With scythe to guard the pass,
His hand cut off, as if to teach
That flesh is still but grass.

But yet a gallant warrior's boast,
  Might to his wounds bring balm;
For though his hand the hero lost,
  He bore away the palm.

He could aver that in the fray
  Where balls and bullets fly,
He had on that eventful day
  A finger in the pie.

And what a wondrous change took place
  When of his limb bereft!
He found, when thinking o'er his case,
  His right hand was the left!

The furious foe, in joyous glee,
  The bleeding hero scanned,
And bade him then in irony
  To get an iron hand.

But Langley, with his sabre bright,
  Struck at the boasting clown.
To crown the labors of the fight,
  He cut him through the crown.

His iron hand henceforth he wore,
  His various works to settle,
Thus proving then just as before,
  Himself a man of mettle.

The following curious will was made by a namesake, probably a relative of his, who also fought at Clonmel :—

I, John Langley, born at Wincannon, in Somersetshire, and settled in Ireland in the year 1651, now in my right mind and wits, do make my will in my own handwriting :

I do leave all my house, goods, and farm of Blackkettle of 253 acres to my son commonly called Stubborn Jack, to him and his heirs for ever, provided he marries a Protestant, but not Alice Kendrick, who called me "Oliver's whelp." My new buckskin breeches and my silver tobacco-stopper, with J. L. on the top, I give to Richard Richards, my comrade who helped me off at the storming of Clonmel, when I was shot through the leg. My said son John shall keep my body above ground six days and six nights after I am dead; and Grace Kendrick shall lay me out, who shall have for so doing five shillings. My body shall be put upon the oak table in the brown room, and fifty Irishmen shall be invited to my wake, and everyone shall have two quarts of the best aquavitæ, and each a skein, dirk, or knife laid before him; and when their liquor is out, nail up my coffin and commit me to earth whence I came.

This is my will. Witness my hand this 3rd day of March, 1674.

JOHN LANGLEY.

Some of his friends asked him why he would be at such a charge to treat the Irish at his funeral, a people whom he never loved. "Why for that reason," replied he, "for they will get so drunk at my wake that they will kill one another, and so we will get rid of the breed. And if every one would follow my example in their wills, in time we should get rid of them all."

www.ingramcontent.com/pod-product-compliance
Lightning Source LLC
Chambersburg PA
CBHW031427020726
47499CB00005B/1635